48.4138

Education
for Musical Growth

JAMES L. MURSELL
TEACHERS COLLEGE
COLUMBIA UNIVERSITY, NEW YORK

GINN AND COMPANY

BOSTON · NEW YORK · CHICAGO · ATLANTA · DALLAS · COLUMBUS
SAN FRANCISCO · TORONTO · LONDON

To

LILLA BELLE PITTS

with affection and gratitude

PREFACE

It seems to me that the reader of this book may be helped to find more repayment in it if I tell him something of how and why it came to be written. So, instead of beginning with the usual rather formal descriptive preface, that is what I propose to do. The book is by way of a progress report in an adventure in thinking which still continues, and in which I hope that at least some of those who read it may be moved to join.

Several years ago there dawned upon my mind the thought that the concept of growth promised quite extraordinary fruitfulness if it could be brought to bear aright on the problems of music education. I was aware that the concept of growth has an immense currency in modern education, and I sensed and felt that it must have an immense significance in the field of music. But the idea was vague, hardly more than a hunch, although I found myself coming back to it again and again. What, exactly, did the concept of growth mean? More particularly, what did musical growth mean? This question, dimly sensed at first, forced itself inescapably into the central focus, and as a result of many meditations and discussions came to seem crucial.

For a long time I thought I was wrestling with something baffling, theoretical, remote from practical issues, almost academic. But little by little I came to see that here was something both exceedingly simple and also very practical indeed. What did musical growth mean? Surely it could only mean growth in human responsiveness to the essential values, and intimations, and meanings of the art of music itself. It could only mean the process of *becoming musical*. About this I had to be clear, and I had to try to make it clear to the reader. Here I found the parallel between music and poetry extraordinarily helpful and suggestive. This is why the parallel is so strongly emphasized in these pages. There is, I am convinced, an essential and illuminating identity between musical and poetic responsiveness. Indeed, the same identity could be demonstrated as between all the arts; for we are dealing with the essential aesthetic responsiveness of human beings, and music education is simply a phase of a broader process which is sometimes called "aesthetic education." Thus the idea of musical growth clarifies itself as something of very far-reaching cultural and intellectual significance.

Yet it is extremely practical too. It has been to me an amazing experience to discover, bit by bit, to how many of the practical problems of music education it provides the key. We concern ourselves with the teaching of note-reading and the score, the teaching of technique, the teaching of theory, the organization of general music, the selection of educative experiences and activities in music, the planning of a vital curricular sequence, the co-operation of staff action. To all such issues and many others I believe that the conception of musical growth provides the true and constructive answer. Moreover, I have found that it yields a set of new operating conceptions—musical awareness, musical initiative, musical discrimination, musical insight, musical skill—by which to take hold upon the practical problems of music education. The power of this conception as a resolver of difficulties has startled me again and again.

Yet in all this adventure in thinking I have had a constant sense of familiar things. There is nothing in this book that I do not seem to have known these many years. All I can claim is that it may have come through a little more clearly, a little more universally, a little more directly, and perhaps with some crudities and discrepancies smoothed away. Also I believe that every inspired teacher of music has always done by instinct the very kind of things that, by dint of a laborious intellectual process, have come to seem to me to be right. For every such teacher knows within himself that he is not a drill-master or a setter and hearer of lessons, but an exponent and revealer of musical beauty. And this is just what I find myself trying to say.

In the course of this adventure in thinking I have come to owe much to many people. They all have my gratitude. But I want specifically to mention two groups. First, there are my friends and colleagues of the Music Department of Teachers College, Columbia University. My association with them has been a constant pleasure and a constant stimulus. Then there are those friends in the University of Southern California who bore with me while I tried out on them some of these ideas which were yet in a sadly half-baked condition. In their generosity and kindness they gave me an experience memorable not only because it was happy but also because it was for me truly developmental. And I should like to tell all these friends of mine, and all who may read this book, that to me it is not a fixed and final formulation but a stage in a continuing quest, and to ask them to accept it as a message from a fellow journeyer who is trying to tell what he has seen, who has learned and is learning by their side, and who hopes to go on in their good companionship to wider vistas and a clearer vision.

JAMES L. MURSELL

CONTENTS

Education for Musical Growth

PART ONE

THE CONCEPT

OF MUSICAL GROWTH

CHAPTER ONE

The Developmental Approach in Music Education

All power and all fulfillment come through growth. This is a nutshell summary of the developmental point of view. It is true of every field of human endeavor, certainly including music. It should be built into every kind of teaching, all the way from typewriting to higher mathematics. To show how to build it into music education is the purpose of this book.

I

The central idea of the developmental approach in music education is very clear and very simple, even though the job of organizing it into an educational program is complex and many-sided. It comes to this: All musical activities, experiences, endeavors, and learnings should be thought of and planned as episodes in a process of musical growth. Singing a rote song, studying the notation, engaging in rhythm band activities, listening, practicing, working at technique, learning theory, playing in the high-school orchestra, to mention some conspicuous examples, should always consciously center on the development of musical responsiveness. This is the process of musical growth. It should always and everywhere be the focal consideration. All special achievements and learnings should be treated as means for fostering it. The emphasis should always be on musical growth. It is the very heart of a well-organized scheme of music education.

An illustration from another field will help to show just what this means. Ballroom dancing is nearly always taught with the emphasis entirely on step patterns. For instance, one famous "system" breaks down the rhumba into twenty different steps. The pupil masters them one by one, and then he is supposed to be able to rhumba, after some experience on the dance floor to gain confidence. Now this is the exact opposite of the developmental approach. The trouble with it is that there is something more fundamental about the rhumba than any one of these steps or all of them together. That something is the basic rhythm itself. It is quite definite, quite easy to grasp. Yet nothing is done to play it up or emphasize it. The pupil is told, for instance, that he must finesse his movements in various ways if he is to keep exact time to the beat and co-ordinate his partner with it. But he is not helped toward a clear awareness of the pattern of the beat. He is all the time trying to remember the steps, and to get their fine points just right; but he is left to pick up the beat as best he can. This slows down his progress, and is the cause of many of his difficulties and hesitations.

Why not put first things first? Why not start the pupil off by making him aware of the basic rhythm of the rhumba? How can it be done? By letting him sit and listen to the music, or count it out, or beat it out with his hands and arms, or walk freely in time to it without bothering about any particular step, or by giving him a look at the score. Anything to avoid confusions and distractions! anything to get that rhythm! Surely that ought to be simple enough, and very helpful too. Once he has got it, the steps are far easier to learn, because they are its manifestations or embodiments. Points of finesse become easier, too, because the beat is there to guide him. Also, of course, as he learns the steps, his grasp of the rhythm itself improves and develops. Moreover he has no problem of confidence, because he does not first learn by arithmetic, as it were, and then have to change over into control by rhythmic feeling. What is happening is that a rhythmic responsiveness and sensitivity are going through a process of growth.

This simple illustration tells the whole story. It shows exactly what the difference is between developmental and nondevelopmental teaching; and it shows why one is good and the other is bad. The developmental approach means that in anything we are trying to teach, we should pick out and emphasize the inner, living essence in the first place, rather than the external manifestations. It means giving the pupil a grasp of this inner, living essence right from the very start, and seeing that his grasp of it improves as he works at this, that, or the other of its external manifestations. In the rhumba, the rhythm is the inner, living essence; the steps are the external manifestations; and the rhythm should be emphasized all along the line. In mathematics, relational thinking is the inner, living essence; sums, calculations, rules, formulae, are the outer manifestations; and relational thinking should be emphasized all along the line. In Eng-

[4]

lish composition, clear communication is the inner, living essence; rules of grammar, punctuation, and usage are the external manifestations; and clear communication should be emphasized all along the line. Of course we want these external manifestations to appear. Not to care about them would be quite idiotic. But the question is how best to get them. Well, the best way to get fruit from a tree is to pay particular attention to the growth of the tree. There you have the whole idea of developmental teaching.

Just as it applies to all the types of teaching we have mentioned, so also it applies to the teaching of music. It means promoting a process of musical growth from which we expect to get the fruits of musical achievement. It means seeing that the pupil, in everything he does, is developing a better and better grasp of the inner, living essence of music.

But what is this inner, living essence of music? Surely this question should not be too terribly puzzling. It is simply the tonal and rhythmic pattern itself. What else could it be? The skills, and techniques, and theoretical rules, on the other hand, are ways of dealing with this tonal and rhythmic pattern, as it is symbolized in the score or projected with the voice or by some instrument, or made up out of one's head. So they are the external manifestations. But direct perception of, and responsiveness and sensitivity to, the tonal and rhythmic pattern are the inner essence. This seems so very obvious that one wonders how anyone can doubt it. Indeed it is questionable whether anyone really can! After all, the fact that shapes, qualities, colors, arrangements, refinements, nuances, subtleties, interweavings of tone and rhythm can project emotional and expressive values is what makes music music. This is what human beings have always responded to in it, all the way from the tyro with his feeble apprehensions to Toscanini with his highly developed ones, all the way from the bushman with his little songs to Beethoven with his majestic symphonies, all the way from the untutored auditor to the sophisticated artist. What else is there?

This is where the idea of growth comes in. The development of relational thinking is mathematical growth. The development of the power to communicate is growth in literary expression. The development of rhythmic responsiveness is terpsichorean growth. In the same way, the development of a keen perception of the tonal and rhythmic pattern, of a free ability to image and think it, of a refined sensitivity to its expressive and emotional values, is musical growth. All special musical achievements should be treated as its manifesta-

[5]

tions. All musical doings and learnings should be planned to help it along. It is the thing always to emphasize in all music education.

There is another way of putting the matter. Relational thinking is what makes a person a mathematician. The power to communicate is what makes a man a writer. Rhythmic certainty and resourcefulness are what makes a man a dancer. Why not say, then, that the business of education is not so much to teach people mathematics, or writing, or dancing as to make them into mathematicians, or writers, or dancers? Not highly developed mathematicians, or writers, or dancers, perhaps, but human beings of a certain kind, with a certain slant in their lives, with the "root of the matter" in them? So too with music. What makes a person musical is responsiveness to the tonal and rhythmic pattern. It is what might be called the *musical quality* in a human being. Why not, then, say that the business of music education is to evoke this quality, to enable a human being to realize his musical potentiality, to help him to evolve into a musical person?

II

Now that the central idea of the developmental approach has been blocked out in outline, it needs to be explained a little more precisely, and a couple of questions it suggests need to be discussed.

The quality which makes a person musical—the musical quality, or musicality, as it is often called—is a characteristic organization of auditory feeling, perception, and imagery. This puts the matter in precise psychological language. There is here an exact analogy with the quality that makes a person a visual artist. That quality is a characteristic organization of visual perception and imagery, and of feeling for visual values. Its development is far more important than the acquisition of any specific techniques. As a matter of fact, the techniques of the painter grow out of his visual responsiveness. The essential thing for him is to become more and more responsive to color, form, line, mass, and organization in the visual world. He is, *par excellence*, a man who has achieved a way of seeing, a way of imaging, and a way of responding emotionally to visual values. This is an exact parallel with music. It is true that music requires much more sheer manipulative skill than painting. But that is all the more reason for approaching it in a musically meaningful manner. It is not skill in and of itself but the ability to perceive, to image, to think, to respond emotionally to tonal and rhythmic design that makes a person musical. One might say that the core of art education is visual

[6]

education—education in seeing. In the same way, the core of music education, considered from the developmental point of view, is aural education.

As to the importance of this musical quality, nobody connected with music can have the slightest doubt about it. Nothing can take its place. When a person has this quality, it shows up unmistakably in everything he does with music. When he touches the keyboard, he sounds like an artist and not like a carpenter, even though his skill may be limited. When he expresses a judgment about a performance or a composition, be it a lengthy masterpiece or a little song for children, he goes right to the vital point, because he is guided by direct musical perceptiveness and sensitivity. When he gives a lesson or conducts a rehearsal, he creates musical values. The unmusical person can do none of these things, because he deals with music always roundabout, by way of intellect, fixed rule, and second-hand opinion.

Furthermore, the musical quality makes a person a good learner when it comes to the specialized or technical aspects of music. He can learn to read as he should, because he sees musical meanings in the score. He can study theory as he should, because he is directly con-scious of the values and relationships to which the rules refer and which make them meaningful. He does not memorize by beating music into his head, but by grasping it clearly and completely. Techni-cal drill becomes a repaying endeavor, not an arid grind, because he is interested in learning to project what he apprehends. What teacher of piano, or voice, or theory, what director of an orchestra or choir, would not feel lucky to work always with persons whose musical per-ceptions were clear and refined, even if their technical equipment was, for the time being, imperfect? Surely the case is crystal-clear. Does it not then evidently follow that music education should be mobilized, first, foremost, and always, to evoke the musical quality, to foster the process of growth through which persons become musical?

This may seem reasonable and convincing so far. But two very serious questions loom up. Is not the musical quality a hereditary gift rather than something that can be acquired and developed? If its acquisition is theoretically not impossible, how, as a practical proposition, can this be done?

1 Musical persons, it may be said, are born, not made. Some have the musical quality. Others lack it. There is nothing we can do about it. If so, of course the whole case collapses.

[7]

However, there is no need to go into an elaborate technical argument to see that this cannot possibly be true. The musical quality is a characteristic way of responding to tonal and rhythmic design. If you will think for a moment of the place of music in human affairs, you have to admit that this way of responding, far from being confined to a few individuals, is almost universal, although it is usually not well developed. All races, all kinds, all conditions of men have made music and enjoyed it. They may not make it very well, or enjoy it very wisely, but still it means a great deal to them. Human beings, from childhood on, are sensitive to music and use it as a natural means of expression and pleasure, although their sensitivity may not be highly cultivated. When a lay audience respond to the music of Beethoven, they may grasp only a little of what he is projecting, but they certainly do not feel that he is talking an unintelligible and foreign language. This amounts to proof that between Beethoven and the layman there is something in common, something shared, and that something can only be the stuff and substance of music. One can only conclude, on the basis of really overwhelming and very obvious evidence, that responsiveness to music is a universal, and not a special or limited endowment. It is the person who lacks it who is unusual, not the person who has it.

Of course not everybody has this quality to the same degree. No one will deny that there are differences in musical endowment, just as there are differences in human endowment of every kind. No sensible person is likely to claim that it is possible to make a Mozart out of a mediocrity. But Mozart and the mediocrity are not completely different creatures. The things that Mozart did can please the mediocrity. He can understand them and enter into them up to a certain point. He can even do the same kind of things himself, again up to a certain point. The musical quality is certainly not what psychologists call an all-or-none ability. It is not either present or entirely absent. As between different persons it manifests itself in different degrees.

But even this might seem to wreck any hope of developing it. If a person is granted a certain measure of this gift by nature, how can it be increased? There are many things that it is tempting to say about this question, for it is based on some very dubious assumptions. But let us resist, for the time being at least. For the moment it can be answered very well by another question. How many people ever realize anything like their full possibilities in any field? That answers itself, does it not? So it is always feasible and always important to develop the gifts that people have, to invest their talents wisely in-

stead of burying them in the ground. The most hard-shelled heredi-
tarian will find this a hard argument to crack, and it is enough for us
so far. Admit that Mozart and Beethoven could develop musically a
great deal further than most people. Yet even they had to develop.
Neither of them could have written their greatest masterpieces in
their teens. So also ordinary people can develop, though not so far.
The case, then, seems clear. Musical development is entirely possible
for all normal people. There is no theoretically fatal objection to the
idea of a developmental scheme of music education.

2 But admitting that the musical quality can be cultivated, one
may still ask how to do it. Quite probably there are a good many
teachers who will find this question quite a sticker. If they really feel
this way, however, it is for a curious reason. The answer is so simple
and obvious that they niss it.

How do you get a person to improve his musical responsiveness?
By making sure that he always really is responding emotionally,
perceptually, imaginally to the content of the music itself, and not
only to something extraneous, such as symbols, rules, or manipulations. If a young pupil is studying a Chopin Nocturne, you make
quite sure that he is getting hold of the flow of harmonic color and
melody and the layout of phrases on the beat, instead of thinking only
of the notes and the movements needed to get them. If you are
teaching children a rote song, you are careful to have them attend to
the expressive contour of the melodic line. If they are preparing a
piece for an assembly program, and it shows some signs of falling
apart, you may have them sit quietly and think it through, or catch
the swing of the rhythm by means of physical movement. If you are
dealing with advanced students, you may take a leaf from the book
of a distinguished piano teacher who used to make his students build
up a complete mental picture of a composition from the score before
they touched a note of it. If you are teaching children to read, you
go as far as you can in having them see how the music ought to sound
before it sounds, and think how it sounds while it is sounding. If you
are in charge of a high-school orchestra, you will not think rehearsal
time wasted if you spend some of it analyzing a new work with them,
and analyzing it not verbally but aurally. If you are teaching a course
in theory, you will enrich it with all kinds of musical illustrations and
applications, and some of the assignments you will make will be to
find more illustrations and applications instead of doing more exercises. You will think this worth while even if it slows your headlong

progress through the textbook. These are just a few illustrative suggestions. They are by no means models to be copied under all circumstances. They are intended to show the answer to the question about how to develop the musical quality in people. One does this in a very simple way. One does it by putting music into music teaching.

A developmental program of music education comes down to just exactly that. It puts an absolute priority on musical perception, musical imagery, musical thinking, musical feeling. It sets up a whole scheme of activities and learnings—and they can range all the way from playing tunes on bottles to writing double fugues—to highlight these values. One finds it a little odd to have to make an argument on behalf of the art of music to music teachers. But a haunting sense that this is necessary, and a conviction that it is vitally important, is the motive for presenting this book. The essence of its message can be put in a sentence. The developmental approach in music education means emphasizing and playing up musical verities at all times, on all occasions, and in all possible ways.

III

A further understanding of the developmental approach can be gained by contrasting it with its antithesis. This is the mechanistic approach. Mechanistically organized teaching, in music and everywhere else, has two characteristics by which it can always be known. It operates in terms of accumulation or assembling; and it works from the outside inward.

1 Mechanistic teaching is planned to promote a process of assembling or accumulation rather than a process of growth. Its assumption is that any complex ability is gained by acquiring its elements and putting them together, just as a wall is built out of bricks, or a machine is made by assembling its parts.

The constituent elements on which mechanistic planning concentrates are sometimes called habits and sometimes called items (or bits) of knowledge. The distinction does not amount to much. If a child holds his violin properly, one may say that he has formed the habit of doing so, or that he knows how to do so. If he says that Beethoven wrote the *Eroica Symphony*, one may call this a bit of knowledge or a habit of mind. So we will not argue about the terms. The point is that the mechanistic approach always promotes the accumulation and assembling of constituent elements, or what are supposed to be such, as the pathway toward achievement.

[10]

There is no lack of illustrations. Mathematics is set up as a series of operations and processes, Latin as a series of vocabulary items and grammar rules, punctuation also as a set of rules, history as a series of items of information. The same plan is followed in much of the teaching of physical skills, such as golf, skiing, skating, and of course ballroom dancing. It constantly appears in music teaching. The notation is broken down into its symbolic elements, which are presented in some kind of serial order, to be learned, retained, and combined. Motor technique is analyzed into its components, with the idea that they are to be acquired and accumulated. In theory, learning and teaching are centered on a series of topics to be mastered and stored away. So everywhere. The wall is made of bricks. The machine is made of parts. Pile the bricks. Assemble the parts. Then the job is done.

2 Mechanistic teaching is externalistic. It always works from the outside in. It emphasizes external manifestations, and neglects the inner essence, perhaps in the hope that it will arrive of its own accord.

Dance instruction, typewriting instruction, ski instruction, golf instruction, emphasize the pattern of movement, and do nothing to emphasize the inner rhythm or co-ordination. Instruction in mathematics emphasizes the techniques of computation and does nothing to emphasize relational thinking. Instruction in English composition emphasizes rules of punctuation, grammar, and usage, and does nothing to emphasize clear communication. So in music education, there is often an emphasis upon notational symbols and a neglect of the tonal design, an emphasis upon facility in technique and a neglect of musical and expressive values, an emphasis on the right notes and a neglect of the tonal pattern which makes their rightness significant, an emphasis on theoretical rules and a neglect of the direct tonal perception and imagery to which the rules refer.

These two characteristics, taken together, are an acid test. They will infallibly show whether any given scheme of teaching is mechanistic or developmental. Is there any clear-cut core of essential meaning, direct, intelligible, simple, that runs through the whole business and is brought out in different ways as the work proceeds? Are there any concrete plans and suggestions for emphasizing and conveying it, particularly at the start, but also all along the line? Are the various doings and learnings expressly treated as manifestations of this essential meaning, as episodes in a plot, so to speak? If so, the plan is

[11]

concentrating on growth, and is developmental. If not, it is concentrating on accumulation, and is mechanistic. One often sees school courses of study in music which begin with noble statements of aim, explaining that the purpose is to develop musical appreciation, musical discrimination, musical power, musical fulfillment, and so forth. But then nothing seems to be done about these professions of faith. What follows is simply a sequence of lessons to be learned one by one, habits to be formed, items of knowledge to be acquired. Apparently the far-reaching values which form the overture are expected to come by magic. Such plans, it need hardly be said, are in no sense developmental. They amount to a mechanistic organization dressed up in fustian. In order to have developmental teaching, it is necessary to do something about development.

The distinction, however, is not between order and disorder. To think that mechanistic teaching is orderly, whereas developmental teaching is chaotic, is a very great mistake. All good teaching is orderly, but there are different kinds of orderliness. The moment some people see any orderly sequence of work they are inclined to call it mechanistic. Nine times out of ten they are right, but they are guessing just the same. One must look deeper. One must find out whether it is externalistic and whether in practice it emphasizes accumulation, for these are the decisive features of the mechanistic approach.

IV

There are two arguments against mechanistic teaching. It does not work out well in practice, and it is based on a false psychology.

1 The mechanistic approach does not work out well in practice. Usually it does not deliver good results; or if good results are forthcoming, they arrive so slowly and cost so much in time and effort that permanent damage is done. Many a capable violinist or pianist has paid such a high price for his skill that he is impoverished musically, culturally, and personally in every other way. In some school systems a certain number of children do learn to read music, but everything else is sacrificed to it, and those who do not come through the mill are lost to music from then on.

The failure of mechanistic teaching is an old and familiar story. Millions of children have been taught the components of the musical score. But how many people in America today could read a folk song at sight? Great numbers of music students go through a high-pressure routine in theory. But the average practical musician could not write

[12]

a decent four-part harmonization, or chord out an accompaniment for community singing, if his life depended on it. To argue that he has few uses for theory is putting the thing back to front. If he could really handle it he would find plenty of uses for it. The author of a widely used book of piano studies says in his preface that he has isolated all the problems of the pianistic technique, and that anyone who will go through his material two or three times a day for nine months will have a good equipment. Try it and see!

It is the same story everywhere. Children memorize the so-called addition facts, and begin forgetting them by the time they start multiplication. They take ninth-grade algebra, but seem to have lost most of it when they enter tenth-grade physics. They study English grammar, but it has no appreciable effect on their written style. They take four years of Latin, and then cannot read a page of Livy or an ode of Horace. They are put through American history, line by line, bit by bit, and a few years later have to go through it all again, even after which not very much sticks.

We have no right to ignore such obvious ills. They are needless and curable. Above all, we have no right to say that the answer is higher pressure, harder work, longer hours—in effect, more of the same. If most of the cars turned out by a factory did not run, it would seem like a good idea to change the system. That is just the point here. The mechanistic plan of teaching has been tried out on an enormous scale. The universal answer is that it does not deliver the goods.

2 The mechanistic approach is based on a false psychology. This is why it does not work out well. Its fundamental assumption is that the acquisition of any ability is a matter of retention and accumulation. Superficially this looks reasonable. But examine it closely, and you will find that it falls to pieces.

Consider the acquisition of a physical skill, such as dancing, typewriting, skiing, or playing an instrument. Does a person really become a good dancer by first making the steps habitual and then adding them up? No, he gets away from step-wise reactions altogether. It will not do to say that they become so ingrained that he need not think about them any more. He comes more and more to respond to the rhythm, and to move freely to it. Surely, then, the sensible thing is to have him from the very first concentrate on what must control him when he is a finished performer. But mechanistic teaching makes him concentrate on the wrong thing, with the idea that somehow, in some mysterious way, he will come to concentrate upon the right one.

[13]

Perhaps indeed he will do so. But why not help this "mysterious" process along, instead of deliberately hindering it and leaving it to chance? We want the learner to get away from his early adjustments, not to stay with them. This is the true psychology of the situation. But we talk and act as though we wanted to make these early adjustments into ironclad habits. This is psychologically quite false, and it shows at once why mechanistic teaching is inefficient.

Or consider the acquisition of mental abilities. The same argument applies to them. Everyone knows that a person becomes good at history, or mathematics, or science, or language study by thinking and understanding. But all that mechanistic teaching emphasizes is routine memory learning. Even in mathematics, which is pure thinking *par excellence*, examinations have to be set up so that they can be passed by sheer memory answers. But no examination will show real mathematical grasp unless it is at least ninety per cent original problems. The idea that we can build thinking out of something that is not thinking, that we can develop insight out of routine memory tasks, simply does not make sense. Assuredly it is a very peculiar kind of psychology. Yet that very psychology is put into practice in mechanistic teaching.

Our own field of music education contains a prize instance of this fallacy. Theory teachers admit that composers, even including the sacred John Sebastian Bach, simply do not follow the rules. But they say that a person must habituate himself to the rules before he can be free of them. Let us deliberately learn in what we know is the wrong way, and then sometime we will perform in the right way. Let us follow the wrong path for a long time and very diligently, and then it will bring us where we want to go. This argument achieves a veritable Mount Everest of absurdity. Yet in it the whole psychology of mechanistic teaching stands revealed. Mechanistic teaching deliberately stresses the routines, although it is as clear as day that any real efficiency depends in getting away from them. The mechanistic doctrine is that the routines must be made habitual; but if this very thing were done, it would be an irremediable disaster.

The opposite doctrine is to stress not the parts, not the routines, but the essence of the thing itself—the essence as it appears in the most highly developed performance. At first the essence is not clear or fully grasped, but it is there, and it is always the guiding thread. Instead of forming habits, the learner should develop effective and meaningful special adjustments. That is the contrasting, the developmental point of view.

[14]

Does developmental teaching promise good results? Indeed it does. From among many possible illustrations one is particularly worth noticing. Jacques Dalcroze, at his school at Hellerau, conducted a careful study of the effects of his procedures. He watched a group of children who had been given a year's introduction to music through the medium of bodily rhythm and then were started on the piano. He found that in a year's piano study they made four times as much progress as a comparable group who had begun piano without this preliminary development. Many similar examples could be given, from foreign-language study, from the teaching of English composition, from instruction in typewriting, and from plenty of other fields as well. They make a conclusive case. The way to get results is to play up the developmental line, because the practice is psychologically sound. The way to fail to get results is to hammer on separate parts and constituent elements, because this is psychologically false.

V

But mechanistic teaching is exceedingly widespread. Does not this at least suggest that there must be strong arguments in favor of it?

1 One great argument for it is that it makes everything clear in the mind of the learner at all times. If we have a series of twenty lessons, we can make sure that the learner knows the first nine before taking up the tenth. This is what it means to say that one can go from the known to the unknown. And perhaps we can even do better than this. Perhaps we can arrange our twenty lessons in an order from simple to complex. Then the learner can go not only from the known to the unknown at every step, but also from the simple to the complex. Surely this means that his mind will always be in a state of crystalline clarity, which is a very great help indeed.

Unfortunately these two famous dogmas, of going from the known to the unknown and from the simple to the complex, do not stand analysis. Clarity, indeed, is very important, but it is not obtainable by either of these techniques. In fact it is not attainable at all by the mechanistic approach.

A. *Consider first the idea of going from the known to the unknown. One hears it repeated again and again in a most unreflecting way. Yet it is based on two quite untenable assumptions.*

[15]

(*a*) It assumes that each lesson in a series is learned to the point of mastery. Obviously this does not happen in fact, and most teachers do not even seriously try to make it happen. But beyond this, it could not happen anyhow. What does it mean to have "mastered" the dotted quarter note, or the six-four chord, or the double trill on the piano? If we are talking about real mastery, which is necessary for real clarity, it can only mean a rounded and complete understanding, an ability to deliver the goods in any and every situation. But is anything of the kind even contemplated in teaching? Obviously not. What mastery actually means in practice is the satisfactory completion of certain tests and exercises. And even if this is done, which is not always the case, there can still be plenty of confusion and jumble in the learner's mind.

(*b*) It assumes that the earlier lessons will remain firmly in the learner's mind as the later ones are taken up. This also is untrue in fact and impossible in theory. To hear some teachers talk, one would think that they had never even heard of the process of forgetting. Yet forgetting is a normal and by no means baneful function of the human mind. We forget far more than we remember, and there is simply no way of avoiding it. What actually—and inevitably— happens is that the earlier lessons are progressively forgotten. Could not properly placed reviews take care of this? No! Properly placed reviews are rare in any case. And is there any reason why a review cannot be forgotten, just like anything else?

B. *Turning now to the idea of going from the simple to the complex, we have here yet another array of untenable assumptions. There are many fields of study where the idea obviously will not apply—the teaching of history, for instance. But even where it seems applicable it is shot through with fallacies.*

(*a*) The order of difficulty of tasks is an extremely subtle and difficult problem at best. In arithmetic, for example, it is found that multinomial fractions can be actually easier than mononomial fractions, which is the very opposite of what one might expect. In music a Bach Two-Part Invention may be harder than a Schubert Impromptu, and four-part diatonic harmony may be harder than chromatic jazz. As to the relative difficulty of the figurations of the score, it is entirely unknown.

(*b*) It is assumed that there must be a fixed order of difficulty in any set of tasks, if one can discover it. But this will not hold water. The difficulty of any given task is affected by the order of the series. The dotted-quarter-note-eighth-note figure or the third position on the

[16]

violin have one index of difficulty if approached in one way, and another if approached differently.

(*c*) It is assumed that there is an order of difficulty which is the same for all learners. This is transparently false. Different people do not find the same task equally difficult. But if this is so, how are we going to set up a simple-to-complex arrangement that will be the same for everybody? Is not any arrangement of this kind sure to help some and to confuse others?

So these two classic dogmas of going from the known to the unknown and from the simple to the complex look rather pitiful when exposed to the sunlight. All that really remains of them is that it is a bad idea to throw problems at a learner that are sure to baffle and frustrate him. Has anyone ever thought otherwise?

But beyond all this, and more generally, the mechanistic approach is the wrong approach to clarity. Clarity is not achieved by setting up a series of lessons to be mastered one by one. The paper outline looks clear, but the learner's mind is not. What actually develops in his mind is a lengthening trail of fog. The simple reason is that his mind does not operate by retention and accumulation. It operates by growth, and the approach through growth is the right approach to clarity. The notation can be taught by a series of experiences more and more clearly revealing how musical meanings are expressed in visual symbols. Theory can be taught by a series of experiences revealing more and more clearly the focal considerations in organizing the tonal and rhythmic pattern. Technique can be taught in terms of experiences more and more clearly revealing the nature of adjustment to the instrument and to music. This, however, is not the mechanistic approach. It is the developmental approach. This too stresses clarity. But it does not deal with it by trying to add one clear thing to another, which is hopeless anyway, because they do not stay clear. It deals with the problem of clarity by instituting a *process of clarification*.

2 Another great argument for the mechanistic approach is that one must work down through the externals to the essentials. The word "must" in this sentence can have two meanings. It may mean that this in general is the only right way to work; or it may mean that this is the only way we know how to work. On either interpretation, the statement is false.

A. *The idea that one must always go from externals to essentials is often expressed by saying that one cannot do a job without the tools.* One cannot

[17]

read music without the notation, or play an instrument without technique, or compose without theory. This is all perfectly true, and perfectly irrelevant. The question is how to get the tools. If one is making a machine one collects them beforehand. If one is creating an ability, one creates them on the job. Indeed they are indistinguishable from the job itself. If we try to learn techniques beforehand and independently, we always have to learn them over again with vital changes when it comes to applying them. This is a very wasteful process at best, and it can easily be a fatally frustrating one. The prize example, once again, is first learning all the rules of theory, and then unlearning them when one composes. This does not mean that there will never be any formal or isolated practice or drill. But it does mean that such practice will arise out of functional situations. It is the mature artist, not the beginner, who can get most out of large doses of isolated study and practice. The reason is that he has experience enough to be aware of its relationship to actual musical uses and applications.

B. *As for the idea that we do not know how to put essentials first, it is completely false.* A grasp of the auditory content of music can be developed with very little external scaffolding,—for instance, by rhythmic movement, rote singing, playing by ear, extemporizing, and so forth. In the same way, the rhythm of the rhumba can be conveyed before a single step is taught. The reason why teachers miss these possibilities is that they are so very simple and obvious. But they are of the highest importance.

3 A third great argument for the mechanistic approach is that it is systematic and orderly. This is probably the most important reason why so many teachers cling to it. But on examination the claim turns out to be spurious.

A. *The orderliness of mechanistically organized courses and sequences always turns out to be very superficial.* It is often spoken of as the "logical" organization of subject matter. Really it is no such thing. There is not a school textbook on mathematics which really exhibits the logic of the field. There is not a school textbook on language which really exhibits the basic logic of linguistics. Such things are beyond the horizon of the immature learner. What we actually find is a collection of topics arranged à la filing system, in a manner calculated to make any logical rigorist writhe. So also with music. The distinction between diatonic and chromatic harmony is not a real one in terms of

[18]

the logic of music. It is merely set up for convenience in writing text books and teaching courses. There is no compelling logic in covering all the triads before tackling the sevenths, or for putting scales ahead of arpeggios. On the logic of the notation, one would presumably have to begin with whole notes instead of quarter notes. The so-called logical order is really only a more or less convenient order, slightly influenced by psychological considerations that are usually not well understood.

B. *Granted that a mechanistic organization may look very neat and orderly, it may still be hopelessly wrong and confusing to the learner.* This, indeed, is, precisely the case. The attempt to break down achievement into separate, integral units, to be acquired, retained, and combined, is foredoomed from the first. It is like trying to create a picture by first cutting a piece of wood into separate segments like a Chinese puzzle, next painting each segment separately, and then fitting them together. This might be a very orderly process, but it would yield a queer picture.

C. *If we want a really orderly and logical approach, then the developmental approach and not the mechanistic approach fills the bill.* The developmental approach centers upon the essence of the field of study. It goes straight to the root of the matter, without beating about the bush. The young beginner has the same kind and quality of experience as the highly developed expert, the only difference being in degree. It treats the essence of mathematics as relational thinking, the essence of writing as communication, the essence of music as aural responsiveness. That is just how the expert feels. It deals with all specializations and techniques as embodiments of this essence, as expressions of it in various aspects. That too is just how the expert feels. And it mobilizes lessons, learnings, doings, not for the sake of storing this or that in the mind, or for the formation of habits, but for bringing about a clearer and clearer grasp of the essence.

It is a very strange thing how often both the friends and foes of developmental teaching fail to realize its essentially orderly character, how often they seem to take it as the equivalent of chaos. True, it brings in a far wider range of experiences, activities, learnings, doings, endeavors than mechanistic teaching. Rhythm bands, water glasses, notational study, making toy instruments, playing harmonicas and melody flutes and autoharps, jazz, listening, creative work, classes in applied music, the choir, the orchestra, the band, the small ensemble,

[19]

the glee club, contests, festivals, are all of them potential grist for its mill. But it does not use them at haphazard, or merely because they seem to be interesting, or because they present themselves by chance. It uses them to promote a line of development which is envisaged with the utmost clarity—the development of musical responsiveness, which is the heart of all valid music study. It uses them as influences for musical growth, for the making of musical people. Surely such a plan is to the highest degree orderly and indeed logical, even though it may be and must be almost infinitely flexible and variable.

QUESTIONS FOR DISCUSSION

1. Consider some teaching procedures in music, under which you yourself have worked as a learner, that seem to you to have been externalistic. In what precise sense may they be so characterized?

2. It is claimed on behalf of many courses of study in music that they are arranged in a simple-to-complex order. Examine a few actual examples, and in the light of them review our criticism of such an arrangement.

3. What reasons can you find to explain why so much teaching, in music and other fields, is externalistic and mechanistic?

4. Can you agree with the claim that every normal person is at least to some extent musically responsive?

5. Can you think of ways in which a piano teacher, a theory teacher, or a teacher of grade-school singing could emphasize musical responsiveness in his work?

6. Widespread attempts are made to teach children to read music in the elementary school. For the most part they fail. Why? What should be done about it?

7. What evidence can you find in your own experience and observation that most people who study music make far slower progress than they might and should?

8. How would you set about trying to make a person musical? What changes would you expect to notice in him? Do you think the thing could be done?

9. Why do you think so many children dislike their music lessons and quit as soon as they can?

10. Have you ever had a teacher who stressed consistently the inner essence of music? How did he do it?

ADDITIONAL READINGS

EMMA D. SHEEHY. *There's Music in Children.* Henry Holt and Company, Inc., 1946. (This little book concretely describes the developmental approach in dealing with little children. As you read it, ask yourself how the essential ideas could be applied, with necessary changes in detail, to older learners also.)

DAVID BARNETT. *They Shall Have Music.* George E. Stewart, Publisher, Inc., New York, 1944. (This book, like the preceding, should be read as a whole, which is possible because of its brevity. It deals with a special situation, but gives an excellent insight into the developmental position.)

INGA OLLA HELSETH. *Living in the Classroom.* Edwards Brothers, Inc., Ann Arbor, Michigan, 1939. Chapter 14, "Growth in Children." (This chapter presents many concrete instances of the developmental idea. They are not drawn from music, but they will help to make it clear.)

TOBIAS MATTHAY. *Musical Interpretation*, 3d ed. Boston Music Company, Boston, Massachusetts, 1914. (This book, by a famous piano teacher, turns essentially on the developmental idea as applied in his special field of work.)

JAMES L. MURSELL. *Successful Teaching.* McGraw-Hill Book Company, Inc., New York, 1946. Chapter 1, "Successful Teaching, Its Meaning." (This chapter emphasizes the importance of results and shows that in mechanistic teaching they are not forthcoming. Music is not dealt with, but the parallelism is obvious.)

CHAPTER TWO

Musical Responsiveness

I

Musical growth has been defined as growth in musical responsiveness. To put the matter in another way, it is the process of becoming a musical person. It is the central and determining purpose of any sound scheme of music education to foster and promote this process. This is the position that has been reached so far.

But a great deal more analysis and explanation are necessary before the idea can be effectively used as a guide in all the various practical decisions involved in conducting a program of music education, such as the shaping up of curricula and courses of study, the planning of units and lessons, the devising of techniques for teaching and evaluation, and so forth. A general distinction between developmental and mechanistic teaching has emerged, and it is of obvious and far-reaching significance. But the nature of the developmental approach must be understood far more specifically before we can see just how to put it into operation.

There will be a series of questions which must be answered, but the first that presents itself is this: What, exactly, does musical reponsiveness mean? What does it include? The broad significance of the idea is, perhaps, fairly evident. But this is by no means enough. To understand just what is to be developed is very necessary before it is possible to deal intelligently with the practical problems of developing it. So the first step must be to give an account, as specific and understandable as possible, of the nature of musical responsiveness.

To musicians and music teachers who have, perhaps, hardly given the matter a thought this may look like a very dubious undertaking, and perhaps not a very useful one. They are apt to think that the art of music and the nature of our basic response to it are so intangible and mysterious that no analysis of them is possible. And even if such an analysis could be made, and carried to something like definitive conclusions, they may ask how it could bear upon the everyday working problems of teaching, rehearsing, performing, practicing, and composing. Everything that follows in these pages amounts, in effect, to an answer to these two suggested difficulties, for it will be shown at length that the musical response is understandable, and also that there is nothing about the art of music more worth understanding for anyone who works with it. But the case may be stated summarily in advance.

First there is a very considerable body of investigation and analysis all of which tends in the same direction. Taken together it yields a remarkably clear and convincing picture of what the essential nature of music is, of how it affects us, and why. In the second place this material, while of great theoretical interest, is full of the most fundamental, vital, and fruitful practical implications. It indicates a way of dealing with music which the best musicians and the best teachers have constantly exemplified in their work, because they have instinctively felt that it was right. But the wisdom of the best teachers and the best musicians has hardly ever been systematic. It has been a matter of scattered gleams, and hints, and intimations. They have not usually been able to give solid reasons for what they did and what they believed, or to follow it out consistently in all its consequences, or to find answers to those who might and did say that they were wrong and foolish. This systematization, this defense, this complete formulation, is exactly what the material before us makes possible. It offers what is of the highest value for every working musician and music teacher—a practical aesthetic and educational doctrine to guide his efforts.

II

The very heart of that doctrine can be put in a single pregnant sentence: *Music is wordless poetry.* The basic response to music is a poetic response. Music is never rightly dealt with, whether by a composer, or a performer, or a listener, or a teacher, whether by a mature adult or by a little child, except in terms of such a responsiveness.

But what does this mean? What sense does it make? Where does it get us? What does if offer in the way of practical helpfulness for music education? I must ask the reader in whose mind these very reasonable questions arise, and who finds the idea startling and confusing, to be patient until he has read further, for everything in this book develops and expounds it. But also I owe him at least a brief preliminary explanation here and now.

[23]

Comparisons between the arts are not at all uncommon. Architecture is sometimes called frozen music. Painting is sometimes called frozen dancing. Such statements are quite familiar currency. But what do they amount to? Are they nothing better than showy and striking epigrams, superficial clichés, certainly not intended to be taken seriously? This is very far from true. The fundamental unity, the fundamental identity, of the seemingly different arts is one of the profoundest, truest, and most revealing of insights. It has been recognized again and again by the greatest minds and the supremest creative spirits that the world has ever known. As Schumann put it: The aesthetic of all the arts is the same; only the medium differs. And this identity is nowhere more evident, nowhere more illuminating, than in the relationship between music and poetry.

What is poetry? What is it that makes a poem a poem? Obviously not rhyme or meter, still less the use of flowery words. Grammatical rules or a string of dates can be expressed in rhyming and metrical verse, but this certainly is not poetry. On the other hand, there is plenty of poetry that has no rhyme, and some at least without any fixed meter. So these things cannot be of the essence. The vital point is this. A poem is a work of art which expresses and projects a way of feeling. It is this which makes it a poem rather than a sheer account of facts, or perhaps a versified argument. In the same way a piece of music is a work of art which expresses and projects a way of feeling. It is this essential identity of purpose or of psychological function that constitutes the identity of the two arts. It is this identity that was in the mind of Beethoven when he spoke of himself as wandering in the woods and "making poetry, or, as they say, composing."

But surely there are differences? Yes, obviously there are. But they are wholly in the means used to achieve the central purpose,— in the "medium," as Schumann put it. And even here they are not nearly so great as one might think at first sight. The great difference, of course, is that the poet uses words, while the musician does not. The poet can tell us explicitly that he is expressing sadness, or gladness, or love. He can describe imagined scenes and events explicitly and in detail, and these can evoke definite emotional values. The musician can do none of these things, or at any rate can hardly do them. But with this exception the tools used by the poet and by the musician are amazingly similar. Both of them use sound, and they use it for purposes of emotional expression. If you will listen to some of the recorded poetic readings listed in Appendix II, you will realize at once that this is so; for the sound, the flow, the rise and fall of the language is one of the most important means used by the poet to produce the effect he desires. This is why a poem does not fully come to life until it is heard, and why the oral reading of a poem is an act exactly parallel to the performance of a piece of music. The only difference here is that the musician makes a fuller and more controlled use of sound than the poet, exploiting it more completely as an expressive resource. And when it comes to rhythm, even this difference fades almost to nothing, for poetic and musical rhythms are exceedingly similar, and both are once more used as expressive resources and for expressive purposes. Poetry uses words, and music does not. Music uses sound more fully than does poetry, but poetry uses it, too. Both use rhythm equally. In both these arts the words, the sounds, the rhythms are simply means to an identical end, tools for achieving an identical purpose, which is the projection and expression of emotion.

Clearly, then, when we say that music is wordless poetry we are not saying something superficial or fantastic. But are we also saying something helpful in a practical sense? Most assuredly we are. What is being said is this: *Music is in its very essence and down to its very roots an expressive art.* It must always be so understood and so treated if it is to be dealt with rightly. Music is not a formal art, an art of pure design. A great work of music is not great because it is a superb solution to a problem of tonal arrangement, any more than *Hamlet* is a great play because of the skill of its internal dramatic plan. A fine musical performance is not fine simply because of its formal, chiseled perfection, but because of what it conveys. When we listen to a piece of music, what we respond to is not a display of expert tonal geometry, but a living and moving message for which the pattern of tone and rhythm is simply the vehicle.

The story has come down to us of how Vergil read the just-created *Aeneid* before Augustus and his court, of how a profound emotion gripped the listeners, of how at that superb passage which speaks of the heir apparent dead before his prime the empress swooned, and of how the emperor paid to the poet a gold coin for each golden word. This was no mere display of skill, but a supreme and moving utterance. So, too, when Wagner secretly composed and rehearsed the *Siegfried Idyll* and astonished Cosima by performing it outside her door on her birthday dawn, he was not demonstrating his virtuosity, but expressing his love. These two acts were both poetic acts, and in them stands revealed the identity of the two arts.

What is the practical value of all this? It saves music education from a sterile narrowness which falsifies all its values and goes far to stultify all its endeavours. When any person, young or old, listens to music, he should be helped to catch its poetic values, which are its central values. When any person, young or old, learns to perform music, he should be learning to release and project the poetry which is its essence. When any person, young or old, composes music, he should be led to feel and know that this is a poetic act. The essence of musical responsiveness is poetic responsiveness—responsiveness to expressive values. Any scheme of music education true to psychological realities has for its central focus the development of just such responsiveness.[1]

III

Having blocked out the general position, our next business must be specific analysis. And here at once a crucial question lies in wait. How is it possible for an art that uses nothing but tone and rhythm still to express emotion? How can music be wordless, and still be poetry? The answer must begin by pointing out the psychological significance and potency of tone.

It may be taken as established that the original and basic responsiveness to music is simply to tone itself. The claim is often made that human beings, and particularly little children, are primarily interested in the rhythm or the melody of music. They are interested in these things, and in harmony also. They do respond to them. But there is something more fundamental still, without which this interest and responsiveness would not exist. This is the tonal content itself.

Tone is a very special and unusual kind of stimulus. Indeed it is an unusual kind of sound. By far the majority of the sounds we hear are noises. Acoustically, a tone is usually said to be a sound in which there is nothing present except the fundamental and some of the series of overtones, the components of the so-called "chord of nature." A noise, on the other hand, is a disorderly jumble of components. But it is the psychological rather than the acoustical difference that is important here. And this turns upon the fact that a tone is organized about, and apprehended in terms of, a definite pitch, whereas a noise is not. The distinction is by no means clear-cut. There are many natural sounds which impress us as either deep or high, although we might not be able to assign them a definite pitch-level. There are some whose pitch-level may seem almost, although not quite, specific.

[1]I wish to say here, with the greatest possible emphasis, that every musician and music teacher will find it rewarding and illuminating to make himself a student of poetry.

Such sounds lie on the borderline between noise and tone. Music, too, always contains plenty of noises, some of them produced deliberately by the use of special media, others the results of the accidental and unavoidable squeaks, thumps, rattles, and puffings of the machines which we call musical instruments. But the broad distinction is sufficiently clear. From the psychological standpoint tone is sound dominated by a pitch component, and it is interesting to notice that such sounds must usually be produced by deliberate and artificial means. Color, for instance, is a far more common natural phenomenon than tone.

This very special, highly selected type of stimulation is known to have profound and very striking effects. Indeed these effects are by no means confined to human beings, but also manifest themselves among the lower animals. A considerable number of investigations have dealt with what is called "animal musicality,"[1] that is to say, the responsiveness of the lower forms of life to tonal stimulation. A striking instance, familiar to everybody, is the howling of dogs in response to music, which in all probability is not an expression of distress at all, but rather of a general emotional perturbation, on the whole seemingly pleasant rather than otherwise. The fact that a dog under such circumstances sounds distressed to human ears means nothing at all. The significant thing is that he does not usually run away, which he would presumably do if he did not like what was going on. On the contrary, he stays and sings! This is only one example of a great multitude of such phenomena. There is widespread evidence that musical tone has a remarkable and powerful stimulating and attractive effect upon a great many of the lower animals—horses, cattle, sheep, birds, and snakes, for instance. The legend of Orpheus, who tamed and subdued wild creatures by the sound of his lyre, is an old-time recognition of the psychological fact of animal responsiveness to tone. And, of course, cowboys who sing while riding round the herd at night are putting this piece of psychology to a very practical use.

For music education considered from the developmental point of view, these findings are highly significant. They mean that we are dealing with a type of stimulation to which a great many forms of life in addition to human beings are profoundly responsive. Animals are not affected in any way by the visual or literary arts. But they are affected by the tonal art. Of course, the musicality of a dog, or a sheep, or a bird cannot be developed, whereas that of a human being

[1]Charles Diserens, *The Influence of Music on Behavior* (Princeton University Press, Princeton, New Jersey, 1926), brings together a great number of such studies.

can be. But the root of the matter is the same for all. It may seem a far cry from the majestic and compelling inspiration of a Beethoven to the calming effect of a cowboy song upon a cattle herd, but there is a common element just the same. Profound and inescapable organic responsiveness to the special stimulation of tone is the factor that makes both manifestations possible.

When we turn from animal to human musicality, its foundation clearly rests on this unique and striking responsiveness. It has been shown again and again, and quite conclusively, that tonal stimulation has remarkable physical and mental effects upon human beings. When a person in an experimental situation is subjected to the impact of musical tone, certain changes are almost certain to take place. There are alterations in the heart beat, and in the depth and regularity of the breathing. These functions do not tend in any way to keep time to the music. What they indicate is a general imperative change in the person's emotional condition. In the same way, the external blood pressure tends to rise, and the chemical constitution of the blood is temporarily altered, due to the special action of the endocrine glands. Tonal stimulation also affects the psycho-galvanic reflex, that is to say, the resistance of the body to electricity, which is used as an index in some forms of "lie detector." Tonal stimulation, too, has a definite effect upon the digestive processes, and other things being equal, it tends to produce a freer flow of gastric juice and an increased gastric peristalsis. Furthermore, it can partially eliminate the effects of fatigue. Experiments have been conducted in which subjects repeated a movement of the hand from the wrist or of a finger from the knuckle until the muscles became paralyzed by fatigue products so that the movement could not be continued any longer. But if, at the moment when this point is reached, music is played, the paralysis is likely to be overcome for the time being, and its final onset postponed. Similarly, experiments have been carried out which show that a person's capacity for extreme muscular effort is increased by tonal stimulation. Finally, and perhaps most striking of all, tonal stimulation has been shown to increase the sensitivity of other senses. Experiments have been performed in which subjects were shown oculists' charts and told to read down as far as they were able. Then music was played, and they could discriminate another line while it was sounding.[1]

[1]Again see Charles Diserens, *The Influence of Music on Behavior* (Princeton University Press, Princeton, New Jersey, 1926). Also see his more technical summary of the literature, "Reactions to Musical Stimuli," *Psychological Bulletin*, Vol. 20, 1923, pp. 173–199.

Tone, then, is a stimulus of great psychophysical potency. This goes a long way toward explaining many common musical experiences. A good band can furnish a very definite pickup for weary troops on a route march. At the Six-Day Bicycle Race it is very often noticed that the fatigued contestants speed up the moment the band begins to play. Many people find that they do certain kinds of work better with the radio on, and it does not matter much what is coming out of it so long as it is tone, and so long as it is not actively annoying or otherwise obtrusive. Music has been used with definitely favorable effects in factories and work rooms. It is a desirable accompaniment to a meal. When it goes on behind dramatic action, at the movies or elsewhere, it has a very substantial and potent emotional effect, which enhances all the values of the play. In the days of the silent movies, many actors were unable to "emote" satisfactorily in front of the camera unless music was being played. And of course these remarkable psychological effects have from time immemorial been exploited for religious and patriotic and social purposes, and in connection with ceremonials of all kinds.

It is important to notice that the basic effects of tone do not seem to depend directly on the kind or the art quality of the music. When music is used to stimulate work, or to add to the enjoyment of a meal, all that is necessary is that it shall not be intrusive, that it shall not attract attention, and, more particularly, critical attention to itself. Elaborate vocal music, for instance, has been found to slow down work in factories, whereas symphonic music tends to speed it up. The reason is that the workers interrupt themselves to listen to the vocal gymnastics, whereas they just let the instrumental music carry them along. In the same way, a fugue would not be a good accompaniment for a dinner, whereas a blues song probably would be. Again, neither the poem nor the music of *God Bless America* is of a very high artistic standard, but when the two are put together and sung with a great volume of tone, they have an extremely marked effect upon everybody whose reaction is not consciously critical and negative. Once more, the English national anthem, *God Save the King*, is certainly no masterpiece, either in its words or in its tune; but when one hears it thundered forth in the grand style in Westminster Abbey, with all the reinforcing reverberations of the great Gothic church, the effect is overwhelmingly impressive. The point always to recognize is the astonishing organic and emotional potency of sheer tone, which manifests itself not only in human beings but in the lower animals as well. This is the core, the foundation of musical responsiveness. In fact it is the ultimate "why" of the whole art of music.

[29]

This brings us to an issue more obviously related to music education than the questions discussed so far—the question of what is sometimes called "child musicality." There are strong reasons for believing that a young child's primary responsiveness to music is first and foremost to tone itself, and not, as is sometimes asserted without any good evidence, to rhythm or to melody. Of course the remarkable calming effect of croonings, and songs, and lullabies is a matter of universal human experience. But there is more than this. Students of infant behavior have pointed out that about the third month of life there appear in the vocal patterns very characteristic babblings and lallings that go on spontaneously. These are, in effect, comfort sounds. They do not belong definitely in the category of either speech or song, but are the matrix out of which both develop, and they have an appreciable tonal content. It has been argued that such experiences and reactions are the original sources of what later becomes aesthetic pleasure in music and in the sheer sound of language. Also it has been suggested that deliberate encouragement at this stage may have an important bearing upon what appears in later life as inborn talent.[1] Furthermore, investigations have indicated that during the preschool and even the kindergarten period, the child is much more preoccupied with the tonal content and appeal of music than with anything else about it. Children at this age were found to be quite indifferent to really atrocious harmony, and quite pleased with music which contained it, although adults in the same room were hardly able to tolerate it, the reason being that the balance of responsiveness was different.[2] This, of course, is not an argument for using bad harmony or no harmony with little children, or for ignoring melody and rhythm. Children are by no means entirely unresponsive to these components, and of course we want their responsiveness to develop in just such directions. What the facts strongly indicate, however, is that there is something still more basic.

Ultimate musical responsiveness, then, is organic, perceptual, and emotional responsiveness to tone itself. This manifests itself far beyond the orbit of human life. It is prepotent in the musical experience of the little child. It is the basic reason why music has a strong appeal for unsophisticated and untrained people. And highly sophisticated and musically trained persons are influenced by it far more than they

[1]M. M. Lewis, *Infant Speech. A Study of the Beginnings of Language.* New York, Harcourt, Brace and Company, 1926.

[2]Sophie Belaiew-Exemplarsky, "Das musikalische Empfinden im Vorschulalter," *Zeitschrift für angewandte Psychologie*, Vol. 27, 1926, pp. 177–216.

sometimes recognize. Nobody, indeed, can escape from it if he responds to music at all.

This at once means that music is not a purely formal art, an art of abstract design. It is, like poetry, an expressive art. This is so because of the nature and the psychological effect of the medium it uses. A musical composition is, of course, a pattern, and often a very intricate pattern. But it is made out of a material to which the human organism and the human personality respond in a profound and far-reaching fashion. When a creative artist elaborates such a pattern he may believe and even claim that he is simply manipulating and refining a delicate scheme of relationships between the parts of a whole, and that here lies the whole significance of his work.[1] But this really cannot be so, because the emotional effects and values of the medium he uses are inescapable, and cannot help but be controlling. Also to perform such a work cannot be a pure exemplification of technique or skill. It is bound to be an emotional projection, either well done or poorly done, because once more of the psychological effect of the medium. This is why music, though it tells no stories, presents no ideas, and does not explicitly impose a sequence of imagery, can still be an expressive art. It does not use language, but it uses tone. And for this reason it is essentially a wordless, a tonal poetry.

This is of fundamental importance for music education. The tendency has been to place the whole emphasis upon problems of pattern, organization, skill, technique, and intellectual understanding. These matters, as we shall presently see, are without doubt of importance. But they are the branches, not the main trunk. Many weaknesses, many failures, in music education come from cultivating them in isolation from the stem out of which their life flows. A developmental scheme of music education will most assuredly foster a wide variety of musical achievement, experience, and expertness. But in and through and during all such endeavors it will always assiduously cultivate that responsiveness to emotional and expressive values which is the living principle of the art of music itself, and which springs from our profound natural response to the medium of tone.

[1]Just such claims are in fact made by some modern composers.

[31]

IV

It is a matter of common experience that our general emotional responsiveness to tone particularizes itself in certain characteristic ways. This has been supported by a number of investigations, so that certain quite definite statements can be made with a good deal of confidence.

1 There seems to be no doubt that music is capable of creating and supporting a fairly definite response in the way of a determinate mood. This carries our exposition of music as wordless or tonal poetry a step further, because the effect of music is to produce something more than a general and vague though perhaps strong excitement. A musical composition, like a poem, is capable of producing or expressing a definite emotional state or mood, which may be said to constitute its meaning.

Although one might think that this much would be accepted without question, some people have been inclined to express doubts about it. One of the chief difficulties is that it is often hard to describe in words the mood produced by a musical composition. Experimental subjects have been given lists of words indicating various mood values, and asked to check the one that seems best to convey the mood value of music to which they listen. On the surface there usually seems to be considerable disagreement. But when one looks more closely, it turns out that although quite a number of different words will be checked by different persons in connection with a given piece, all these words are likely to mean about the same thing. For instance, the Turkish March from Mozart's A Major Sonata may be described as happy, lively, peppy, or bright. But although these words are different, they probably stand for about the same thing in the minds of the persons responding. No one would be likely to call the music gloomy, or sad, or depressing. So the divergencies are more apparent than real. Also there may be another reason for them. A great many pieces of music do not maintain the same emotional tone and suggestion throughout. For instance, in a minuet and trio, the minuet may sustain a mood of gaiety or sprightliness, and the trio one of wistfulness, or calm, or meditativeness.[1]

When these allowances are made, all our evidence is that music is capable of engendering remarkably consistent mood responses among different persons. Indeed these effects even seem to cut across cultural

[1]In this whole connection see Kate Hevner, "Expression in Music; a Discussion of Experimental Studies and Theories," *Psychological Review*, Vol. 47, 1935, pp. 186–204. This is one of the best treatments of the subject.

and racial barriers, for it has been shown that similar tonal figurations and arrangements occur in our own music, in that of the North American Indians, and in that of certain African tribes, to express similar sentiments, such as those associated with love, war, victory, and grief.[1] Also a number of eminent composers, who consented to act as subjects, were asked to create phrases or fragments of music which would express or embody certain stated moods. These men worked independently, but there were recognizable similarities in the music they produced to convey each defined mood.[2]

There seems, however, to be an interesting limitation upon the expressive capacity of music. It does not appear to be well able, in and of itself, and without any external suggestions, to produce the definite emotions of everyday life. When groups of subjects, mainly college students, were asked to write down freely their emotional reactions to music, such feelings as love, fear, and hate were conspicuously absent. The explanation offered was that in order for such feelings to arise, it is necessary to have somebody to love, or some person or object to fear or to hate. This of course, the music cannot supply.

If this is so, then, while a piece of music may and probably does arise out of some specific circumstance in the composer's life, it does not express the literal content of that experience, but rather its general emotional values. The music of Schubert's *Hark, Hark! the Lark* does not tell about a lark, or even about the actual content of the poem from *Cymbeline*. But it conveys the emotional values of the poem. The *Pastoral Symphony*, as Beethoven himself said, paints no pictures of country life, but conveys the joy of a return to it. Even overt program music does not literally tell the story of the program. And while it is perfectly legitimate to seek the "meaning" of a piece of "absolute" music, we must not think that it is "about" something, like a piece of descriptive prose. A meaning it certainly has—a meaning which stems from some experience in the life of its creator. But that meaning turns upon its emotional effect, which can never be wholly translated into words.

[1] R. H. Grundlach, "Factors Determining the Characteristics of Musical Phrases," *American Journal of Psychology*, Vol. 47, 1935, pp. 624–643; "A Quantitative Analysis of Indian Music," *American Journal of Psychology*, Vol. 44, 1932, pp. 133–145; "An Analysis of Some Musical Factors Determining the Mood Characteristics of Music," *Psychological Bulletin*, Vol. 31, 1934, pp. 592–593.

[2] Julius Bahle, "Die Gestaltübertragung im vokalen Schaffen zeitgenössischer Komponisten," *Archiv für die gesammte Psychologie*, Vol. 91, 1934, pp. 444–451; "Psychologie des Einfalls und der Inspiration im musikalischen Schaffen," *Acta Psychologika*, Vol. 1, 1935, pp. 7–29.

Now the case is almost exactly the same with poetry. The famous sonnet by Keats *On First Looking into Chapman's Homer* does not tell us anything about Chapman's translation of the *Iliad*. But it projects in colored words and subtle rhythms, and a succession of wonderful images, the poet's joy in a great discovery. Shakespeare's *Hark, Hark! the Lark* and Shelley's *To a Skylark* are neither of them literal descriptions of the bird, but projections of the spiritual and emotional meanings of its song and soaring flight. Further illustrations of the basic function of poetry, which is to convey emotional meanings rather than literal content, will be found in Appendix III at the close of this book. So here again the parallel between music and poetry holds good. This is what Schumann had in mind when he insisted that the composer should determine the title of his piece only after it is finished, because the title should have a poetic truth and fitness. The only difference seems to be that poetry can perhaps define and establish emotional values more specifically than music.

But even this is none too certain. It may well be that the reason why the emotional meaning of a piece of music seems vague and indeterminate is that our response to it is superficial. This point has been argued by Ferguson,[1] and his reasons for it will be found elaborately set forth in the musical analysis presented in Appendix IV. He contends that if we really grasp everything that is in the pattern of tone and rhythm, its emotional values define themselves with unmistakable clarity and decisiveness.

So we conclude that music is capable of establishing and conveying mood-values or spiritual values which can, perhaps, be quite specific. Indeed to do this is its essential function, just as is the case with poetry. This brings us face to face with educational conclusions of the very first importance. When a person undertakes to perform a piece of music, he must do what a person does who undertakes to read a poem aloud. He must project its emotional and spiritual meaning. This is true all the way from the simplest grade-school song to the most elaborate symphony. So the education of the performer turns on developing at the same time a sensitiveness to these meanings and values and an ability to translate them into sound. Again, when anyone composes music, be he a little child or a mature artist, he functions as a poet who uses tone as his medium. He uses this medium to express spiritual and emotional intimations and values; and once again his education turns upon a developing sensitiveness to such

[1]Donald N. Ferguson, *On the Elements of Expression in Music*. University of Minnesota, Minneapolis, 1944.

values and a developing command of expressive resources. So, too, with listening. The development of the power to listen well, which is surely one of the capacities of the musical person, means a growing ability to catch and respond to the subtle emotional intimations and values of the music.

For some people the mood-wise response to music is all-absorbing and exclusive. They go to concerts or listen to recordings solely for a kind of emotional debauch. They may even object to any explanations of the structure of music or of the technical aspects of the performance. This, of course, is an immature and unsatisfactory kind of reaction, if it is the only one a person makes. But the extreme analytic attitude of some trained musicians is unsatisfactory and immature, too. The mature musical person is one who responds to music to which he listens, or which he performs, or which he composes, as a wordless poetry whose basic function is to embody and express emotional and spiritual intimations, and which does this not superficially or vaguely, but through all the refinements of its structure.

2 A second type of musical responsiveness is in terms of association and imagery. This is less important and fundamental than mood-wise response, but still by no means negligible.

All the investigations on the subject have shown that with a great many people music has a remarkable power to call up old memories and associations, and to set going a flow of imagery which is usually visual, but which may also be verbal. There are, in this respect, wide individual differences, and with some persons effects of this kind are not prominent at all. Responsiveness of this kind, however, is very common. It is by no means confined to so-called "program" music. Imagery and association are very generally elicited by the purest of "abstract" compositions. One point of interest, that contains not a few suggestions, is that in the mental pictures called up by music, movement is nearly always an important component. Flowing brooks, waving trees, dancing forms, and so forth, are elicited, rather than scenes of still life.

It must not be thought, however, that the imagined or remembered scenes and episodes evoked by a piece of music are in any sense its "meaning." If twenty persons are listening to a march, or a ballade, or a nocturne, perhaps eight or ten of them will respond in terms of fairly definite visualizations, but they will all be different. Five more, perhaps, will have vague and fleeting visual associations and images, which again will vary widely. The rest may have no such impressions

[35]

at all. If these people listen to a highly programmatic composition, such as *Till Eulenspiegel*, or *Siegfried's Journey to the Rhine*, without being told what it is supposed to be about, pretty much the same thing will happen. With some, perhaps with a majority, there will be a more or less copious flow of visual or verbal imagery and association. But it is most unlikely that any one of the twenty will hit upon the program that the composer had in mind.

Nevertheless these associative and imaginal responses have a very definite rationale. They are by no manner of means merely arbitrary or haphazard. They all of them embody, in various forms, the determining mood of the music. A funeral march may suggest night, darkness, the motion of heavy clouds or somber waves. It will not suggest scenes of rejoicing, peasant weddings, and the like. Such imagery and associations are, in fact and in essence, poetic projections of the emotional values of the music, and certainly not direct interpretations of it. In the Wagnerian music drama, for instance, the dramatic action is a comment on the music, and the music is a comment on the action, and both reinforce one another, although neither is a direct and literal interpretation of the other.

Quite a number of sophisticated musicians are apt to be contemptuous of all such literary and visual values in the musical response. The reason probably is that they themselves have been intensively trained in other directions and toward other interests. To the psychologist, however, this looks like a very real limitation. Daydreaming to music is a perfectly legitimate type of response. It occurs not only among enormous numbers of human beings, but in some of the greatest composers as well. It becomes objectionable only when forced, or carried to extremes, or thought of as a search for some cryptic and hidden meaning. It should be encouraged rather than discouraged, never, of course, as a fixed assignment, but by way of suggestion and stimulation, and for the sake of establishing and reinforcing the proper mood. Just what psychological and neural mechanisms are involved we do not know, although it is a fact that there is a connection, and with many people a close connection, between the auditory and visual centers of the central nervous system. It may be said with certainty that here we have to do with a perfectly normal and perfectly legitimate type of musical responsiveness, which ought to be recognized and fostered in a developmental program of music education, although it should never be compelled.

Here once again the comparison with poetry is interesting and illuminating. One might be inclined to say that music tends to give rise to free imagery; that is, imagery in producing which the person concerned has almost absolute *carte blanche*, whereas poetry gives rise to controlled or suggested imagery. But this would have to be qualified. The mental pictures called up by a poem—let us say by the description of Pandemonium in the first book of *Paradise Lost*—will certainly not be exactly the same for everyone; so they are not entirely controlled. Also the mental pictures which might go along with the Chopin Funeral March will not be absolutely random; so they are not entirely free. So the contrast between music and poetry here is only one of degree. Also the poetic images, which are directly suggested by the words, are media of emotional expression, just as the images suggested by music are organically related to its emotional values. Milton, in *Paradise Lost*, describes the hall of Pandemonium as a Doric temple, which instantly suggests remoteness from the present, formidable majesty, vast size, and austere perfection of detail, all in perfect keeping with the values of the great scene in which the fallen spirits hold conclave. So the less definitely suggested imagery called up by a piece of music will all be more or less in keeping with its values—and this will hold true to some extent even if a deliberate attempt is made to parody it.

This parallelism between music and poetry can be carried a step further and brought to a very practical focus. Some time ago it was shown that the evocation of imagery is definitely related to poetic appreciation.[1] Most people, it was found, gain in enjoyment when their attention is called to the imagery of a poem. Moreover there can be such a thing as deliberately coaching oneself to look for and evoke images when reading suitable poems. Even vague imagery was often found to be definitely helpful. However there is danger in overemphasis, and a deliberate search for images is likely to spoil appreciation. Moreover there are wide individual differences in susceptibility to suggestions in the way of imagery. It would, no doubt, be rash and improper to transfer these findings wholesale to music, but they certainly suggest interesting possibilities. They show that imagery is associated with mood, and that it can be used to evoke and intensify mood-wise response. They warn us against prosaic literalness and over-forcing. They remind us of the fact of wide individual differences. All this adds up to very good advice in using imaginal content and suggestions in connection with music, although of course the two arts are not on quite the same footing; and such suggestions will help a

[1]C. W. Valentine, "The Function of Images in the Appreciation of Poetry," *British Journal of Psychology*, Vol. 14, 1923–1924, pp. 164–191.

larger proportion of people in connection with poetry than in connection with music.

3 A third type of responsiveness, not by any means as basic as the two that have just been considered, but still important and characteristic, is visual responsiveness to music. There is a strong tendency to look toward any source of sound. This is very obvious at piano recitals, for which the seats on the left-hand side of the hall always sell first. It is also obvious when half the audience will turn round to look in the direction of an echo choir which begins to sing. All this is a great deal more than a matter of accident, and seems to have quite deep and significant roots in human psychology. It has been shown that sound becomes, perhaps not literally more audible, but certainly better articulated and structured when the action of the two ears is equalized. So there is a tendency, when listening to patterned sound, to bring the source of it into the median plane of the head. Also, of course, there is the factor of sheer attentiveness, which naturally manifests itself in looking at or toward what one is noticing.

This explains why people sitting in the back seats at a concert will peer so anxiously to see the performer, why people will sit and watch the radio or the phonograph as though something were likely to pop out, why at an organ recital they will watch the pipes and wish they could watch the organist. And it certainly suggests many things in organizing significant musical experiences. Thus one of the values of "live" music is simply that there is something to see going on. Or again, little children sometimes find a great deal of interest and an appreciable value in watching the action of a piano while it is being played. And of course this all gears into the use of symbolism and of the score, which makes it possible to look at what one is hearing, and to look at what one is playing or singing. The general point is that vision affords psychological support to audition—that to see what one hears tends to enable one to hear it better. There is, of course, no close counterpart to this in the case of poetry.

V

The general mood-value or emotional meaning of a piece of music, and the associations and images connected with it, are established by responsiveness to the constitutive elements of its tonal-rhythmic pattern. What these crucial elements are, and what psychological effects they have, are at least reasonably well understood. They will be found displayed in the aesthetic analyses of music presented in Appendix IV. And once more the parallels and contrasts between music and poetry are highly instructive here, for the constitutive expressive elements of a poem, other than the meanings of the words themselves, are very much like those of music. This can be clearly seen by comparing the analyses of music to which reference has just been made with the similar analyses of poetry presented in Appendix III.

1 A piece of music depends for its expressiveness first of all upon various kinds of tonal constituents. It is not possible to set up a clear classification of these tonal components, because they all affect one another and do not act separately. But if this is remembered, the following discussion, which is based upon nothing more than a convenient organization, need not be misleading.

A. *First there are the various types of tonal color, or, to use a more precise psychological term, of tonal quality.* The word "quality," however, is a little misleading, because a great deal more is included here than tone-quality or timbre, as ordinarily understood. The color effects, or sheer quality effects, of the tonal content of music include chord colors and key colors as well as what is commonly spoken of as tone-quality or timbre itself. All such effects are primarily agencies for musical expression, and they contribute toward establishing the mood-value or emotional meaning of a piece of music.

Chords are basically experienced as colors, as sheer qualities, and not as logical patterns organized above a chord bass. It is as colors that children naturally deal with them, experiment with them, enjoy them, and come to know them. Grieg reported that when he was five years old he was thrilled by "the wonderful mysterious satisfaction with which my arms stretched out to the piano to discover—not a melody—that was far off—no, that there is such a thing as harmony. First a third, then a chord of three notes, then a full chord of four, ending at last with both hands. Oh, joy! a combination of five, the chord of the ninth. When I found that out my happiness knew no bounds."[1] This is a very typical and an exceedingly valuable kind of childhood musical experience, which ought to be fostered and encouraged. It features a kind of musical responsiveness which is basic and also very much neglected. One of the great defects of conventional music education is that it always deals with chords in

[1]From Henry T. Finck, *Grieg and His Music.* Quoted by Emma Sheehy in *There's Music in Children.* Henry Holt and Company, Inc., New York, 1946, p. 41.

terms of logic and analysis,—that is, as entities produced by a juxta-position of parts, organized above a bass, and displaying certain res-olution trends. Of course these effects are there, and of course they are important. But there is something more fundamental still in the harmonic experience, and that is its sheer color value.

Chord colors or qualities in music have a similar place to word colors or qualities in poetry, although their relative importance is greater in music. A number of examples of effects produced by the sheer qualitative sound of words in poems will be found in the ana-lyzed material in the Appendix. Or consider the following three lines from the seventh stanza of Keats's *Ode to a Nightingale:*

> The same that oft-times hath
> Charmed magic casements, opening on the foam
> Of perilous seas, in faery lands forlorn.

One of the most distinctive values of this passage is created by the use of the wonderful and plangent word "forlorn." To be sure, the word has a grammatical relationship in the sentence, which is of ex-pressive importance. But in one of its aspects it is a sheer piece of verbal color, extraordinarily like a uniquely tinted chord in music.

Moreover such color effects, or qualitative effects, are essentially expressive agencies. They are used in this way by composers, almost without reference to resolution trends. They should be felt and pro-jected for this purpose by performers, and apprehended in this way by listeners. Responsiveness to chord color is grievously neglected in conventional music education, and this is one reason why so many persons have a very poor grasp of harmonic resources even after a very considerable amount of musical training. It should be cultivated from the first, and cultivated continuously, because it is one of the determining factors in musical responsiveness.

What has been said about harmonic color applies also to key color and to tone color proper. Here too the poetic analogy holds good. The major and minor keys and the various modes are not primarily schemes of relationship, but schemes of determining and often subtle color value. There has been quite an extensive technical discussion in the psychology of music as to whether the minor mode is essentially sad, or dark, or gloomy, and considerable experimental research has been devoted to the question. The upshot is that while the mood-value of a piece of music depends on all its components, so that it may still be gay although it is in a minor key, yet the minor tonality in and of itself does produce the characteristic sad, or gloomy, or dark effects ordinarily attributed to it. Tone quality, or timbre, too, belongs to the class of tonal color effects, and has the same function in music as word colors have in poetry. That is to say, it is essentially an expressive agency, one of those components responsiveness to which helps to establish the mood-value or emotional meaning of a composition.

B. *The second type of tonal component in music is melody.* This again has its counterpart in the "speech tunes" which are used when poetry is read aloud expressively.

A musical melody, like a speech tune in poetry, is not in the first place apprehended or responded to as a series of separate notes but as an entire, organically unified, flowing curve, with its beginning, its ending, its points of emphasis and subordination, its periods of rapid and retarded motion. Here again illustrations will be found in Appendix IV. The notes into which a melody is broken down do not themselves create it. They merely define the points through which it passes, and also they are used as conveniences in notation. The melody, however, lives in its organic unity, and it should be responded to as such, for on this depend its expressive and emotional values.

This extremely important point has been beautifully and decisively brought out in what is by far the best of all investigations of the melodic responsiveness of children.[1] It has been shown that children always tend to respond to melody as a living totality, not as a structure built out of notes. When they make mistakes in singing back a melody by ear, such mistakes are not true note-errors at all, but misapprehensions of the total melodic shape, in which it is perhaps simplified by reducing the size of the interval skips or by leaving out some fine point of nuance, or otherwise distorted. Moreover the investigator reports that when a melody is transposed into another key, very young children are apt not to recognize it at all.

Refined responsiveness to melody as a living whole is not only natural, but also a highly musical type of response. It is the way composers work, for they are very far from working out melodies note by note. It is the basis of a great deal in expressive performance. It has a great deal to do with facility and certainty in technique. It is a factor in memorizing. When a teacher of musical dictation tells his students that they should not try to spell out melodies note by note, but rather attend to the total shape involved, he is putting the

[1]Fritz Brehmer, "Melodieauffassung und melodische Begabung des Kindes," *Beihefte zur Zeitschrift für angewandte Psychologie*, No. 36, 1925.

idea into practical operation. This basic melodic responsiveness should be fostered from the first and all along the line in a developmental scheme of music education.

C. *The third type of tonal component in music is tonality.* This means the system of tendencies, of leadings, of attractions and repulsions, of points of rest and movement which establish themselves among musical tones. A chord can be treated both as a color or quality, and as an element in the logical system of tonal relations.

Is there anything in poetry that corresponds to tonality in music? Yes, there is. It is the grammar of the language. But—and this is an absolutely vital point—grammar in a poem is constantly used for expressive purposes. In the following excerpt from Milton's *A Paraphrase on Psalm CXIV*, much of the majestic and eloquent effect is produced by what is essentially a grammatical device. This is the postponement of the two principal clauses to the end of the sentence (they are run in italics), so that everything else piles up toward them and culminates in them.

> When the blest seed of Terah's faithful Son
> After long toil their liberty had won,
> And passed from Pharian fields to Canaan **Land,**
> Led by the strength of the Almighty's hand,
> *Jehovah's wonders were in Israel shown,*
> *His power and glory were in Israel known.*

It is because the grammatical structure of the English language lends itself to such treatment, that this highly distinctive emotional effect is made possible. Poetry is full of instances in which the poet has manipulated and exploited grammatical relationships for the sake of an expressive effect.[1] This is an exact counterpart to tonality in music.

[1]A still more magnificent example is the wonderful opening sentence of *Paradise Lost*, in which the subordinate clauses pile up to the principal clause (again italicized), and then fall away, so that the whole effect is like a majestic wave which swells, culminates, and irregularly recedes:

> "Of man's first disobedience, and the fruit
> Of that forbidden tree whose mortal taste
> Brought death into the world, and all our **woe,**
> With loss of Eden, till one greater Man
> Restore us, and regain the blissful Seat,
> *Sing, Heavenly Muse,* that, on the sacred top
> Of Oreb or of Sinai, didst inspire
> That shepherd who first taught the chosen **seed**
> In the beginning how the heavens and earth
> Rose out of chaos."

For musical tonality is not mere grammar, not mere logic, not mere pattern. It is expressive grammar, expressive logic, expressive pattern. What this means can once more be seen in the material in Appendix IV.

So the reason why people should develop a responsiveness to the tonality relationships in music is that they are living elements of musical expressiveness. From this it follows that they should be explored, used consciously, and enjoyed long before they are standardized as scale patterns or in terms of theory. Tonality does not derive from the scale. It derives from and manifests itself in music. The scale is not its origin, but only its standardization. And like all other standardizations, when taught too soon it has a cramping and frustrating effect instead of an enlightening one.

2 We turn now to the rhythmic component of music, and to the kind of responsiveness that it ought to evoke.

What, exactly, do we mean by the rhythmic content of music? The term is very far from exact, but perhaps it can be clarified. To make a start, we might say that the rhythm of a piece of music is everything that is left when the tonal content is eliminated. This, to be sure, is a very artificial idea, and a violent and distorting abstraction, but at least it may help to clarify matters so long as we always remember that we never experience anything of the kind purely in isolation. Tonal factors and rhythmic factors constantly affect one another, and there is an intricate interplay between them. This most certainly should always be born in mind. But still let us ask what would be left of a piece of music if all its tonal content were stripped away. Surely an intricate pattern of stresses and releases of various intensities, and of durations and pauses of varying lengths. But what gives this pattern its distinctive character that we call rhythmical? Shall we say that it is regular recurrence? Look and see! Certain arrangements or constellations of stress, release, and duration are repeated again and again. They are indicated in the score by the measure bars. Yet even they do not always recur with absolutely the same gradation of intensity all the time. The strong beat is sometimes a little stronger and sometimes a little weaker in relationship to the weak beats. Nor is the timing absolutely regular. But beyond all this, there are a great many patterns or constellations of stress, release, duration, and pause which are anything but regular, and which may occur only now and then, or even only once. These, of course, are the musical phrases. Yet they too are most certainly rhythmic entities, and must be experienced and delivered as such.

[43]

Thus regularity and recurrence cannot be the real bases of rhythm. Where, then, shall we look? The answer seems to be this: *Rhythm is a pattern of stress, release, duration, and pause organized for an expressive purpose.* Let us apply this idea to fields other than music. When a golfer makes a stroke, he executes a pattern of movement which of course involves stress, release, duration, and pause. Can it properly be called a rhythmic movement? No, not unless we want to use the word so inclusively that it means virtually everything, which is equivalent to virtually nothing. The movement pattern must be co-ordinated, and it must be well co-ordinated. But, in and of itself, it expresses nothing at all, and so it is not properly a rhythm. If, however, a dancer were portraying a golf shot in a ballet, everything would be different. The idea would not be to hit a ball a certain distance in a certain direction, but to express and convey certain aesthetic and emotional intimations and values. The movement would still be co-ordinated, but the co-ordination would be expressive, and this would put it into the category of rhythm. Or, to turn to another field, what is the difference between verse and ordinary expository prose? In both cases we have a sequence of co-ordinated language patterns, that is, constellations of stress, release, duration, and pause. But in the prose these co-ordinations are not in and of themselves expressive, whereas in the verse they are. There lies the distinction. It applies also to music. The pattern of stress, release, duration, and pause which is a component of the musical complex is not rhythmical because it is regular, but because it is expressive in and of itself, because it embodies and conveys aesthetic and emotional values. Regularity itself is not *ipso facto* rhythmic. It only becomes so when utilized to convey certain values, as with the steady beat of a tom-tom, the steady pulsation of the drum in the second movement of Tchaikowsky's *Symphonie Pathétique*, or the steady iteration and reiteration of the phrase in the Ravel Bolero.

Responsiveness to rhythm, then, is responsiveness to an *expressive* pattern of stress, release, duration, and pause. This must determine our whole educational approach to and treatment of it. A purely arithmetical approach to it is, of course, quite hopeless. A rhythmic pattern yields certain time values, obviously. But to try to get at it by emphasizing the time values is to deal analytically with the end results instead of with the thing itself. To approach it purely by way of physical movement is also insufficient, though it is a good deal better. Rhythm is more than physical movement. It is expressive physical movement. Here, as everywhere else in teaching, phases of

[44]

analysis are absolutely necessary. But so are phases of synthesis. In general, rhythm must be felt and apprehended in terms of its expressive function if it is to be experienced and learned aright. Rhythm as part of the beauty of music, not merely part of its formal mathematics, is how the musically developed person apprehends and deals with it. If anyone has the least doubt that conventional educational practices for teaching rhythm are disastrously wrong, let him ask himself how many members of the average senior high-school orchestra, or for that matter how many professional musicians, have a sure and flexible grasp of the rhythmic component of music.

Both poetry and music teem with wonderful and instructive examples of the expressive value of rhythm, which indeed is its very essence. The ones that are most likely to come to mind, however, are perhaps rather commonplace—heavily accentuated poems, such as some by Kipling, marches, waltzes, and the like. In contrast I offer here a poetic example which is both very subtle and very revealing. It occurs in the first two lines of Milton's sonnet *On the Late Massacre in Piedmont*. In prose the passage looks like this: "Avenge, O Lord, thy slaughtered saints, whose bones lie scattered on the Alpine mountains cold." One's tendency would be to read the words of the subordinate clause beginning with "whose," in a fairly even and unaccentuated tone. To do so would make the sense perfectly clear, and it might be accomplished quite expressively. Yet a certain subtle but very powerful value which Milton intended would be lost. In his sonnet the passage stands as follows:

> Avenge, O Lord, thy slaughtered saints, whose bones
> Lie scattered on the Alpine mountains cold.

The word "bones" is placed on a strong element of the beat. It is placed at the end of a line so that there is a very brief pause after it. This produces a gradation in what would otherwise almost certainly be a clause of uniformly delivered words. At once, because of this subtle difference, the values are profoundly altered. What would otherwise have been a not unaffecting but perhaps rather commonplace statement is transformed into a piece of majestic eloquence. And it is all done by the rhythm! Music is full of effects like this. Anyone who wants to apprehend or to deliver its expressive values should never think that these are created by superficial, or obvious, or arbitrary means. One might sentimentalize Milton's words in their prose setting forever and a day without getting their unique and

[45]

intended effect. So also anyone who hopes to deal with music expressively should pay the closest attention to its rhythmic component.

3 The third and final type of musical component to be considered is its architectonic content,—its broader structure. Here the emphasis should by all means be upon the kind of analysis which has been exemplified in our Appendices III and IV—that is to say, upon what students of the aesthetics of literature call functional rather than abstract form. The important thing about a sonnet, as they remark, is not that it consists of fourteen lines divided into an octave and a sestet, with a certain fixed rhyming scheme, but that it has a central, focalizing idea, which its structure organically conveys. This illustrates the distinction between organic and abstract form in poetry, and exactly the same distinction holds true in connection with music, or indeed any other art.

What is the consideration of primary importance about a Beethoven symphony, regarded as a piece of musical architecture? To be able to identify in the first movement the first subject, the second subject, the development section, the recapitulation, and so forth? To decide whether the second movement is a rondo, or an air with variations, or an A-B-A pattern? By no means. Such matters are by no means negligible, but they are not at the top of the list. The first thing is to realize that here is a vast, tapestried development of a single pregnant musical idea, which is the living unity of the whole immense and intricate organism. That is how the music grew in Beethoven's own mind, as we can see very clearly from his sketch books, and judge from his numerous self-revelations. It is what he intended it to convey. That is what it must convey, if it is not to miss the intended mark. Everything began with a single fertile idea. The distribution of its movements, the elaboration and arrangement of its themes were not achieved by any process of addition. They took shape as the limbs and organs of a developing embryo take shape in the womb.

The vital thing about a symphony, as with any other work of art, is not the external specifications of its architecture, but the pregnant musical and expressive idea that grew into this particular shape. This is the way to approach musical architecture, all the way from the B Minor Mass to a simple folk song. There can be no question but that it is aesthetically and educationally sound. The first thing to notice about the architecture of a folk song is not that it consists of three phrases, one repeated at the beginning and at the end, and the other two contrasting, but that it is the development of an expressive

[46]

musical and poetic conception. This is also the essential thing to see about the musical architecture of the Mozart *Requiem*, the *Christmas Oratorio*, and the *Ninth Symphony*. It is how the composer himself feels about his work. It is how the mature and sensitive musical person responds to it.

For the sake of illustration, let us compare the expressive value of the architecture of a certain poem and a certain piece of music. The poem is Keats's *On First Looking into Chapman's Homer*. It goes as follows:

> Much have I travel'd in the realms of gold
> And many goodly states and kingdoms seen;
> Round many western islands have I been
> Which bards in fealty to Apollo hold.
> Oft of one wide expanse had I been told
> That deep-brow'd Homer ruled as his demesne:
> Yet did I never breathe its pure serene
> Till I heard Chapman speak out loud and bold:
> Then felt I like some watcher of the skies
> When a new planet swims into his ken;
> Or like stout Cortez—when with eagle eyes
> He stared at the Pacific—and all his men
> Look'd at each other with a wild surmise—
> Silent, upon a peak in Darien.

This is one of the masterpieces of English literature, and it contains innumerable subtleties and expressive beauties. But let us concentrate on its architecture. Formally it is a Petrarchan sonnet, divided into an octave of eight lines and sestet of six, with a fixed rhyming scheme. But this tells very little. What does it express? A great and thrilling discovery! Not only the discovery of Chapman's Homer, but the self-discovery by Keats of the fullness of his own poetic genius, than which surely nothing could be more moving and exciting. The idea of a quest appears in the very first line—the idea of search, of exploration. Fulfillment arrives in the eighth line, with the reading of Chapman. But this is not the whole story. More and greater things are still to appear. All the metaphors in the octave are limited in scope—the Ionian Sea, the isles of Greece, the rumor of an unknown and wider region. The octave terminates in what in music would be called a half-close, something that brings it to an end, yet is not wholly conclusive. Then the same theme of exploration and discovery is taken up again in the sestet, but now with a wider compass and more sweeping metaphors—the sky, the planet, the vast Pacific instead of the narrow sea. And everything comes to a terminal point in one of the most wonderful cadential effects in literature—the image of the explorers silhouetted against the sky, silent, motionless, gazing at each other in the presence of the revelation. It is in this way that the architecture of the poem expresses its meaning.

The piece of music is the Air with Variations which constitutes the first movement of the Mozart A Major Sonata. All the sequence of the variations taken together amount to a progressive exposition of the emotional values implicit in the theme. Variation III (the Minore) comes like a gentle sigh in the midst of wistful happiness. The feeling elaborates itself with constantly shifting—though, save for this one case, never sharply contrasting—colors and values. The patterns in which it conveys itself become more and more intricate as the evolution proceeds. It is this sense of a steady unfolding, a making explicit of certain values delicately established in the original statement of the theme that constitutes the whole life and meaning of the architectural form as here used by Mozart.

VI

So, in concluding this perhaps rather analytical chapter, we return once more to its central contention. Music is wordless poetry, tonal poetry. Its function is to express and convey human feeling. It does this by utilizing certain resources which have been briefly surveyed here, though they have been very far from scrutinized in all their fullness. But enough has been said to explain what musical responsiveness means. It is an emotional responsiveness determined by the constituent elements of the expressive pattern of tone and rhythm and design. This responsiveness must control composition, and performance, and listening. It is the very heart of music as a psychological and cultural factor in human life. To develop it is the central task of music education at all levels and in all its branches. This does not imply any neglect of skill or knowledge. On the contrary, such an emphasis is the surest and quickest way of achieving both. When properly understood and conducted, growth in skill and in knowledge is inseparably bound up with growth in musical responsiveness. This is what the developmental approach in music education means. The prevailing defect of too much of our current practice is that it emphasizes skill and knowledge as independent ends in themselves, and thus deals only with externals, leaving the vital essence of the matter to mere chance.

[48]

QUESTIONS FOR DISCUSSION

1. What parallels with music do you find in the aesthetic analyses presented in Appendix III?

2. Examine some children's songs to see how the constituent elements of the music convey emotional values and meanings. What does this suggest about the teaching of these songs?

3. What practical conclusions can you draw from the finding that tone quality is an outstanding factor in musical responsiveness?

4. In what respects does the reading of a poem aloud resemble the performance of a piece of music? If possible consider this question in the light of the readings listed in Appendix II.

5. Discuss the values and dangers of encouraging imagery, association, and "literary" interpretations generally in connection with music.

6. Suggest ways of evoking responsiveness to (a) harmonic coloration, (b) expressive rhythm with young children and older pupils.

7. What implications for music education do you find in the fact that many species of lower animals are responsive to music?

8. What does the contention that a melody is an organic whole, not a composite of separate notes, suggest as to the significance and value of vocal experience?

9. To what extent is it possible to express the emotional meaning of a piece of music in words?

10. Which of the aspects of musical responsiveness can and should be emphasized in early music education? Must any of them be postponed to more advanced stages?

ADDITIONAL READINGS

R. M. OGDEN. *Hearing*. Harcourt, Brace and Company, Inc., New York, 1924. Chapter 13, "Aural Education." (This chapter deals with sensory and emotional education from a broad psychological standpoint.)

ALBERT R. CHANDLER. *Beauty and Human Nature*. D. Appleton-Century Company, Inc., New York, 1934. Chapter 13, "Rhythms of Speech." (Repays careful study, though overloaded with detail, for it clarifies the nature and function of rhythm in both poetry and music.)

JAMES L. MURSELL. *The Psychology of Music*. W. W. Norton and Company, Inc., 1937. Chapter 1, "Introductory: The Appeal of Music." (This chapter develops at length and with numerous references the fundamental conception of music here presented.)

VERNON LEE. *Music and Its Lovers*. G. Allen and Unwin, Ltd., London, 1932. (This remarkable book contains a wealth of material throwing light upon the nature and varieties of musical responsiveness.)

CHAPTER THREE
Characteristics of Musical Growth

I

Having explained what is meant by musical responsiveness, the next thing is to explain what is meant by developing it. What is the process of musical growth, which should be the center and focus of music education? It is precisely not a process of addition or accumulation. Rather it is one of living evolution. This much we have already seen, and some of its fruitful practical implications have already become clear. A program of music education should not consist of a series of lessons or units, each one set up to be learned and retained. Nor should it be organized as the study of a number of isolated specialties. On the contrary, it should consist of an array of developmental influences, all centering about a common focus in musical responsiveness. This gives us something to go on in practical planning. Indeed it gives us a good deal, but it is not nearly enough.

The nature of the growth process itself needs to be understood much more specifically than it has been so far. It will be found to have certain definite characteristics, and to exhibit certain typical rhythms. These two considerations will be the topics of the present chapter and the one that follows it. Then the distinctive features of a developmental influence or a developmental experience will be discussed. As to the general characteristics of musical growth, which are dealt with in this chapter, there are four of them which will come up for consideration.

II

Musical growth, like all mental growth, is a process in which essential meanings are clarified, deepened, and broadened. This is the first of its four characteristics. A few non-musical illustrations will help to explain the idea.

A little child becomes able to walk by a process which is much better described as growth rather than as learning. The first intimations of the new pattern of behavior manifest themselves long before he is able to assume an upright posture, or to take a single step. As he lies on his back, he tends to thrust his legs strongly against anything touching the soles of his feet. He makes more and more decisive and energetic attempts to raise his body from the supine position. When he is held sitting, he is likely to squirm and wriggle in the general direction of an erect posture. After a time he is able to assume this posture for a moment. Then balance and control become better, and at last true independent locomotion appears. To anyone watching his behavior over a period of months, it is evident that an intelligible and definite action-pattern is establishing itself. At first there are only hints, and fleeting and imperfect intimations. But these grow more and more definite, until they coalesce and crystallize into the complete, meaningful, co-ordinated organization of behavior.

When the sculptor Rodin produced his bust of Balzac, the finished work was a product of growth which took place in the artist. He searched for suitable models, and considered appropriate materials. But beyond this, he read every published line of Balzac, and visited every place where he had spent any considerable time. Rodin saturated himself in the life and personality of Balzac, so that the creation of the bust itself was the focalization of a great sweep of insight, comprehension, and meaning.

When a person achieves a grasp of mathematics, the essence of the affair is a process of growth. Mathematics itself is precisely relational thinking. The child discovers that one thing is bigger than another, that there are more objects in one pile than in another, that when one pile is combined with another the result is a third pile larger still. Then he begins to comprehend the use of symbols, such as numbers, plus, minus, times, and the like, and his grasp of relationships become clearer, deeper, broader. After a while he passes on from arithmetical to algebraic symbols. He finds that the symbolic language can convey geometrical relationships. He goes still further, into the more abstract and inclusive concepts of calculus. Always there is a continuous gain in power and insight, a firmer and firmer grasp of relational thinking itself. So the central meaning of mathematics becomes clearer, deeper, broader. This, in the very briefest outline, is what the developmental approach would mean in the teaching and learning of mathematics.

It will be clearly seen from these three instances, how greatly the process of growth differs from a process of addition or accumulation. The child does not become able to walk by assembling the components of the locomotor pattern. Rodin was not accumulating a mass of knowledge about Balzac, but trying to realize the essential meaning of the man's life, and work, and personality. The proper learning of mathematics is not an affair of mastering a series of separate skills or processes, but of achieving a new understanding, a new way of thinking. Growth, as contrasted with accumulation, is a process of clarifying, deepening, and broadening.

This applies also to musical growth. When a performing artist is working on a new composition he does not break it down into fragments, learn each of them one by one, and then put them together— not, at least, if he knows his business. He conceives of his job as a process of growth. He may, it is true, from time to time concentrate on fragments, even on very small fragments. But this is always in the light of the whole, and as part of the job of evolving a clear, articulate, intelligible pattern. What he is doing is to transform something vague, indefinite, and therefore imperfect into something specific, definite, and controlled. He may slave at details, and spend long hours at manipulative problems. But what he is always working for is the creation of an interpretation. What mastering the composition really comes to is getting its essential meanings into his fingers, his mind, and his feelings.

This same sequence of growth is beautifully illustrated in the process of musical creation. From many autobiographical fragments, from the sketchbooks that he left, and from the comments of contemporaries, we know quite a good deal about how Beethoven worked as a composer. His starting point was often a mere fragment of harmony, or melody, or rhythm—an *aperçu*, as it has been well expressed. This tonal or rhythmic *aperçu* would grow in his mind as a seed grows in the ground. It would expand, ramify, take on shape. Very often it is possible to trace this sequence of development, at least in part. One can see how the pregnant meaning of the original hint came to be more and more explicit and complete, how its possibilities were realized, often slowly and with many errors and falsifications. Thus his great works were not built, were not fitted together out of separate pieces. They grew like living things. So, as we listen to them now, we are aware of their profound organic consistency.

You might be inclined to think that a great composer like Beethoven would exemplify in his work certain psychological processes which have no place in the musical undertakings of young people and children. To some extent this is true, but the identities are far more fundamental than the differences. Here is an example of musical

[52]

composition carried on by a group of children which involves precisely the same point that has just been brought out. These children were five-year-olds in a nursery school. Each morning for a week they had been playing homemade instruments with very little in the way of formal direction. They enjoyed this activity very much, and used to come to school early each day to help carry the drums to the playground and get first turn in using them. One day, as they played with well-accented rhythm, they started chanting the words: "You better watch out for your whole life!" The chant kept getting louder and louder. It went on and on, and seemed as though it would never stop. Suggestions that music has changes in it, that often different parts are used, and so forth, had no effect. Next day's performance was the same, except that it was still louder, with more of the group joining in. After that, however, changes in intensity and the first beginnings of organized form began to manifest themselves. After three days the following arrangement had established itself:

DRUMS AND VOICES
  You better watch out for your whole life!
  You better watch out for your whole life!

VOICES ALONE
  Better watch out—better watch out!
  Better watch out—better watch out!

VOICES ALONE (*Hushed*)
  Shoo, shoo, shoo, shoo
  Shoo, shoo, shoo. . . .

DRUMS AND VOICES
  You better watch out for your whole life!

VOICES (*Shouting*)
  Watch out![1]

These children were doing, in a very humble, simple, elementary way, to be sure, exactly what Beethoven was doing when he composed his symphonies. They were starting with an expressive musical idea, and they were shaping it up, bringing out its meaning. They were discovering and utilizing certain musical resources, particularly those of rhythm and architecture, to express a way of feeling. There was a meaning from the first, and it became clearer, deeper, better defined, more sharply realized. In other words, this was a process of musical growth.

[1]This episode is told by Emma D. Sheehy in *There's Music in Children* (Henry Holt and Company, Inc., New York, 1946), pp. 23–24.

[53]

What happens in all the three instances just discussed—that of the virtuoso, the master composer, the child composers—is precisely the refinement, the clarification, the deepening of musical responsiveness. Expressive meanings, emotional values are first dimly and partially seen. More and more of what they imply, of what is in them, is brought out as they are shaped up by the use of the expressive resources of the art of music. Every musical undertaking—singing a song by ear, making up a tune to be played on water glasses, learning how to use the notation, working at a problem of theory or technique, joining in a rehearsal—should have precisely this character. Indeed this must be so if the undertaking is to be psychologically and educationally as well as aesthetically valid. There must be an emotional intimation which comes into clarity. There must be a growing grasp, in terms of this particular undertaking, this particular problem, of the meaning and resources of music as an expressive art. And the whole long sequence of a person's musical education must consist of a varied succession of just such revelations of the meaning of music as an expressive art.

Let it be remembered that musical responsiveness is essentially poetic responsiveness. The very little child begins with simple pleasure in tone, which is the basic medium of the art of wordless poetry—with tone that he makes himself or hears. Through multifarious experiences extending over the years—through rhythmic experiences, through creative experiences becoming more and more complex, through singing songs, through playing homemade instruments and standard instruments, through taking part in ensemble performances—he comes to realize more and more of what tone can express. His study of the notation, or of an executant technique, or of musical theory is pointed toward an increasing mastery of the expressive resources of the art of tonal poetry. His study of the history of music is a revelation of how this art of tonal poetry has been used and what it has stood for in days gone by. Thus, in all such multifarious doings and learnings, there is a coherent thread of meaning. In and through them all he discovers more and more of the significance of musical responsiveness, and of the significance and possibilities of music. He finds that to sing, or to play, or to compose, or to listen, or to work at a problem in theory or technique are all different ways of coming to grips with the poetry of music. So the germ develops. What was at first implicit becomes more and more explicit. What were at first vague hints become more and more fully realized possibilities. Musical responsiveness itself becomes clearer, deeper, broader, more significant, and the possibilities and values of the poetic art of music rise more and more completely into consciousness.

This implies, of course, that all the endeavors, activities, and learnings that make up the music program must be consciously centered upon promoting musical responsiveness. One learns to sing, to play, to read, to compose, always with the central emphasis upon the musical response, the poetic response, the projection of emotional values by the resources of the tonal art. And so that response itself becomes more and more adequate and assured. This is what the first general characteristic of growth implies for music education.

III

Musical growth, like all mental growth, is continuous. This is the second of its general characteristics.

To begin once again with a non-musical illustration, consider how a child comes to be able to read the English language. He is brought up, let us say, in a stimulating home environment. He is surrounded by people who have intellectual, or at least cultural, interests. There are books and magazines about. He hears them discussed in conversation. Older members of the family read to him, and he enjoys it. Almost insensibly he gets the feeling that to be able to read to oneself is desirable. From time to time he is encouraged to do so, perhaps quite casually, and people show him how to set about it. This hardly seems like a business of lessons, but more like a natural development. Later on in life he may not be able to remember a moment when he crossed a watershed between non-reading and reading. Of course when he has reached a certain point he needs to be helped to look at printed English properly, and to understand the symbols that he sees. But all this may come about gradually, incidentally, and not at all as a clear-cut, consciously defined stage. In fact, if reading is set up as a sort of block skill, to be started from scratch on a certain day, without any developmental background, and carried through on a schedule of lessons, it may never be mastered very well. For one grows continuously into the ability to read, under the impact of various developmental influences, among which, of course, may be certain specific techniques of instruction.

Musical growth, too, has the same essential continuity. This must always be remembered in practical educational planning, for discontinuity is psychologically destructive, and is sure to make trouble. What this means may be made clearer by showing how the idea applies to three specific problems.

Music reading should always be treated as one special phase of a continuous sequence of musical growth. It turns upon the visualization of music as represented in a system of symbols. Long before a child begins to study these symbols, his musical responsiveness should have gone through a considerable development. The melodic and rhythmic components of music, and its distinctive mood values should have come to mean something to him. Then as he begins to be able to see what he hears and what he responds to, the symbols themselves are learned in terms of meanings that are actualities in his experience, and the learning of them further refines and clarifies musical responsiveness.

Piano study, again, should be initiated as a process of reinforcing and defining a musical responsiveness already organized to a considerable extent. The child should already have had considerable experience with music through listening, through singing, through bodily movement, through the rhythm band, through the use of toy instruments, and so on. He should have gotten to know what the piano is, by hearing people play it, by strumming on it and picking out notes, perhaps by looking inside of it to see how it works. Then the definitive approach to piano study comes as a further shaping up of these evolving musical responses.

Again, when it comes to the study of theory, a person should have had ample experience with melodies, chords, rhythms, architectural patterns, and so on, before he undertakes the study of triads, sevenths, part-writing, and all the rest of the familiar material. These experiences should have come through many avenues—listening, singing, playing, extemporizing, creating melodies, and the like. A fairly mature and organized musical responsiveness should have been established. Then the study of formal theory supports this evolving responsiveness, and carries it further, by intellectualizing it.

The vital, indeed the universal point exemplified in these illustrations is that the new study should not come as a bolt from the blue. It may well come as a dramatic development, but it should not be a sheer novelty. Rather it should have the quality of revelation, of a fuller and wider realization of something already apprehended. Many of the most refractory difficulties in music education come from ignoring this essential continuity. The problems of notation, of the pianistic technique, of the materials of theory, are presented as brand-new challenges to be surmounted. Many of us can remember that in our first course in theory we found ourselves grappling with matters of which we had not even faintly dreamed, and for which past experience gave virtually no clues whatsoever. How can this fail to make trouble of the most serious kind? A good deal of attention is given to better "methods" of teaching note reading, piano playing, theory, and other branches of music education. One cannot say that they are nothing more than time thrown away. But they are only alleviations, not cures. The real trouble lies in setting up the new study in such a way that it is approached without any developed musical-mindedness. This means that it is in essence musically unintelligible. It has to be handled by a routine, by what amount to mechanistic procedures, because there is no living musical responsiveness to be carried forward to greater depth and precision. Even the cleverest methods cannot fully compensate for such a lack. They have to do with the organization of the study within itself, whereas the root of the difficulty lies in its lack of relation to musical growth.

This idea of developmental continuity means that every musical activity, endeavour, or learning, throughout the whole gamut of maturity, should involve the same kind of musical experience. The youngest child should sing or play as the masters sing or play, compose as the masters compose, listen as the masters listen. He should be doing on his level of capacity the self-same thing that they do on theirs. He should be coming to apprehend the essence of the tonal poetry more clearly, to feel it more truly and deeply. The principle holds for every human endeavour. The little child at the very beginning of mathematics should be doing what Einstein did when he discovered the mass-energy formula—coming to understand relationships. The beginner at English composition should be moulding language for expressive ends, just as all the greatest writers have done. In his early approach to history, the child should, in his own measure, think and feel as the historian thinks and feels. True, the child is immature. But so is the greatest master! There is no such creature as the ultimate, the "finished" mathematician, or writer, or historian, or musician. There is no finality. There are only degrees of maturity, of clarity, of profundity, of amplitude in the grasp of meanings. And everywhere and always, musical growth is progress in the apprehension of the essential poetic values of the art of music. So, in an ideal developmental plan, every experience, every activity, every learning will be one that illuminates and clarifies these values.

This clearly involves a reconsideration and to some extent a rejection of various popular and widely held ideas.

[57]

1 Musical growth cannot be subdivided into a series of self-contained stages. Various suggestions of this kind have been made, but they are in conflict with the idea of developmental continuity.

According to one old-time theory, the individual repeats in his lifetime a sequence of stages through which the human race has passed. This is the theory of recapitulation. According to it, a person goes through a period of savagery, then a period of barbarism, and finally reaches the status of civilization. It used to be taken very seriously. Methods of instruction and discipline, and the content of the curriculum itself were to be determined by the stage through which the pupil was passing. Thus stories of heroes and the Homeric poems were considered appropriate for a certain age, because they belong to the childhood of the race. So far as I know the theory of recapitulation in its strict sense has never been applied to music education, although the notion of definite stages certainly has been. The positive value of this theory lay in its recognition of the importance of mental development. But it is now well recognized that there is no evidence of an individual's mental growth being determined by racial development. A civilized child is a very different being from a primitive adult. And above all, human individuals are not held to any rigid, predetermined sequence of mental growth, as they would be if they recapitulated the alleged racial sequence.

According to a more recent theory, children pass through a sensory stage, an imaginative stage, a stage dominated by memory, and finally reach a stage dominated by reason. Quite a few attempts have been made to apply this idea to educational practice. For instance, it has been thought that the best time to start a foreign language is around the age of twelve, because that is when memory is prepotent, so that the child can then learn vocabulary and grammar best. Again it has been claimed that the education of little children should chiefly be a matter of sensory stimulation, that imagination should be evoked later on, but that studies calling for the use of reason should be postponed until adolescence. Ideas of this kind still have some influence in music education, although they have been abandoned by responsible psychologists. Many criticisms could be made of them, but here it is sufficient to point out that the human mind and personality always develop as a whole. A child is reasonable enough in his own way. So is an adult. But neither is perfectly reasonable. A person has just as much imagination at thirty as he did at eight, though he probably uses it differently. Rich and diversified sensory stimulation remains all through life a very fruitful and desirable type of influence.

So the idea that certain mental processes are segregated at certain ages is a fallacy.

2 The idea of developmental continuity bears on the problem of preparation. How ought a learner to be prepared for some phase or type of music study? This is a question that bulks large in the thinking and planning of many music teachers. Let us deal with it first by way of a specific application, and then try to formulate a general answer.

Many teachers of applied music, and particularly teachers of wind instruments and strings, devoutly believe that a beginning pupil must establish certain automatisms at the start of his work. So they conclude that introductory study should center chiefly and even exclusively upon the technical mechanics of the instrument. Some of them even go so far as to insist that a serious student should work at nothing but formal technique for months on end, before he undertakes to play any music at all. A case has actually come to my notice where a teacher summarily refused to go on working with a pupil because the pupil found this unbearable, and was wicked enough to break down and play a piece before he was told to do so. Now for young pupils this is most certainly a clear breach with the idea of continuity. It loads them with novel and difficult problems absolutely unrelated to anything else in their experience. Only a musically mature person could derive much nourishment from such a routine, and if he could do so it would be because he was aware of the musical significance of what he was trying to accomplish, so that the new problems were to him really musical problems, and not an affair of sheer, unmitigated acrobatics and manipulation.

What, then, is the alternative? The abandonment of all study of technical mechanics? Trying to play the instrument anyhow, in the pure light of nature, for purposes of self-expression? This too has its advocates, but it seems sentimental, superficial, and unrealistic. A musical instrument is a machine which imposes certain unavoidable conditions. The bowing hand of the violinist, for instance, must establish a straight-line motion which is difficult because the limbs are levers which move in circular arcs about their fulcra. There is no use pretending that such conditions are unreal. Anyone who tries to ignore them will certainly find that they trip him up.

It is, however, a fair question to ask whether preparation for playing the violin is only or chiefly an affair of acquiring certain automatisms. This, quite simply, is untrue. The great impediment in learning to play the violin is a lack of developed musical responsiveness. *Per aspera ad astra?* No doubt! But if a person has hardly caught so much as a glimpse of the *astra*, the *aspera* are very likely to defeat him. If one starts this person to climbing an interminable range of arid hills, encourages him with tales of vast views and flowing streams far ahead, and refuses on principle to give him so much as a drink of water, he is exceedingly apt to leave his bones by the trail.

There are, indeed, two imperatives here. The automatisms must be mastered. Granted! A developing musical apprehension and responsiveness must be promoted. That must be granted, too! These two necessary conditions require planning in the following terms. (*a*) Pay most careful attention to the pupil's guided musical growth before he begins the study of the violin—and long before. (*b*) When he begins the study of the violin, and from then onward, never let the automatisms obscure the musical values. This nearly always means teaching them gradually and incidentally, except with musically mature students, who are a little rare. (*c*) Rationalize the automatisms to the limit, and teach them with maximum efficiency, so that they are acquired as easily and speedily as possible. Wonders can be done along this line, for as a usual thing technical mechanics are taught with maximum inefficiency so that their difficulties are magnified beyond all reason.

The approach to applied music, and in particular to the violin, exemplifies the problem of preparation in its most acute and difficult form. This was the reason for choosing it as an illustration. The general principle is that under no pretext whatsoever must a new study be introduced in such a way as to constitute an irrelevant interruption of the continuity of musical growth. If this can be avoided in violin teaching—and it certainly can—then it is avoidable anywhere. Instrumental and vocal teachers in the high-school should not demand that pupils come to them from the elementary school able above everything else to read. They should demand very urgently that pupils come to them with a developed musical sensitivity and responsiveness. Such sensitivity and responsiveness can very readily be shaped into the specific pattern of reading. Theory teachers should not demand that pupils come to them able to play the piano as the supreme desideratum. Once again they should ask for, and even shout for, pupils having a developed musical sensitivity and apprehension which can very readily be organized into a conceptual framework. If this wise policy is followed, instrumental and vocal teachers need not worry about their performing organizations, and theory teachers need not fear that their subject will have the daunting reputation of a desert journey. For the true preparation for anything in music is always continuous musical growth, which solves the most refractory problems in all specialties.

3 The conception of musical growth as a continuum has a bearing upon what is called readiness. The term is being widely used today in educational discussions generally, and has been imported into music education.

It is said that a child should not be introduced to the formal or technical aspects of any study such as language reading, note reading, formal arithmetic, work on a musical instrument, and so forth, until he is psychologically ready. This, in a sense, is a return to the old problem of preparation, although in a new and interesting form, and handled with more than traditional intelligence. Thus a child is not supposed to be "ready" to read English when he has memorized the alphabet, but when, through a variety of influences, his desire to read has been fostered, and his language-patterns fairly well organized. "Readiness" for formal arithmetic, again, is brought about by many experiences with quantitative situations and problems which are interesting, concrete, and within his mental grasp. So far the idea is entirely acceptable. The trouble begins, however, when readiness is supposed to be a definite point, a break in the continuum. Up to that point everything is pleasant, stimulating, beneficial. Beyond it every-thing changes. The child is lured through an oasis of flowing streams and flowering foliage. But there comes a moment when he is suddenly pushed out into the desert. This is a precise inversion of older notions about preparation. According to old-fashioned doctrine one first ate one's bread and then got some cake. But the newfangled idea is to begin with the cake, or at least with some *hors d'oeuvres*,—and then provide nothing but bread. Both notions ignore the vital truth that growth is a continuum.

Let us deal with the problem of readiness in general by way of a specific application, namely to note reading. The proper approach to note reading is not to beguile the child on his way through the first three grades with various intriguing musical trivialities, to decide that by the fourth grade he ought to be ready to take it, and then to let him have it with both barrels. No one is apt to be ready for an ex-perience like that. There is no magic in the lines, the spaces, the dots, the clefs, the sharps, the flats, the numbers, which makes life begin anew from the moment one first beholds them. The affairs of men

[61]

may move toward a divine event, but the introduction of the musical score is no part of it. If the promoting of readiness to read music means working toward a supreme moment when all things are changed and serious study really starts, it is preposterous.

But if it means organizing a continuum of musical growth in which an understanding of the score is a contributing element, then indeed it makes sense. What the introduction of the score should mean is that the ear, in its grasp of tonal poetry, is more and more supported by the eye. Even if there were a sharp dividing line between reading and non-reading, which is not true, experiences before and after should be of the same kind, and should differ only in organization and precision. Early experiences should not be trivial. Later experiences should not be arid. Both should be poetic experiences. So the concept of readiness, if it must be used at all, should never suggest that there are definite, separable stages in musical growth, but should only stand as a warning not to try to impart something to a learner before he is capable of benefiting from it, which is tolerably obvious though much neglected advice.

4 There are many ways in which the notion of developmental continuity bears upon the organization and planning of a program of music education. Three of them will be considered here.

A. *First it bears upon the sequence of lessons or topics, particularly in the elementary school, but in fact everywhere.* One constantly finds elementary school courses of study in which the year's work is blocked out in a series of lessons, or topics, or units, usually centering about problems of notation—the quarter note, the eighth note, the half note, the dotted quarter note followed by an eighth note, the rests, the key signatures, and so forth. The sequence is controlling, and musical material is organized in terms of the indicated topics. This is a thoroughly familiar form of pedagogical arrangement, to be found in many subjects other than music.

Now the essential thing to say about it is that it probably does no great harm *if it is not taken seriously,* and if the musical material itself is abundant and good. But if it is regarded as the sacred order of learning instead of a mere convenience at best, and above all if the music is cramped, distorted, and carpentered together to illustrate the topics, then it becomes disastrous. Children do not grow musically by a discontinuous process in which they learn first one thing, then another thing, and then another, and finally add them all up. They grow musically by a continuously developing poetic responsiveness.

[62]

It may very well be that in connection with some revealing experience in the way of listening, or performing, or composing, the ingenious notational device of the dotted quarter note followed by an eighth may bring matters to a sharper focus and a happier outcome. That is the moment when it is nourishing. To have a book in which one can look it up and which provides examples may be a great convenience. But to become a slave to the book and its table of contents is deplorable, for our loyalty should always be to the children and to the art of tonal poetry.

B. *Second, the idea of developmental continuity bears upon the grade-wise and school-wise organization and subdivision of the program.* That program should be conceived and organized first and foremost in terms of the evolving musical responsiveness of the human beings with whom we are dealing. The fact that some of the experiences and learnings in and through which this evolution is brought about are carried on in the first-grade, others in the third-grade, and others in the sixth is not the primary consideration, for the grades themselves are only administrative conveniences and operative devices, not psychological realities. They are means, not ends. So it is a fundamental mistake to allocate certain designated achievements or masteries to each grade in a hard and fast fashion, with the thought that when the whole sequence has been run off, a sum total of achievements will have been attained. In the fundamental sense, just one thing ought to happen in all grades —the evolution, deepening and broadening of musical responsiveness, and just how this is brought about depends not on the numerical designation of the grade concerned, but on the proclivities, the impulses, the interests, the personalities of the children with whom we have to do. In the same way there is no essential difference between the music program in the elementary school and the secondary school. The basic controlling factor in all planning should be a continuous musical growth, brought about by the organized influences of the educational system, and extending throughout all the years during which the child has dealings with it and it has dealings with him.

C. *Third, the idea of developmental continuity bears upon the relationship of general music to the various specialties.* This will be considered more fully at a later stage of our discussion, but it is germane to the present topic. Briefly put, it comes to this. The specialties are the branches. General music is the trunk. As the music staff contemplates the entering first-grade child, it is realized that he may develop some kind of musical specialty before he is through with school. This is a subject about which very large amounts of very bad nonsense are talked. Some people dream of infallible tests which will show that a six-year-old boy is destined to become a bassoonist. Others think that the youthful prospect should, at the very first possible instant, be high-pressured into some kind of specialty, and in particular the one they represent themselves. The truth is that children should grow into their musical specialties, and that the program should encourage and stimulate such growth, just as a gardener takes measures to encourage a tree to grow into a well-balanced and desirable shape.

Here are the children, fed into the program in the first grade or the kindergarten. It is hoped that some of them will blossom out as pianists, some as singers, some as violinists, some as horn players, a few as tympanists, a very few perhaps as composers, and a great many of them—all, if possible—as musically interested persons. This looks like a stunning problem until we remember that nature will help us a great deal with it if only we will let her. The proper origin of all musical specialties is the same. All of them have a great deal in common, at least in their earlier stages. The pathways begin to divide only at the upper levels, and even then they should not be nearly so segregated as they usually are. By all means shape up the whole program with an eye to the development of specialization. This is a natural and desirable outcome of musical growth. By all means use the various specializations as influences in the elementary-school and the junior high-school. This can greatly enrich and vitalize the program at these levels. But think of these influences not as aimed at providing recruits, but at developing musical persons. Playing toy instruments, playing "social" instruments, interesting demonstrations of band and orchestral instruments, listening to "live" instrumental performance, using the piano keyboard, piano classes, instrumental classes, voice classes, are not mere recruiting devices. They are effective means of musical growth, and should be so considered and so handled. Not every child in an instrumental class in the elementary school will go into the band. He may go into the choir. He may go into no musical organization at all. So what he ought to get from his instrumental class is an all-round development of musical perceptiveness and sensitivity in an instrumental medium. This is the best way of turning him into a good oboist, if such is his destiny. It will be of great value to him if he becomes a vocalist. And also it will be a lasting benefit if he remains an almost unspecialized amateur. A good music program works all the time for the development of musical responsiveness. Certainly this can branch out into specializations of various kinds. But such specializations are living offshoots of such a program, not independent sequences. It is this evolution of musical responsiveness which is the substance of what is called general music, an idea often understood far too narrowly. General music is the trunk of a developmental program of music education, not a course at a certain level, and the various specialties are its branches.

IV

Musical growth, like all mental growth, is a purposive process. This is the third of its general characteristics.

The essential idea can be very well illustrated and explained from the example which has already been used of the process of becoming able to walk. The baby, in his first vague and groping reactions, raising himself up, squirming for a moment to an erect posture, thrusting with his legs—is trying to *do* something. His efforts are not co-ordinated. The goal, as it appears in his behavior, is not clearly defined, although an observer can tell what it is. Gradually, however, the whole pattern becomes clearer, more articulated, more focalized upon its purpose. One can see success coming closer and closer, until at last it arrives.

It might be argued that this particular sequence is not a good illustration for our present purpose, for the reason that in it nature does most of the teaching. Surely, it will be said, the baby becomes able to stand and walk because an impulse to do so is born in him, and this produces all the restlessness, striving, and endeavour. Environmental influences may seem to have very little to do with the matter, and even if the baby is physically restrained for many months —something that has actually been done—he begins to walk very quickly after he is set free. Compared with the business of becoming able to walk, most of the developmental sequences with which we have to do in school may appear rather artificial, and if they are dominated by purpose, that purpose is surely engendered by circumstances rather than implanted by nature.

There is some truth in all this, but the distinction is very far from absolute, certainly where musical growth is concerned. Babies have an inborn tendency to walk. *They also have an inborn tendency to respond musically.* It has already been pointed out that tonal experience has profound, astonishing, and very impressive effects. Anyone who watches a baby calming down when his mother sings him a lullaby or hears him emitting comfortable lallings, babblings, and cooings as

[65]

he kicks up his heels, can see the future musician in this small person. There, beyond the slightest doubt, is the musical impulse. It can be frustrated far more easily than the walking impulse. It depends far more upon circumstances, outside influences, encouragement. But it is no artifact. Nature is indeed setting a goal for all who have eyes to see. Growth, in a word, is always a quest. Locomotor growth is a quest for walking. Musical growth is a quest for a better realization of the poetic values of music. In both cases nature herself establishes the goal. In the case of walking, the purpose is difficult to frustrate. In the case of music, this can be done all too easily. Yet it need not and should not happen.

Thus a musical learner should always be treated as a person who has a natural impulse to be musical, to seek a clearer, deeper, broader, more varied musical responsiveness. Everything should be done to encourage this. Nothing should be done to hinder it. And encouragement simply means revealing the poetic values which are the essentials of music. Here is the reason why harsh and insensate yelling can be cured simply by revealing to the children what beautiful yet free vocal tone is and what it can mean, why a beautiful and singable song can do so much in bringing out the voice, why a piano pupil can get amazing technical benefits from a piece he longs to play, why a high-school student can get so much good from composing, with suitable help, a piece of music of his own. These are all fulfilling revelations, in which a natural purpose moves towards its goal. Conversely, here is the reason why the teaching of the notation simply as an abstract symbolism, or the formal study of technique or theory, yields such poor and slow results. The reason is that no natural impulse is involved. All such work is unrepaying unless it is organized—and it certainly can be so organized—as a fulfillment of the natural will to be musical.

All this has many important practical implications for the program of music education, a few of which may be considered here.

1 The prevailing emphasis of a developmental program of music education must be upon doing things with music rather than upon learning about it as an end in itself. It is exactly the person who wants to do something with music who is most "ready" to learn about it, and to do so in the right way. Thus preparation for a public performance or an assembly program should be, and can be, a challenge to clarify, realize, and project a musical message—to enjoy and share musical beauty. To explore music for oneself by means of the phonograph is another way of "doing" something with it, rather

than simply learning something about it. Yet such exploration opens up all kinds of inciting challenges to learning. Get people to use music for the purposes for which it is obviously adapted, namely the enjoyment, creation, and projection of tonal beauty, and there will be no difficulty at all about getting good learning.

There is no subject in the curriculum which is richer than music in natural expressive outlets. In this respect, indeed, it is more like an extra-curricular activity than a curricular subject. The performance of music, and particularly ensemble performance, has in itself an intrinsic attractiveness. If there can be an audience situation, even a very informal one, much added pulling power is produced. Music invites the listener, and to hear and enjoy it is to "do something with it." To create or compose music of one's own is a peculiarly rewarding and intriguing undertaking, and things can be started in this direction by some systematic and planned encouragement and incitement. So there is nothing impossible about organizing a program of music education in which the emphasis from beginning to end is upon musical activities rather than music lessons.

2 Musical activities are opportunities for teaching. They are necessary opportunities, for without them teaching is almost sure to be lifeless, pointless, mechanistic, and ineffective. But they are nothing more than opportunities. Everything depends on what is done with them. They may be capitalized or they may be thrown away. Also they may be set up in such a way that it is almost impossible to take proper advantage of them.

A contest, for instance, is a very compelling musical activity. It ought to give the local music teachers a first-rate chance to promote genuine and substantial musical development. Too often it does nothing of the kind. There is very little latitude in choosing the work to be presented. Standards of adjudication are very rigid and often arbitrary. The whole emphasis is placed on interminable drill, on the over-cultivation of a very small plot. Then the opportunity is largely wasted. This is by no means necessarily an argument for the abandonment of contests. It is, however, an argument for using this very powerful force for much more wisely chosen ends.

Again, if a sixth-grade choir is invited to appear at a Parent-Teacher Association meeting, or at an assembly, or at graduation exercises, a real opportunity is created. It is not, however, primarily an opportunity to put on a show, but to further the all-round musical development of the pupils in terms of a solid and

[67]

genuine purpose. The children will want to do as well as possible. That is the motive, and it is a fine one. Very well, let them have a hand in deciding what music to present. Let them discuss problems of interpretation and tone quality. Help them to gain some understanding of the musical pattern upon which all expressive effects depend. Help them with simple vocal techniques through which musical intentions can be realized. This is an instance of what is meant by saying that a musical activity should be treated as an opportunity for musical growth—for the development of musical responsiveness.

Toy orchestra performance and rhythm band work in the grades, again, can be intriguing and purposeful activities which are fruitful influences for musical growth if rightly managed. Discussions and decisions about the distribution of parts, on-the-spot elaboration of parts, the notating of parts perhaps by means of the standard score or perhaps by some simpler homemade symbolism, the use of songs which the children have learned or are learning are among the possibilities that suggest themselves.

In general, any sequence or course of music study can and should be vitalized by relevant and purposive musical activities. This is true not only in cases such as have been mentioned, but also of classes in applied music, in theory, in the history of music, and indeed everywhere and at all levels. It is, for instance, possible to organize the history of music largely around a series of concerts in which members of the class play compositions of various periods. One of the great advantages of this way of working is that it naturally, indeed almost inevitably, carries music study and musical growth beyond the school. Home study is almost always thought of in terms of stated assignments imposed under the threat of a check-up soon to be faced. If, however, pupils have before them a really appealing and compelling activity, which involves a sense of responsibility, and if they are shown how to prepare for it in ways that foster musical growth, the carry-over beyond the classroom and beyond the school itself becomes a perfectly normal expectation and will probably need little forcing. This, of course, is just as it should be. It is exactly what must be involved if genuine purpose is aroused, and perhaps the surest of all signs that it has been aroused. To have in operation a developmental program of music education should mean that the school is a center for a whole series of musical activities and undertakings designed for the optimum promotion of musical growth, and stimulating relevant and fruitful music study both in and out of the school.

[68]

V

Musical growth involves a shaping up, a reorganizing, a reorienting of the entire personality. This, of course, is what is meant by saying that it is the process of becoming a musical person.

Human beings shape their lives by opening up avenues of fulfillment. A person who learns to play chess or to ski does a great deal more than acquire an internal or, as it were, purely private ability. He tends to bring himself into a whole new set of relationships, personal, social, and economic. A man who makes himself a scholar in the field of history is doing much more than learn a great deal about the subject. He is on the way to becoming a certain sort of person, with interests, preoccupations, ambitions, hopes, ways of feeling, ways of acting, tendencies to seek certain kinds of occupation, which can readily mold the entire pattern of his life.

The same is true of anyone who is in process of becoming a musical person. The inner side of this process is the organization of perception, imagery, feeling, and standards and judgments of value. Its external counterpart is the opening up of a whole range of living. Associations, contacts, friendships, avocations, opportunities for service and for pleasure are brought within such a person's compass. A musical person, in other words, is not merely one who has music in his head. He is also one who has music in his life, which means a great deal, most of it exceedingly practical. Moreover, as always, the relationship is reciprocal. Musical associations, contacts, and doings are not only fruits or outcomes of musical growth. They also stimulate and fertilize the process.

Now here is a consideration which needs to be borne in mind in organizing the music program. At the universities of Medieval Europe the professors were not regarded as belonging to an entirely different caste from the students, nor was it merely their function to shower wisdom from on high and then retreat into their private *arcana*. The undergraduates were considered to be junior or apprentice members of the scholars' guild in which the professors were master workmen. That is exactly how students and pupils in school ought to be treated by their music teachers—as junior members of the guild of musical persons. Take them into confidence, let them know what goes on in the world of music, open up its realities to them even if they are sometimes rather daunting, create chances for them to meet distinguished artists and to discover that these luminaries are also human, take them around to meetings, or at least take selected representatives who

[69]

can report back, encourage the formation of informal music clubs, disseminate some of the commercial musical periodicals. Open up music, not only as a beautiful art, which it is, but also as a slice of real living, which it is as well. That, emphatically, is one line of policy to follow in the promotion of musical growth, for the human mind develops best, not in a holy vacuum, but in close contact with mother earth.

A point quite often made in connection with music education is that young people ought to develop skill in musical media which they will have plenty of chances to use in after life. For instance, few men of thirty and onward will have much chance to play the tuba, and so it is contended that they ought to study the piano, or the violin, or voice. The same problem arises in physical education when it is said, and not without truth, that golf and tennis have a much more promising future in most people's lives than football. Many a good and conscientious band director has felt that there is force in the argument, but he is puzzled just the same. Certainly he does not want to exploit any student by forcing him to learn an instrument the use of which in after life would almost surely get him evicted from any apartment house in the country. On the other hand, the band needs a tuba player. It seems like an impasse.

But is it really? I have seen an old and faded daguerreotype photograph of the student orchestra at an obscure Polish conservatory. There in the back row, as large as life, unmistakable in spite of his youth, stands none other than Ignace Jan Paderewski—holding a trombone. So at least there has been one person in the world whose musical prospects were not seriously damaged by a large and raucous brass instrument. Perhaps, indeed, trombone playing was not an altogether arid episode in this great man's musical development.

The point is simply this. If skill with any medium is learned as a narrow and unrelated specialty, to be acquired as a circus elephant acquires the technique of standing on a tub, it is extremely likely to wither on the vine, and this is true even of the tenor saxophone. If, however, it has been learned as a specialization of a broad musical growth, and if it has been made a ticket of entry to broad and happy musical living, then its values are likely to remain, even if it is laid aside, and this is true even of the tuba. For the aim is not to produce tuba players, or piano players, or violin players or any other kind of specialized acrobats, but musical persons. What instrument is a boy of sixteen most likely to play when he is sixty? Who can possibly tell? So far as I am aware, no curriculum committee or music staff has access to the Delphic oracle. How can we prepare for a future which almost by definition is unknown? The answer is easy. We cannot! But it is possible to shape and create future probabilities by bringing to bear certain influences. Creation rather than preparation is always the function of any curriculum. It does so by shaping personality, by orienting its growth. This, too, is the ultimate function of the music program. The tuba probably will not be used much by most students in their future years. Music probably will be, if they get a good chance at it, here and now. Therefore the policy is to mobilize all possible influences, one of which may be the tuba, to promote musical growth and to produce musical persons.

QUESTIONS FOR DISCUSSION

1. What are some of the most serious discontinuities which conventional music education introduces into what should be a continuous sequence of growth?

2. What are some of the implications of the idea of growth as continuous for the teaching of reading, of theory, of instrumental performance?

3. In what sense should a child's musical experience be similar to that of a mature artist? In what sense should it be different?

4. Consider carefully what is right and wrong with the notion of readiness. Indicate some practical implications.

5. What basic natural purpose can one count on in fostering musical growth? How may it be evoked? How may it be stifled?

6. If musical growth is essentially purposive, ought one to try to make music interesting? What is legitimate and what is misleading about this idea?

7. How soon do you think a child's musical education should begin to be concentrated on some specialty, for example, piano lessons? What might be the alternative?

8. Mention some changes in the personality that one might reasonably hope for as outcomes of musical development. How might one seek to bring them about?

9. Consider some specific ways in which pupils in the grades or in high school might be treated as "cadet musicians."

10. What dangerous fallacies are involved in the idea of preparation?

ADDITIONAL READINGS

James L. Mursell. *Successful Teaching*. McGraw-Hill Book Company, Inc., New York, 1946. Chapter 13, "The Principle of Sequence and the Organization of Learning." (A compact statement of the nature of mental growth.)

Myrtle McGraw. *Growth: A Study of Jimmy and Johnny*. D. Appleton-Century Company, Inc., New York, 1935. Chapter 10, "General Principles of Growth." (This chapter brings together the author's conclusions from the famous study of growth here reported.)

Carl E. Seashore. "When to Begin a Musical Education," *Child Study*, 1928, Vol. 5, No. 7, pp. 7–8. (A brief but very effective statement of certain aspects of developmental music education.)

Arnold Gesell and Catherine E. Amatruda. *Developmental Diagnosis*. Harper and Brothers, New York, 1941. (This is a work of major importance which ought to be examined and studied by everyone who wishes to understand the growth process.)

CHAPTER FOUR

The Rhythm of Musical Growth

I

Musical growth is a continuous process in which the living values of the wordless tonal poetry are apprehended and realized ever more deeply, more broadly, more subtly, and more purposefully, and in which the personality moves toward a new orientation through the opening up of avenues of fulfillment. This is the point to which our discussion has so far brought us, and in reaching it many things of high practical significance for music education have revealed themselves. But much more still remains. This process has a characteristic, unmistakable, and recognizable rhythm, and to this rhythm the developmental teaching of music must conform.

The rhythm of musical growth is an organic, not an additive, rhythm. It is the rhythm of life, not of construction. It is the rhythm which is exemplified when the seed puts out shoots and tendrils and becomes the plant, when the bud appears and becomes the flower, when the flower becomes the fruit. It is not the rhythm of construction, in which parts in themselves inert and meaningless are assembled in some convenient sequence to form an inanimate machine. It is a rhythm of unfolding, not of the mechanical putting of things together. This is the rhythm which must constitute the basic pattern of a developmental program of music education.

Put in these general terms the idea may seem hard to understand and hard to apply. But it can be made more specific and manageable, for the organic rhythm of musical growth can be characterized in many ways. It is a movement from crudeness toward precision, from the concrete toward the abstract, from the immediate toward the universal, from vagueness toward clarity, from hesitation toward certainty. It is a rhythm of synthesis, analysis, and synthesis, of re-organization and emergence. All these statements are different ways of expressing the same idea. They reveal different aspects of the selfsame organic rhythm of growth, in and through which the poetic values

[73]

and meanings which are the essence of the art of music are progressively better realized. As they are considered one by one, the central conception itself will become both more understandable, and more evidently and specifically applicable.

II

Musical growth is a movement from crudeness toward precision. It is a process in which a grasp of musical values that is always living and authentic, but at first full of imperfection, becomes progressively refined and perfected. This sloughing off of error, this progressive emergence of precision and exact control is one of the characteristic aspects of its organic rhythm.

The early musical experiences of little children, or of adolescent or adult beginners, should always turn upon the poetic intimations and values of music. They should be experiences of conveying emotional intimations and meanings in the music that is sung, or played, or composed, of responding to the emotional intimations and meanings of music that is heard. Such attempts are bound to be crude, bound to be full of faults and errors. But this does not matter, because the crudities will eliminate themselves, and the faults and errors slough away in the course of time by virtue of the vital process of growth. The rhythm band, the toy instrument ensemble, the harmonica band, are crude means of making music. But if through such agencies the children discover what music-making really is—namely the expression of poetic values in the tonal medium—then such crudeness matters not one whit. When children or older beginners undertake to compose music, they are sure to make what theorists would call mistakes. But again this does not matter if they are discovering that the composition of music is in essence the projection of poetic intimations in the tonal medium. A homemade poster devised by a second-grade group to show the pitch relationships and note-lengths of a melody by means of some simple *ad hoc* symbolism is a crude device compared to the standard notation. But if it helps the children to grasp what they hear and what they sing or play because they can see it represented, it is a legitimate and desirable agency for musical growth. There are all sorts of musical intricacies and refinements that can probably never be brought out simply by singing songs by ear. But if the singing of many songs by ear develops a responsiveness to the expressive musical line, then it is a powerful influence for musical growth, and a proper foundation for work with more exacting and precise media.

Again, the proper way of introducing any composition that is to be performed is to emphasize not its detail but its general import. This is true all the way from simple songs to be sung by little children to elaborate works to be performed by advanced orchestras and artist soloists. The little children may listen to the song sung to them by the teacher, and then sing it with her, preferably with a piano accompaniment. The mature artist may be able to form a conception of the composition by studying it in the score. The means do not matter, and they may vary widely. The important thing is to start by blocking out the import of the music, even though at first it can only be crudely grasped and very imperfectly rendered, and then going on to refine both the conception and the execution. This is how painters and sculptors and writers operate when they first block out a job of work fully aware that there will be many crudities, and then proceed to refine and polish up the details. It is highly characteristic of the organic rhythm of growth.

To play up the point by way of contrast, here are some of the things that should not be done. In general, a beginner should not be put up against problems that demand high precision, or at any rate high precision should not be required or attempted in his first attack upon any musical problem. This applies both to the child and to the adult who is just starting with music, and also to the musically mature person who is learning to play a new piece, or listening to a new composition, or engaging in the process of composing. Complicated notation, elaborate rules for part writing, or the study of a difficult and confining instrument are instances of such problems that come readily to mind. In the early stages of learning the performance of a piece of music there should not be a pressure of anxiety to avoid mistakes. When pupils are given the chance to discuss and decide upon points of expression and interpretation—and this should most certainly be done from the very beginning—the emphasis at first should be upon broad effects rather than finesse. In listening, again, broad contrasts and broad structural and emotional intimations and factors should be the focal considerations at the beginning. And no musical endeavor should proceed by getting one detail or small segment precise and perfect before going on to the next.

Now this may seem like exceedingly dangerous doctrine. Many earnest and experienced teachers may consider it downright destructive. Certainly their opinions deserve careful and respectful examination. There are three points which are often energetically urged. 1. The right start is crucially important. This is true in starting a new song or a new piece. It is true in starting the study of music. It is always true. A beginner who is allowed to fumble and to fall into all kinds of crudity and error is apt to get going in the wrong direction, and may never recover. 2. Mistakes are always dangerous and may be deadly, because they easily become ingrained. This is true of technical errors, of errors and crudities of interpretation, and of the sort of mistakes a person will make if he tries to compose without a thorough grounding in theory. Therefore, mistakes should always be avoided if possible, and strenuously attacked whenever they occur. 3. Crudity and error are always unfortunate. To pretend that they can have any constructive value or that they can be influences making for growth is obviously absurd.

The answer to these sincere and serious arguments is to point out more explicitly the reason for what has been said, which has already been indicated. The reason for tolerating early crudity is not at all that it is good in itself, but that an anxious emphasis on precision in the initial stages of growth obscures essential meanings. What a learner should have in the forefront of his mind, first, last, and all the time, is the poetically expressive content of music. Anything that blocks this off is all to the bad. A little child cannot concentrate on the notes of a piano piece without losing sight of everything else. Therefore give him a homemade instrument so that he can concentrate on the music. A third-grade group cannot spell out the notes of a folk song with careful precision and still have any thought left for its poetic intimations. Therefore let them sing it by ear, perhaps with some visual assistance. To be more specific, immature pupils cannot concentrate both on the right notes and the rhythm of the beat, which is one of the most subtly expressive of musical components. It becomes necessary to choose. If the notes are exclusively or very strongly emphasized, the rhythm is pretty sure to be obscured. If the rhythm is emphasized, a good many notes may be missed. Which is the more important? To build the right notes around the framework of the beat is a natural and straightforward development. But every teacher knows to his cost how difficult it is to establish the beat once the note-patterns have been ingrained without it. So the band director or the piano teacher insists on the correct notes from the beginning, and thinks he is doing his duty. Then he finds that the rhythmic structure has all the shapeliness of a jelly fish on the sand, and laments that the youngsters mysteriously lack a "sense of rhythm." What else can he expect, when he has done virtually nothing to develop it? He has made them concentrate on the trees. Why should

[76]

he be surprised when he finds they have no idea of the configuration of the wood?

This specific illustration contains in itself the whole general contention. A grasp of the beat is of enormous importance in learning a new piece fast and well. So is a grasp of its melodic patterns, its phrase patterns, its harmonic patterns, its structural organization, its expressive values. Very well! Does it not make sense to put these things in the forefront when the piece is being learned and to let nothing obscure them? Something has got to be sacrificed, because one cannot reach perfection in a single bound. But surely it should not be these things. They should be stressed from the very first, no matter what the cost, for they are the essential guide-lines of development. They should be given a priority. They should be grasped as clearly as may be from the very start, and as precision builds up and error is eliminated by work oriented by them, they themselves become clearer and clearer. This, surely, is the best way to develop mastery of any specific piece of music. And a piece of music so studied is an episode in the total process of musical growth, which itself turns on a developing musical perceptiveness, imagination, and sensitivity.

Consider how this bears upon the three objections mentioned above. 1. The right start is of crucial importance? Indeed it is! But what is the right start? A centering upon musical content, meanings, and values! Anything that disturbs this makes a wrong start. The vocal approach, humming a melody before one plays it, using toy instruments, fumbling through a new piece, all such procedures, are good for one reason only. They make the music easy to come at. To do this is always the first and great commandment. 2. Mistakes tolerated and repeated are apt to become ingrained? Yes and no! It all depends on the kind of mistakes. Mistakes of one sort or another there are always going to be. A pupil may practice a new piece a hundred times, and by a *tour de force* play not one single wrong note. But his work may be full of dreadful crudeness just the same—unrhythmic, badly phrased, performed with a self-defeating physical rigidity. So we have to take our choice among mistakes. By far the worst and most ineradicable of them are failures of musical grasp. A pupil guided by a musical apprehension that is becoming surer and surer will clear up his note errors readily enough. A pupil who fumbles from note to note, like a blind man fumbling from post to post in constant fear of missing one, may never apprehend the music at all. 3. The position here taken amounts to a glorification of crudity and error? This is a **very great mistake.** What is glorified is the music itself, and its vital

[77]

sense. Crudity and error are regrettable, but unavoidable. They have to be accepted to avoid obscuring a dawning musical apprehension which grows brighter as the work proceeds.

As a footnote to this discussion it may be helpful to touch upon a problem that may seem peculiarly difficult and crucial. What about the mechanical adjustment imperatively required by certain instruments, for instance the violin? The instrument must be held and handled in a certain way, otherwise it will not sound and cannot be played. Must not this adjustment be learned with full precision from the beginning? Yes, it must. But this is not the whole story. First, such an instrument should not, in ideal at least, be taken up in the early stages of musical growth. It is without doubt a barrier, and the growing creature should be strong enough to get over it before he tackles it. Second, the essential adjustment should be taught with maximum efficiency and directness, something that is by no means always done. Third, the pupil should begin, at the very first possible moment, to use the instrument for the purpose for which it was invented, namely the making of music—even if he also makes mistakes!

III

Musical growth is a movement from the concrete to the abstract. In general all abstract formulations, such as symbols, including those of language itself, rules, laws, principles, and so forth, are tools for the manipulation of concrete experience, and for making behavior more effective. They should always be taught and learned with this in mind, for otherwise they are meaningless and confusing, and their purpose is defeated. This is just as true in music as anywhere else.

Consider for instance the musical notation, which is one of the most important abstract systems in this field. It is capable of representing pitch direction, harmonic content, the duration of notes and rests, the placement and structure of the beat, key or tonality, dynamics, and to some extent the beginnings and endings of phrase units. That is to say, it picks out certain crucial aspects of the musical pattern, and designates them by means of symbols. A great many of the problems in dealing with it come from the fact that pupils are simply not aware of these crucial features in terms of direct, concrete, perceptual experience, or at any rate only dimly and partially aware of them. They may know that music rises and falls or that notes differ in length, but they are not conscious of the precise relationships displayed. Their

[78]

feeling for the beat, for the key, and for harmonic content will not be entirely absent, but it is apt to be hazy. Then suddenly all these considerations are thrust upon them, not in concrete form, but in abstract symbolism. Two misfortunes almost inevitably follow. They never really master the score, because they do not understand what it has to tell; and work with it does nothing to improve their musical responsiveness.

Clearly what needs to be done is to approach the score by way of musical development. There should be wide experience in singing, playing, and composing by ear, in listening, in bodily rhythmic response. But this experience should not be a mere undifferentiated mass. It should turn on the explication of musical verities, of the expressive realities of the musical pattern. Children should discover that you can make music better if you know what you are doing with it, that you can enjoy listening to it better if you know what you are hearing—if you are aware of its coloration, of its movement up and down, of its rhythmic arrangement, of its tonality relationships. These are its expressive components, the components that make it a wordless poetry, and the more keenly one responds to them the better one grasps its values and intimations. Such responsiveness should arise out of the activities just mentioned—singing by ear, playing by ear, composing by ear, listening, and bodily rhythm. Their effect should be to begin the transformation of a mass response into an articulated pattern. Then the symbols of the score have something to take hold of, so to speak, and the study of them can carry the development further.

There are, of course, in music several other important systems of abstraction besides the notation itself. One of these is the widely used and much debated movable "do" system. Its whole value is to point up and shape up musical perception, and to guide musical action—to show the learner what to discriminate, and what to do about it. The so-called ear-training drills often used in the elementary school, involving tone-matching and the singing of designated intervals, are also abstractive procedures, though of a less systematic kind. The elaborate array of definitions, rules, techniques, and devices—often rather dubious ones—which goes by the name of musical theory is another case in point. Always the thing to remember is that the purpose and meaning of such abstractions is to give form and contour to musical experience, and control to musical action.

The proper educational treatment of all these abstract devices and systems can be summarized rather definitely.

[79]

A. *They should never be projected as brand-new problems, unrelated to anything that has been evoked by previous experience.* Any abstract formulation should always come as a recognition of something of which the learner is already aware, and as a revelation to him of its further significance.

B. *They should not be projected on an undifferentiated mass background of musical experience.* To think of getting ready for the notation simply by a good deal of "rote" singing, or getting ready for theory by a good many years of music lessons, is a definite misconception. A person may sing and listen to music for a very long time, or may take piano lessons for ten years, and still be blissfully unconscious of the crucial elements in the musical pattern. Many a person has played *America* a thousand times without any discriminating consciousness of its harmonic coloration. Such mere mass experience is by no means what is needed. The crucial differentiations—the ups and downs, the longs and shorts, the beat, the tonality, the harmonic coloring—should have already established themselves in concrete perceptual experience. Then their names, their symbolic designations, and the rules for handling them, instead of being so many quasi-mathematical problems, can come as revealing illuminations.

C. *The very idea of background is misleading.* We should not think in terms of first building background, and then building notational or theoretical competence. What ought to take place is a continuous developing consciousness of the crucial aspects of the musical pattern, into which the abstractions are introduced for the sake of carrying it further.

D. *The abstractions ought always to be introduced for the immediate enrichment of musical experience and the immediate improvement of musical action.* The best time for the use of certain simple ear-training drills, or for the introduction of the syllables is when they will help in the singing of some enjoyable song. The fortunate instant for getting acquainted with the diminished seventh chord may well be when one has to play a cadenza based on its appeggio.

E. *The great and fatal error in dealing with the abstractions is to teach them out of relationship to functioning musical experience and action.* In these matters teachers are prone greatly to underestimate the need for immediate, concrete, organized experience. Far more is necessary than a casual illustration here and there. Everyone knows how poorly children in school learn the notation, and how poorly conservatory

[80]

students learn theory. The reason is simple. The abstractions are unrelated to a developmental context, and are treated as problems with little musical relevance, whereas they should be considered as the more advanced levels of a continuous musical growth.

IV

Musical growth is a movement from the immediate to the universal. It is said that Pestalozzi, the father of modern elementary education, used to begin the study of geography with the crack on the blackboard. It is worth pondering this as an alternative to starting with the boundaries of the state of Iowa, the rivers flowing into the Pacific, and the products of Borneo. On the grounds of every psychological insight we possess, the example of Pestalozzi is by all means the one to follow in music education. For organized completeness and systematic universality are the outcomes of mental growth, not its beginnings.

In the teaching of music, as indeed in education everywhere, one constantly finds work organized in terms of dealing with all significant aspects of a field of study. To be sure, comprehensive completeness is usually recognized as not feasible, but the effective ideal is clearly to cover everything, or at any rate as much as possible. In elementary-school programs we find careful plans for the systematic presentation of as many of the notational symbols as possible, omitting only those likely to be least used, such as unusual key signatures. Courses in theory are usually organized with the evident purpose of dealing in a given time with all the important topics of diatonic harmony, chromatic harmony, and so on. The same idea is exemplified, though not so clearly as a general thing, in the teaching of applied music, where pupils are set to going systematically through all the technical problems of the medium as a separate and distinct phase of study. Occasionally this is carried to extremes by teachers who insist that a student must master the whole range of the technique before he undertakes to play any music at all. And in many courses in the history of music, or in chronologically organized appreciation, the very evident aim is to cover the whole field systematically.

Now of course there is an argument for this kind of organization. Any person is hampered if there are serious gaps in his equipment. Systematically complete grasp of any field of achievement is of great and undeniable importance. So the argument runs that a beginner ought to have what is called a "thorough grounding" just as soon as

[81]

possible. And the "thorough grounding" is taken to mean the systematic study of all its pertinent aspects or constituent topics. Admittedly such work may be dull and arduous. The learner may not see the applications of the things he is learning until he has learned them all. But it is the only way for him to lay a solid foundation for future achievement. If he dies off before he reaches the end, it may be due to weakness of character or lack of talent. But the inexorable condition is that he must win through to freedom by a more or less lengthy period of servitude. If he can last out his seven years, then he may have his Rachel.

This argument is put forward in all sincerity by a great many serious educational workers, although in practice many of them falter before the formidable prospects opened up, and in fact temper the wind considerably, though against their convictions. One may commend the firmness of those who insist on ploughing the grim furrow to the bitter end for the sake of what they honestly consider the ultimate good of their pupils. But one cannot admire their insight. For the true nature of a "thorough grounding" is misconceived.

To get to the heart of things is always incomparably more important than to "cover" a great many of them. The desideratum is always vital and authentic experience, and any abstract systematization which does not grow out of such experience cannot be other than spurious. By way of an illustration, of which many could be offered, consider the scheme for teaching key signatures which is often found, with minor variations, in the elementary-school program. The key signatures constitute a remarkable abstract system. It is supposed to be part of the "fundamentals" of music, and therefore to have a place in a "thorough grounding." So it is taught in many elementary schools. To be sure, it is not taught *en bloc*, but over a period covering several grades, and the attempt is made to have the pupils learn the signatures most commonly used. Yet it is exceedingly doubtful whether key signatures can be made to mean anything to children whose chief musical activity consists of singing. Considerable instrumental experience would seem necessary at the very least, and probably considerable experience in actually writing music. But what can and should be done in the elementary school is to develop an awareness of tonality relationships as an element in musical expressiveness and enjoyment, and to develop it in the setting of actual musical undertakings where such relationships are important. This feeling for tonality as an expressive and poetic element in music is the real "fundamental." The development of it is part of a "thorough grounding" worthy of the name. The logical scheme of key signatures belongs to the superstructure, valuable for musically mature persons, but meaningless for anyone else.

The same principle applies in the study of technique, or of theory, or of music history. The right starting point is always an immediate musical problem or challenge. There is a passage to be executed that contains technical difficulties. The learner should be shown how to deal with them for the sake of making the passage sound musically expressive. What he should get out of it is not one or two technical tricks to be put in his bag, but a growing sense of what it means to project poetic intimations in a musical medium. The study of what is called theory should be an incidental adjunct to performing, listening, and composing, brought to bear as and when immediate problems arise, for a long time before it is taken up as a rounded abstract system. As to music history, there have been absurd arguments as to whether it should begin with the remote past and work forward, or with the present and work backward. Neither answer is the right one. The study of music history should begin with any experience, activity, or endeavor which initiates a revealing process of musical exploration. Its systematization in terms of periods, interpretations, and chronology is meaningful and repaying only as an outgrowth and organization of wide and rich musical awareness.

Not one word can or should be said against systematic completeness, or a universal and comprehensive grasp. But mature workers who have achieved it, as far as human beings ever can, are prone to be greatly mistaken about the road that led them there. Even if, in their young days, they were put through a typical "thorough grounding," this certainly was not the true cause. It was a living seed that somehow or other survived the desert journey, and blossomed out as soon as it found water and nourishment. Why, then, the desert? It seems a total loss except perhaps as a test of character. The truth is that the human mind cannot achieve universal comprehensions ready made, but must grow into them. And the starting point of such growth is always immediate experience which possesses meaning and vitality, whatever other characteristics it may possess or lack.

V

Musical growth is a movement from vagueness to clarity. All mental growth is like exploring a tract of country shrouded in the mist. There are only the haziest of intimations, and probably many of them

[83]

are deceptive. The important thing is not to fan away the fog so that the small patch of ground on which one stands is revealed in sharp detail. The important thing, by all means, is to find the right clue.

Consider an example: A child has the vaguest notion of the passage and the longer subdivisions of time. To him a month seems like eternity, and the difference between a person of thirty and a person of fifty is virtually indistinguishable. How, then, can one bring home to him the significance of the dates of the life of Beethoven? It simply cannot be done. He can be forced to learn them like a parrot. But a whole mass of experience must be digested and slowly co-ordinated before these clear-cut figures can become landmarks in his mind. Clear and distinct formulations always have a most delusive look of simplicity. But if we try to teach them just as they stand to immature learners, we are guilty of the most arrant externalism; for real clarity is one of the most difficult achievements of the human mind, and the infallible mark of the mature personality. A Bach chorale has a beautiful and penetrating clarity. But try to write one like it! For better or for worse, we human beings always begin with a hazy and impeded vision at best, and grow toward any clarity we ever gain.

Consider now a problem. What does it mean to say that a child has a clear grasp of scale patterns in the notation? Does it mean that he can look at any scale passage you would like to show him in the sort of material he is used to, name each note by its letter name and its syllable name, tell its duration value, its relationship to the beat, its relationship to the key signature, tell whether the passage itself is a whole phrase or part of a larger one? This would certainly be a large order, but it still might not be clarity. He might be able to do all these things like a little parrot, without a vestige of grasp of their musical significance. Clarity with a scale passage must surely indicate the power to perceive, and image, and feel, and execute it musically. This is what one admires in the work of a great artist, who projects such a passage, and perhaps quite a simple one, with exquisite lucidity and finesse. He presumably knows just what he is doing at every point. He could no doubt explain all the details very well. But such technical knowledge is merely the supporting structure, whereas the musical organization of his mind and body is the living essence.

From this we can derive a general principle of procedure. In every experience, activity, and endeavor try to clear up musical perception, musical imagery, and musical feeling as far as clarification can go. Never mind if at the start the fog is thick and the confusion great. See to it that the learner has the right clue. Introduce knowledge and

[84]

terminology and technical devices for helping along the immediate clarification, and for no other purpose. They themselves are not the clues, useful and even necessary though they may be. Think of the whole sequence of music education, in one of its aspects at least, as a series of just such clarifications. A developmental program of music education is precisely a sequence of such musical projects. They may be enormously varied in type and content. But they are all of them active, dynamic undertakings, in which music is enjoyed, performed and created. An emphasis which should inform every one of them is the attainment of a clearer grasp of the content, the verities, and the values of this music which is being experienced here and now. The syllables, the notation, items of information and explanation, the medium used, the devices of its technique, the concepts of theory should be brought to bear for one reason and for one reason only—to take the mud out of the music. Is it not as obvious as the nose on one's face that this is the best possible way of making human beings into musical persons? This is the process of musical clarification, which is one momentous aspect of the process of musical growth.

What has been presented is the converse of the doctrine that learners should always be perfectly clear about everything up to the point they have reached. A group of children are preparing to present a program of characteristic folk music at a school assembly. They have gone as far as the dotted quarter note followed by an eighth note, and the key of four flats. Up to that they know everything perfectly, and beyond it nothing at all. Will this give them much useful guidance? Hardly! What they ought to be consciously working for is a musical utterance as clear and convincing as they can make it. If they knew everything about the score, it would be nice. But since we cannot have everything, we must choose what is most important. These children should have the right clue already in their hands, and should get a firmer grip of it in their new adventure. And if this clue is being followed, the supporting apparatus will not be hard to acquire, and will help still further to dissipate the fog instead of adding to it.

VI

Musical growth is a movement from hesitation to certainty. Watch a man who has played hardly anything but wind instruments as he struggles in a class in keyboard harmony. He bends over the keyboard, rigid with anxiety. He shapes his hand to clutch a chord. He is full of strain, full of tension, full of hesitation. He grabs, and

[85]

gets it wrong! How are we going to transform this anxious fumbling into a smooth-running, certain pattern? Not by drill alone, not by work alone, though both are necessary. There must be a process of shaping-up which goes on inside him, and which affects both mind and body. There must be a process of growth.

Let us examine the psychological requirements for an immediate, certain, and facile response in this situation. The teacher has told our student to play the dominant seventh chord of the key of A flat. He understands at once the meaning of the words, that is, the verbal symbols. He has an aural image of the chord, that is an inner "mental" awareness of how it sounds. He has a muscular or kinesthetic image of how his hands will shape themselves in playing it. He sees it like a ghostly pattern on the keyboard. He makes his movement, and the aural and kinesthetic images pass over into actual perception. He must be able to react to the chord as a musical entity which is known by name, by aural imagery and perception, by motor or kinesthetic imagery and perception, by visualization as a pattern on the key-board—in every way that it can be known except in the visual symbolization of the score. So the problem is to co-ordinate all these avenues of awareness, to open them up and get them to coalesce. If only one of them is open, he is pretty well doomed to hesitation and inaccuracy. For instance, if he knows that a dominant seventh chord is a triad on the fifth degree of the scale with an added seventh above its root, and that the key of A flat has four flats, he can get his solution, but only by figuring it out. If he has a clear mental image of what a dominant seventh chord sounds like, he is better off. But still what he has is not good enough, for the name and the aural image must be associated with a motor image and a visualization. A good teacher of keyboard harmony will not want this student to work entirely or chiefly by figuring out the specific consequences of an intellectually comprehended concept, by saying to himself in effect: "The dominant seventh of A major means thus and so. Therefore it follows that if I hit this key, and this key, and this key, and this key, I shall get it right." He will want the student to use all the avenues of approach, and he will help him to do so, and even insist on his doing so. For the teacher will be aware that the crux of the matter is not the application of a formula, but the development of a musical apprehension. This is the way from hesitation to certainty in keyboard harmony. And, of course, it is also what makes keyboard harmony an effective influence for musical growth in general, because musical apprehensions are clarified and defined by dealing with them in a number of media.

[86]

What is true in this particular case holds everywhere. Assured musical response is always a function and outcome of clear and mature musical apprehension. Parrot-wise learning always makes for risk and uncertainty. When a person is playing a piece from memory, and has for his only clue the feel of his hands on the instrument, he is taking some long chances, and usually knows it very well. What he needs is a visual, auditory, and intellectual grasp of the music itself. When he has mastered or seemed to master a difficult technical passage, perhaps one involving an awkwardly placed and fingered trill, entirely in terms of the external movement-patterns, he is again in a risky spot. What he needs to pull him through is a clear grasp of the musical shape, and more particularly of the rhythm. When a person is conducting an orchestra by performing conventional baton patterns, and with only a vague idea of what is happening and is supposed to happen, he often has a nasty feeling that almost anything can happen —and he is not far wrong. What he needs, and very urgently, is a clear-cut apprehension of the layout of the musical pattern on the skeletal structure of the beat. So the basis of all certainty in musical action is clear musical apprehension, which is the outcome of guided musical growth.

This is further illustrated by the extraordinary assurance of the best jazz musicians, and of certain extemporizers. These people may, and do from time to time, make mistakes, in the sense that they may play notes that they did not intend to play. But they are not the sort of mistakes that make one fall flat on his face—only slight stumbles and imperfections which are almost unnoticeable in the sweep and fluency of the utterance. The listener does not get the impression of an agonized progress from hand-hold to hand-hold above a yawning abyss. But such fluency is not attained by feats of lightning calculation in the application of formula. These musicians are simply carried along by the dynamic musical pattern itself.

Now we may not want to make people into good jazz players or even good extemporizers; but musical assurance is undeniably a very desirable artistic virtue. Yet a great many artists and a great many amateurs rather sadly lack it. This is a certain sign of something fundamentally wrong with their training, because confident response is a natural outcome of healthy growth. What is wrong with it is also sufficiently clear. It is prevailingly mechanical and externalistic rather than prevailingly musical and developmental. It places a tremendous emphasis upon the outward forms and manifestations of skill, and very little emphasis upon that living, inner apprehension that is the guide-line of all skill. Under these circumstances skill becomes approximated to stunt, and the musician becomes approximated to the acrobat. We may admire his performance, but it makes us grit our teeth and break into a light perspiration for fear of an accident. And it has the same effect on him.

This whole discussion bears upon two problems which loom large in the minds of all musical people—nervousness in public performance and tension in technique. The public performance of music is very much like public speaking, which is simply the act of telling other people something that one has clearly in one's mind. A great occasion may produce a little goose-flesh, but the act itself is not particularly formidable, so long as it is done in this way. If, however, the orator gets somebody else to write his speech, memorizes it word for word without understanding it very well, and then tries to recite it, he has something to be frightened about. This is pretty much how many musical performers approach the podium—scared to death of details, scared to death of forgetting, with no blessed clue to guide them if they falter. It is no use advising them, on the analogy of the speaker, to have in mind a clearly apprehended and emotionally meaningful musical pattern, and then to walk onto the platform and tell it to other people, because their training from childhood on has not enabled them to have clearly apprehended musical patterns in mind.

As to tension and relaxation in technique, there are a good many things to say which must be postponed. The relevant point here is that it is by no manner of means a problem of movement pure and simple. The key secret of relaxed action is not to breathe deeply, or to close one's eyes, or to adjust one's diaphragm, or to lower one's wrist, or to play from one's shoulders, or to call on Buddha, but to have a very clear awareness of what one is aiming at. There is more to it than this, but this much is essential. Uncertain, vacillating action, disoriented action, is almost certain to be tense, unless indeed it is simply indifferent. One can, of course, always flop, but this is quite different from relaxation in technique. Aimed action, when the aim is vague, is almost bound to be under tension. The real enemy of placed and patterned relaxation in musical performance is an unclear and rudimentary awareness of just what one wants to say musically. So the way to work for relaxation, as with everything else in music education, is from the inside out. Develop musical perception, musical imagery, musical feeling, keen and clear musical apprehension, and there will be a focus about which to organize clear and facile technical action-patterns.

VII

Musical growth is a rhythm of synthesis, analysis, and synthesis, in which occurs a process of transformation or reorganization. These two aspects of the matter are so closely related in actual practice and experience that they cannot be distinguished, but for the sake of clarity it seems well to consider them in order one at a time.

1 Fulfillment or achievement always involves a dramatic interplay of synthesis, analysis, and synthesis. This is not only a point of psychological doctrine. Its truth and crucial practical importance have been recognized again and again by effective workers. For instance, a great many writers, all the way from Horace to Rudyard Kipling, have explained their working methods precisely in these terms. They begin by blocking out their material in a first draft, as well as possible. Then they put it away for a time. After an interval they come back to it with fresh minds, and see various imperfections and inconsistencies which they did not notice at first, which they proceed to correct. First there is a synthesis, that is, the original blocking out of the job, then an analysis leading to an improved synthesis or revision. This too is put away to simmer and mature. After a while it is taken out again, and the need for more and more delicate alterations becomes apparent. So the process goes on until the writer feels that he has done as well as he ever can.

This is a good example of what is meant by the rhythm of synthesis, analysis, and synthesis. Of course the stages are not always so clear-cut, but the essential nature of the business can be clearly seen. A person starts with an over-all idea for a speech, or a story, or a poem. It is likely to be crude, vague, limited, and uncertain. These, as we have seen, are the characteristics to be expected in the early stages of any growth process. He works at it here and there, reorganizing, shaping, selecting, rejecting, altering. He does this in a great many ways—perhaps by writing out drafts, perhaps by making notes, perhaps by studying references, perhaps just by meditating. But in spite of all these surface differences, what is really going on is a process of analysis. And as this analysis proceeds, the work itself—the synthesis—is becoming clearer and more adequate. All human achievements, all the way from planning a military operation to painting a picture, are brought about by this sequential rhythm of synthesis, analysis, and synthesis, and it needs to be recognized, emphasized, encouraged, and facilitated in the teaching of music.

For instance, the first thing to do in taking up a new piece is to get some kind of overview, either by listening to it, or playing it over, or reading it through in the score without playing it, whichever seems most feasible. This is the preliminary synthesis. The point is to start with something intelligible to work on. The work itself consists in concentrating on selected details and polishing them up, and at the same time getting a better organization of the whole thing. Again, in writing a harmony exercise—or what is likely to be much more beneficial, a simple composition—the first stage of the game should be an over-all blocking out, like that recommended by Horace and Kipling. Then one proceeds to tackle the details, and, as one does this, the entire job begins to assume a new shape. The selfsame idea applies to much longer and perhaps less well-defined sequences, such as learning to read the score or to develop a technique. These also are wholes, or totalities, or as it were organisms. They are at first vague, clumsy, feeble, and full of imperfections and even contradictions. They improve little by little, as now this weakness is cleared up, and now that one. The sequence of interweaving synthesis and analysis must go on for years; but this is the essential nature of the process.

What has just been said means that the playing of a piece, or the writing of an exercise or a composition, or the ability to read, or technical facility is attained by growth. It is the exact opposite of the idea that such things are attained by accumulation or construction—the very opposite of the mechanistic doctrine. A mechanistic plan of practicing would be to start at the beginning of a new piece, without any overview or idea of its expressive and aesthetic values, and get each little section right before going on to the next. A developmental plan of practicing would be to start with this overview, this guiding conception, and to refine it by picking out details for study anywhere in the piece at any time. A mechanistic plan for sight reading would be to teach the various symbols one by one, making as sure as possible that each was well learned before going on to the next, introducing them very carefully so that there would be only one unknown thing before the pupil at a time. A developmental plan for sight reading would be to use music that the learner wished to sing or play, and to show him how its expressive components were indicated in the visual symbolism, taking them up as they happened to arise, and not necessarily dealing with all or nearly all that were involved in any one composition. These are two out of innumerable illustrations of the developmental approach. It may be relied upon for far better and more effective results than the mechanistic approach, because it is

[90]

psychologically sound, and because it is how the best workers always work.

Does this developmental process mean that there should be no systematic or "formal" work? Both the friends and foes of the idea often think that this is so. But they are both quite wrong. Systematic and formal work has a very important place indeed. And that place is in the later stages of development. The formal study of musical theory can be fascinating and illuminating—if there has been a genuine and significant musical development beforehand. But it is a very bad starting point for musical development. The formal study of technique, which means practicing scales, arpeggios, figurations, etc. perhaps for hours on end, is enormously valuable—if there has been a genuine and authentic technical and musical development beforehand. Otherwise it is a barren desert of sand and dry bones. Both of them are essentially analytic phases of the rhythm of growth. Analysis should always be present from the very first. But it should only become very stringent toward the end. The learner must always be conscious that he is analyzing out and resolving his own difficulties—difficulties of which he is conscious and which bother him in a functional situation—or he is not really analyzing at all, but only going through the motions.

Does not this developmental process call for purpose and intelligence? Indeed it does! How much easier, how much simpler, how infinitely less exacting to divide the stuff into little bits, to set up each little bit as a lesson, and to expect the learner to tackle each lesson submissively because he is told to do so! If the rhythm of analysis and synthesis is to go at all, the learner has to think about his problems, and the teacher has to help him do so by thinking with him. Also the learner has to care about his problems, to want to solve them, so that he feels a real excitement and illumination when with the teacher's help he begins to find out how to do so. Yes, the rhythm of analysis and synthesis does demand intelligence and will. But what effective achievement is possible otherwise? Also, if we happen to be interested in our pupils' characters, as well as in their musical achievements, as we ought to be, it is well to remember that work of this kind is exceedingly good for the soul.

The general idea of the rhythm of synthesis, analysis, and synthesis may perhaps now seem fairly understandable. But there is still one more point to be brought out, perhaps the most important of all: this whole rhythm should invariably center upon musical content, musical expressiveness, musical responsiveness. A learner runs into what seems like a technical difficulty. A tremolo passage in a piece is muddy, insecure, refuses to go. He isolates it, and practices the movement-pattern, but it does not clear up. What is the matter? To analyze the difficulty is certainly the proper treatment, but analysis has not yet penetrated the core of the problem. The trouble may not lie in the movement-pattern, but in a defective grasp of the rhythm itself, which is one of the expressive elements in the music. If this is picked out, analyzed into clarity, and put back again, everything may succeed! A learner is having trouble with a supertonic triad in a harmony exercise. He pulls it out of context, and analyzes it as an isolated entity that has to be treated according to certain rules. Very likely the whole emphasis of the teaching leads him to work in this way. What he ought to do is indeed to analyze it, but in terms of its expressive and aesthetic function in the entire passage, and the right kind of teaching will encourage this. A group of children is failing to sing in tune or producing unpleasant tone. Should such problems be attacked by having them think about how to breathe or how to place the voice? Not in the first instance, at any rate. Attention should be focused on catching, responding to, and projecting the expressive values of the music, and on what this means in the particular passage that is giving trouble. To hear the passage beautifully sung, perhaps by the teacher or by one of themselves, to establish an ideal image of its expressive delivery is the sort of analysis needed. The rule for all analysis is: *Always go back to the music.*

2 Another way of looking at all these ideas is to say that we are dealing with a rhythm of transformation or reorganization. As a person advances towards maturity, he should be achieving new and better ways of responding, new and better controls.

It is the neglect of or insufficient emphasis upon this vital idea that is one of the chief reasons why mechanistic teaching does not give good results. In mathematics, pupils are taught to compute, and it is hoped that somehow they may take to thinking. In English, they are taught rules of punctuation, grammar, and usage, and it is hoped that somehow they may take to communicating. In music reading, they are taught the separate symbols, and it is hoped that somehow they may take to seeing musical meanings in the score. In musical performance, they are taught the separate adjustments and movement-patterns, and it is hoped that somehow they will take to clear and expressive musical enunciation. In musical theory they are taught the various procedures, and it is hoped that somehow they will take to

[92]

projecting meaningful musical patterns. Every teacher who thinks about the matter at all has to admit that the functioning ability itself is just as different from its elements as a finished picture is from the blobs of pigment on a palette. But too often he provides only the blobs of pigment and leaves the job of combining them to providence. .· It is really amazing how blind teachers can be to the obvious need to encourage and guide these combinings, these creative fusions, these higher integrations. Pieces are taught simply in terms of the right notes, and pupils are left entirely to their own devices to make the vital discovery that the right notes embody meaningful and intelligible musical patterns. Music is taught with the whole emphasis upon technique, and pupils are left to their own devices to make the vital discovery that a melodic line can be expressively rendered. Theory is taught as a collection of rules, and nothing at all is done to reveal to the student, in and through his own experience, that these rules are neither more nor less than practical directions for making creative statements in the tonal art.

Why? One encounters several reasons, if such they can be called. First it is said that talented pupils, and only talented pupils, will become able to apprehend and respond to musical content, to perform with intelligent expressiveness, to project musical conceptions. This is a dialectical boomerang if ever there was one. It amounts to saying that we teach so clumsily that only a genius can get the point. It is even bad business, for the implication is that very few people can ever get from music study the only valuable thing it has to give, in which case there should be very few music students. The truth is that the appeal to special talent is an appeal to magic and a confession of ineptitude, for the teacher's business is not to make things difficult, but to make them easy. Second it is said that free musical responses, in the way of expressive performance, or creative utterance, or adequate appreciation are possible only after the notes, and the chords, and the details of technique have been thoroughly acquired. This is another fundamental misconception. The learning of the notes, and the chords, and the techniques should itself be a conscious progress towards increasing musical freedom and adequacy. For instance, the mastery of the harmonic components of a Chopin nocturne should bring with it revelations of new possibilities of expressive utterance and motor control. We are not dealing in any such situations with two processes of an entirely different kind—the routine and the creative or expressive. We are dealing with a musical responsiveness which continually transforms itself into greater adequacy. Lastly it

[93]

is said that free and adequate musical response—that is to say, expression, creative utterance, fine appreciative discrimination, and so forth,—cannot be taught, and that only the routines can be taught. The only answer one can make to this contention is that it is simply and flatly false. Obviously a person can be taught to perform in terms of attending to, working for, and projecting expressive values. Obviously a person can be taught what is called theory with a primary emphasis upon the creation, at a simple level no doubt but still authentically, of musical values. Indeed, this is just how such things should be taught. Far from sacrificing a thorough mastery of the routines, this is how to get it, because such mastery comes through the process of growth.

VIII

In this chapter and the preceding one we have been doing the very thing that was discussed in the preceding section. We have been going through a process of analysis. We have been looking at a great many distinguishable aspects of musical growth. But analysis must lead to better synthesis if its purpose is to be fulfilled. So now it is necessary to bring everything together again. It is necessary to face this question: In view of our analytic study, what better and clearer understanding of musical growth as a whole has emerged?

Let us begin by reminding ourselves of the way we have come. Musical growth is a process in which a living core of meaning becomes more and more perfectly apprehended. It is a process marked by an essential continuity, and which cannot be broken down into separate stages. It is a process in which purpose becomes more and more explicit and effective. It is a process which alters and moulds the entire personality. In this process crudeness evolves into precision, concrete experience comes more and more under abstract and symbolic controls, the universal and systematic implications of immediate experience become explicit, what is vaguely apprehended becomes clarified, and hesitation evolves into certainty. When one looks over all these points, stated in such a brief and summary fashion, there are so many of them that they may seem rather bewildering. Yet they are nothing more than different perspectives on one single thing. What is this one thing? What do all these points come to, when one holds them together in one's mind?

Musical growth is essentially creative. That is what they all come to. It is a process in which a person creates for himself a way of perceiving, imagining, thinking, feeling, and acting. Developmental

[94]

teaching fosters, guides, and assists this creative process by organizing conditions which help it along. Mechanistic teaching, on the other hand, concentrates on the learning of separate lessons, at best lets the creative process take care of itself, and nearly always does a great deal to hamper it.

A few concrete illustrations will probably help to show just what this means. If you will call to mind Alexander Graham Bell's invention of the telephone you will find in it all the features of growth which have been discussed. There was an idea which ran all through his work—the idea of transmuting sound into physical impulses and these back again into sound—and it became clearer and clearer as he went on. He experimented along many different avenues, and ran into some extremely dramatic turning points, but there was a living continuity in all he did. His purpose became defined as he saw more and more adequately on what to concentrate. His work shaped and moulded his entire personality. Much of his early work was crude and fumbling, but it became more and more precise. As he experimented with this and that concrete and immediate problem, general principles and general ideas developed in his mind. At first he saw vaguely, but his vision narrowed down, sharpened up, clarified, and came to a focus. He was beset with hesitations, but gradually certainty established itself. He went through endless analysis, and endless attempts to reach better syntheses, until at last the invention emerged. This is the story of a creative process, which is also precisely a process of growth.

The same thing happened in Beethoven's creation of the *Ninth Symphony*. We know that for many years he was haunted by the idea of a great work which should combine the values of choral and instrumental music. Beyond a doubt it had a pervasive influence on his life. His output as a composer and the drastic self-discipline he gave himself were, in a real sense, a preparation for it, a growth towards it. Twice he thought that the time might be ripe and that he might be ready, and produced compositions combining voices and instruments on a large scale. But he knew within himself that the synthesis was not yet complete. The *Ninth Symphony* was the outcome of these years of creative growth and striving, and so was the Beethoven who was at last able to write it.

A good friend of mine has told me how, in his student days at a conservatory, theory was for a time the bane of his life. He was passing his courses, but he had a maddening sense of missing something essential and precious. This bothered him so much that one summer

[95]

vacation he engaged a young man who had done some composing to give him tutoring. The young composer, it turned out, was an anti-conventionalist. "You want to work with me?" he said, in effect, to my friend. "Very well. But we'll take an entirely new tack. I won't put you through those textbooks. We'll just get down and compose music, and I'll help you out. If things go well I'll let you pay me. If not, I won't take a cent." During that summer all the features of growth displayed themselves—emerging meanings, clarifying purposes, a fumbling movement from the crude to the precise, from the vague to the clear, from the immediate to the general, a series of small dramas of analysis and synthesis. "As I look back on it," my friend told me, "I remember how I felt—as if a weight had lifted, a light had broken in upon me. What I sort of halfway knew became as clear as crystal." One might call that a process of growth or a process in which a new power was created. They are both the same thing.

When a little child in a rhythm band gets hold of the great fact that music has a beat, a new power is being created. When a boy of twelve gets hold of the great fact that a musical melody "says something," and can be shaped expressively to say it better, a new power is being created. When a student in a voice class hits upon the natural co-ordination of mind and body which produces the act of song, a new power is being created. When a student in a theory class discovers that the harmonic colors, the trends of resolution and tonality, the melodic combinations that he has known for long enough as immediate and concrete experiences have systematic meanings and can be handled by a symbolic apparatus, a new power is being created. When a violin student hits upon a new mode of attacking a technical problem that has baffled him for years, a new power is being created. Whenever we really achieve anything, we always have in our very bones, the sense that in us at any rate, a new thing has been created. Yet the process that brings it to birth is the process of growth. Nor does it matter in the least that something very like it has been born in millions of other lives. When a child becomes able to walk, it is *his* capacity to walk that has been created. Every rose is very much like every other rose. But each rose is a new birth of beauty, a new result of growth, a new creative outcome.

So the conception of musical growth as a creative process—a process in which musical apprehension and sensitiveness are creatively evolved through many endeavors and experiences—brings together all the points that we have been studying one by one. It leads us through analysis to a better synthesis, a better vantage point. From this vantage point it is possible to see more clearly the profound difference between mechanistic and developmental teaching. That difference does not consist in one being orderly and the other chaotic. Both are orderly. But with one the order is that of blindly putting a machine together by separate operations whose meaning is never clarified, and with the other the order is that of inventing the machine. Mechanistic teaching works for results by considering them as finished products, analyzing them into their components and assembling these components. Developmental teaching works for results by redis-covering them anew. Mechanistic teaching proposes to make a flower out of its petals, its stamens, its pistil, its stem, and its leaves. Develop-mental teaching proposes to grow the flower. Mechanistic teaching patterns itself on the assembly line of a factory manufacturing tele-phones. Developmental teaching patterns itself on the creative adventure of Alexander Graham Bell in inventing the telephone. So much now seems visible from our vantage point. So once again we see that power and all fulfillment come through growth.

QUESTIONS FOR DISCUSSION

1. Does the sequence from the concrete to the abstract mean that at a certain point concrete experience should stop, and after that nothing but abstract notions should be presented?

2. Is there any conflict between beginning with the immediate and beginning a new song by giving the children an over-all idea of it?

3. Show specifically how the rhythm of growth described in this chapter differs from a sequence of topics to be mastered one by one and retained.

4. How may a simple and immediate musical experience contain in itself the germ of systematic theory?

5. Show how clear musical thinking can help to eliminate nervousness, hesitation, and tension.

6. Carefully analyze the idea of "the right start" in learning a new piece of music. Why is it important? What fallacies are often involved?

7. What is the place of (a) synthesis, (b) analysis, in learning a rote song, a new instrumental piece?

8. In what sense may a person's whole musical development be described as the achievement of better and better syntheses?

9. Admitting that error and crudeness are not good in themselves, for what positive and constructive reasons should they be tolerated?

10. Does the achievement of a genuine musical responsiveness require special talent?

ADDITIONAL READINGS

JAMES L. MURSELL and MABELLE GLENN. *The Psychology of School Music Teaching.* Silver Burdett Company, Inc., New York, 2d ed., 1933. Chapter 3, "Musical Learning." (Deals extensively with the notion of analysis and synthesis as an aspect of learning.)

HENRY COWELL. "The Process of Musical Creation," *American Journal of Psychology*, 1926, Vol. 37, pp. 233–236. (A very personal account of the author's own musical growth, revealing many aspects of the process.)

RUDYARD KIPLING. *Something of Myself for My Friends.* Doubleday, Doran and Company, Inc., New York, 1937. Chapter 8, "Working Tools." (Kipling's account of his creative methods reveals and illustrates many of the rhythms of growth.)

POLLY AMES. "Children and the Teaching of Painting," *Progressive Education*, 1939, Vol. 16, pp. 535–542. (A very interesting account of artistic development, full of parallels with music, and illustrating many of the points in this chapter.)

CHAPTER FIVE

Developmental Experience in Music Education

I

The prime mover in musical growth is *developmental experience*. All of us, looking back over the past, can think of certain impacts, doings, discoverings, learnings, which have had a profound and perhaps even a fateful influence upon us. They may be of the most varied kinds—reading a book, engaging in a conversation, making a friend, seeing a picture, going on a trip, taking up and following a hobby, working at a new job, getting into a new subject of study, finding a better way to learn an old subject, achieving a success. They may be colorful and dramatic happenings, or have all the aspect of sober drudgery. But however they differ in content and appearance, they are the same in effect. They bring about a reorganization of thought, action, interest, and purpose. Such vital influences as these are what we are going to call developmental experiences.

On the other hand, there are innumerable experiences which do not seem to have any such striking effect upon us. We meet people casually, we go on journeys, we walk about strange cities, we read magazine articles and stories, we go to concerts and plays and movies, we study required subjects, and it does not seem to make a great deal of difference. No doubt this is a matter of degree. Presumably everything that comes into our lives affects us to some extent, even if it only creates indifference, or mental numbness, or downright dislike. Perhaps, too, it is partly our own fault that every person we meet, every place we visit, every conversation we have, every lesson we study, does not have a deep and lasting effect upon us. But the plain fact is that they do not, or so it would seem. These at least relatively sterile and ineffective| happenings are the opposite of developmental experiences.

The argument based upon this contrast is that *the substance and staple of a program of music education should consist of developmental experiences in music, deliberately designed to bring about musical growth.* The ideal program of music education consists of nothing but musically vital experiences. Every merely routine lesson, every languid and indifferent activity, every undertaking without any grip and drive about it is a dead spot, and to that extent a failure.

This may seem like an impossible ideal. You may say that one cannot tell in advance whether a given experience will have a developmental effect, and one cannot be sure about its influence while it is going on or after it is over. Such objections certainly must not be shirked or minimized. But there are several things to be said before the discussion proceeds.

First, one can spot genuine developmental experiences better than might be imagined, if one starts looking for them. I once visited a third-grade room to watch the work of a young music supervisor. She was dutifully following the course of study, and had what seemed to me a rather dull lesson on intervals, using the notation and the syllables. However, she had a beautiful voice, and she sang the intervals in a way that was a pleasure to hear and a pleasure to watch. I thought to myself that she had something right there to offer to the children, the value and possibilities of which she seemed quite unaware. She made the dull intervals sound like music, but nobody seemed to notice, she least of all. There was a nugget of developmental experience lying right at her feet, only waiting to be picked up. All that was needed was for her to notice it and recognize its value. That often happens, so perhaps this business is not so terribly difficult after all.

Then there is a second thing to say. A teacher who is on the lookout for developmental experience, and recognizes its supreme importance, will in the course of time be able to tell pretty well in advance what will go and what will not go. Also he will become pretty well able to tell whether something is getting across, or has done so. Actors, speakers, writers learn to do this, because they know very well that their stuff must have vitality. Teachers can learn to do it too. And if a whole teaching staff is on the lookout for such experiences, and if it pools its learning and discovering, a great deal can be done. It is quite true that there will always be some failures. No one can ring the bell every time. But if one tries to, one can ring it a good deal of the time. On the other hand, if one does not even attempt to ring it, if one does not feel that ringing it is important, if one does not even realize that there is a bell to be rung, then its sounds will be few and far between indeed. So difficulty recedes a step further, and impossibility is blotted out.

Thirdly, it is possible to formulate the general characteristics of a developmental experience. One cannot be hard and fast about it, to be sure. But a reasonably definite bill of specifications can be drawn up. What features must an experience have if it is to be developmental? How can one tell whether it is having, or has had, an appreciable developmental effect? What must one look for? These questions can, in a real measure, be answered. So the ideal of a music program made· up of nothing but vital developmental experiences, ceases to seem like a dream of some quite unattainable Utopia, and becomes a feasible goal for planning and action, even though, as with all human endeavours, we· never manage to achieve perfection. To a discussion of these general characteristics of developmental experience we now turn.

II

A developmental experience has five characteristics. It is arresting, impelling, revealing, fulfilling, and conscious.

1 A developmental experience is *arresting*. It imposes itself. It grips the attention. It is like a barrier thrown across a stream, against which the current checks and eddies before finding a new direction. This is one of its most striking and recognizable characteristics.

A very notable phenomenon of mental and behavioral growth is what is called exaggeration. When a new behavior pattern—a new action, a new word, any new performance—emerges in the development of a little child, he is very· apt to use it to excess. He emphasizes it, exults in it, repeats it endlessly. It is a taking-off point, and he pauses on it for reorientation. It is as though nature had told him to dwell on it, because it is pregnant for the future. Exactly the same phenomenon is seen on the highest developmental levels in the inspiration of great artists. Wagner hearing the Beethoven symphonies for the first time and being unable to get the music out of his head, Keats sitting up till dawn to read with his friend from the borrowed copy of Chapman's translation of Homer, Beethoven and Schubert seized with a creative inspiration in the company of friends and being visibly transformed and carried away, all exemplify the same phenomenon. They are instances of the creative pause, the check upon

[101]

the ordinary stream of living, the imperious arrest which is characteristic of developmental experience.

I have seen a beautiful example of this very thing in a piano class. At the close of the period the teacher, after a short announcement and explanation, sat down and played Schumann's *Träumerei* to the pupils. One of the boys was instantly and visibly fascinated. The pause, the arrest, were quite dramatically apparent. The boy waited for a moment till the others were gone, and then came up and asked the teacher whether he might be allowed to try to learn the piece. She was inclined to be doubtful, because she had something else in mind. But she consented, and very wisely. The boy went home and practiced like a fiend. For a week his other school work suffered. He was rather more than lax about his domestic tasks. He had to be prevented from wakening his family at five in the morning with the so delightful strains. It was as true a case of the creative pause, the imperious arrest so characteristic of all developmental experience, as ever was seen by Schubert's friends when he dashed off *Hark, Hark! the Lark* on the back of a beer-garden menu.

The reason why a developmental experience must be arresting is this. It comes as an opportunity to function in a new and better way. This is to fulfill the most profound and vital of all natural needs. It is the taproot of happiness, itself the most powerful of all tonics, for through happiness we grow stronger. The music supervisor comes into a third-grade classroom. Instantly there is a stir of welcome and anticipation. One can see the languid current check and pile itself up, ready to sweep into a new channel. She has a reputation for inaugurating activities that have the breath of life in them. What will she bring this morning? A new song to be learned! It will take some careful work, some hard study here and there. Never mind. Indeed, so much the better. While it is going on, nothing else is thought about. This is because she teaches, not only the notes, but also musical enjoyment and fulfillment. After the minutes are over, something has been established in hearts, and minds, and voices. It is something more than that particular song—a modest something, perhaps, but real just the same. A developmental experience has taken place.

Alas, one often sees the very opposite happen in school classrooms. It is a seventh-grade class in general music. A lady, doubtless well-meaning but apparently quite bored, appears on the dais. One gets the impression that she has just been rummaging through her files for enough material to fill, or perhaps kill, about forty minutes. Part singing, it appears, is to be this morning's treat. Nobody sings the songs particularly well. Nobody seems to care. They have, as the expression has it, "gone through the work." Languidly the period limps to its lingering close. If one must characterize the occasion the word that rises to the mind is "unimportant." It has not been arresting. Nothing has been changed, unless for the worse. It has not been a developmental experience.

All this, you may be inclined to say, is very well as far as it goes, but it does not go far enough. It does not yet answer the really practical question: How can one organize an arresting experience? What makes it arresting? Is there any tangible reply forthcoming?

I think you will always find that what makes the kind of experience we are talking about arresting is that it throws into high relief some facet or aspect of the music itself. Think of the examples we have already considered—the beautiful singing of the young supervisor, the teacher's playing of *Träumerei*, the visit of the supervisor with the reputation for inaugurating vital activities. They all tell the same story, and you will find it clearly repeated in all the illustrative cases in the rest of this chapter. It is the music itself that arrests, and grips, and holds. Of course the whole situation in which it is played up and made apparent is important, just as the setting of a jewel is important. But the jewel itself is what makes the impression. The seventh-grade class in general music was a failure, precisely because the jewel was obscured and covered up.

So the way to set about organizing arresting musical experiences is to be eager to project some kind of authentic musical message every time you meet with an individual learner or a class of learners. How you do it depends on the circumstances, and the learners, and to a very large extent on you yourself. If you are an extrovert you go to work in one way, if you are an introvert, in another way. One of the most unobtrusive teachers I know has developed an almost uncanny power of projecting experiences which instantly grip and hold her pupils. She has built up a battery of devices and techniques peculiarly suited to her own personality, such as ways of taking attendance, making announcements, starting the period, assigning responsibilities to members of the class, dramatizing the arrangement of her materials and of the room. For instance, I once saw her present a lesson on Wagner to a junior high-school group. She had a number of striking imaginative pictures of scenes from the operas, which were arranged ahead of time on a large bulletin board by three carefully chosen members of the class. They had been told to keep it a dark secret, and on a private signal from her to bring in the display and place it where everybody could see. The effect was just what she desired. It staged the music and the discussion perfectly. Yet one could not recommend it as a universal practice, for with some people, and in some situations, it would not work at all. But after all, it was nothing but her particular way of creating a setting to throw the jewel of music into high relief—or, to put it more technically, to establish an attitude and to focalize an interest. It was by no manner of means a show put on for its own sake. She wanted very much to convey certain musical values and meanings, and she used this procedure to dramatize them and make them stand out.

Or consider the application of this idea to what is called drill, by which is meant intensive work at a more or less isolated problem. Such work must be arresting, or it does very little good. The learner must concentrate during drill, if he is to get much out of it. It is not the least use simply telling him to concentrate. One must give him something to concentrate on, indeed something that actually compels concentration. This is exactly what all really good drill masters (who are somewhat rare birds) know that they must do. What is the best thing to concentrate on? By all means the musical content. To get the notes right, the passage smooth, hang onto the music, its tonal content, its rhythmic content. It is very hard for an individual practicing scales or the clarinet players of an orchestra to concentrate by just hammering away. It is very easy for them to concentrate if there is a perceived or imaged musical effect that they are trying to create. The analytic study of movement should be part of the business, but it cannot be the most important factor, let alone the whole picture, because the goal of skilled movement is the production of a musical effect, and an awareness of the goal helps very much to control the movement.

The great obstacle to organizing and projecting arresting experiences is lukewarmness on the part of the teacher, and the lack of any urgent musical message every time he meets a learner or a group of learners. Of course there may be good reasons for this, such as an exhausting schedule, an unbearable pupil load, or an ironclad course of study. But whatever the reason, the effect is inevitably the same. Indifferent teaching means lackadaisical experience. If one always tries to come before a class urgently desiring to project some facet of the charm, the power, the meaningfulness of music itself, one's feet are on the right path. There will be failures. One must learn to use one's own resources and to proceed in terms of one's own powers. One must acquire the art of fabricating the right setting. But as time goes on, failures decrease and successes mount. One finds oneself increasingly able to project experiences which have the first necessary characteristic of any developmental influence, that of being arresting.

2 A developmental experience is *impelling*. It inaugurates action, and shapes future choices. It induces not merely a strong immediate reaction, but also a chain reaction.

Two boys were members of the wood-wind section of their high-school orchestra. They were fairly interested, fairly industrious, fairly effective in their work and contribution. Then George Barère came to town with his ensemble for a wood-wind concert. The orchestra director persuaded these boys to attend, and arranged for them to have front-row seats where there would be a good view. He himself sat in the balcony and kept an eye on them. He could see that they were fascinated. They listened with all their ears, watched with all their eyes. Clearly the experience was arresting. So far so good. But he knew that this was not enough. What would happen afterward? He made it his business to find out. What developed was that they talked about the concert for weeks, practiced harder, took their responsibility as orchestra members much more seriously. It was quite evident that the experience was not only arresting, but also impelling.

The members of a sixth-grade chorus voluntarily come to school half an hour ahead of time three days a week. The members of a high-school orchestra return to town for rehearsals six weeks before the opening of school in the fall. Students who have been under the influence of the work in music in a large school system go in large numbers into the adult musical organizations of the city. Several children in a third-grade ask to sing a certain song which they had learned a couple of weeks ago. A boy in a high-school course in general music buys a recording of the Schubert *Erl King* after hearing it in class. Two or three high-school pupils inquire about getting some work in theory after an effective discussion of the structure of a Schubert impromptu in a piano class. A high-school girl, after the first two meetings of her course in general music, writes on her own responsibility to some prominent people for help with her music notebook. These are the kind of symptoms to look for. They are among the best proofs we can have that genuine developmental influences are at work.

From all this two practical considerations emerge.

A. *Everything turns on the vitality and the driving power of the experience itself.* It must be capable of arousing an impulse which, so to speak, spills over. Here as everywhere, the talisman is music itself. The normal effect of an authentic and living musical experience is not only to grip us while it is going on, but to make us want some more. One can hardly say as much for studying the dotted quarter note, the proper fingering of a trill, the dates of the life of Beethoven, or the rules for resolving a dominant seventh chord, except in so far as they are embedded in genuine musical aspirations. But to listen with deep enjoyment to a composition that charms us, to find ourselves able to participate effectively in the singing of a delightful song, to have before us a piece that we long to be able to play for ourselves, to participate in the rehearsal of music whose power and beauty we deeply feel, to capture and crystallize in the process of composition our own musical intimations, are among the most naturally intriguing and inviting experiences of human life. It seems very strange that so many music teachers should make so much of the bare bones of their subject, and so little of its living substance. They seem to think that the symbols, the techniques, the rules, the facts are the true essentials, the real foundations. But this is not so. The true essential in music education everywhere is direct experience of the compelling power of music. Moreover we should not think of ourselves as laying the foundations for a building, but as promoting a process of living growth. The primary consideration about anything we bring to any musical learner is not whether it is something that he "ought to know," but whether it is a true developmental experience. And the endeavour should be to make such an experience so arousing that it sets going a continuing impulsion.

B. *Follow-up opportunities should, wherever possible, be organized.* They should, however, be of the nature of opportunities and suggestions, rather than assignments. Like so many other desirable things in teaching, this can be done very simply if one has it in mind. For instance, it may be effective, in presenting a piece on the phonograph, to write on the board the title, the catalog number of the recording, its publisher, and its price. In some schools it is possible to organize opportunities for free listening out of school time. A rental library of records is sometimes a feasible undertaking. Attention can be called to local musical events, and often some of the class activities can be geared to them. A part of every elementary-school music program should be the publicizing of musical opportunities offered in the school system. Many other suggestions along similar lines can be made, but these suffice to indicate what can and should be attempted. Just what it is best to do will clearly depend upon the local situation and its resources.

This is an interesting inversion of the usual relationship between in-school and out-of-school doings. The ordinary thing is to assign homework for check-up in class. This is just the opposite. We are proposing to organize in class experiences which have impelling power, and then do what we can to make such impulsions practically effective. Of course the impelling power of a developmental experience is by no means always overtly observable. For many a pupil the living reality will correspond to the words of Wordsworth:

> The music in my heart I bore
> Long after it was heard no more.

There is no doubt that such inner enrichment is the most important thing of all. It is the living essence of all musical growth, and its attainment should be our constant and conscious goal. But if we center our thoughts on nothing else, and ignore overt manifestations, we can easily deceive ourselves. And indeed without any overt manifestation the inner enrichment itself may not take place. After all, Wordworth himself wrote a poem about his experience.

3 A developmental experience is *revealing*. It opens up a new understanding. It brings a new insight. It affords, or promises, an intelligible solution of a problem. It has an intelligible point.

A student who had been studying piano for a good many years, and thought himself quite advanced, came to work with a new teacher. At his first lesson he went through the first movement of a Beethoven sonata, doing what he considered a creditable job. The teacher, however, did not agree. After some moments of silent meditation he proceeded to analyze and comment, and little by little quite a devastating diagnosis emerged. Then came the prescription. "I want you," he said, "to get a metronome. Set it at a quarter of the regular tempo of this music. For the next two months I want you to go through this music always at this low tempo. Never indulge yourself and just play. Attend very carefully to everything you do, keeping the tempo away down. Do this at least four times a day. You badly need control. This will give it to you." A deadly mechanical routine, do you think? It did not turn out that way. From the very start the student realized that he had been presented with an expert and reasoned analysis, and that there was an idea in it all. As he worked, understanding and insight grew clearer and clearer. He came to

[107]

understand better and better, how to move, how to co-ordinate movement with the music and above all with the onward flow of the beat, how to practice. He came, in a word, to understand how to project musical values through the medium of the piano in a way that he never had before. He found in it all a fascinating solution to a fascinating problem, and neither the problem nor the solution had, up to that time, ever been clearly seen.

Another student majoring in piano at a school of music was taking his required work in voice. He did not want to take it. He did not believe he could do much with it. He did not see the point. During the first half of the term the instruction was quite hidebound, and all his doubts seemed well on the way toward confirmation. Then the teacher became sick, and a substitute took over. Almost at once this proxy assigned him a very "singable" song, with an easy flowing melody. Within a week his vocal approach was transformed, and controls which to all appearance were not there at all had emerged and begun to establish themselves. He never became more than a fair singer; but even this seemed a miracle to him. But singing opened up new musical perceptions and discriminations which had the widest scope and visibly affected his piano playing. The song did what numerous vocalises and drills had failed to accomplish. It revealed the inwardness of the vocal act. It made a cosmos out of the chaos of his vocal reactions. It came as a gleam of light breaking through clouds and darkness, and because of this, it was an effective developmental experience.

These two contrasting examples bring out several points.

A. *First, a developmental experience is quite different from routine mechanical learning.* Looked at from the outside they may sometimes seem quite similar. Nothing could seem more deadly, more mechanically laborious than going over and over a familiar piece at a very slow tempo for two months. It took far more self-control, more self-denial than the ordinary stint of exercises, scales and studies, run off as a duty. But it was, in all its inner values and meanings, an entirely different thing. The difference lies in this: Routine learning is organized with the idea of ingraining something; developmental experience is organized with the idea of revealing something. Revelation may come by keeping one's nose to the harshest of grindstones, or it may come, as in our second illustration, by singing a song that one likes to sing. The crucial consideration is that it shall come.

That, of course, is the trouble with a great deal of teaching—the

[108]

teaching of the notation, of music history, of theory, of technique. It is set up as a series of lessons to be learned, rather than as a series of revealing experiences. In exceptional cases, it is true, a student will transform a series of mechanical lessons into a series of revealing experiences. A girl once told me that she found what I know to have been a highly formalized course in theory fascinating throughout. But the reason was that she attacked each unit as a problem to be solved, as a challenge to insight, and not as a dull and tasteless, although presumably nutritious, capsule to be tamely swallowed. This, however, will only happen once in a thousand times. With children and adolescents it will almost never happen unless we make it happen. So it becomes our duty to make it happen. The girl I have just mentioned learned better than her teacher taught. This was a credit to her, but decidedly not to him.

B. *The second point brought out in our illustrations is this.* Just as a developmental experience is fundamentally different from routine learning, so also it is fundamentally different from an experience that is merely pleasant or attractive and nothing more. Going to a movie, a trip to the beach, are no doubt pleasant, and indeed even "arresting," but they are not for that reason developmental, because nothing opens up, nothing is revealed. The piano-major student whose case has been presented found his new song a pleasure. This was all right as far as it went, but there had to be more than this. As a matter of fact, even desperately hard work becomes arresting and compelling when and if it is also revealing. No conservatory teacher would ever dare to assign the job of copying out the *Forty-eight Preludes and Fugues* several times over. Yet this is just what Beethoven did, and he found it fascinating because it was revealing.

One frequently hears activities and undertakings defended on the ground that they are enjoyed. "The children love it." How often that refrain is repeated! This is all right, indeed even essential, up to a point. If the children hate it (whatever "it" may be), one may be quite sure that "it" is not a developmental experience. But we have not come far enough. What are they finding out, what is being revealed to them, in this activity, this endeavor? Rhythm band work, creative work, the making and playing of toy instruments, can be very good fun. It is altogether right and proper that they should be. But if they are nothing more than this, then they are simply pleasant ways of passing the time. What they should be are experiences in which something about music and one's relationship to it is revealed.

[109]

They should assuredly be both arresting and impelling. But if they are to be developmental influences they must also be revealing.

One very solemn and urgent note of warning needs to be sounded before we leave this topic. A routine lesson cannot be transformed into a developmental experience by giving it a coating of sugar. For instance, I once ran into a "system" for teaching the notation in which the staff was pictured as a wire fence on which little birds and animals were perching and climbing. At the first glance this seemed rather farfetched, although it could be all right. So I had to go deeper. It turned out that the material was set up entirely as lessons to be learned. For instance, a pigeon sitting on the third wire meant a quarter note on B, and if there was a sparrow beside the pigeon, this meant a dotted quarter note. The ingenuity lavished on this scheme was almost shattering, but it was wrongly directed. There seemed to be no idea of organizing experiences in which the children would *discover* that notes move up and down, that phrases flow, that durations vary, that there is a relationship to a key center, and so forth. All this can be done by using posters, and cunning figures, and cut-outs, although it is usually better to have the children themselves make all such devices rather than to present them with an elaborate ready-made apparatus. The reason for this is that one should want them to find something out, to achieve a revelation, rather than to *swallow down* a lesson in which indigestible ingredients are given a pleasant flavor. It is this finding out, this revelation that is an essential characteristic of a developmental experience. It is exactly what John Curwen had in mind a hundred years ago when he promoted the use of the movable do. He insisted again and again that the value of the syllables lay in what he called their "mental effect." His whole intention was to play up and clarify tonal trends and relationships or, in other words, to develop musical perceptiveness in certain definite directions. The debate pro and con that has raged around this particular device is a fine example of misdirected energy and misunderstanding. It has turned very largely on the syllables themselves. But what counts is the "mental effect." Any device whatsoever that evokes this is all to the good.

C. *One further point remains to be developed, and it is perhaps the most important of all.* What should be revealed in a developmental experience in music? Always some facet, some aspect, some application of music itself.

A state-wide high-school orchestra made up of students selected from a considerable number of local schools was rehearsing some of the music from *Das Rheingold*. The harmonization is highly colored, quite different from anything that most of these young people had ever played before. When they tried it, the chords that came out were, to put it mildly, unusual. The visiting director, instead of resorting to drill and repetitive effort, turned to the music itself. He played the chords to them on the piano, and had them listen. He had them build these chords up and hold them, again for careful listening. He organized a musical revelation.

That is exactly what happened to the advanced piano student who worked for two months at a familiar piece at a slow tempo. He found out all sorts of things about music which he already knew in a way, but which were never clear, and never centered on any practical and compelling problem. It is what happened to the piano major who was studying voice. He had been told to free up his vocal action, to attend to breathing and placement. He knew the dictionary meanings of these words, but their musical and vocal meaning had to await a revealing experience. This is just the kind of thing that ought to come out of every musical endeavor, all the way from free bodily rhythm in the nursery-school to advanced counterpoint in the conservatory. Music has literally endless facets, endless applications, endless "angles." Even its supreme exponents never exhaust it. A conductor I know once found Toscanini sitting in the greenroom during a rehearsal, raptly studying the score of Beethoven's first symphony, which one would think he knew to the last sixteenth note. The discovery of these facets, these applications, these intimations, these "angles" is endlessly fascinating. It is the very heart of musical growth, and every developmental experience in music ought to activate it.

4 A developmental experience is *fulfilling*. It conveys a swift, intimate, yet unmistakable sense of enlargement, of illumination, of better functioning, of success or the sure promise of success.

Consider again the case of the representative state-wide orchestra rehearsing *Das Rheingold*. A notable feature of the rehearsal technique adopted by the visiting director was the swift improvement produced. The wind sections, in particular, were having trouble with the unusual harmony, because adjustments of *embouchure* familiar to them were getting them nowhere. If the director had followed the policy of try, try, try, try again, it would have been endless, and probably futile. But his resort to the music itself had an immediate good effect. There was an immediate sense of successful effort, instead of frustration, and it reflected itself both in the morale of the players and in the music that they produced. This was valuable on the basis of the most realistic and hard-boiled practicality, for the organization had only a limited rehearsal time before facing the ordeal of public performance. It was also excellent from the standpoint of musical growth. More than one of the characteristics of a developmental experience are exemplified here, among which the one we are now discussing is not the least prominent, namely, the establishment of a quick and sure sense of success.

In the same way I have seen an expert analytical violin teacher take hold of a new pupil who had already studied the instrument for nearly ten years, and in a single lesson transform his sense of his future prospects. This pupil had drudged and labored for a long, long time, and had progressed with all the blithe alacrity of a glacier. He had about reached the conclusion that either the violin was an almost impossible instrument, or else he was an almost impossible learner. In spite of all his toil he was insecure, and lacking in assured facility. Of course the new teacher did not transform him into an accomplished virtuoso in a week. But one half-hour was enough to bring an intimation, an assurance, a promise. In the things this teacher had him do, in the line of attack he laid out, there was the unmistakable taste and aroma of future success. He went away from his first lesson hopeful as he had not been for a long time, convinced not by any encouraging words that had been spoken, but by the sense of having found in this experience the right clue.

True developmental experiences always have this quality. They bring with them the sense of a success which may not and indeed often cannot be final or ultimate, but is yet sufficient for a convincing foretaste. In this respect they are the diametric opposite of routine and mindless pounding. There is no developmental value in ramming one's head repeatedly against a concrete wall. There is no developmental value in failure and frustration. Failure and frustration are just what a teacher ought to fear and avoid. They occur quite often enough in ordinary life without being deliberately induced by pedagogical stupidity. If one wants pupils to become able to play the violin, give them the promptest possible experience of making music on the violin, even if it is only with the open G string. If one wants learners to respond with a delicate and discriminating sense of the values of the musical phrase, make it possible for them to play or sing phrase-wise with success and enjoyment from the very first. If one wants them to control their performance by musical perception and imagery, set up simple situations where they can really do so. If scales do not run freely, do not pin your faith to endless repetition, hoping for the best. Establish a situation—and it will usually be a musical situation, calling for musical perception and imagery and for expressive values—where they will at least begin to run freely. I have often seen scale-playing dexterity improve very fast, with the learning curves changing from a plateau to a spurt, with the practicing of the scale passages in Chopin's G minor Ballade and A flat major Polonaise. I have seen tremolo figurations improve like magic with the study of the tremolo passages of the third movement of Beethoven's Sonata Opus 27, No. 2, delivered with effective rhythmic and dynamic gradation, when a great many studies had produced very little increment.

5 A developmental experience is *conscious*. It is an experience in which the learner himself is at least partially, though perhaps for the time not fully, aware of what is happening to him, why it is valuable, and what is coming out of it.

In this respect it is in sharp contrast with the conventional routine drill experience. A person taking music lessons is told that he should spend half an hour each day on scales and exercises. The teacher honestly believes that this is both necessary and beneficial. The pupil, who naturally feels that he does not know as much about such matters as his instructor, accepts the judgment and follows the prescription. He does exactly what he is told, that is, he spends time. There is nothing about such technical work that is intrinsically arresting or gripping. It has, in and of itself, no dynamic quality which makes the pupil want to continue with it beyond the time limit under his own steam. It brings little or nothing in the way of revelation, of clarification, of expanding and deepening insight. And there is not likely to be any striking drama of fulfillment. It is, in fact, simply a chore—a necessary chore, perhaps, in the opinion of both teacher and pupil, but a chore nevertheless. Progress is supposed to take place in much the same way as a daily dose of some drug benefits the system. That is to say, it takes place, or is supposed to take place, gradually, imperceptibly, and without any clear consciousness on the part of the learner as to what is happening, why it is happening, and how it is happening.

The whole tendency of such work is to hamper and minimize progress, and even to frustrate it altogether. One may safely say that the alleged benefits of all blind and mindless drill are almost certainly spurious. It is exactly because of reliance upon work of this type that music study is so difficult and tedious, and yields such slow and hesitating advances. The student who was set to practicing the Beethoven sonata for two months at a very slow tempo did not work in this way at all. He was given a hard row to hoe, and it took plenty of character and determination to keep at it. But he knew exactly what he was trying for, exactly why he was trying in that particular way, and he could see what was coming out of it. He was engaged in a conscious and intelligent undertaking, and that made it entirely different from drill carried on in the blind faith that somehow some benefit might accrue. The high-school orchestra members who were helped to hear, perceive, and image the chords they were to produce were again conscious of the process that was being set up, and this once more created an entirely different situation from one in which the director had tried to get them to improve by endless and mindless repetition. The first-rate analytic teacher of violin whose work I have already mentioned does not simply tell his pupils to do thus and so in order to shape up their technique. He makes it possible for them to understand what these things are, and why they should do them. The proper way to help children develop a command of the score is not simply to drill them on the details of the notation. To say that the details must become familiar is true, but at the same time irrelevant to the problem. How are these details to become familiar? That is the question. They ought to become familiar in a situation, or rather a long series of situations, in which the children are helped to understand what they must see, and how they must see it, in order to visualize the music in the symbols.

The point is this. A developmental experience is one that involves the conscious, intelligent collaboration of the learner. It is not enough that such an experience shall be judiciously chosen. The learner himself must be aware of its judiciousness. It is not enough that such an experience shall have a point. The learner himself must see the point. And this cannot be done by sales talk. The experience itself must carry its own conviction, must reveal its own point. Most of us can remember being told in school that the study of geometry would improve our reasoning ability. Perhaps we were sufficiently docile or simple-minded to believe it. But our geometry lessons did not, in and of themselves, bring home the proposition, because nothing of the sort was really happening. Geometry can be taught as a series of developmental experiences involving the use of logic and reasoning. When it is taught in this way—which happens

[114]

far too rarely—the effect is so clear and evident that it cannot be missed, and hardly needs to be mentioned. But when it consists of unenlightened memorizing of theorems and blind fumbling with problems, the claim that reason is being trained is an insincere rationalization. Geometry is full of logic, but it must be attacked as a conscious challenge to logical thinking if that logic is to do the learner any good.

What is true of the teaching of geometry is true everywhere, including the teaching of music. If you propose to set up a developmental experience, one of the things you must do is to secure the conscious, intelligent collaboration of the learner. He must see with his own eyes, and understand with his own mind, the point of what he is to undertake. This will usually involve a certain amount of verbal explanation, although just how much of this to use will depend on the age and maturity of the persons concerned. In teaching rhythmic organization and values through bodily movement to preschool children, one would certainly not go into a long disquisition about why to walk, or run, or skip, or gallop, or move the arms and trunk and head in such and such a way. The exposition might be a marvel of logic and judiciousness, but it would miss fire. The obvious thing to do would be to see that the movement-patterns help rather than impede a developing awareness of the rhythm, to help the children to grasp the point in terms of very immediate experiences, and to say just enough to be of assistance. On the other hand, if one were dealing with the members of a senior high-school orchestra, it might be quite legitimate to set up the generalization that they should always be able to perceive and image the total musical pattern as well as their own parts, and to let them recognize for themselves the validity of this advice in all kinds of concrete situations. The point always is to help the learner to be conscious of the point of the experience, so far as he is able, at his own level of maturity. This, of course, is easier to do with highly developed learners, but it is just as necessary and just as possible with little children. The difference between the child and the adult is not that one grows mentally through routine, and the other through insight and intelligence. Both develop through insight and intelligence, the only difference being that the child has a little less of them than the adult.

III

In the section that has just been completed we have been going through a phase of analysis. Various aspects, distinguishable though

[115]

kindly, and with the best of intentions, even though the undertaking is chosen with the most judicious care and set up in the most orderly fashion, all the conditions are right for routine learning. Some pupils may avoid this, but if so, they are going against the tide. As to the majority, they may be amiable and well behaved, and really wish to please. But the chances are that there will be no real steam behind their efforts. This is the way to stay in grooves, not to get out of them. And growth and achievement, as we have repeatedly seen, depend precisely upon getting out of grooves. If one asks why imposition from above does not favor development, the only answer is that human beings are that way. This may be annoying, but it happens to be true. People may not violently object to being driven and commanded. Indeed they may even rather like it, because they find absence of effort and the dodging of problems on the whole rather comfortable. But there is no doubt that they grow and flourish best when they have to shoulder responsibilities which they themselves have undertaken.

Let us return for a moment to an instance already discussed, that of the piano teacher who assigned the Schumann *Carnaval Suite* to a student for the sake of his all-round pianistic development. The teacher in this case began by discussing the whole problem with the student. He treated him as an intelligent being, who was anxious to make an improvement. The teacher himself functioned as an expert consultant and adviser, who was able to make an effective diagnosis, and to suggest a promising prescription. But the student's own doubts, questions, wishes, and suggestions were considered quite extensively. When the decision was finally made, it was an outcome of joint thinking. Nor was it imposed as the last and infallible word of wisdom, but only as a solution which might work out in this particular problem, although neither of the two parties could be quite sure. Thus all the student's practicing on the *Carnaval Suite* was dominated by intelligent choosing, intelligent analyzing, intelligent evaluating, and intelligent collaborating. His study, in fact, became a joint undertaking; and when striking improvement did in fact take place, it was not because of some magic in this particular piece, but because of the heightened effort and the constant analytic experimentalism evoked by this very intelligent management of the situation.

Thus, it is always better to have pupils choose their own undertakings rather than to tell them what to do. It is always better to have them find out their own ways of working rather than to tell them how to work. It is always better to have them select and perhaps even devise their own drill exercises rather than to set the next ones in the book. It is always better to have them find out their own answers rather than to give them the answers out of hand. It is always better to have them appraise and criticize their own efforts rather than to offer purely external evaluations. Of course it is always a matter of more or less. One must not simply leave them to fumble around in the dark. If this were the best way, what would be the point of having a teacher at all? Also it is quite true that the more mature the individual, the more responsibility he can profitably take. But the business of the teacher in dealing with any learner, all the way from early childhood to maturity, is to suggest choices that may be feasible, to indicate solutions that may work out, to stimulate questions and suggestions and experimental lines of approach that seem promising. This is how the teacher's resourcefulness, knowledge, and expertness should be brought to bear. When people say that the teacher ought to control the situation because he knows more than the learner, they are quite right up to a point. If this means that he should play the part of an expert and sympathetic consultant, who is collaborating with less expert persons who want to improve, and who exercises leadership because of his superior equipment, it is perfectly correct. If it means that the teacher's function is simply to command, while the learner's function is simply to obey, and that there should be no collaboration at all but only domination and submission, then it is perfectly incorrect. This is not the way to promote growth. It is not the way to get results. As a matter of fact it is precisely the meagerly equipped teacher who is most likely to behave like an infallible autocrat, because he knows only one line of procedure, and is lost the moment he takes a single step off the beaten pathway.

A developmental experience, then, must be a co-operative undertaking rather than an imposed task. The patterns, grades, and methods of co-operation are innumerable, but the thing itself is essential. It appears very differently with little children and with adults, very differently in individual teaching and in class teaching. But appear it must, for the reason that co-operative responsibility breeds a high working morale, which in turn activates those creative transformations upon which growth and improvement depend.

3 All that has been said in this chapter culminates in the conception of the program of music education as a sequence of varied developmental experiences, designed to promote and foster musical

growth. This, admittedly, is an ideal, and a very exacting one, but it is the goal of all improvement, and the determining factor in all planning. It bears directly upon all practical matters, such as the preparation of courses of study, the development of resources, the internal co-ordination of the various phases of the work, the relationship of music to other subjects in the curriculum and to the extra-curriculum, the setting of standards, evaluative practices and techniques, and the pre-service and in-service training of teachers. All these topics will come up for treatment at a later stage of our discussion, but the broad picture has already defined itself. For the moment, and to round out the subject now before us, there are two final points to be made with regard to its implications for the teaching process itself.

Developmental teaching is essentially experimental. Every lesson, every unit (or whatever one calls it) is, in ideal, a developmental experience. As one plans it, one must have in mind the conditions which this imposes. Is the contemplated experience likely to be arresting, impelling, revealing, fulfilling, and consciously convincing? How can it be made so for this particular group of learners? One can never be sure in advance. One can never be sure while the work is in progress. Indeed one can never be perfectly sure at all. What is really happening is that an experiment is being conducted, the success of which must be judged, as well as possible, by some fairly well defined criteria. Complete certainty, either before or after the event, is not possible. However there is one thing sure. If the work is not consistently approached in this experimental spirit it is sure to be more dead than alive.

Again, developmental teaching is essentially a matter of artistry rather than of routine. Each lesson, each unit, each experience calls for the artistic handling of a human situation for the sake of certain outcomes. Teachers constantly want to be told just what to do and just how to do it. They want a fixed course, and a set of fixed procedures. One cannot have developmental teaching on these terms. In the old monitorial system of instruction, in which one teacher handled several hundred pupils all at once, lessons in arithmetic, geography, and so forth were printed on cards and taught by the teacher to the monitors, who then took the cards and relayed the lesson to the pupils. All of the monitors knew exactly what to do, and the system was a highly efficient organization. The only trouble was that nobody learned a great deal of arithmetic and geography, for the fostering and promotion of mental growth cannot be conducted in any such way. It is entirely possible to provide a teacher with a wealth of helpful suggestions and resources, including guiding principles, just as the same thing can be done for an artist or a composer. But every developmental experience he organizes must, in the last analysis, be his own individual creative projection, fashioned in the light of the personalities and backgrounds of his pupils, of his own personality and background, and of his understanding of what he wants to accomplish.

QUESTIONS FOR DISCUSSION

1. Does the fact that children enjoy an experience make it a developmental experience? Does that fact have any relationship to the educational value of the experience?

2. Consider an ordinary routine lesson. Show how it differs from a developmental experience in the light of the five criteria in the chapter.

3. Must a developmental experience always be pleasant?

4. Must a developmental experience always be interesting?

5. Plan, in as much detail as you can, several developmental experiences in music, with specific groups of pupils in mind.

6. If you were actually presenting these experiences, how would you judge whether they really did have the intended developmental effect?

7. How do you explain the fact that a formalized and apparently mechanistic course may sometimes and for some people have great and genuine developmental value? Would this probably be true only in special cases, or in general?

8. If it is possible to learn a great deal from one experience, what becomes of the idea that learning requires repetition?

9. In the light of our criteria of developmental experience consider rnythm band work, toy orchestra work, rhythmics, learning songs by ear, orchestra rehearsals, lessons in theory. Show how they might be managed to make them really vital.

10. Bring together and discuss instances of developmental experiences that have occurred in your own musical education.

ADDITIONAL READINGS

FRANK HAYWARD. *The Lesson in Appreciation.* The Macmillan Company, New York, 1917. (This little book deals most effectively with developmental experience in connection with poetry, but what is said applies admirably to music also.)

INGA OLLA HELSETH. *Living in the Classroom.* Edwards Brothers, Inc., Ann Arbor, Michigan, 1939. (This entire book should be scanned for concrete instances of developmental experience, in which it is very rich.)

EMMA D. SHEEHY. *There's Music in Children.* Henry Holt and Company, New York, 1946. (Another small and valuable book, which contains many concrete instances.)

PART TWO

AVENUES OF MUSICAL GROWTH

CHAPTER SIX

Growth in Musical Awareness

I

Having dealt with the general nature and characteristics of musical growth, and with what they imply for a program of music education, we are now to approach the subject from a different point of view. Developing musical responsiveness manifests itself in five directions, to wit, as growth in musical awareness, in musical initiative, in musical discrimination, in musical insight, and in musical skill. These are the five broad avenues of musical growth. The present chapter is devoted to the first of them.

However there are certain preliminary points that must be considered.

1 An identification of the directions along which musical growth must proceed provides the framework for a developmental curriculum in music. The general notion of musical growth has by now been made fairly clear. It is growth in musical responsiveness, in responsiveness, that is to say, to the poetic values and meanings of music, and to the expressive resources which establish these values and meanings. Moreover the process of growth has certain recognizable characteristics and rhythms. All this, as we have seen, involves many important practical consequences. But something more is needed.

Along what specific lines must musical growth be fostered? What kind of things must a musically growing person become better and better able to do? These questions must also be answered as far as possible. In general, such a person must become broader in his awareness, more active in his initiatives, keener in his discriminations, deeper in his insights, and more proficient in his skills. These are what might be called the broad avenues of his development. Moreover each one of the five can and should be rendered more specific by means of further analysis. The outcome of such an analysis is a working map of the developmental curriculum. The curriculum itself is set up by organizing, at all levels, appropriate and effective developmental experiences for the sake of promoting musical growth in the designated directions.

2 The five broad avenues of musical growth are by no manner of means mutually exclusive or separable from one another. They cannot be, because they are simply aspects or outer manifestations of the same thing, namely a developing musical responsiveness. It is often difficult to tell with which one of them we are dealing—whether, for instance, we are dealing in some given case with musical discrimination or musical insight. But there is no need to become pedantically concerned over such problems, because they are not of primary importance. Like all classifications of natural phenomena, the one here proposed is to a certain extent arbitrary, and cannot help but involve much overlapping. It is, indeed, nothing more than a tool for getting hold of events, and for the guidance of thought and practice. So all the five avenues overlap one another at many points, and to remember this is to save oneself considerable needless concern. Nevertheless, it is still well worth while to think and plan in terms of them, because this is the best possible way to avoid lack of balance. For example, many programs of music education are seriously out of balance because of a narrow preoccupation with skill. Now skill certainly is, or can be, one important aspect of an avenue of musical growth. But it is very important to be reminded, in all our planning, that there are others too which are just as important. Many a conservatory curriculum heavily emphasizes skill, does something about insight, touches upon awareness, but hardly fosters initiative and discrimination at all, except perhaps incidentally. But the moment one begins to think in terms of all five, the weakness becomes apparent, and the basis for a proper reorganization is revealed. It is for practical reasons like this that a comprehensive formulation of the avenues of musical growth is important and valuable, in spite of overlapping.

3 All five avenues of musical growth intimately and continually affect one another. Musical awareness, for instance, provides some of the best and most powerful of all incentives for the generation of musical insight and musical skill. Capacity to perform opens up possibilities for musical initiative, and is reinforced when such possibilities are realized. When, for instance, a high-school choir decides largely on its own initiative to put on an important public perform-

ance, there is a powerful impulse toward doing the best work possible. Or again, when a pupil studies a piece because he himself has chosen it, and wants to be able to play it, this is an incentive for the most repaying kind of technical work, or the most illuminating kind of analytical study. Or again, musical initiative in such matters as the building of a program, or the choice of compositions for one's own study is obviously hampered without a wide awareness of what music there is to be considered. Innumerable further instances of such inter-play and inter-relationship readily present themselves, and attention will be called to many such as we proceed.

Of course the reason why these five avenues of development cross-fertilize each other is that they are not really separate at all. They are simply five distinguishable aspects of the process of becoming musical. One becomes a developed musical person partly by an expanding awareness, partly by a stimulated initiative, partly by a finer capacity for discrimination, partly by deepening insights, partly by increasing skills. Reciprocally, these are the five chief natural manifestations of a growing musical responsiveness.

So we reach two statements of principle which are of momentous importance in planning the music curriculum. (*a*) *Each avenue of musical growth should be promoted in organic relatedness to all the rest.* (*b*) *No one of them can be slighted or neglected without weakening all the others, and stunting and warping the process of musical growth itself.* These two principles will appear again and again in many connections in our later discussions, but they are quite important enough to be made explicit and strongly emphasized at the outset.

II

The first broad avenue of musical development is growth in musical awareness. This is the process in and through which the great world of music, in its immense richness and its kaleidoscopic appeal, is opened up as an inheritance to be entered upon, explored, and enjoyed. In its broadest sense it is a process of becoming conscious of the place and manifestations of music in the affairs of man. To become aware of music is to become aware of its literature, both past and present, classical and popular, of its traditions and personalities, of the uses to which it is put, of the men and organizations who present and promote it, of its realities as an aesthetic, and social, and economic complex in the world.

[127]

In planning the music curriculum, one of the main things to have in mind is the fostering of growth in musical awareness. This does not mean merely courses in appreciation or history, or listening lessons in the grades, though they have an important place. It is an avenue of development which should run through the entire program. It should be emphasized in applied music classes, which means that so far as possible a variety of music should be used, instead of everybody studying the same thing at the same time. It should be emphasized in the study of theory, which means that such study should be enriched with much actual music. It should be emphasized in orchestral, band, and choral rehearsals. One of the defects of the contest system—and this does not mean that it is without any values—is that it tends to limit repertoire, and therefore to limit musical awareness. One of the arguments for a set-up of small ensembles is that it opens up a variety of musical experiences, and thus promotes musical awareness. The fostering of musical awareness does not belong in one special place in the curriculum. It should be undertaken wherever opportunities can be created.

This, however, should not be left as an attractive but nebulous ideal. It should be set up as a definite working scheme. The music staff should develop and codify in writing a definitive master plan for the promotion of musical awareness. This means breaking down the general notion of musical awareness into specifics, which amount to specifically formulated developmental lines. Here is the way to set about it.

Imagine that you are a guide in a very large and beautiful park. You are facing some visitors who know very little about it. You want to help them to know and enjoy it as fully as possible. What will you do? Presumably the first thing would be to think over the various trails, and outlooks, and scenic features that the park contains. You might not be able to take your visitors personally to all these places. Indeed they might even enjoy them better if they found them out for themselves. But you would make quite a definite plan, so that they would not miss anything you knew to be important and repaying, and so that they would not simply wander around in the woods without getting much of anywhere. To be sure, you would have another problem on your hands. How would you get them to start in the directions you think advisable, and to keep on going? That too must come up, but one thing at a time is always a good idea. So let us stay for the moment with the various journeyings your visitors must take if they are to develop an awareness of your park, and if your own conscience is to be satisfied.

The park, of course, in this case is the art of music. You, as the guide, want your visitors, that is to say your pupils, to develop the fullest possible awareness of it. The various trails and directions are the lines of musical awareness that you would like them to follow up. I am about to suggest a list of scenic features, outlooks, and trails that seem to me worth-while. But before I do this there are one or two words of warning and advice that I must offer.

Do not take this list, or any other list, as the last word of wisdom. It is nothing of the kind. There is no last word of wisdom. I happen to think that the trails and points of interest that I would suggest are worth visiting. Probably most people would agree, more or less, but they might not agree completely. You yourself may not like some of the trips on my schedule; or I may leave out some that are special favorites of yours. That is quite as it should be. Again, you may wonder about priorities. Which of these proposed trips would you especially recommend? Are there some which your visitors simply must not miss, and •others again which they might do without, although it would be a pity? On that point, I fancy, you will have to make up your own mind, because it depends on the circumstances, on the background and interests of your visitors, and last but not least, on your own proclivities and enthusiasms. That, once more, is just as it should be. But one thing is very important indeed. Give them as many and as varied trips as you possibly can. Do not think that, because the list looks rather long, the whole idea is impossible. Always plan as comprehensively and ambitiously as you are able, and then execute as much of your plan as you can.

With this by way of preamble, I now present my schedule of exploration and discovery in the park of music. I think your visitors should be helped, encouraged, and incited to become aware of the following scenic features:

1. The treasury of song: School songs, popular songs, patriotic songs, folk songs, religious songs, art songs, part songs.

2. The treasury of instrumental music: Popular music including jazz, light classical music, classical music.

3. The treasury of piano music.

4. The treasury of operatic music: Popular and movie dramatic music, semi-classical and light opera, grand opera.

5. Various types of music: Occidental music of various periods from "modern" back as far as you like, "exotic" music—that is, that of other cultures.

[129]

6. Outstanding musical personalities: Composers and performers (the living and the dead), their lives, their work, their characteristics, their influence.

7. Outstanding musical organizations: Orchestras, opera companies, associations.

8. The musical media: Orchestral and band instruments, the piano, the organ, the voice, the phonograph, motion-picture music, jazz instruments, old-time instruments.

9. The place of music in human affairs: How it has been and is used, enjoyed, created; how it has developed out of certain ways of living; how it has influenced people.

10. The place of music in your own community and school.

11. The realities of a musical career.

I hope this makes the idea of musical awareness at least fairly definite—more so, at any rate, than it has been before. One would be inclined to say that a well-rounded, fully developed musical person would have an awareness of all or most of these matters. Therefore it follows that the development of such a many-sided awareness is part and parcel of musical growth. Do not, however, think that this list is complete or in any way final. It is simply a schedule of suggested explorations, of directions which your visitors might profitably follow. Do not accept it as gospel. Use it to stimulate your own thinking. You wish to set up a developmental program which, among other things, will promote musical awareness? Then the first thing to do is to work out a schedule of trips. Your schedule may not be identical with the one just presented, but it will look something like it. It will give you an overview. It will enable you to feel pretty sure that you are not missing something important and attainable. And you can constantly refer back to it when you get on the job of showing your visitors where to go.

In one respect you may find this rather discouraging. It looks like a tremendously large order. All that exploring, you may think, would surely take a lifetime! But do not be downhearted too soon. It is a pretty large order, and in fact much larger than one often finds undertaken in various programs of music education. But it is by no means as impossible as it might appear. This will become clear from the discussion in the following section.

III

How is the development of musical awareness to be promoted? This, as you may remember, is the second of the two questions you would naturally ask yourself. You have mapped the musical landscape. You have listed the trails you would like your visitors to follow, the scenes you would like them to behold. Now, how to get them started, and how to incite them to continue?

1 The first and most basic consideration is this: *You are dealing with a process of musical growth, not an accumulation of knowledge.* The important thing is not for your visitors to get to know the landscape of the park, but to create in themselves a developing musical responsiveness. This responsiveness will not develop adequately unless they come in contact with a good deal of the landscape, and in fact a wide variety of it. The more the better, indeed. But the landscape is the means, not the end. The responsiveness itself is the end. Also there is a reciprocal relationship. The evolution of responsiveness will itself create an eagerness to come in contact with more scenery and different scenery. This is what it means to say that you are promoting a process of growth, and not a process of accumulation. It hints, at least, at the right answer to the objection that one cannot cover so much ground. It is not the ground covered that matters, but the effect on the person who covers it.

Let us suppose for a moment that we are talking about a real park, and that you yourself really are a guide. What has just been said comes to this: You ought to be interested in promoting in your visitors a developing responsiveness to natural scenery and its values and meanings in human life, and you ought to use the various sights and opportunities of your park for this purpose, and as means to this end. Does this strike you as farfetched? It should not. Surely it is more or less what the National Park Service has in mind as one of its objectives. It does not merely want to make people familiar with the geography of the Yellowstone, the Yosemite, the Glacier, and the other national parks. It hopes to create and foster in the public a responsiveness to the beauties and riches of our natural scenery, so that they will have it as a benefit for themselves, and also become supporters of the park service and its enterprises. Even for a real guide in a real park, the fostering of such a responsive awareness is a feasible and understandable undertaking. And when it comes to music, the idea is even more convincing and comprehensible. There is nothing farfetched in talking about the development of musical responsiveness. Indeed, it is exactly what should be aimed at all the time in connection with musical awareness. All the specific developmental lines of musical awareness converge on this objective.

Here as so often the parallel with poetry is exceedingly helpful and clarifying. When a person is influenced to read poetry widely, shown what to read, and helped to read it as he should, the main purpose is not to have him accumulate a large stock of knowledge. In one famous course in English Literature given for many years at Harvard University, students were required to memorize numerous lengthy passages from Shakespeare. Even so, however, the instructor's intention was not to have them stock their minds with an enormous mass of content, but to establish a certain attitude, a certain interest, and to put it on a solid foundation. As a matter of fact, the plan worked out exactly in this way for many of them, and many of the students who took the course, and sometimes rebelled against what seemed a very arbitrary demand, found later on that there had been created in them a feeling for Shakespeare and for poetry which carried on as a precious asset throughout their lives. So the wide reading, and even the extensive memorizing of poetry should result in an appreciative awareness of what the poets have expressed and how they have expressed these things, rather than in knowledge for its own sake. This, clearly, is one aspect of what might be called poetic responsiveness. And without such a wide awareness the poetic responsiveness of even a sensitive and gifted person would be greatly limited.

This is a precise analogy with music. In working for musical awareness what is being promoted is a developing responsiveness to wordless poetry—that is, to the expressive potentialities of tone—brought about through a wide and varied range of experiences. It is this responsiveness, above everything else, which ought to come out of explorations of the treasury of song, the treasury of instrumental music, of various types and kinds of music, of outstanding musical personalities and organizations, of the various musical media, of the uses to which music has been put in human life in general and in one's own community and school in particular, and of the realities of a musical career. Singing a wide variety of songs, playing or listening to a wide variety of instrumental compositions, reading such books as Marcia Davenport's *Of Lena Geyer* or Lang's *History of Music in Western Civilization*, to bring together two violently contrasting instances, can and should all be revelations of what tonal experience actually does and actually means in the affairs of human beings, and therefore of what it can mean and do in one's own life. Notice that this is quite a different thing from accumulating a large stock of knowledge. Notice, also, that it goes a great deal further than what is ordinarily called "music appreciation." Certainly it is important, and indeed essential, to appreciate music directly through listening and performing. But when one reads Paderewski's autobiography, and learns about the sacrifices and arduous labors endured by a great artist for the sake of his art, or finds that the music of wandering minstrels was one of the unifying influences of medieval Europe, such things broaden and deepen one's responsive awareness of the art of tonal poetry.

This idea has numerous and important practical implications.

A. *In the promotion of musical awareness a primary consideration will always be the mood values or the expressive meanings of music.* This will affect both the experiences that we select and our way of dealing with them. Why, for instance, introduce some of the music of Palestrina, or of Prokofieff, some of the music of China, or of southern Negro field laborers? Not chiefly for the sake of accumulating knowledge about certain composers, or certain civilizations or social groups. The determining reason is that these are distinctive and sharply differing types of tonal poetry, and when properly presented and experienced, either through listening or performance, can widen the horizons of musical responsiveness. Here is what music has meant to others; here is what it can mean to us. Such is the argument.

The case can be pointed up by reference to a matter of familiar experience. Many young people much prefer the music of Tchaikovsky to the far greater music of Bach, just as they often like the poetry of Swinburne better than that of Shakespeare. Now it is quite clear that we cannot make people like things by telling them that they should, or by trying to force them. On the other hand it is equally clear that such preferences indicate a limited range of aesthetic awareness, and an immaturity of aesthetic responsiveness. What has to be done is to emphasize always and at all times the expressive, the spiritual, the poetic values of music, and to try, by precept, example, and direct experience, to help the learners to discover poetic revelations to which, for the time being, they are unresponsive. When a youngster says he likes Tchaikovsky, the confession should be welcome, for Tchaikovsky is well worth liking, and to like him is to reveal an authentic musical responsiveness. When he adds that he does not like Bach, this means that there are musical realms which

[133]

he has not yet been able to explore, and refinements of emotional and musical responsiveness into which he has not yet grown. Our duty is clear. We must welcome the maturity that has been achieved, the authentic responsiveness that has emerged, and we must seek to carry it further, not by a process of forcing but by a process of growth.

B. *Another implication is that in the promotion of musical awareness, the human setting, the associations, and the suggestions of the music should be an important consideration.* It has been pointed out that music has a remarkable power of arousing imagery and association. Its power to do this is part of what makes it quite literally a wordless poetry. Musicians who dismiss such associations and suggestions as irrelevant or undesirable are not only flying in the face of psychological reality, but treating music itself as a formal rather than an expressive art. Yet the associations and imagery that music so readily arouses in many people are not in and of themselves its meaning. Their importance lies in the fact that they are compatible with its mood, and can reinforce that mood and point it up. What, then, to do about it?

First of all, imaginal and associative factors should not be ignored. There are some people who argue for avoiding them, and say that music should be left to make its own impression in its own way without any of what they consider adventitious aids. But this is purism run wild, and also bad psychology. And like all bad psychology, it does not make sense. When one learns about the overwhelming scene in the Budapest opera house when the *Rakozcky March* was played at the world première of Berlioz's *Faust*, does not this add something to the musical impression itself? If one could have sat at the beer garden table while Schubert composed *Hark, Hark! the Lark*, would not one's responsiveness to the sheer beauty of the music have been enhanced? Is not something added to a cowboy song when one remembers how it was sung at lonely campfires in the remoteness of the great plains? Surely such questions answer themselves. Music is full of suggestive values. It is a projection of human experience. When it is treated as nothing more than a tonal and rhythmic abstraction, no matter how beautiful, the experience that it produces is impoverished.

Should one, then, indulge in all sorts of fantasies and fairy-stories which are supposed to interpret music? Should one encourage children to do the same? To mention one specific procedure, should one encourage them to make interpretive pictures, or to compose interpretive poems or dramatic scenes? So far as I can see, there is nothing to be said against such procedures, and a good deal to be said in favor of them, so long as the intention is always to establish, point up, and reinforce a mood, and not to search for some unique correct interpretation. Let us admit that elaborate interpretations of the *Moonlight Sonata* as the story of a tragic love affair can be stickily sentimental, and that the title itself is rather cloying. Still, we are probably dealing with youngsters at a stage of life when they are peculiarly susceptible to sentiment, and such suggestions may help to develop their musical responsiveness a great deal better than a businesslike analysis of the architectonics of the work. An academic musician may bring himself to agree so far, but still may insist that such subjective and arbitrary fantasies belong, at best, to an immature stage of development, and should be got over as soon as possible, like measles or whooping cough. Even this, however, is a matter of individual differences. People vary widely in their associative and imaginal responses to music. After all, Wagner himself conceived the *Flying Dutchman* during a mist-shrouded night voyage; and Wagner is usually considered quite a mature musician. To declare war on all the imaginal intimations of music is quite as great a mistake as to insist upon them in and out of season.

Moreover there is an effective line that may and should be taken, and that can be recommended as highly constructive. This is to bring out the human circumstances under which a piece of music was created and has been used. What sort of person was the man who composed it? Under what circumstances did he compose it? What did he think about it? What did he say about it? What did he call it? Why? Here, of course, we come down to actual fact. Moreover such facts are revealing and important. Music is always an emotional interpretation of some happening or trend in a man's life, and the closer we can come to the generating circumstances the better we are likely to be able to respond to the music. Material bearing on the actual human conditions under which music has been created is of very great value for teaching in general, and for the promotion of musical awareness in particular. Teachers are strongly advised to accumulate files of such material, for which many uses can be found.[1]

C. *Another implication is that in the promotion of musical awareness there should be an emphasis upon the expressive constituents or components of music.*

[1]Probably the best source of such material in English is Helen M. Rees, *A Psychology of Artistic Creation*, Teachers College, Columbia University, New York, 1942.

[135]

It must always be remembered that there are a great many people strongly responsive to music, deeply interested in it, eminently capable of developing musical responsiveness in terms of awareness although never likely to achieve much technical skill, but with very little notion of what makes it sound as it does, or of the elements on which its effects depend. Also it is a fact that there are a great many people who take what are called music lessons for years without developing any apprehension of the expressive content of the art. This is, without a doubt, a very great limitation, and an impediment in the way of musical growth. The analyses both of poetry and of music to be found in the appendices at the end of the book, although, as they stand, on much too high a level for use with children, do undoubtedly show how aesthetically revealing a consciousness of the expressive components of a work of art can be. I well remember the shock I once received when a highly cultivated and musically interested man once asked me what was meant by a musical "phrase." It seemed a most elementary question coming from a man who had attended concerts for years. Such ignorance was obviously limiting, and just as obviously quite avoidable. And undoubtedly there are many such persons.

Now the expressive constituents of music, as we have seen, are tone color, chord color, melody, tonality, rhythm, and architecture. These are the elements which make possible the expressive tonal poetry, which establish the mood, and elicit association and imagery. But it might seem that responsiveness to them has to do rather with musical insight than with musical awareness. It is quite true that here we have one of the numerous points of significant overlapping between our five main avenues of musical growth. Nevertheless there is a distinction well worth making. What is being advocated here is the promotion of a responsiveness to these elements in a setting of extensive, wide, and varied experience, instead of in one of intensive study. Let us illustrate.

A very distinguished musician of my acquaintance was once talking to a musically interested but untrained friend of his about a symphony concert that they were both planning to attend. He remarked that the second movement of a symphony they were to hear contained a modulation that had always struck him as peculiarly beautiful.

"But," said his friend, "I know nothing about music. How can I recognize it?"

"I am sitting a few rows ahead of you," was the answer. "Just before the moment comes, I will raise my hand like this, so that you can catch the passage."

[136]

The little device worked! It seems decidedly better to speak of what took place as a development of musical awareness rather than of musical insight, because of the setting of the experience in a broad context in which it played a more or less incidental part. This man was being helped to listen more selectively in a setting of general awareness.

Procedures essentially similar in principle are used at the concerts for young people given by the American Youth Orchestra under the leadership of Mr. Dean Dixon. Various ingenious devices are employed for high-lighting constitutive aspects of the music. For instance, at various points in the music the section of the orchestra which is carrying the principal part will stand, thus calling attention to differences in tone quality. Sometimes the audience is asked to count the beat, for the sake of centering attention on it. Again, mimeographed sheets with "quiz" questions are distributed, with blanks for quick responses to be made while listening. Three out of fifteen such quiz items on the first movement of the Brahms *Second Symphony* are as follows.

1. Opening horn theme has 6/7/8/9/10 notes. 2. After each tympani roll the brass figure has/has not contrary motion. 15. Ending chord major/minor.

Once again, one cannot call these in any sense lessons in theory. Clearly they have to do with the development of musical awareness. The difference is that this selective responsiveness is organized in an extensive setting, and not with the intention of intensive analysis. If you will turn back once more to the eleven suggested lines or pathways of musical awareness, it will be evident to you that here is a great variety and range of musical experience. Out of it should come, among other things, an evolving ability to notice and respond to the constitutive factors of tone, melody, rhythm, harmony, tonality, and architectonics. To repeat the essential point, it is not a tremendous encyclopedic knowledge of music that we should have in mind, but a highly developed responsiveness to it. Evidently a wide range of experience is very helpful in bringing this about.

All emphasis upon the constitutive elements of the tonal-rhythmic pattern which is made in connection with musical awareness should be in terms of their expressive values. This is a point of very great importance. We must not use wide and varied musical experience for the sake of teaching a formal or intellectualized musical grammar if we want to foster musical growth. But to be able to pick out and enjoy the subtleties, refinements, nuances, and modes of treatment

[137]

that make the music beautiful and establish its expressive meaning is altogether desirable. This is precisely the intention of Mr. Dixon with the American Youth Orchestra. It was precisely the intention of the distinguished musician who helped his friend to notice and appreciate an expressive modulation.[1]

Here, of course, is the answer to those who claim that with increasing musical maturity there should be more and more attention to the so-called intrinsic contents of music, that is, its structural elements, and less and less to such so-called extrinsic factors as mood, meaning, association, and imagery. The truth is that we do not have two separable lines of development, but an increasing and deepening responsiveness to the poetic values of music and to the resources by means of which those values are established. The musical person in whom musical growth is fulfilled is neither a grammarian nor a sentimentalist, but a person keenly responsive to the expressive intimations of music which are conveyed by the subtleties of its content.

D. *There are many ways of listening to music.* They range all the way from response to dinner music which is nothing more than a pleasing and stimulating sound in the ears, through the musical daydreaming and the absorption in sheer mood in which people often indulge when listening to the radio or at a concert or opera, to the most intense analytic preoccupation with the performance or with the structure

---

[1]The very idea that modulation is an expressive rather than a purely technical device may come as a surprise to some people. Yet this certainly is so. The effect of modulation is beautifully illustrated in poetry in the consummately skillful Sonnet XXXIV of Shakespeare, in which the whole expressive value revolves about the wonderful and dramatic change from a plaintive, almost anguished minor to a rich and throbbing major tonality in the last two lines.

> "Why didst thou promise such a beauteous day
>   And make me travel forth without my cloak,
> To let base clouds o'ertake me on my way,
>   Hiding thy brav'ry in their rotten smoke?
> 'Tis not enough that through the cloud thou break,
>   To dry the rain from my storm-beaten face,
> For no man well of such a salve can speak
>   That heals the wound, and cures not the disgrace:
> Nor can thy shame give physic to my grief;
>   Though thou repent, yet I have still the loss.
> Th' offender's sorrow lends but poor relief
>   To him that bears the strong offence's cross.
> *Ah! but those tears are pearl which thy love sheeds,*
> *And they are rich and ransom all ill deeds."*

of the composition. The point to remember, and it is a vital one, is that all are legitimate, and all, in their place, desirable. The average trained musician is too consistently analytic, and this is so even when he does not analyze any too well. The average layman is impoverished in his musical responsiveness because he has no analytic resources at all. The tendency of the average musician is to think that his way is the only right way, that everybody ought to listen in the same way, or at any rate wish that he could, So he forces the issue, insists on an academic approach, cramps responsiveness into a set pattern, and probably does irremediable harm. He is not only oblivious to his own limitations in responsiveness. He is even proud of them.

Some writers on the subject have drawn a distinction between hearing and listening. Hearing is supposed to be a more or less vague, global response to "extrinsic" factors. Listening is an analytic response to "intrinsic" factors. The whole distinction is open to radical objections. In the first place it is far from clear-cut. In the second place, what is called listening should not be thought of or promoted as primarily an intellectualized response. It is, of course, like any other good response, selective. Certain features in the complex of musical impression are thrown into focus and others, for the time being, subordinated. But such selectivity is not for the sake of understanding as such, but of deeper and more adequate pleasure. We do not wish people to be able to distinguish the two themes of the first movement of a Beethoven symphony for the sake of knowing about them, but for the sake of adequately responding to the message that the composer is projecting.

The truth is simply this. There is a repertoire of types of responsive awareness to music. Growth in musical awareness means, among other things, the development of this repertoire. One should be able to respond to music in various ways. One should be able to find in it many facets of interest and appeal. It seems pretty clear that this can best be brought about by a wide variety of musical contacts and experiences. Thus we see once again that the promotion of musical awareness does not simply mean covering ground for its own sake, but covering ground for a purpose. Extensive experience is indeed essential. Explicit plans should be made with this in mind. As wide a range and variety of experience as possible should be included in the curriculum. But the basic reason for this is not because we wish to accumulate knowledge, but because extensive and varied experience is beyond all doubt a most valuable instrumentality in fostering the development of musical responsiveness.

[139]

2 Growth in musical awareness should always be thought of and planned as a continuous and not a discontinuous process. This, of course, is one of the basic characteristics of all growth, and it bears directly on our present problem.

A. *Many a teacher, confronted with our eleven suggested lines of musical awareness, will wonder just at what level this or that material or experience belongs.* Should one use the *Nutcracker Suite* in the third-grade? Should one keep back the *Great G Minor Fugue* of Bach for the secondary course in general music? Do simple folk songs belong chiefly in the elementary-school? When should one introduce a lesson on the life of Mozart? At what age is it best for children to find out something about the Boston Symphony Orchestra? In short, the practical question of grade placement arises.

If this question is handled in an externalistic way, it introduces an essential discontinuity. Moreover there is no means of finding a really satisfactory answer. How can one tell just where any piece of music, or any lesson, or any experience belongs? Look at the problem from the outside, and it becomes simply rule-of-thumb. One finds out that in one's own work, and with one's own procedures, this or that seems to "get across" in such and such a grade. Then one expands one's special experience, which is based on very vague criteria, into a universal principle. This is just how most of the graded lists of material one sees are actually determined. They are the outcomes of some person's seemingly more or less successful experience, presented as though they were the ten commandments.

The whole difficulty comes from thinking of the experiences, the materials, the lessons, the contacts, as ends in themselves. As such they are different from each other, and therefore necessarily without a living continuity. The right question to ask is always: What will such and such an experience do to the development of musical awareness? Will it carry the growth process forward in some determinate direction? We propose to use the *Nutcracker Suite*. What for? Not just so that the children will know the music and the name of its composer. We ought to use it with some specific type or types of responsiveness clearly in mind. Of course we must use our material at some suitable level. This is one of the practical requirements of our work, and it must be met. But we should be very suspicious, indeed, of universal and absolute recommendations on grade placement. Everything turns on the developmental effect to be produced. It is in this that the continuity resides.

[140]

B. *Another question which arises is whether the fostering of musical aware-ness is chiefly a matter of listening, or whether the actual performance of music should be introduced and strongly emphasized.* Here again a threat to continuity arises. Listening and performing are far too sharply sun-dered in the minds of many music teachers, and also in their practices. The two types of activity are supposed to have quite different values and effects. What this is apt to mean is that listening becomes purely passive or else very academic, and that performing becomes a musi-cally impoverished experience.

The truth of the matter is that we should always fix our minds upon developmental effects, upon the type of musical responsiveness we wish to foster. We propose, let us say, to use *Home on the Range* to project awareness of mood, of association and imagery, and of melody. In this case it will be a good idea to have children listen to a good recording, talk the whole thing over, perhaps show some pictures, and sing the song themselves. We propose to use the first movement of the *Eroica Symphony* to project mood, associations, melody, and rhythm. Listening, then, will clearly be our chief resource, but it may well be a good idea to have our learners sing the principal theme, and move to the swing of the beat. As one item of developmental material we set up a unit on the life story of Paderewski. We want to bring this story to the children, not as a set of facts, but as a revealing human and musical drama. We will show them pictures, and if possible motion pictures. We will have them listen to some of his interpretations, per-haps contrasting them with those of some other virtuoso. And if some of the class can play a piece or two of his, we will certainly feature this opportunity. Nor will we necessarily think it profanation to arrange some work of his for performance by a pickup ensemble.

In summary, then, there is no magic virtue either in listening or performing. It is all a question of convenience, and of what we are trying to do. The right kind of performance certainly can high-light developmental values in the way of musical awareness. But it must be the right kind! We must courageously play up the values that we want to emphasize, even at the risk of letting other authentic values go. Nor should there be any sharp distinction between listening and per-forming. There should be a constant, easy, natural switch-over from one to the other. The singing of a symphonic theme, the building up and holding of a striking chord heard in a choral recording, the beating out of the rhythm of a fugue are, in their degree, activities in the category of performance. The conventional wall of division be-tween listening and performance is a very cramping, not to say pernicious, influence in music education. As a matter of fact, what many performing artists grievously lack is an easy, natural, often occurring transition between listening and doing, for both can be and should be agencies of musical growth in general, and of growth in musical awareness in particular.

C. *An interesting issue arises here concerning the repetition of material, or its reduplicated use at different levels.* We have the *Nutcracker Suite* in the third-grade. Shall we also use it in the seventh-grade? Questions of this kind often come up.

The general answer is that any going over of old ground, any review, should never be merely a matter of repetition. The return to it should be both a renewal of something old and the emergence of something new. One of the numbers of the *Nutcracker Suite*, perhaps, has first been presented for the sake of projecting a mood. Later on it is used again for the sake of emphasizing musical architecture. But the mood also reappears, and is deepened and rendered more definite. Thus the old experience comes back for the sake of recapturing it with a new vision, and responding to it with a new appreciation of its values. Of course much more must be done than the persistent tilling of one small patch of ground. But from time to time old scenes should be revisited, old paths trodden again, old acquaintances renewed, because in such experiences can come a rebirth both of pleasure and understanding.

3 Growth in musical awareness should always be treated as a purposive process. Here is yet another of the basic characteristics of all growth that applies to our present problem.

What it means is that the promotion of musical awareness should be thought of and organized as the promotion of *musical exploration*. Here is another consideration which bears upon our very practical problem of how to cover enough ground. If one looks at any adequate blueprint of musical awareness, such as the eleven-point list already suggested, the impression may very well be one of impossibility. If one has to do all that in a music education program, you may well think, when will there be time for anything else? The point, however, is not even to try to cover the whole area of music in school, or in direct contacts with learners. The promotion of musical awareness does not imply setting up an enormous and so far as possible complete survey pattern, running through the elementary-school, extending well into the secondary levels, and designed to give pupils a thorough acquaintance with as many phases and facets of music as possible.

The proper policy is to do everything possible to stimulate pupils to explore for themselves along promising lines. The thing to try to do in school is to indicate the trails, to show how inviting they are, and also to show how they may be followed.

No doubt, if one is going to do this successfully, it will call for the use of a good deal of varied material. For instance, the singing repertoire of the Cleveland Junior High-School in Elizabeth, N. J., during the school year 1933–1934 consisted of fifty songs, classified as school songs, folk and popular songs, religious songs, art songs, and part songs.[1] This in itself is by no means a negligible range of awareness. But certain questions still remain. The songs were not all learned in one year. They represented a repertoire accumulated from grade-school music, and expanded in the junior high-school. To what extent was their acquisition an expression of the stimulated purposes, the aroused curiosity, the exploratory tendencies of the pupils? To what extent did they arouse an appetite for more? These are the crucial considerations. This particular repertoire, like all similar ones, should better be thought of as a fine and ample assemblage of *hors d'oeuvres* than as a complete meal, planned, served, and finally eaten and assimilated.

Now this puts a very different aspect on the matter. Once you have mapped out the trails in your mind, you are by no means committed to conducting your visitors personally over every foot of them. Indeed it would not even be a good idea to try to do so. They will get more out of it, and develop a better and more authentic responsiveness to the scenery if they do a good deal of exploring for and by themselves. It is, however, very necessary to indicate to them what there is to explore, to make it possible for them to explore, and to make them want to explore. This should be the urgent and constant aim in promoting musical awareness, beginning away down in preschool, and carrying right through to the twelfth-grade and beyond. The entire music staff of the school system should get together and block out a control list of significant types of musical manifestations. These are the trails to be followed. Then a large number of intriguing samples of each of these various types of musical manifestations should be assembled. These are, so to speak, the bait. They should be presented in the most effective manner possible, through listening, through performance, through out-of-school and in-school activities. The point should be to make them as dynamic as possible. Attention

[1] Lilla Belle Pitts, *Music Integration in the Junior High School*, pp. 24–28. C. C. Birchard and Company, Boston, 1935.

should be given to making carry-over and initiative feasible for the pupils, by such practical measures as letting them know where they can get more songs, where they can buy or borrow more records, where they can listen to records, by suggesting radio programs, concerts, musical opportunities, interesting readings, press notices of concerts and musical affairs, local library resources, motion pictures with particularly interesting music, and so forth. This is what the promotion of musical awareness as a process of growth, as a process of exploration, means in practical terms.

Clearly this is an altogether different affair from simply covering ground, even a great deal of ground. It turns precisely on the organization and stimulation of purpose. Moreover an outstanding implication is that the promotion of musical awareness is not to be segregated in any one spot in the program, or in any one course—for instance in general music, or in classes in appreciation. To be sure, there will be certain courses, among them general music, appreciation, and music history, where musical awareness is a very prominent consideration. But if everyone on the staff, and in fact everyone connected with the teaching of music, including the grade teachers, has it in mind, and if there is a definite over-all plan which is straightforward, simple, reasonable, and practicable—as it can be—it will happen in one way or another everywhere and all along the line. If this policy is followed, a great deal can be done. Everyone can contribute to it, including the grade teachers. The idea is simply this. Everyone connected with the teaching of music should have, as one of his constant aims, to encourage and stimulate pupils to become musical explorers, and to use whatever means seem best in the light of the maturity of the pupils, the resources of the situation, and, last but not least, whatever the teacher in question likes to do most and is able to do best.

4 It has already been pointed out that the prime mover of mental growth is developmental experience. If, then, we desire to promote musical awareness, each and every experience organized with this purpose in mind should be developmental in character.

A. *An experience designed to promote musical awareness should be arresting.* There is a little book, published thirty years ago, but still very much worth reading, which embodies the essence of this idea and offers many practical suggestions for putting it into effect.[1] Hayward, the

[1]Frank H. Hayward, *The Lesson in Appreciation: An Essay on the Pedagogics of Beauty.* The Macmillan Company, New York, 1917.

[144]

author, deals particularly with poetry, but what he has to say applies just as well to music. He insists that the lesson in appreciation should be treated as what he calls a "red letter lesson." There should be preparation well in advance. The children should be made aware that on such and such a day there is to be a specially delightful and interesting experience. The teacher should build up anticipation by comments and suggestions. Any difficult words or references which might detract from their enjoyment of the poem should be explained ahead of time. The actual presentation should be carefully stage-managed. The class should be in good order and quiet. The poem should be read as effectively and impressively as possible. Everything should be done to give the experience a maximum impact.

What is valuable and instructive about this scheme is not its details, which are open to question, but its basic idea, which is admirable. That a genuine developmental experience should indeed be a "red letter lesson" is indeed true. But that such lessons should be great and extraordinary exceptions, which Hayward more or less suggests, is not true at all. The more of them the better! All the time if possible! The idea of a special build-up, too, is open to objection though the principle is entirely sound. What one should try for is a whole sequence of vital experiences, which build up a momentum of their own, so that pupils expect something manifestly worth-while whenever music is involved. Everything that Hayward says about the actual presentation, however, is very much to the point as far as it goes. By all means it should be planned for effectiveness and impressiveness. But he limits his discussion to listening to a poem being read, or a piece of music being played, or to looking at a picture. Experiences which involve performance should also be included in our thinking, and his ideas can readily be extended to cover them as well.

B. *An experience designed to promote musical awareness should be impelling.* One of the surest tests of a developmental experience is its carry-over into the pupils' lives and their self-initiated choices. An experience designed to promote musical awareness should have an effect beyond itself. It should start a process of exploration. Partly this depends on its intrinsic power and appeal. Partly it depends on various practical measures which have already been suggested, such as making sure that the children know how and where to get recordings, musical scores, readings, how to locate radio programs, musical opportunities, and so forth, and also making sure that facilities are actually available.

C. *An experience designed to promote musical awareness should be revealing.* Hayward deals with this consideration in a very interesting way. He says that after the experience has taken place—after the poem has been read—time should be given to what he calls "aesthetic discussion." This again applies very readily to music education. Aesthetic discussion is not primarily intellectual analysis, still less a matter of quizzing on facts. It is just what the name implies, a guided discussion of the aesthetic content and effects of the experience. How much has one enjoyed it? What has one liked about it? What has one not liked? Has one missed certain values? What can one do about it if one has missed them? These would be fairly typical questions. The whole point is that the experience should not merely be impressive and stimulating, but also that it should reveal new possibilities of musical responsiveness.

The two other characteristics of developmental experience, that of being fulfilling, and that of being conscious, are clearly involved in what has been said. In particular, the importance of a conscious awareness, not indeed complete but still genuine, of the values and meanings of what one is experiencing, is well recognized in Hayward's idea of aesthetic discussion.

IV

All this lengthy and perhaps rather elaborate analysis is for the sake of achieving a better synthesis. Out of it should emerge a clear idea of what to do and what not to do, what to try for and what not to try for, in promoting musical awareness.

1 Let us return once more to our eleven pathways. What they suggest is by no means the covering of an enormous amount of ground in stated lessons based on a comprehensive syllabus. The point is not how many songs children learn in a year, how many symphonies or operas they can recognize, how many musical personalities and organizations they know about, how many of the band and orchestral instruments they can describe, how much information they have about musical manifestations and affairs either current or historical, how many facts they have in mind about the realities of a musical career. The very last thing in the world that we ought to be doing is to prepare them directly for a comprehensive musical memory test. The essential issue is the vitality, the arresting, impelling, and revealing power of each experience. How much does it open up? How much does it suggest? To what extent does it incite to explora-

tion? Those are the questions on which one should always center. If the range of experiences is very narrow, their impelling power will be limited. If the content of the experiences is musically devitalized they will be impotent and infertile, and incapable of initiating growth. If one rushes through an enormous number of them with the idea of covering everything, or at any rate as much as possible, the life will be crushed out of them. The same thing happens if one always insists on very intensive analysis, and goes on the policy that nothing is any good unless it is polished to the highest attainable pitch of perfection. The promotion of musical awareness means an extensive and varied sampling of musical experiences, each designed to incite exploration.

2 There are certain types of activity and patterns of pedagogical organization upon which our present discussion throws considerable light.

A. *All social occasions for the making, sharing, and enjoying of music are very rich in developmental opportunities.* It should always be borne in mind that whenever a group of learners come together, chances are created for them to learn from one another, and to be stimulated by one another. Teachers constantly throw away such chances with an obliviousness and lack of imagination that one can only call amazing. They treat a class simply, solely, and always, as an opportunity to teach the same thing to everybody at the same time. This amounts to ignoring the rich veins of gold which are in the hills right at one's feet, and which even come to the very surface of the ground. To do this is perhaps particularly deplorable in connection with musical awareness. If a musical experience stimulates some people and not others, use those people to spread the influence. Encourage pupils to strike out along lines of musical exploration for themselves, and if anyone makes even a feeble start, help him along and see if a few others will not join with him in the good work. If different responses are set up in different members of a group, bring out the differences and capitalize upon them. When experiences in the way of listening or performing are set up, try to create that powerful, almost hypnotic group facilitation to which music peculiarly lends itself. In general, use a group situation not for uniformity, but for its dynamic potential. The skilled teacher plays upon a group as a virtuoso plays upon an instrument, eliciting values otherwise unobtainable, and evoking developmental influences which the mere togetherness and inter-action of a number of human beings make possible.

[147]

B. *The so-called "integrated" activity, or unit, or project involving music has become a rather prominent feature of present-day educational practice.* What should our attitude towards it be? Certainly we do not want to sell music down the river for the sake of social science, or to put on a song and dance to enliven some unit in economics. Still, one wants to co-operate. But there is a difference between being co-operative and losing one's virtue. The controlling principle would seem to be as follows. From the standpoint of the legitimate interests of the music program, an integrated project is an asset if it can be shown to foster musical growth, and particularly growth in musical awareness. It offers a musical experience in a novel setting, and perhaps of a novel kind. This is all to the good, but it is not a final answer. Here as everywhere, everything turns on the authentic musical value of that experience. If it brings out some new facet of the poetic meanings and possibilities of music, if it emphasizes some new way of responding to those meanings and possibilities, or if it renews and reinforces an old way, then the case is made. But if it is simply a shallow and trivial piece of propaganda for somebody else's stock in trade, then it should be resisted as an affront to music and an injury to the pupils. Children should not sing Hopi Indian songs in order to sugar-coat some pill of information about the Hopi Indians, but because the singing of such songs can be a musical challenge and a poetic revelation.

C. *The bearing of this whole topic upon the teaching of the history of music is of particular relevance and interest.* The relationship of the history of music as a school subject to musical awareness is like that of the study of systematic theory to musical insight, a matter which will come up for later discussion. In each case we have organized patterns of learning and teaching which belong to the higher developmental levels, and which must be so considered and so treated if they are to be fruitful. The study of the history of music should systematize and universalize a great body of previous musical experience. Properly understood it is precisely a high-level synthesis. Like all synthesis, it does not terminate the sequence of development, but opens up still further possibilities. Also like all synthesis, it brings together and re-orients much that has gone before. A scholarly course in the history of music, imposed upon people whose musical development has been very impoverished, and whose musical awareness is extremely limited, can be a singularly sterile experience. Study of this kind can be re-paying only on one condition—that it is an organic projection of a

[148]

long sequence of development. To put the matter in blunt language, one needs to have gotten a great deal of music into one's head and one's heart in order to profit as one should from a systematic course in the history of music.

Neglect of this vital point is undoubtedly one of the chief reasons for the hostility to musicology found in certain quarters. The subject is recognized, though on a decidedly limited scale, in our colleges and universities. But without a genuine developmental setting it is certainly condemned to aesthetic sterility. It can, of course, be regarded as an intellectual discipline and nothing more. But in that case it has no claim whatever to belong within the orbit of musical or aesthetic education. It then becomes one segment, and perhaps not a very important segment of general history, to be pursued by a few specialized scholars. If musicology is really part of music education, then like everything else in music education, its primary business is to make people more musical. Undoubtedly this is possible, whether or not it is in practice probable. Judging by the type of work actually offered, and the vision or lack of vision of many of its devotees, one has one's doubts. Still, it is certainly true that scholarly knowledge, and illuminating categories of interpretation are in no way antipathetic as such to genuine and growing aesthetic responsiveness. Quite the contrary! But there must be something for the categories to illuminate! If not, the whole thing becomes merely a matter of playing with words, or perhaps better laboring with them. To understand music more perfectly, to apprehend it more comprehensively, is certainly a valid aim, and one can only wish that more musicians recognized its potentialities and rewards. But merely to verbalize about it is aesthetic dust and ashes. If our institutions of higher learning take the curricular claims of music seriously—and assuredly it belongs to the great tradition of Western education and culture—then they should use their influence to encourage an adequate developmental sequence of musical awareness from nursery-school on. Then their intellectual mills—and let us admit that they should be intellectual—will have some grist to grind on.

D. This leads to one final comment, subsidiary perhaps, but interesting and revealing just the same. It has been said that the promotion of musical awareness is not a matter of ground-covering, but of vital and purposeful exploration. In particular, it was pointed out, the thing we should not have in mind is the comprehensive musical memory quiz. Strange to say, however, the very best way to prepare

[149]

for such a quiz is by a broad, fertile, self-impelled development of musical awareness. I myself have had some responsibility for giving what is, in effect, a comprehensive music-memory test, not, I may say, without misgivings. But consistent experience has shown that the people who do best with such a test are well-rounded, enthusiastic, growing musicians, and not those who simply try to cram for it.

3 Various hints and suggestions have been made from time to time as to the importance of musical awareness. It seems desirable at the close of our discussion, to pull these threads together in a comprehensive explicit statement.

The value and importance of musical awareness turns on the fact that it involves *extensive* musical experience. Psychological investigations in other fields have clearly shown that extensive experience, that is, the covering of a great deal of material without much intensive analysis, has a distinctive and beneficial effect upon learning and growth, and that there is no sufficient substitute for it. This is undoubtedly the case with music. A program of music education which ignores or belittles it, is without question radically defective.

Musical awareness can be carried a very long way, and can yield a very significant development of responsiveness, without any marked development either of insight or skill. This is not, to be sure, desirable, but it is certainly possible. If one must be one-sided in one's emphasis, it is better to be one-sided in favor of musical awareness than in favor of skill or insight. Conversely, musical awareness is of extraordinary value in the promotion both of skill and of insight. Anyone who has had a beginning piano pupil who has developed a genuine musical responsiveness and enthusiasm from a wide range of musical experiences, knows what an enormous difference it makes even in terms of sheer technical progress. Exactly the same is true with a student beginning the study of theory. In fact all the other four aspects of musical growth are greatly impeded without wide musical awareness and greatly facilitated by it. Moreover any musician whose musical horizons, sympathies, and responses are narrow and limited is seriously crippled. He tends to the status of a mere technician. Yet there are a great many such. The reason for all this is that extensive experience is peculiarly capable of eliciting and developing genuine and many-sided musical responsiveness. Yet extensity of experience, valuable as it is, is not an end in itself. The ultimate end is always the development of musical responsiveness which is the essence of musical growth.

[150]

QUESTIONS FOR DISCUSSION

1. Does the promotion of musical awareness mean the same thing as teaching music appreciation?

2. Discuss the importance of "extensive," that is, wide-ranging musical experience as part of a person's musical education.

3. Does musical awareness simply mean knowing a great deal of music?

4. Make your own list of specific lines of musical awareness.

5. Pick out one or two specific lines of growth in musical awareness and consider how you might go about promoting them with some specific group or groups of pupils in mind.

6. Why would you expect wide musical awareness to be an important factor in making a person a better learner when he studies performance on some instrument, or musical theory?

7. Find and discuss instances of so-called "integrated units" involving music, some of which are desirable, and others undesirable. Upon what does the difference turn?

8. How may the history of music be taught to foster musical awareness? Should it be taught chiefly with this aim in mind?

9. How do you explain the fact that musical exploration stocks the memory with music much better than cramming?

10. Consider specific practical ways and means of encouraging musical exploration.

ADDITIONAL READINGS

James L. Mursell. *The Psychology of Music.* W. W. Norton and Company, Inc., New York, 1937. Chapter 6, "The Psychology of Musical Listening." (While dealing with many aspects of musical responsiveness the immediate relevance of this chapter is its treatment of types of listening.)

James L. Mursell and Mabelle Glenn. *The Psychology of School Music Teaching.* Silver Burdett Company, Inc., New York, 2d Ed., 1933. Chapter 5, "Appreciation." (This chapter deals with many aspects of musical awareness and its promotion.)

David Barnett. *Living with Music.* George E. Stewart, Publisher, Inc., New York, 1944. (This little book contains admirable illustrations of the inter-relationship of the avenues of musical growth, and particularly of the relationship of awareness to all the others.)

CHAPTER SEVEN

Growth in Musical Initiative

I

The second broad avenue of musical development is growth in musical initiative. This means the desire and the power to make choices of one's own, to strike out for oneself in matters musical, to think of things to do with music, to want to do them, and to do them. The appearance of such initiatives is one of the surest of all signs that anyone is really becoming a musical person, for it means that music is really coming to play a part in his life because of his own wishes and desires. The fostering and strengthening of such initiatives is one of the best of all ways of making anyone into a musical person, because it means not only learning music in the narrow sense, but doing something about it.

This is why the fostering of musical initiative should be a major consideration in any developmental scheme of music education. Yet in a great deal of music teaching it is more or less completely left out of account. For instance, there are plenty of piano teachers who have in mind nothing but the development of a command of the instrument. How the pupil may use this command, what he may do with it, what it may lead to, is not the teacher's business, or such at least is the working assumption. If he plays to his friends, or takes part in a concert, or pays out his money to attend a piano recital, or buys piano recordings, that may be all to the good. But there is nothing in the lessons themselves to suggest or encourage such enterprises. Indeed, there are not a few teachers who go a good deal further than this along the wrong road. They seem positively to resent any kind of initiative on the part of their pupils, and may even take active measures to discourage it. If a pupil says he would prefer to study one piece rather than another, he is apt to be snubbed; and if he proposes to appear on some kind of public occasion, the teacher may raise objections. This same neglect and even suspicion of initiative which is so common in studio teaching appears also in the teaching of music in the schools.

As one surveys many a program of music education, all one can find in it is a series of stereotyped and imposed procedures and activities, extending right through to the twelfth-grade, with very little opportunity or encouragement for free choice and active self-expression either by individuals or groups.

This is a very serious defect; and as every experienced worker in the field knows perfectly well, it is a quite unnecessary one. It is a serious defect, because people do not become musical by having more and more music, as it were, poured into them, but by getting more and more music into their everyday actions and choices. It is a needless defect, because music offers so many, and such natural, rewarding, and enjoyable lines of initiative. This is particularly true in a school situation, with its wealth of social opportunities and contacts. So one of the test questions to ask in judging any program of music education would be how much music it is getting into the lives and actions of the pupils considered as social beings, and not merely how much music it is getting into their heads or their nervous systems.

II

In order to understand exactly what we are talking about in discussing musical initiative, and also to see how to plan for it in the music curriculum, the idea must be broken down into a bill of specifics. This was done in connection with musical awareness, and the same treatment must be followed here. It is not nearly enough to talk about musical initiative in general, or to emphasize its importance. What kind of initiatives does one want to promote? What kind of initiatives can be promoted in a given situation, keeping in mind the physical facilities, the time schedule, the backgrounds of the pupils, the capacities of the teachers, and so forth? These are the questions that need to be answered, and they should be answered in black and white. The essential step here is to write down a list of desirable lines of musical initiative, adding to and revising it from time to time, and using it as a reference point in practical planning.

The making of such a list is always a job of custom tailoring. It cannot be done properly on a wholesale basis. One cannot say that such and such musical initiatives are essential, or that they should always have top priority irrespective of circumstances. For instance, in a general music course in a boys' vocational school, a great deal was done to encourage the pupils to make musical instruments in connection with their shop work, with very happy and far-reaching

[153]

results. In another school system a teacher vitally interested in vocal work was able to develop singing groups made up of pupils not hitherto interested in musical performance. She met with these groups twice weekly in the evening for voluntary rehearsals. These are both admirable instances of the promotion of musical initiative, but there are plenty of situations where they would not work out. So in the last analysis you yourself must do the job of selecting and listing. The important thing, however, is not to leave the whole idea hanging in the air, as something to receive an occasional respectful genuflection, and then to be ignored in actual practice, but to bring it down to a bill of particulars.

But although you should not look for or indeed wish for a final and authoritative list of desirable lines of musical initiative, concrete suggestions can still be a great help, just as they were in the case of musical awareness. The list I am about to present is by no means complete. It is not arranged in order of importance, which would in any case be difficult and perhaps impossible to ascertain. Many of the suggested items may not be suitable for this or that situation, or on this or that level. It is presented simply to show in general how any such listing might look, and what kind of items it might contain. It is, in fact, a starting point for your own planning, rather than a ready-made plan handed to you on a silver platter.

Another important point is that while the list goes down to rather specific items, these are grouped under a small number of broad classifications. To do this is very desirable. Otherwise one simply puts down anything and everything that happens to come to mind, which means working in a haphazard way, and probably coming out with a haphazard result. Moreover, when one classifies specific musical initiatives into a few broad types of categories, it gives one an overview of the whole problem, and shows how everything comes together and what it signifies. Still you should be warned that the classification here adopted is not the only one possible, and also that its subdivisions are not watertight. Other significant and useful classifications could be set up, and I think it would always be true that the various categories or types would overlap a great deal, which is certainly the case here. This latter, however, is not a serious objection, for any such classification is a means and not an end. It is simply an instrumentality for making sure that nothing important is overlooked, for securing a proper balance of emphasis, and for getting an organized grasp of the whole problem.

The following types and lines of musical initiative seem to me important, valuable, feasible in many situations, and well worth considering and promoting:

1. *Initiatives having to do with musical experience.* a. Attending concerts, operas, and musical performances of any kind of one's own choice
b. Selecting and tuning in on specific radio programs
c. Reading articles and reviews dealing with music. Finding such articles and reviews
d. Obtaining from libraries or purchasing books on music and musicians
e. Selecting from rental and other collections phonograph records and listening to them
f. Building up a personal collection of phonograph records
g. Building up a personal library of musical scores
h. Informing oneself about local musical events
i. Informing oneself about the musical opportunities and activities offered in the school system

2. *Initiatives having to do with musical activities.* a. Seeking for and availing oneself of opportunities for individual musical performance, in formal and informal situations. Creating such opportunities for oneself and one's friends
b. Becoming a member of volunteer performing groups, such as choruses, small ensembles, and the like. Working with such groups in various ways. Organizing and leading them
c. Composing music

3. *Initiatives having to do with music study.* a. Devising and developing one's own methods of practicing and studying
b. Deciding upon the best interpretation of music one is learning to perform, or in group situations participating in such decisions. Interpretation is understood to include expression, instrumentation, and so forth
c. Deciding upon some new line of music study, for instance a new performing medium, musical theory, music history, etc.
d. Exploring the demands and conditions of a musical career

This amounts to saying that a musical person will show enterprise in seeking and enjoying musical experiences, in carrying on musical activities, and in the study of music, so that a well-balanced musical growth will manifest itself in these three directions. A musical person is not merely the possessor of certain skills and certain knowledge. He is a person who does things with and about music. If this is granted—and it can hardly be denied—the immediate implication is that the promotion of musical initiative is one of the prime re-

[155]

sponsibilities of music education. It cannot be left to chance. Organized provision must be made for it. The teacher, or the staff, or the institution whose only idea is to cram as much music as possible into the learners, and then to cast them adrift to make whatever uses of it they may, is putting a premium on self-frustration.

III

There is a very definite reason why the promotion of musical initiative should be an integral part of a developmental scheme of music education. The point is not that it seems like a good idea in general to have musical doings of the kind that have just been listed going on. It is far more specific and convincing than that. The basic argument for musical initiative is that it is both a natural expression of musical growth, and also a very powerful and, in fact, an indispensable influence for fostering it and carrying it forward.

In this there is nothing in the least remarkable or mysterious. The same holds true in every field of human endeavor. People constantly find that they learn more about the inwardness of writing in a few months on the job as reporters than in all their courses in English composition; that they learn more about the inwardness of teaching and of the subjects that they teach in a few months on the job as teachers than in all their college years. Swimmers, dancers, stenographers, tennis players—learners of all kinds—get something from going ahead and doing the best they can on their own account, which they never get under tutelage. Not, of course, that tutelage is unimportant, or has no value! But a situation in which the undertaking itself is the challenge, in which the person knows perfectly well that the responsibility rests upon him and nobody else and that he himself must make the essential choices can have a developmental effect never produced by one in which he depends ultimately upon a teacher to determine standards, requirements, and procedures.

This is a matter of common experience. It is universally recognized. It is the reason why so many schools of journalism send their students out on independent assignments as part and parcel of the curriculum. It is the reason why so many good teachers' colleges set up plans of cadet teaching, in which the student is to a considerable extent on his own. It is the reason why good dance teachers want their pupils to go ahead and dance instead of doing nothing but taking interminable lessons. It is the reason why a good tennis coach will want a pupil to play tennis during the period when he is receiving instruction. These are all what might be called "initiative situations," and their value, indeed their indispensability, is universally admitted. Such initiative situations often occur only after schooling is over, that is to say on the job. But every teacher in every field knows very well that if a student who has been on the job for a while comes back to school, his instruction can pay very high dividends if it is rightly directed. Such a student has a much better idea of "what it is all about" than one who has never had any experience other than more or less passive tutelage. Here, then, is the argument for organizing initiative situations as integral elements of a person's education. Teaching, in one of its aspects, may consist of standing over a learner, telling him just what to do, just how to do it, and just how well he has done. But in another, and equally important aspect, it consists of putting him on his own and letting him find out a few things for himself—things which no other person can ever tell him.

This is the point of view to have in organizing and encouraging musical initiative. Some teachers may feel dismayed or even hostile when it is suggested that they ought to do something about encouraging their pupils to build up record collections or personal libraries of musical scores, to read and own books about music, to seek opportunities to perform, to join musical groups, to try to compose, to elaborate on methods of practicing, to think out interpretations, and so forth. They may be inclined to say that the sole business of the teacher is to teach music, and that it is the pupil's business to make whatever use of it he pleases after he has well and truly learned it. Such a division of function, however, is psychologically unsound. The pupil who is an independent user of music—a musical enterpriser on his own account—will be a much better learner than one who is not, always provided that the teacher has enough gumption to handle him not as a passive recipient, but as an individual who is growing in musical independence. What I am advocating here is by no means a dizzy round of musical activities for their own sake—an enormous extra-curriculum which has no relationship to the serious business of organized instruction. The point is that if a learner is to function best as a learner, he ought to be treated as a cadet musician, just as a student in a teachers' college needs to be treated not as a mere receptacle for wisdom but as a cadet teacher, or just as a dance pupil needs to be treated not as a being to be drilled on certain skills but as a cadet dancer. A policy of this kind is sure to give a teacher innumerable golden chances, obtainable in no other way, if only he is smart enough to see them and to take them. Or to use the analogy of swimming, the music teacher should do something more than teach all the strokes, and the motions, and the fine points of breathing. He should also convey to his pupil the thought that the water is fine, and that it would be a good idea to jump in and do some swimming on his own account.

This implies that musical initiatives should not be fostered on a haphazard, hit-or-miss basis, but for their developmental value. They should, in other words, be regarded and treated as expressions or outcomes of musical growth, and as influences for the furtherance of musical growth. This leads directly to a number of controlling considerations.

1 The purpose always is to deepen, broaden, and refine musical responsiveness. Doing this in terms of musical initiative means encouraging autonomous choices and activities whose outcomes, values, and relative success and failure are to be brought under consideration.

For instance, a fourth-grade group is to present some numbers at a Parent-Teacher Association meeting, or at an assembly program. What numbers shall be chosen? Give the children as much part in deciding this as may be possible. Instead of discussing the matter only with the whole group, it may be a good idea to have a small committee selected to consider the problem. Perhaps the group already has a sufficient repertoire of songs or other music from which to make a choice. Perhaps it may be well to suggest a little voyage of exploration in search of program material that they may like better or that might go better than anything they now have. If the school, or the teacher, or some of the pupils have phonograph records available, they may be useful for this purpose; or the committee or certain designated individuals who are taking piano lessons may accept the job of looking through music books or song books for suitable material. Or it may be that one or more of the youngsters will be able to offer constructive suggestions on their own account, if encouraged to do so. Having decided on the numbers to present, how are they to be handled particularly in regard to interpretation? Again encourage suggestion, choice, initiative, as far as possible. Stimulate discussion on how the music ought to sound, what mood ought to be projected, what impression it is desired to produce on the audience. Nor is it necessary to stop even here. Questions of phrasing, tone-quality, rhythmic accentuation, and perhaps the balance of parts can come up, so that the expressive problem merges into the technical problem as it should. Individuals or small subgroups can be pulled out to listen to the group

[158]

performance as it comes along, to report on how it sounds, and to make suggestions for improvement. Then, when the numbers have been presented, and the occasion is a thing of the past, there can very well be a discussion of its values, its success, and the points where it has not been all that might have been wished. This is one instance of what the fostering of musical initiative can mean in a specific situation. It means treating the performing group, not as a passive instrument at the disposal and under the direction of the teacher, but as a collection of human beings who are contributing to a desired result for which they feel a genuine responsibility in terms of their own musical choices, and who are thereby growing musically.

One finds exactly the same principle operating with younger children. In rhythm band work or toy instrument work, the pupils should be encouraged to choose their own instrumentation, to experiment, to try out alternatives, not because of any mystic or far-fetched respect for personality, but because they can learn and grow musically both from their successes and their failures. Very often, again, little children are given the experience of "realizing" or expressing a piece of music in rhythmic bodily movement, or in some kind of dramatization. Such experiences are a sort of half-way-house between listening and performing. By all manner of means the initiatives of the children should be evoked in such situations. One of the objections to Dalcroze Eurhythmics is that, while it is a very beautiful and highly developed expressive system, it usually leaves nothing to the choice of the pupil, whether it must operate in this way or not. The children should be encouraged to decide on their own rhythmic or dramatic expression. They should be helped to do so, partly perhaps by suggestions from the teacher, but even more so by organizing situations in which individuals will really feel free and able to make suggestions of their own in the knowledge that they will be heeded. And all this, once again, is desirable not because of a metaphysical respect for personality which may or may not be legitimate, but for the much more convincing and common sense reason that self-initiated and self-criticized expressive choices are peculiarly effective in revealing the expressive values of music.

Once more, and more generally, every teacher in every phase of music study at every level should constantly have in mind the desirability of inciting pupils to strike out for themselves, to find and follow lines of their own. He should organize situations to make this possible. He should throw out hints, enticements, suggestions, and whenever such suggestions bear fruit, he should make much of it.

[159]

A certain high-school theory class was dealing with the topic of modulation. One of the boys, in response to various suggestions of the kind just mentioned, brought in what he thought was a good example from a Haydn sonata which he was studying with his private piano teacher. The music, as a matter of fact, was not very closely related to the particular problem before the class, but the teacher recognized the value and possibilities of the example presented. She broke off the regular planned sequence of the lesson and, working extemporaneously, developed an excellent and revealing discussion of the music brought before her. In so doing she encouraged the musical initiative both of the pupil concerned and also of others in the class, and undoubtedly fostered musical growth far more effectively than she would have done by a slavish adherence to the syllabus.

In a certain general music course the teacher in charge was a specialized and excellent vocalist, as well as a person with a broad and constructive educational outlook. Between the start of the school year and the Christmas vacation she had stimulated a strong interest in vocal performance. She did this partly by using recorded music, partly by encouraging concert attendance, partly by her own singing, partly by class singing, partly by assigning some very inviting books and articles in the vocal art. Also she kept on throwing out suggestions that perhaps some members of the course, which was run in several sections, might like to form a singing group of their own. A little before Christmas these suggestions and influences bore fruit in the form of a petition that just such a group be organized. Most of the petitioners had never before shown the least interest or ambition in the matter of musical performance of any kind. But the group was set up. It worked for the rest of the year out of school time, partly under the direction of the teacher, partly under that of competent pupil leaders who were interested enough to volunteer their services. It made several presentations in various sections of the course, and as a culminating undertaking participated creditably in an assembly program. The activity of this volunteer group was exceedingly fruitful. It opened up the art of music in a new and effective fashion for its own members. And it projected a vital musical influence both throughout the entire enrollment of the course and throughout the school.

In another general music course the discovery was made early in the school year that several of the pupils were building up record collections of their own as a hobby. This was immediately seized upon and used as a leverage for the promotion of fruitful initiative. The planned syllabus suffered, but the pupils benefited. These enterprising individuals were given a chance to display their treasures, to play them to the group, to talk about them, to say why they liked them, what they thought of them, what other records they hoped to obtain, how they ran across them, how much they cost, and so forth. Discussion was very active, and interest and emulation were strongly stimulated. The initiatives of these enterprising individuals were themselves strengthened and pointed up towards more effective outcomes; and their example had a palpable effect on many of their classmates.

A certain teacher of class piano has adopted the practice of encouraging his pupils to devise their own technical exercises. Instead of assigning exercises from one stated book, he refers them to a fairly large collection of books on piano technique, with the suggestion that they select whatever seems most helpful. Moreover he does not stop there. He asks them to invent exercises of their own, usually after they have looked through a good deal of material, to try them out, to bring them to class, and to report on their values. These pupil-invented exercises may not be as neat and pretty as those published under the awe-inspiring names of Czerny, Hanon, Joseffy, and Moscheles, but they have something that is lacking in the handsome and embalmed material. That something is the principle of life! They embody real thought about technical problems, real experimentation, real endeavors to make music sound like music in the face of manipulative difficulties.

These are all illustrations of how musical initiative can foster and further genuine musical responsiveness. One additional example may serve to clinch the point. Back in the twenties a young woman was hired by a small school system to inaugurate a music program. Thus she had a pioneer job, and it was a tough one with everything still to be done. One of her troubles was the really appalling quality of the singing, if such it could be called, in the elementary-school classrooms. Everyone yelled, with little reference to pitch or anything else, and most of the boys were quite convinced that music was an extremely "sissy" proposition. How did she cope with the problem? One of the first things she did was to organize in the elementary-school a boys' glee club, and then a girls' glee club, as volunteer organizations. Within a very few months matters were visibly—and audibly—coming under control. It was the magically right solution, far better than scolding, admonitions, drill on syllables, and disquisitions about that light, charming head tone. The multitude was confronted with groups of its own members who actually chose to sing, who actually enjoyed singing, and whose singing was actually enjoyable. Musical initiative did the trick when lessons out of the book would almost certainly have failed.

2 Musical initiative is a very important and valuable agency for self-discovery and self-revelation. Books on psychology and education frequently remind the teacher of the obvious and very important truth that individuals differ, yet it often happens that he carries on his work almost as though he had forgotten all about it. A determinate sequence of procedure is set up, apparently with the idea that it will be suitable for all persons and all occasions, as the deacon said about the Doxology. Those who seem to get little out of it, and who fail to flourish according to expectations, are categorized as lacking sufficient inner ability. Nobody knows quite what to do about them, and on the whole the policy is to think about them as little as possible while they slide into a decent obscurity along the assembly line without undergoing the indicated operations. This is what is often called "the problem of individual differences," and it manifests itself in every curricular field, including music.

Now it should always be understood that any stereotyped program or sequence in educational work is bound to be limiting. What suits some is bound not to suit others. The teacher of a junior high-school course in general music once informed me in a public conference that while her work seemed to be effective for a certain proportion of the pupils, it was undoubtedly a total loss for a great many of them. She asked me if I had any suggestions to offer, in view of a statement I had made to the effect that music has a very wide and indeed, probably a universal appeal. This struck me as a rather unusually honest and realistic facing of certain facts which are often dodged, so I was interested. What, I asked her, was she doing in this course? She replied that she was trying to convey the most important and essential things in music. This certainly sounded promising, but I was still not quite satisfied. What were these things, I wondered. It then appeared that almost her entire emphasis was placed on turning these children into good readers, and that her eyes were firmly fixed upon the very excellent performing organizations in the senior high-school, which were really setting her standards and determining her procedures. There, undoubtedly, was the answer. For some of her pupils what she was doing was at least in part the right thing, and they themselves knew it. But for others, who had no ambition to be members of the orchestra, or the band, or the *a cappella* choir, it was quite meaningless. She had a one-track setup, which she had formulated according to some definite specifications. Those who had wheels of the proper gauge rolled along fairly well. But those who were so constituted by nature, circumstance, or inclination that they did not fit on the rails bumped over the ties for a while, and then subsided into the ditch.

Were those who made nothing of this particular course, and were thereby lost to music so far as the school was concerned, lacking in talent? Not necessarily so. Many of them may have been definitely able people who simply did not want to go in that particular direction. It is sometimes suggested that the way to deal with individual differences is to set up work adapted to the "fast learner," or the "slow learner," or the "average learner," this being the polite and modernistic way of referring to persons who are supposed to be hereditarily bright, or dull, or mediocre. Such a policy, however, is a grave over-simplification. Neither the "fast learner," nor the "slow learner," nor the "average learner" is a universal type. Differences within these categories may be just as real and important as differences between them. For there are differences also in interest, intention, and background—qualitative differences, that is to say—which may be of determining effect. A naturally brilliant child can be just as hopelessly bored and baffled by something outside his *metier* as though he were stupid. Indeed, in such a situation, and for all practical purposes, he *is* stupid. So it would not have been legitimate for the good lady who was handling the general music course to flatter herself that she was reaching the talented pupils, and only letting the culls fall by the wayside. What she was really doing was to reach only those who were suited by her kind of work, whatever their talent might be.

Now there is no doubt that the range and complexity of differences, both in quality and degree, that a teacher has to face, amounts to an extremely difficult challenge, and that success to the degree of one hundred per cent is something only likely to occur in the happier kind of dream. But also there is no doubt that the systematic organization of initiative situations is the right policy, and that it can get further than one might readily suppose. Give pupils plenty of chances to do different things and to choose different things in connection with music, and what will show up will often be very surprising, and pleasantly surprising, too. The refractory monotone, for instance, is an impossible problem ʃonly in a sequence committed to the slogan

"Sing or bust." Suppose he receives a little gentle encouragement to bring a few records to school, play them to the class, and talk about them. A boy who is high-pressured into an applied music class in the grades, where he has the mentality of a resentful draftee, is almost sure to give a fine imitation of a musical moron, even if he is no such animal, and the director of instrumental music is left lamenting because so many fish slip through the meshes of this well-intended net, instead of at last swimming happily in the tanks of his secondary-school organizations. But what if this same boy had been given a chance to explore the musical resources of the community, to report on motion picture music at the local theatre, and so on? Then the final picture might have been altogether different, and he might even have ended up playing the tympani in the high-school orchestra, than which, of course, nothing could have been more desirable.

So it goes. The plain truth is that the teacher who only knows his pupils in stereotyped and imposed learning situations will never know many of them musically at all. Also pupils whose musical opportunities are all along a single predetermined line run a very real risk of never discovering that music has for them anything of particular value or distinctive appeal. In a certain very large junior high-school there has been operating for years a special scheduling device which brings a great many pupils into varied contacts with the work in music. Considerable numbers of them are at one time or another assigned to the instrumental studio or barn, and of these latter an appreciable proportion have no instrumental background or intentions whatsoever. The teacher in charge has been able to devise a whole set of subsidiary optional activities, such as caring for and distributing the instruments, sometimes making minor repairs, conducting some of the more routine activities of the department, and the like. Busy work, one might say, and to some extent quite truly. But the fact remains that a good many, though by no means all, of these non-instrumentalists are actually reached and influenced year by year, and that a really worth-while number of seeds of musical growth do indeed take root.

3 Musical initiative is a function which exhibits a process of growth. If this is understood and borne in mind, many apparent difficulties in promoting it will be found to clear up.

A. *It must manifest itself first in crude, simple, easily handled situations.* There would, for instance, be very little use in asking the members of a senior high-school orchestra to discuss and make suggestions about

[164]

the interpretation of an important work if their whole musical up-bringing had been in terms of stereotype. To do this would be foreign to their whole way of thinking and acting. Years of musical depend-ence and docility might have given them a fairly smooth technique, but they certainly would not be in a position to try their wings in a difficult and exacting flight. But if they had been systematically subjected to the influences of a program emphasizing initiative, the outcome might be very different. Away down in the grades they would have been encouraged to select and decide upon rhythmic or dramatic interpretations of music heard or sung. Further along the line in their instrumental and vocal work the question of varying interpretations would have been raised again and again in many situations and in more and more sophisticated forms. They would have come to recognize, in and through their own assisted choices, how the mood values of music and also its structural content determine the nuances of its projection. Then the orchestra director in the senior high-school might well find himself facing a group of enter-prising and judicious cadet musicians, instead of more or less efficient and docile robots. He would need to be a good man to handle such a problem, for a weakling would assuredly find it embarrassing. But if he could deal with it, very far-reaching possibilities would be opened up.

So, too, with initiatives having to do with methods of music study. A great many music students simply have no independent idea about how to practice, how to carry a part with a group, how to work up an accompaniment, the reason being that all their experiences in music education have turned simply on doing what the teacher said. But suppose that from the very first they had been shown how to analyze their problems, how to vary their attack upon difficulties, how to use the content and values of the music itself as a guide—shown these things simply and easily at first, but with an increasing analytic insight—then by the time they reached the upper levels they would manifest that self-guidance in difficult and delicate situations which is the mark of every really superior student, and which is welcomed by every good teacher.

B. *Again, growing musical initiative is associated with growing resource-fulness.* A musical person who is relatively mature ought to have pretty far-reaching ideas about the music he himself would like to learn to play or sing, or about the music that would be suitable for this or that group, or this or that program or occasion. If he has

[165]

narrow and limited ideas about such matters, or perhaps hardly any ideas at all, it is a sure sign of a limited musical development. Then, of course, some very important and valuable types of musical initiative become impossible. But such resourcefulness does not come about by magic. The young learner ought to experience, listen to, discuss, talk about, think about, react to a good deal more music than he actually performs. He should from the very first be encouraged to make choices of his own, at first very immediate and limited, but steadily increasing in scope. To want to hear this piece repeated, to want to sing this song again, to suggest that this other song or piece might be a good one for the class to try—these are the beginnings of musical initiative of this type. The point, it should be noted, is not to build background in the ordinary sense of the term. One should not try to cram the learner to the bursting point with an enormous repertoire of familiar, half familiar, and barely familiar music, and then invite him to display high level initiatives in selecting performing repertoires or setting up programs. What should be done is to or-ganize and promote choices based on an expanding area of awareness.

C. *Growth in musical initiative must be regarded and treated as a continu-ous process.* This is implied in everything said so far, and indeed it has several times all but broken through into explicit statement.

According to a rather curious view current some years ago, there is a fundamental distinction between secondary and higher education. The difference is alleged to turn upon initiative. According to this view, the secondary-school student is entirely under tutelage. He does what the teacher tells him to do, only that, and nothing more. When he bursts into the more exhilarating atmosphere of higher education, however, a great change takes place. He knows what he wants to do, what he wants to work for, and how to work for it. The teacher, instead of being a dictator, turns into a guide to short-cuts, and has uses not dissimilar to library card catalogs, bibliographical indexes, style books, and other similar conveniences for the intellec-tual worker. The only thing not clearly explained by the ingenious author of this fantasy is how the mysterious transmogrification takes place. Usually it does not. The person who has learned nothing but docility up to high-school graduation is more than a little apt to remain a dependent although possibly dutiful and industrious worker up to college graduation and in fact well beyond. The person who shows independence and powers of self-guidance in college is pretty sure to have been manifesting them for years before he got there, even in the face of considerable lack of appreciation on the part of his teachers. For if we really want high-level initiative at the upper levels, it is a good policy to start cultivating it just as soon as possible.

This whole theory, and its obvious rebuttal, can be transplanted entirely from general education into the special field of music. How old must a child be before it is "wise" or "safe" to begin encouraging him to show musical initiative? Old enough, let us say, to babble. If one holds him down somewhat before that, no very radical harm is likely to be done. To frame the answer somewhat more seriously, one should begin promoting musical initiatives of all types from the start, and keep right on. Of course at first they will be very simple initiatives—little choices, little preferences, little projects. Of course, too, we may never put him up against the most stringent of challenges, such for instance, as making crucial musical decisions on behalf of a ninety-piece orchestra on the eve of a public performance before five thousand people. But it may be quite feasible to have him work during his high-school years with a small and perhaps informally organized ensemble where there can be a great wealth of initiative situations having to do with technique, interpretation, choice of repertoire, methods of practicing and rehearsing, and public and semipublic appearance. If a young learner is encouraged to seek and take initiatives will he make blunders and errors? Certainly he will, but no one can grow without making blunders and errors. And the most psychologically cramping, crippling, and impeding of all faults is to be afraid to take one single step on one's own account without the kindly guidance of a teacher to show one how to lift one's foot, how to move it, and just where to set it down.

D. *The ultimate goal of growth in musical initiative is musical independence.* The mature musical person is independent in his quest of musical experiences, in his carrying out of musical activities, and in his methods of music study. This does not mean that he has no use whatever for teachers, coaches, and critics. But he translates what they have to offer into terms of his own needs and processes. Every teacher worth the name should welcome any sign that a pupil may give of an active, personal, reflective, critical response in place of mere docility. When a pupil expresses wishes and opinions of his own, when he strikes out on lines of his own without asking for permission or even for help, the teacher should throw his hat in the air. These are signs that the teaching process is succeeding. They are signs of life and growth. In a well-organized program of music education

[167]

in a school system, one of the constant preoccupations of the staff should be the promotion of just such choices, just such initiatives, just such independence, because they are both outcomes and causes of musical development.

IV

There are a number of points in connection with the promotion of musical initiative already implied in what has been said, that are important enough to be made explicit.

1 Listening experiences should be organized, selected, and pointed up with a view to the encouragement and support of musical initiatives of many kinds.

A. *So far as possible pupils' choices and preferences about what music to listen to should be elicited and heeded.* They may from time to time be asked whether there is any music they would specially like to hear, or whether they would like a repetition of some selection already heard. On the upper-grade levels, discussions and readings about music and musicians can be shaped to bear fruit in requests for the hearing of this or that composition. The course in the history of music and also the work in theory can be made rich in initiative situations of this kind, for the teacher, instead of presenting nothing but a predetermined list of compositions, can encourage requests for music to illustrate some period, or the work of some composer or some theoretical problem.

B. *Free listening out of class, and undirected reading about music are both very desirable initiative opportunities, if facilities can be provided.* The value of such activities can be increased if pupils are encouraged to report informally in class about what they have heard or read.

C. *There should be deliberate efforts to encourage pupils to contribute to the listening experiences and opportunities of the class, by bringing records of their own to school, or by volunteering their own performance.*

D. *One outcome toward which the whole range of listening experiences should be pointed is to broaden the basis of musical choice as maturity increases.* By the time senior high school is reached many pupils should have a fairly wide range of music from which to choose works they wish to learn, or selections for programs and occasions of many kinds.

2 Similarly activities by way of musical performance should be pointed up for the encouragement of initiative. From the very first, questions of treatment, interpretation, and technique should be opened up as matters for discussion. Budding performers should be able to find opportunities to perform in their own class groups, in other classes, at club meetings, on assembly programs, and so far as possible, on more formal occasions outside the school altogether. Opportunities to show initiative in performance which are within "the range of challenge," that is, not so difficult as to be frustrating, but not so easy as to be futile, should be organized as extensively as possible. Glee clubs, dance bands, small vocal ensembles, and small instrumental ensembles have great values here. They give the as yet immature but growing musician a chance to make his own choices along many lines in situations with which he can cope, but which are still significant enough to be true developmental influences. If it is thought that a set-up of small ensemble work would call for an impossible expansion of the music staff, part of the answer is that it can, to a very considerable extent, be organized under student leadership.

3 Musical composition was mentioned in the list of types of initiative but nothing has been said about it so far. It is undoubtedly, in some respects, a special case. But there is no doubt at all that we have here a kind of initiative of great value and rich possibilities.[1]

Musical composition, from its humblest to its highest levels, is an act in which feeling is transmuted into a pattern of tone and rhythm. Thus it is an act in which all phases of musical responsiveness are evoked. It should be so understood and so treated. It occurs very naturally in a milieu of rich, varied, stimulating musical experience, and above all in one in which initiative and self-confidence with the art of music are being developed. This undoubtedly is its true psychological and social origin in the child-lives of the greatest composers. It is how it ought to arise in the life and experience of any

[1] I definitely prefer to talk about musical composition rather than musical creation. The word "creation" has become greatly fatigued of late. As used it often seems to me a weasel word which enables one to sound grand and mean nothing. Certainly it requires very careful definition if it is not to be intolerably slippery. I know what I mean by musical composition. I mean making up music of one's own and probably writing it down, or getting it written down. If it is said that little children cannot do this with high effectiveness, I quite agree. But they write letters, and notes, and essays, and stories, and we call that English composition, not English creation. Why not use the same factual and honest term in connection with music?

[169]

child, even though he may be no Mozart. What should be done is to encourage and help him to project his own feeling in his own melodic formation. That is the gist of the matter. Such encouragement and help can be given at any point—in connection with singing or listening or playing toy instruments or standard instruments. Part of this encouragement and help may consist of nothing more complicated than suggestion and opportunity. Part of it may consist of writing down his melody for him if he is unable to do it himself. Such original melodizing should, above all, be as spontaneous as possible. That is to say, he should not be handed two or three phrase patterns and told to carpenter up a melody out of them. To do this defeats the basic purpose, which is the development of responsiveness to what is the true essence of the art of music. Moreover such melodizing should not be used for ulterior purposes, such as teaching the notation. Beethoven did not compose the Ninth Symphony to get more practice in writing out the score; and to convert sincere, spontaneous, and often very appealing melodic composing into an under-the-counter lesson on the lines and spaces is an insult to the child's individuality and to the art of music.

Musical composition may very properly be fostered not only in the lower grades, not only in the elementary school, but at all levels and in a great many situations. As musical composition becomes more mature it begins to make increasingly specific contact with musical insight. But let it be remembered that theory is the servant of composition, not its master. A mastery of theoretical skills is of great importance for composition, but it is by no means the root of the matter. The essential thing, by all means, is initiative, freedom, and confidence with the art of music, with a resulting responsiveness to its true essence and meaning. Children talk before they know grammar. If they talked only *via* grammar, their linguistic responsiveness would certainly be cramped and confined, to say the least. I am inclined to think that one of the basic troubles with many of our standard plans of music education is that they hold people to stereotypes for many years, and crush out of them that musical originality, individuality, and confidence for which even the best of skills are no substitute at all.

QUESTIONS FOR DISCUSSION

1. How do you explain the fact that many music teachers seem to fear and resent initiative on the part of their pupils?

2. What is the relationship between this discussion of musical initiative and the idea, previously presented, of treating pupils as "cadet musicians"?

3. Make out your own list of specific lines of musical initiative, and if you so desire, your own classification also, and compare your results with those presented in the chapter.

4. Should a teacher welcome any and every kind of musical initiative, or should he consider that some are better than others? What might make them better?

5. To what extent is musical initiative possible for young children? What can be done to help them achieve it? In what ways might it be made impossible?

6. If you had a pupil who very much wanted to study a piece which you knew was beyond him, what would you do about it?

7. Would there be any truth in saying that musical composition is very difficult largely because it is organized in ways that are bound to make it very difficult?

8. With some specific group of pupils in mind, consider how you might encourage them to try to compose music.

9. In this chapter the term "composition" is preferred to the term "creative work." Discuss the reasons for and against this choice.

10. How can the promotion of musical initiative help to take care of individual differences?

ADDITIONAL READINGS

Lois Coffey Mossman. *The Activity Concept.* The Macmillan Company, New York, 1938. (A broad philosophic discussion which, however, comes down to cases pretty much in terms of initiative and has many implied bearings upon music.)

James L. Mursell. *Successful Teaching.* McGraw-Hill Book Company, Inc., New York, 1946. Chapter 10, "The Principle of Socialization and the Appraisal of Teaching." (Deals with social situations which permit and encourage initiative.)

CHAPTER EIGHT

Growth in Musical Discrimination

I

The third broad avenue of musical development is growth in musical discrimination. This means the development of a sensitivity to musical values in the performance of other people, in one's own performance, and in compositions themselves.

Such value differentiations are of two chief kinds: First there are those that are in terms of better and worse. A person who is mature in his musical discriminations not only knows but intimately feels that the third movement of the *Ninth Symphony* is immensely superior to *To a Wild Rose*, that the *Great G Minor Fantasy and Fugue* is immensely superior to *Alexander's Ragtime Band*, that Melchior is far superior, as an artist, to Frank Sinatra. He may have catholic tastes. He may be able to enjoy and appreciate inferior work so long as it is good after its kind. But he will have no doubt that there really are grades of aesthetic and musical excellence, and this not on a basis of critical theory or accepted opinion, but of direct personal experience.

But musical discrimination is concerned with a great deal more than ranking artistic manifestations in a scale of relative excellence. Is the music of Mozart superior to that of Bach? Is Palestrina greater than Wagner? Is the *Londonderry Air* a finer piece of folk-type music than *Swing Low, Sweet Chariot*? Is Toscanini's interpretation of the *Eroica Symphony* better than that of Bruno Walter? Uninformed laymen often ask questions like these. But the person of mature musical discrimination will refuse to answer, because he is aware that they neglect a fundamental consideration. There are kinds of excellence as well as degrees of excellence, and to these also he is sensitive. Musical discrimination, then, has to do both with degrees and also with kinds of excellence in musical manifestations.

That musical discrimination, as so understood, is a capacity of the highest importance, that it is a natural and inevitable expression of musical responsiveness, that it is a characteristic quality of a truly

[172]

musical person is so obvious that no one is likely to question the proposition. When Beethoven greeted a bad composition with roars of laughter, when Handel greeted a bad performance with yells of rage, when Schumann instantly recognized genius in the work of Chopin, they were behaving just about as might be expected of musically sensitive and exacting persons. For there is no surer sign that anyone has the root of the matter within him than his decisive responsiveness to relative and comparative values.

Bearing this in mind, then, is it not astounding to what an extent musical discrimination is neglected in most conventional schemes of music education? In effect nothing whatever is done about it. It is left to pure chance. Every musician or music teacher who thinks about the matter for more than ten seconds has to admit that good taste, good judgment, wise and refined critical standards are of the highest value. Yet in how many conservatories, or schools of music, or school music programs is there any vestige of a constructive and intelligent plan for fostering them? Teachers cannot resist talking incidentally about them, for their importance is manifest. Students are vitally interested in them. I have heard many an informal student seminar after a conservatory recital which turned entirely upon value judgments. Laymen, too, are interested in knowing how to recognize, appreciate, and respond to musical excellence; and many more of them would be interested if they could be shown simply, intelligibly, and at an early age what it is all about. But by and large there is no guidance at all. And if it is proposed to deal with the matter by means of some kind of working plan, a great many people would not have the vestige of a notion how to set about organizing one.

There is a very good reason for all this confusion, and for this disastrous gap in our scheme of work; it is the prevailing externalism of music education at all levels and in all its branches. This inevitably sets up standards of value which have nothing to do with authentic musical discrimination. In performance all along the line, an overwhelming and distorting emphasis is placed on sheer skill, simply as an end in itself. Are the right notes being played? Are mistakes being avoided? Is the technique facile? These are the kind of questions which inevitably dominate the learner, the teacher, and the critic, so that the musical values which constitute the whole meaning of the act are either entirely submerged, or treated as a kind of epiphenomena, nice if they happen to appear, but not part of the really serious business of music study. The teaching of theory again, where the emphasis is even more obviously illegitimate, is prepossessed with a

[173]

concern for sheer skill. The desired outcomes turn on facility in producing correct solutions to formal problems, which may be and usually are very remotely related to authentic musical values. A recent survey of theory courses offered in American colleges has shown that in most of them not one scrap of actual music is used, which is a sufficiently shocking commentary. On such implicit assumptions the *Eroica Symphony* would be a great work because it was a very successful exercise in musical composition. The teaching of music history again is obsessed with facts, and emphasizes memory rather than musical responsiveness. There are many courses in this field in which not one note of music is heard from start to finish. The present emphasis on appreciation is perhaps a gesture in another direction, and praiseworthy so far. Unfortunately, however, such offerings are usually of a very superficial and unenlightening kind.

Now when music is approached in this way, effective discrimination cannot be constructively fostered, because the basis for discrimination is not there. All one has to judge on is sheer skill and sheer knowledge. The most sophisticated audiences in America will go into raptures when a pianist rips off some showy piece of virtuosity. Apparently if the man would play blindfold and with gloves on, the impression would be still deeper. Now in all conscience there is something perverse and humiliating in appraising a serious artist as though he were a circus acrobat. Yet when we train people from youth up with the emphasis nine-tenths on skill and at most one-tenth on authentic musical values, this is exactly what we are aiming at. Or once again, there are plenty of people—and among them not a few trained musicians who are trying, poor souls, to be democratic—who intimate that jazz music must be taken very seriously because it is often very skillful, whereas the plain truth is that most jazz music is artistic trash of the most debased and contemptible kind.

There is only one possible basis for musical discrimination, and that is responsiveness to the constitutive values of the art of music. This, by all means, is what ought to be taught right from the very start, and all along the line. The development of skill would not suffer thereby. On the contrary, it would be facilitated, for the great obstacles to the acquisition of musical skills are not manipulative but psychological. Such a scheme of music education would emphasize always the inner, living essence, and move from it to the external manifestations. Its central aim would be the development of musical persons who, among other things, are musically discriminating persons. It would, in short, be a developmental scheme, rather than a mechanistic one.

II

It becomes alarmingly clear at this point that we are facing a problem of the most formidable dimensions. What is a good musical performance? What is a good musical composition? What makes good music good? These are questions often asked by dialectically inclined persons who wish to be embarrassing, and as a general thing they are dodged with great agility. Yet we must face them and deal with them somehow, or else stop talking about musical discrimination altogether. For discrimination without a criterion is a contradiction in terms.

We shall be able to come at an answer by reminding ourselves once again of the essential nature of music itself, aesthetically and psychologically. Music is an art capable of establishing and imposing all the conditions of a distinctive emotion, a distinctive way of feeling, but in the absence of the object or circumstance that gives rise to that way of feeling in ordinary life. It is capable of doing this because of the expressive means it employs. It uses a medium, the medium of tone, which in itself gives rise to profound, far-reaching, and commanding emotional and organic effects. It uses the relational values of tone, the so-called tonal logic, to give specific form to the general emotional and affective stir and lift produced by the impact of this kind of stimulation. These relational values or factors, as we have seen, consist of tone quality with its various nuances and differences, pitch with its levels and its rise and fall, harmonic quality with its nuances and differences, melody with its movement up and down and its beginnings and endings, tonality with its patterns of attraction and repulsion and of rest and movement, rhythm with its moving flow of stress and release, and the larger architecture in which musical formations are developed, juxtaposed, and contrasted in a moving tapestry. Objectively a piece of music is a kaleidoscopic flow of shapes merging into one another, and this we call its form. But the musical form is not something entirely outside the composer, or the performer, or the hearer. It has a psychological counterpart in a moving flow of stresses and releases, very complex and subtle, but very distinctively shaped, within the organism itself. In this correspondence, and indeed interfusion of objective form with the form of the bodily and mental response lies what must be called the meaning of the music. For the formed and shaped mental and physical response is precisely the substance of emotion, the affective content itself.

This is why music can express and convey the emotional values of experience apart from the experience. Beethoven could and did put

[175]

into music his joy in returning to the country, without telling anything about his journey there, or about his visit, or where the country was. The *Pastoral Symphony* captures, expresses, and conveys nothing but the emotional effect of the experience, and leaves out almost all its literal content. A great deal of music, such for instance as the fugues of Bach, goes further than this, and conveys the emotional values which must have been established in the composer's life by some event or other, without a hint of literal reference. In vocal music, on the other hand, the literary axis of reference is usually fairly explicit, but the music gives us not a literal one-to-one translation or commentary on the words, but a projection of their emotional value.

All this, of course, is a recapitulation and epitome of the analysis presented more at length in the second chapter of this book, offered because of its special relevance to the problem now before us. It leads to a series of propositions bearing on and, in effect, providing an answer to the question: What is good music?

1 All significant music from the greatest to the most trivial is a transposition of a way of feeling into a moving tonal-rhythmic pattern. Musical responsiveness is the transposition of this moving pattern back into the way of feeling to which it corresponds. It is quite possible to invent or manufacture tonal and rhythmic patterns to illustrate problems in reading, or technique, or theory. But the result is not significant music. It is not even bad music. Properly speaking, it is not music at all, any more than the sounds made by a piano tuner are music, or any more than a carefully arranged series of dabs of different colored paint is a work of art. Such material can, of course, quite properly be used for special purposes. But it cannot be made the substance of music education, because it is incapable of evoking musical responsiveness.

2 Ultimately the significance of all music resides in its emotional content and meaning. Great music embodies, expresses, and conveys the emotional quintessence, at his highest pitch of insight and inspiration, of a great man's reaction to life and circumstance, subtly and profoundly understood and felt. Lesser music, which may still be good and indeed admirable, expresses a lesser conception, a shallower insight, an emotion less profound and penetrating. Commonplace music, which may be on the borderline between good and bad, expresses a commonplace way of thinking and feeling. Vulgar music, which is always bad no matter how much it happens to tickle the ear, embodies and conveys vulgar values, vulgar responses to life and circumstance.

[176]

In this respect music is exactly similar to the other arts. Compare, for instance, Tennyson's poem *Maud* with *The Eve of Saint Agnes* by Keats. Both are emotion-fraught interpretations of a similar circumstance in general. Both deal with the theme and values of tragic love. Keats projects his glowing vision against a somber background of varied hues which opens depth after depth of profound significance. Tennyson tells his story well enough, and it is a moving story, yet comparatively speaking a banal one. On the one hand the struggle of love against human evil and the harsh negations of the universe, typified by the bleak and stormy night, all conveyed with a matchless wealth of imagery and language. On the other hand a tale not undramatically conceived and unfolded in tuneful and melodious verse. That is what these two men were able to make of one of the sovereign circumstances of human life, and the difference is obvious. Or compare again the subtle poignancy and vast intimations of the sonnets of Shakespeare with the obvious, though not unharmonious, musings of Longfellow. Once more, the difference is obvious. So, too, with the pictorial art. Compare a Titian Venus, the Bouguereau *Matin de Septembre*, and one of the trashy pretty-girl confections published by *Esquire Magazine*. There you have the gamut. In all three cases the human body is the theme, and you can see its emotional values treated from the universal, through the commonplace, to the vulgar.

To come back to music, compare *Isoldens Liebestod*, Grieg's song *Ich Liebe Dich*, and the average torch song. Once more the theme is human love, but how differently conceived, felt, and treated. Once more you have the gamut—ecstasy asserting itself on the brink of oblivion, a worthy sentiment feelingly expressed, the crude bellowing of a discontented cow. There again the differences are obvious. It is the universal explanation, the universal criterion. Here is the reason why the best music of Beethoven is better than the best music of Chopin, why the best waltzes of Chopin are better than the best waltzes of Johann Strauss. It is a matter of universality, scope, and insight primarily, and not of technical skill in composition. Beethoven is the universal poet. Chopin, though far more limited, catches some intimations below, and above, and beyond the glitter of the present scene. Strauss responds to nothing but its obvious glamor and its surface sentiment. Or again, here is the reason why every one of the Bach chorales is a piece of music superior to *Onward Christian Soldiers*. On the one hand the quintessence of faith, devotion, and prayer; on the other a forthright expression of a much simpler and perhaps

[177]

more superficial religious feeling. Comparisons of this kind could be continued indefinitely, but I think quite enough has been said to make the point.

I should perhaps emphasize again the consideration that much music which cannot be considered great is nevertheless good. A cowboy song, a folk melody, a Negro spiritual, a tune composed by a child can all be good. They can be good because they are direct, sincere, and worthy emotional reactions to circumstance. Sincerity, in fact, is the necessary condition for any kind of artistic excellence. There is plenty of art in the world whose values are not sincere, which expresses not the emotions some person really feels, but the emotions people are supposed to feel, or that they have been told are conventional and expected. Many motion pictures belong to this *genre*. So does a great deal of jazz. So do many revival hymns. Such art is inescapably contemptible. It is just a little above the level of the advertisement which warns against halitosis, and the singing commercial. But although sincerity is a necessary condition for excellence, it is very far from being a sufficient condition for greatness. Anyone who supposes that folk songs, and cowboy songs, and spirituals, and child-composed tunes are great music in any sense is very much mistaken. Nevertheless, they are worthy of respect, and a suitable pabulum for music education, because they are genuine and sincere musical projections capable of evoking a genuine musical responsiveness.

3 The form of the music, in the inclusive sense in which the term is here used, must be regarded as an expressive vehicle for transmitting the emotional intent of the composer. The quality of the tone, the level and the rise and fall of pitch, the shifting harmonic color, the ups and downs and beginnings and endings of the melodic pattern, the trends of the tonality, the moving flow of rhythmic shapes, and the larger musical architecture, are always means to an end, not ends in themselves. The act of composition does not consist in manipulating them skillfully for their own sake, but in utilizing them as agencies to project meanings and intimations. Thus it is that while one criterion in evaluating a musical work will be the significance of the emotional idea which it embodies, another and complementary criterion is the adequacy and perfection with which that idea is conveyed in the form. What has the composer to say? How well does he manage to say it? These are always the two basic questions.

This relationship of form to substance is always fundamental in

[178]

matters of musical taste. For instance one is conscious of a certain disconcerting incongruity when the Schubert *Ave Maria* is sung with the words of the ecclesiastical Latin hymn. Schubert, in his music, was not projecting the values of this hymn, but of quite a different poem; and although both will go well enough to the literal notes of the tune, the hymn is definitely incompatible to the feeling of the music. We sink to a much lower level of sheer bad taste when all sorts and kinds of words are united in shot-gun marriages to instrumental and vocal melodies to which they have no aesthetic relevance at all, simply because the words can be made to fit more or less to the notes, with perhaps a little forcing. And the very lowest depths of vulgarity are plumbed when all sorts of verbal gibberish are hooked up to classical musical motives, simply to make the music easier to remember. This is strictly comparable to treating the Venus de Milo with rouge and lipstick so that one can never forget her. Musicians who do such things should be admonished to feel ashamed of themselves, and music teachers should avoid them like the plague.

The whole question of the use of music out of its intended context, and of transcription is involved here. Ever since the days of Liszt there has been an inveterate tendency to translate music into a foreign medium—songs and orchestral works fixed up for the piano, organ compositions "arranged" for the orchestra, and the like. There is always a flavor of impudence about such doings, and very often they are pernicious. The intent of the composer is chucked away for the sake of glitter. We live in a day when highly paid baton-wielders expect the kind of homage which would be suitable for the greatest creative spirits that have ever adorned the art of music. But one would think that even these essentially derivative artists might resist the intoxication of success at least to the point of keeping their hands off their betters. The same fashion has invaded elementary music education also. No doubt the song that is manufactured simply to exemplify some technical notational problem without saying a solitary thing either musically or emotionally is a deplorable phenomenon. But one has to doubt whether some noble theme dressed up with childish and irrelevant words is really much better. It makes one think of the Hermes of Praxiteles tricked out in costume for a children's party.

In music, as in all the arts, there is always a tendency for form to run away with the whole show. There is always a temptation, to which even the greatest have succumbed from time to time, to produce a glittering surface and nothing more. Berlioz is a type case of the

[179]

artist engrossed in the sheer problems of technique, and able to solve them with uncanny success. The music of Berlioz, in this respect, is comparable to the poetry of Swinburne. Both were incredibly deft in their manipulation of the medium. The orchestration of Berlioz is something to marvel at; but the limitation appears when we realize that he does not have much to say. It is a question whether a good many present-day composers are not manifesting this weakness—whether a good deal of their output is not essentially technician's music rather than a poetic interpretation of life and its values.

So it comes to this. A musically discriminating person will always value and respect music which embodies something sincerely felt, and which projects that feeling in adequately expressive form. Such music may be very simple, even very naïve. It has been produced many a time by untutored men and by children too. It must be taken on its own terms. But if this be done, it can still be found exquisite and repaying. One need not be a colossal genius to produce good music, even though one must be such to produce great music. Musical expression is natural to man, and all that is needed to achieve it is to be a sincere and sensitive person who wishes to tell what he feels in the magical medium of tone.

4 All the values of musical performance turn upon translating the composer's intention into tone—on shaping up the form so that it will carry its message. This should always be the conscious and controlling consideration for the teacher, the learner, and the critic. A good performance is one in which expressive values are clearly projected. Let us follow up this idea into some of its most important implications.

A. *The importance of the right notes.* To hear some teachers talk, and to watch them work, one would think that getting the right notes and avoiding mistakes was the ultimate goal of musicianship. Indeed when one approaches music externalistically, this at once becomes about the most important discriminative criterion we have. But it is a distorted point of view, just the same.

The importance of playing the right notes in music is exactly on a par with the importance of saying the right words when one recites a poem. The seventh stanza of Keats' *Ode to a Nightingale* opens with the following two lines:

> Thou wast not born for death, immortal bird!
> No hungry generations tread thee down.

[180]

Now supposing that one makes a slip, and instead of "tread" comes out with the word "get." The rhythm is maintained, and the literal sense is not too greatly altered. But the whole evocative effect is shattered, and something positively grotesque takes its place. This is exactly what tends to happen when note errors occur in music, and it is the true reason for their seriousness. It should be observed in passing that not all slips of the tongue in reciting a poem are as flagrantly disastrous as this one, and similarly that in music some note errors are far more serious than others. But the point is that they always involve some disruption of the expressive sense of the form.

Accuracy, then, in musical performance, should always be taught, learned, and appraised as a means and not as an end. What are we trying to say musically? What effect do we wish to produce? Those are the questions which should dominate. This attitude and mode of approach should be instilled into children from the time of their first directed dealings with the art of music, and it should be continued and reinforced from then on. Accuracy is an artistic, not a mechanical problem, and it should invariably be treated as such.

B. *The importance of tone quality.* Tone quality, like accuracy, is a means and not an end. Yet many music teachers indubitably treat it as an end in itself, with values of its own independent of everything else. This is well exemplified by the recent fetish-worship of some mysterious entity called the head voice, which in practice means an extremely soft and trepidatious kind of vocalization in which the young singers act as though they were afraid of waking the baby. I have listened to a much-admired grade-school choir using this kind of tone in what the composer presumably thought was a song of praise to the Creator, but which the director evidently conceived as conveying the emotional meanings of passing to a foreign agent some secret about the atomic bomb. Again such notions, in which tone of a certain kind is made an end in itself, are distorted and harmful.

Does this mean that there is no such thing as good vocal tone? Does it mean putting a premium on uncontrolled and indiscriminate yelling? Of course not. What it does mean, however, is that the real controls and the real values are not intrinsic to the voice. A good vocal tone is one that expresses a clear artistic and emotional intention. The voice is, *au fond*, an expressive instrument, and an amazingly sensitive one. The way to get it to work right is not to fiddle around with its internal mechanism, most of which is a *terra incognita* anyhow.[1] The thing to do, by all means, is to use the voice as nature intended it to be used, that is as an instrumentality for the projection of expression and feeling. Children, and older singers also, would do well always to center the control of the voice not in the diaphragm, not in the breathing, not in the vocal chords, not in the masque, not even in the hypoglossal muscle, but in the artistic intent.

I am well aware that this simple idea knocks out a tremendous deal of the hocus-pocus which infests vocal pedagogy, all the way from the kindergarten right up to some of our most respected choral organizations. Probably no field of professional endeavor outside astrology is more rife with poppycock. "Straight-tone" singing, "vibrato-tone" singing, "chest tone" singing, and so on without end! Is it not about time to return to simple artistic verities, and to remember that good vocal tone, like good tone everywhere, is tone that expressively conveys a discriminating artistic intention?

C. *The importance of rhythmic precision.* The rhythmic component of music is never properly taught, properly learned, properly used, or properly appreciated unless it is treated as an expressive instrumentality. The on-flowing steady beat which the German writers have called the *Takt*, and which is one but only one of the constituent elements of musical rhythm, is the spine of the composition. If an organism has no spine, or perhaps a very crooked one, it is not apt to look very handsome. If a composition is given out without a clear sense of the organizing beat, it tends to fall to pieces. All its shapes become distorted and vague, and many of its expressive values are lost.

Many teachers of individual pupils and many directors of ensembles do not realize the sovereign artistic importance of the basic rhythm. They are aware that something is not quite as it should be with the musical outgivings of the young persons in their charge, but their diagnoses are apt to be fumbling. They try to fix up this, that, or the other little thing, and when matters still do not come out right they readily give way to a mild despair, and resign themselves to the hope that some day, somehow these people will really be able to make music sound authoritatively expressive. But a good musical

[1]The plain, unvarnished truth is that very little is known about the facts of vocal action and production. I am inclined to regard this as a wise dispensation of Providence, because it enables us with a good conscience to stop our ears to the nonsensical outgivings of alleged scientists who undertake to tell the world what makes the voice work, their chief sources being elementary textbooks on anatomy, and studies of the gagging efforts of persons with laryngoscopes in their mouths.

trouble-shooter will look at the rhythm of the beat first of all, for he knows very well that if it is not right, nothing else can be quite right either.

But the way to work for rhythmic precision is by no manner of means through mechanics, arithmetic, and isolation. Counting, stepping, moving, and all similar devices for the isolated study of the rhythmic component undoubtedly have their occasional and incidental uses. But they also have their stringent limitations, for one cannot isolate the rhythm from the music without denaturing it. The essential thing is to get a grasp of the composition (and this is true all the way from the simplest folk song to the most intricate symphony) as a living organism, with all its parts, members, and limbs centering upon and moving in an orderly fashion about the onward flow of the rhythmic beat. So the essential approach to the rhythmic component is always by way of its expressive and organizing values. One may from time to time safely diverge. One may take the music apart and try to clean up the rhythmic component, just as a watchmaker takes out a balance wheel and furbishes it. But, as with the watchmaker, the cycle has not been completed until the part has been put back in place, so that the whole organism is a going concern.

D. *Melody, harmony, tonality.* An enormous amount of music teaching goes on in which nothing is done to direct the learner's attention to the components of melody, harmony, and tonality. In fact not a few teachers feel quite astonished when it is suggested that there is something radically wrong with such procedures, and argue that these are lofty flights beyond the capacity of any pupil until he has had at least two years of formal theory. This is what I mean by unmusical music teaching. It is externalism of the most vicious kind.

Melody, harmony, and tonality are not hidden technical mysteries, unless we deliberately make them so. They are not elements of pure and abstract form, suitable only for advanced study to be postponed until the human anatomy is tough enough to take it. They are among the expressive components which make music what it is. As such they can be, in a real measure, apprehended and enjoyed by young children and beginners. They should control musical action from the very first. What is the composer saying in this work? How does he use the melodic flow, the kaleidoscope of harmonic color, the subtle and insistent drama of tonal attraction and of key changes to project his message? No one is really studying a work of music as he should unless these questions are in his mind. The fact that a discord rather than a triad occurs in an accompaniment figure, that the music modulates into the relative minor, that a melodic curve breaks for a moment into a fantastic and liquid variant is not primarily a technical problem or a theoretical problem. Primarily these are all expressive problems, and should always be treated as such. Yet many a pupil approaches them, and is in effect encouraged to approach them, as though the composer were merely trying to be mean and to make trouble.

E. *Dynamics, tempo level, tempo rubato.* These are often called the expressive devices *par excellence.* As a matter of fact, they are means of the second degree—means for means to an end. Their proper use is always to clarify the musical form in such a way that its expressive purpose will be fulfilled. We must set a dynamic level which will give adequate scope for increments and decrements in order to clarify the various components of the form. We must choose a tempo level at which the components will come through with authentic clarity. We shade and modify the tempo in order to set off the beginnings and endings, the delicate points of emphasis and subordination.

Thus it follows that these devices are not subject to any fixed mechanical rules. It is often said that proper *tempo rubato* is determined by the average tempo as a norm. That is, if one slows down at a certain point, one should always speed up somewhere else to the exact degree needed to compensate. This is a gesture in the direction of the truth, but nothing more, for it is incontestable that tempo rubato should not be merely arbitrary. The controlling consideration, however, is not mathematical but artistic. The question always is what a given change of tempo will do to clarify or to obscure the organic components of the expressive form.

F. *The importance of technical facility.* To regard technical facility as a virtue or a value in itself is the last word in artistic and pedagogical externalism. It instantly establishes a false standard of values, a false basis for evaluation, and false goals for endeavor. It reduces musicianship to the level of juggling. Here we are dealing with a factor which is altogether instrumental, and which it is stringently necessary to keep in its proper place. Nevertheless it has a place, and obviously so. Technical facility properly understood means the ability to clarify the musical form without mechanical and motor distractions, and it means absolutely nothing more. It is from this standpoint that technical facility should be evaluated, and this consideration should

[184]

control all endeavors to acquire it, all the time, and at every moment. A fine technique should never be regarded as a thing in itself, and should never be admired for itself alone. Is the performer faithfully, imaginatively, sensitively projecting the emotional intimations of the music in all their fullness and detail? That is always the master question in judging a musical performance, whether by oneself or some other person.

III

One manifest outcome of this whole discussion is that the development of musical discrimination is not a specialized concern, to be treated as a single, limited phase of music education. On the contrary, it should be promoted in and through every aspect of intelligently conducted music study—listening, toy instrument work, work with "social" instruments, instrumental study proper, singing, ensemble experiences, musical theory, music history. This, after all, is directly implied in saying that the development of musical discrimination is one of the main avenues of musical growth itself. Music study which centers upon musical and aesthetic values, as it should always do, is aimed directly at the refinement and deepening of musical responsiveness, which in itself involves those standards of preference and taste which we call musical discrimination.

But here there is a certain danger. Anything that should be present always is quite apt to be so much taken for granted that it is neglected. The fostering of musical discrimination requires conscious planning, conscious action. So, although we cannot limit our thinking to anything less than the over-all program of music education in all its aspects, the following specific points should be borne in mind.

1 Always use music of authentic artistic value, in connection with listening, in connection with performance, in connection with theoretical study, and everywhere else. This, as we have seen, does not always mean the greatest of music, or music by well-known composers; nor does it exclude the use of music specially written for children. What it does mean is music that is significant and expressive in the sense already explained. It does, however, exclude pseudo-music manufactured simply to illustrate technical and notational problems. Such music cannot possibly foster artistic discrimination, because it evokes no musical responsiveness, and is devoid of aesthetic challenge and significance. Also what has been said inescapably im-

[185]

plies that we must accept abbreviations, transcriptions, and arrangements only with great caution and many misgivings. Such tamperings, even though undertaken with the praiseworthy intention of making a composition simple enough or short enough for children, or easy enough to be managed by a strangely chosen ensemble, very readily take on the aspect of murder. Scrupulous artistic integrity, all the way from the kindergarten to the senior high-school orchestra, is a fundamental and imperative condition for the development of musical discrimination.

2 It is always necessary to choose music with reference to the pupil's present capacity for enjoyment. The reason is that it is necessary for him sincerely and genuinely to enjoy music that he hears or performs, if any dividends in the way of developing musical discrimination are to be gained. Otherwise no authentic musical responsiveness will be evoked, and the whole process is frustrated. Thus there will always be a very serious question about the use of lengthy, or extremely elaborate, or highly abstract compositions, particularly with young or immature persons. Also there will be the same question about compositions which project very remote and exalted ways of feeling, far removed from the present emotional experiences of the pupils, such as some of the work of Bach, or of Palestrina, or the later string quartets of Beethoven, even though they represent some of the greatest music ever written. Thus many adolescents enjoy the music of Tchaikovsky a great deal more than that of Bach or Mozart, because of its highly charged and rather obvious sentimentality, and because of the luscious expressive devices which convey its emotional content. But there is no doubt that Tchaikovsky has convinced a great many people that symphonic music is enjoyable, and has set them off on a course of development that has led them far. The same principle applies everywhere, and is even more obvious in dealing with young children in the elementary-school. To repeat, genuine aesthetic pleasure is a necessary condition for the development of aesthetic discrimination.

There are, however, certain qualifications which it is important to observe.

A. *While one must not make excessive or impossibly formidable demands, it is a mistake to assume that standards of acceptance and enjoyment are necessarily very low.* As a general policy one would say that it is better to go through the ceiling than through the floor, if one has to miss the mark in either direction. Teachers who have the courage to experiment will often be surprised at the quality of the music which children find charming. Young people are by no means unwilling to believe that a great work really is great, and that there is much in it to be appreciated, if the case for it is enthusiastically made, if it is well presented, and above all if the teacher himself deals with it with manifest sincerity and respect.

B. *It is definitely a mistake to set up hard-and-fast classifications of music as suitable for designated grade levels.* For one thing, any given school grade is an extremely heterogeneous group. For another thing, any given grade—the fourth-grade, for instance—will have widely varying characteristics from school to school, and often from year to year in the same school. Thus there is no such creature as "the fourth-grade pupil," in any genuine psychological sense, and one cannot choose music on the basis of its probable appeal to a being who is nothing but a statistical fiction. Furthermore there is no such being as "the fourth-grade teacher," save in the most nominal sense. One teacher may be able to handle successfully a type of music that would defeat another. This will depend on something more than the external tricks of the pedagogical trade, and methods of presentation generally. The determining factors are almost sure to be the teacher's own musical enthusiasms, and his sympathetic understanding of children.

C. *It is by no means necessary for children to become discriminatingly aware of every phase, aspect, and facet of a composition the first time they take it up.* One may say that a great and important work is beyond them, and to some extent this may be true. But the question still remains whether it is entirely beyond them. Sometimes this will be the case, but not always. Then the further question arises whether they will be able to make enough of it for it to constitute a repaying experience. In any case one must certainly avoid the assumption that the only proper alternative is all or none.

D. *It is not always necessary for children to take to a piece of music the first time they hear it, or the first time they try it over.* This is particularly true when musical responsiveness and discrimination have advanced to an appreciable maturity. There are certain works of art to which one must be willing to return again and again before one begins to realize their significance, beauty, and power. Indeed one might say that with truly great art this is always necessary. One of the differences between the advertiser and the artist is that the latter is not

[187]

condemned to making a sale at the first contact. Once more the teacher can rightfully assume that children who have begun growing up under proper musical influences will be willing to wait and work until the light breaks. To be sure, it would be a very mistaken policy to exploit this willingness, but from time to time the experience of discovering beauty and appeal, not apparent at the first glance, can be highly beneficial.

3 When any musical composition is being presented in any way, either in listening, or in private or class study, or in rehearsal, always have in mind some specific aspect or aspects of the musical values it embodies, and plan to emphasize them, and throw them into high relief. There has already been presented in this chapter a discussion, somewhat brief and schematic it is true, of the constitutive aesthetic values which appear in the content of musical works, and determine their performance. Much fuller treatments of the topic will be found in the references at the close of the chapter. These values are foci of musical discrimination. The suggestion is to have some of them always in mind, and to stress them, whenever any piece of music is being taken up in any way. It will usually be a mistake to try to cover them all, although if questions come up which carry beyond the intended plan, they should be hospitably treated. The point is that whenever a piece of music is being used in any way, it should be used as an opportunity to bring home to the learners some specific phase or musical expressiveness and significance. The particular experience, the particular undertaking should not be conducted for itself alone. It should be thought of and planned as a developmental influence which promotes musical growth in general, and which in particular establishes new standards of value and opens up new discriminations.

4 Situations in which comparisons are instituted can be very fruitful and revealing. Put side by side compositions of similar type, compositions of contrasting type, compositions of varying excellence, various interpretations of the same work. In rehearsal situations and performances generally this may mean the use of recordings, but the method is less important than the idea. If equipment is available, let pupils hear their own work before and after study. Encourage them to find, bring to school, and present similar and contrasting instances of the music with which they are dealing. Such comparisons, judiciously handled, can do a great deal to clarify points having

[188]

to do with aesthetic values, and to render them meaningful. Such comparisons should, of course, always be pointed up to stress the constitutive aesthetic values which have already been considered. That is to say, they should not simply be presented with the thought that pupils will be able to draw their own conclusions without any particular help.

5 Make much of guided aesthetic discussion. Talk over with the pupils the constitutive values in the content and the performance of the music with which they are dealing. Encourage them to express their own ideas on the subject. Even in the lower grades such guided aesthetic discussion is not only entirely possible, but potentially very fruitful, so long as it is kept within the range of the children's understanding and experience. At later levels it can, of course, become more generalized. Also with older pupils it can be supported and supplemented with readings in books dealing with musical appreciation and criticism, and perhaps even with musical aesthetics. Usually it should turn on some present experience, or some work actually in hand. But it may range quite widely, touching on out-of-school musical experiences and interests.

Guided aesthetic discussion of this kind is potentially exceedingly valuable, and also exceedingly neglected. Music education, as conducted everywhere—in studios, in the general schools, in conservatories, in schools of music—is far too exclusively concentrated on skill, and places far too little emphasis on thought, insight, and aesthetic response. The school, with its group situations, including general music classes, classes in applied music, and rehearsals of all kinds, provides very rich opportunities for rectifying the balance. Aesthetic discussion should by all means be promoted and conducted in all such situations, just as widely as possible, both incidentally to other undertakings such as the rehearsal of compositions by the orchestra or the choir, and as an undertaking planned in its own right. The same practice could very well be carried upward to the levels of specialist and professional training. It may be said with confidence that conservatories and schools of music would find it highly repaying to set up seminars in practical musical aesthetics, in which students would discover and explore the meanings and values of what they were doing.

6 Always remember that aesthetic standards are not created by personal preference. To suppose anything of the kind is to reverse the true order. A composition or an interpretation is not good because

people like it. They must like it because it is good, and they will in fact do so if they have a fair chance and if it has one also.

A great deal of muddy thinking and destructive talk has centered on this point, particularly with reference to the use of jazz, and of so-called popular music generally. One very general argument is that the curriculum must always have reference to the actual experiences with which pupils deal and will deal in their everyday living. But is there any reason why the curriculum should not give them experiences and encourage them to go on seeking experiences which they would not otherwise have? Another argument, slightly less sweeping, is that a teacher must always work at the level of his pupils' experience. But is there any reason why he should not try to raise them to a better level, and to reveal to them things of which they do not dream? Another argument—and I really do not know whether to call it pathetic or shameful—is that a music teacher should be ready to purvey anything and everything simply to show that he is a good fellow and a pal, just like all the rest of the boys. This, however, is a hopeless strategy, and any teacher who follows it will only make a fool of himself, for he will most certainly be defeated by the ineluctable psychological gap between the generations. He had better make up his mind to the fact that, although he need not be a tough customer or an inhabitant of an ivory tower, his job is not to be one of the gang, but rather a wise and sympathetic leader and guide, which is an altogether different affair.

The plain truth is that no rationalization can justify cheapness, insincerity, or vulgarity. If the pupils like such things, then it is high time to persuade them to like something better, and if we cannot do this we have failed. It is not "democratic" to give pupils just what they happen now to like, for no better reason than that it corresponds to their barbaric and untutored taste. If democracy meant anything like that, we would be better off without it. But it does not. What it means is the opening up to young hearts and minds of the matchless appeal of authenticity, sincerity, worth, and greatness. Unless we are willing to accept this much, we had certainly better stop talking about musical discrimination.

Of course musical discrimination can only be established by a process of growth. One must start with the immediate, the crude, the imperfect. One cannot force standards of taste in a series of fixed lessons. One can only bring about their evolution through a series of revealing and commanding developmental experiences. But the point is that when tackled in these terms the job can be done. Musical responsiveness is fundamental to human nature, and it can be developed into discriminations which rise far above the gutter level. Not always, to be sure, and not with everyone. There will be resistances too stubborn, negative influences too strong to be overcome. Also we shall not seldom be defeated by our own limitations and mistakes. These, however, are among the inevitabilities which we must face. All we can ask is a policy which has in it the sure promise of reasonable success. And when we remember the universal and profound appeal of the art which we serve, we cannot deny that so much is possible.

QUESTIONS FOR DISCUSSION

1. Can musical discrimination be fostered in elementary school singing? in piano lessons? Why does this so often not happen?

2. Ought one to allow pupils to use bad music simply because they like it?

3. Ought one to be able to recognize good music as good the first time one hears it?

4. Can music specially composed for children ever be good?

5. Why is accuracy the most often used discriminative criterion in judging a performance?

6. How might sound standards of musical taste affect a person's practicing? What does this suggest as to the inter-relationship of the avenues of musical growth?

7. Could the discriminative standards for musical performance here set forth be used in judging at a contest? Are they so used? Should they be?

8. Do you think that pupils will tend to like good music and good performances if they have the chance to do so? What are some of the reasons why they may often find good music boresome?

9. Expressiveness is the basis of all excellence in music. Consider, discuss, and explain this statement.

10. Bring to bear the standards and criteria of musical discrimination presented in this chapter upon some actual instances of musical compositions and musical performances.

ADDITIONAL READINGS

MATHIS LUSSY. *Musical Expression.* H. W. Gray Company. (An excellent general treatment of the subject, highly recommended by Dalcroze.)

JAMES L. MURSELL and MABELLE GLENN. *The Psychology of School Music Teaching.* Silver Burdett Company, Inc., New York, 2d Ed., 1933. Chapter 10, "Expression." (This is probably the most easily available summary of the principles of expression in music, although it is a comparatively brief statement of the topic.)

CHAPTER NINE

Growth in Musical Insight

I

The fourth broad avenue of musical development is growth in musical insight. Musical insight may be defined as the capacity to identify, understand, and deal with the elements of the tonal-rhythmic pattern in terms of their intrinsic logic and their expressive values. Whereas musical awareness has to do with the cultivation of musical responsiveness through extensive experience, musical insight has to do with its cultivation through intensive experience.

There are several respects in which this definition needs to be amplified and explained.

1 When we speak of identifying and understanding the constitutive elements of music, it is necessary to point out emphatically that the process involved is not primarily intellectual in the abstract sense. A visual artist develops a very fine sense of color values, which can properly be called an ability to identify or understand them, but which is essentially a matter of perception and imagery. In everyday life we identify and understand our friends in terms of direct experience, whether or not we superimpose elaborate verbal analyses and explanations. So too in music one must be able to identify and understand melodic patterns, harmonic sequences, rhythmic shapes, tonality relationships, and so forth in terms of direct aural experience if one is to have anything which can be called musical insight, although to be sure symbols and rules may help.

2 In these processes of identification and understanding both logic and expressiveness are involved. A great deal of work in so-called ear training and theory emphasizes only the logic of tone. Children are taught to identify intervals, and to feel the logic of scale passages and arpeggio passages. Older learners are taught to identify triads, discords, and so forth, and to sense the logic of part-writing, resolution, chord sequence, and melodic juxtaposition. Really

to do these things "by ear" is certainly much better than trying to do them by way of verbal symbols and rules. Moreover the logic is really there in the music, and if it were not, music itself would be impossible. But something else is there too, and it cannot be ignored if musical insight is to be achieved. That something is expressiveness. It is not enough to recognize a skip of a minor third by sound, and to feel its downward tendency. It is also necessary to feel it as "saying something," as conveying some emotional import, some significant beauty, in a musical composition. It is not enough to recognize consecutive fifths when they occur, although this is more than a good many harmony students ever manage to do. It is also necessary to be sensitive to their expressive wrongness when they are wrong (as they sometimes are), and to their expressive rightness when they are right (as again they sometimes are). A visual artist is not only keenly sensitive to the violent clash produced when red and green are juxtaposed. He must also be keenly sensitive to the aesthetic and expressive rightness or wrongness of such a clash in different situations. Thus musical insight is, basically, aesthetic insight, and while this certainly involves responsiveness to the logic of tone, it involves responsiveness to that logic as a medium of expression.

3 Some explanation may perhaps be in order with regard to the meaning of the third item in our definition of musical insight—namely that it involves "dealing with" the musical elements in terms of logic and expression, although what is intended here seems more obvious than in the two previous cases.

A person may "deal with" the musical elements in terms of their logical and expressive values in many situations and in many ways. When a child expressively projects a vocal phrase with a feeling for its shape, he is so dealing with one of the constitutive elements of music. When a pianist plays the second movement of Beethoven's *Sonata Pathétique* with a keen sense of its unity and its rhythmic continuity as the figuration changes from dyads to triplets, he is doing the same thing. Listening to a composition in such a way that one catches at least some of its expressive components, extemporizing, composing, genuinely musical sight-singing are further examples. In all of these situations musical insight is being put to work. Its applicability is part of its very nature, and also the decisive criterion of its presence.

That musical insight is one of the most important and characteristic aspects of musical responsiveness is obvious. It is responsiveness

[193]

to music in terms of its constitutive expressive detail. This specificity is what differentiates it from other aspects of musical responsiveness. Musical awareness means responsiveness to music in and through experiences and learning which are extensive, which cover much ground, which deal with wide-ranging and various manifestations of the art. Musical discrimination indicates responsiveness expressing itself in value judgments and value differentiations. These distinctions, of course, are by no means absolute. All the aspects of musical responsiveness, and all the avenues of musical growth overlap one another and affect one another, and this, of course, is inevitable, because they are simply phases of a single integral process. The value of looking at this process from many viewpoints is that it leads to a rounded understanding, and provides the only safe and sufficient basis for planning a developmental program of music education.

Again it is perfectly clear that the promotion of growth in musical insight has an essential place in any sound scheme of music education, from the beginning onward. The reason is that no one who lacks it can be considered an adequately developed musical person, even though his love for music may be deep and sincere, and even though he may have great skill as a performer. Yet it is worth-while to state in explicit terms just what its place in the scheme is. Here a distinction must be made. Musical insight is not equivalent to what, in educational and musical discussions, is often called "musicianship." Musicianship, if the word is used in any legitimate sense at all, goes beyond musical insight. It includes musical awareness, musical initiative, musical discrimination, and musical skill as well. This at once avoids a perniciously wrong way of thinking, according to which music education has to do on the one hand with musicianship and on the other hand with skill, which are regarded as independent functions, and according to which musicianship means nothing more than competence in dealing with the musical content brought about by intensive study.

One further illuminating distinction needs to be drawn. It will be evident by this time that the study of what is called theory has specifically to do with musical insight as here defined. Now theory is often spoken of as the "grammar of music." In terms of the way of thinking here developed this is a wrong conception. Grammar has to do with structure, with logical relationships, and nothing else. But musical insight, as we have seen, means a grasp of the logical relationships of the constitutive elements of music, and of their expressive values too. Indeed it is not a case of "both" or "and," for the two

[194]

things go together. Without the musical logic there could be no expressiveness. Without expressive values, the musical logic is sterile. Thus it would be better to think of theory in particular and of musical insight in general as having to do with the rhetoric of music rather than with its grammar.

II

Musical insight must be achieved by a process of growth. That process should be inaugurated in the very earliest and simplest of musical experiences and endeavors. It should stem from the crude, the immediate, the specific, the limited. It should be, and, indeed, must be carried forward under the impulsion of purpose and will. It should move toward its ultimate culmination in systematic grasp. Let us consider more specifically some of the implications of this idea.

1 Growth in musical insight should certainly have its origins in actual, functional, meaningful musical experiences, activities, and endeavors—in playing, singing, listening, and composing. The learner should be led to analyze music that he actually enjoys and uses, so that he becomes aware of its constituent elements, their pattern, their logic, and their expressiveness. In other words, the development of musical insight turns upon a process of sequential analysis and synthesis, applied to plenty of actual music, which should be studied not only for its technical problems, but also for its aesthetic content.

There is a close parallel here with language study. Three hundred years ago, in some of the great schools of the Reformation Movement, the early study of a foreign language—usually Latin or Greek, and less usually Hebrew—was entirely grammatical. The rules and principles of the linguistic structure were taught in a purely abstract setting, with no applications at all. This made everything exceedingly difficult. Progress was very slow. For many pupils, success was virtually impossible. If our present notions about individual differences had been current, it might well have seemed to the teachers of those days that real mastery of these languages was possible only for the mentally elect. Under more recent practice it became usual to convey grammatical concepts and principles by means of a fair number of actual applications. For the most part, however, these were silly and trivial. "Balbus built his wall." "The sister of the master was kind to the slaves." "The army of the tyrant took the corn away from the citizens," and so on. This was appreciably better. Progress was still slow and uncertain, but at any rate considerably faster. A person could make a success in his work if he were only somewhat above average in intelligence, without being a genius. Still later, however, language study came to center on the use of interesting and meaningful linguistic material. Direct conversation was introduced from the first. Special reading materials, easy both in structure and vocabulary, but likely to mean something to the students and to be interesting to them, were prepared. The linguistic insights, which of course were still essential, were developed out of experiences of this kind. Once more efficiency increased and progress became faster. Moreover it began to appear that quite an ordinary person could master a foreign tongue, which after all is reasonable enough when we recall that quite a number of Greek, Roman, and Hebrew children have managed to acquire and use their esoteric media without needing an I.Q. of 125 or over to do so.

At the present time the study of musical theory has gone well beyond the first of these three stages. It does not deal with logical principles and concepts in a purely abstract setting. For the most part, however, it has not overpassed the second stage. Illustrations, applications, and exercises are used to help the learner master the concepts and practices. But they are formal, contrived, and musically and aesthetically meaningless. Most of the exercise material in conventional textbooks on theory is about on the level of meaningfulness of the following gem from a first book on French: "Have you seen the coat of your brother? No, but here is the handkerchief of my aunt." To acquire authentic musical insight by dint of such calisthenics may not be beyond the capacity of the human mind, or at least of a really superior specimen of the human mind. But it is certainly a long, doubtful, and very trying process.

Material of this purely formal and illustrative type, whether used for language study or for music study, has a fundamental and manifest defect. It lacks authentically expressive meaning. The language "says" nothing worth saying or communicating. It is simply a pattern put together to exemplify some grammatical principle or concept. Neither does the kind of so-called music either presented or concocted in the conventional course in theory "say" anything. This is its chief deficiency as a medium for engendering musical insight. The identification, understanding, and manipulation of the constitutive elements of the tonal-rhythmic pattern in terms of their intrinsic logic and their expressive values can only be developed in connection with authentically expressive music.

[196]

This, of course, implies that growth in musical insight should be promoted, not in theory courses only, but in every phase and aspect of music study. When a piano pupil is learning a new piece, he ought to study not merely its problems of motor technique, but also the constituent elements of its musical content—its melodic content, its harmonic content, its contrapuntal patterns, its rhythmic content, its architecture. Moreover he ought to study them, not merely as intellectual problems exemplifying the logic of tone, but as generators of expressive beauty. The flow of the melodies with their essential and unessential notes about the harmony, the sequence and resolution of the chords, the alterations and juxtapositions of the melodies should be attended to not simply as problems to be understood, but as factors whose proper management, both in the composition itself and in its rendition, make it an appealing work of art.

Again, when children sing a unison song by ear or with the use of the notation, or when they sing a part song, it is not only very proper but highly desirable to call their attention to the constitutive factors of the musical rhetoric. And the emphasis should be on rhetoric— that is, on expressiveness and beauty—rather than simply upon quasi-grammatical relationships. The rise and fall and onward movement of the melody, its subdivision into phrases, its further definition in terms of specific interval relationships, perhaps its organization about a key center, the steady beat combined with inter-twining fluid patterns which constitutes the rhythm should be featured not simply as grammatical considerations but as elements which are expressive in their logic and logical in their expressiveness. To sing a second part should not mean spelling out one note after another, but coming to realize how one melodic line can be wedded to others to create an organically unified and satisfying whole. It may be quite proper to stop now and then for a moment's analysis, to pull this or that con-stituent element out of the complex for the sake of clearing it up—an isolated interval, a turn of phrase, a rhythmic unit, for instance. But always the immediate and evident purpose should be to reveal more clearly and more convincingly the beauty and expressive meaning of the music, and to help the children to realize it with greater sureness and satisfaction.

Choral and instrumental rehearsals, once more, are peculiarly advantageous opportunities for developing the specific grasp of ex-pressive musical content which is the essence of musical insight. These are serious occasions, both socially, artistically, and education-ally. The endeavor clearly ought to be to make the music being studied sound beautiful. It would seem to follow, then, that the pupils should be helped to "see into" the elements of the musical rhetoric upon which beauty depends.

In all these cases the point to be observed is the use of authentically expressive music in the development of musical insight. Many other such instances and situations could readily be cited. Is it in any way implied that when the promotion of musical insight is taken over in a special course labelled "theory" the use of such music can properly be discarded? Obviously not. The use of actual "composed" music in theory classes is rather rare, but it is eminently desirable. Folk music, symphonic music, string quartet music, piano music, and so forth, can be used as admirable study material in such classes. Nor should it be regarded as extraneous "enrichment," but as an integral part of the course. To see how a harmonic concept or a contrapuntal device is applied in actual music, and to realize how it constitutes an element of expressiveness and aesthetic appeal certainly points the way towards a very effective promotion of musical insight.

2 A great deal of the promotion of musical insight should be deliberately incidental. Indeed it may be laid down, as a matter of principle, that a great deal of such work should be definitely incidental and incomplete.

A piece of music is being studied for performance. It may be a folk song to be learned by ear. It may be an art song. It may be a composition for instrumental solo, taught either in the studio or in the class. It may be an ensemble composition taken up in rehearsal. If it is being approached from the developmental point of view, that is to say for the sake of musical growth, the great essential always is that its beauties, its aesthetic content, its expressive and emotional values must be revealed and to some genuine extent realized. Its general over-all mood has been established, perhaps by listening to a recorded or "live" performance of it, perhaps by discussion and exposition, perhaps by other means, and usually by several means. Now this mood is created and projected by the tonal and rhythmic agencies and devices which the composer has employed. It turns, that is to say, on the management of a great many details of form. Some of these should always be brought to clear consciousness in the minds of the learners.

Take, for instance, Schumann's *Träumerei*. The melody line opens with a movement from the dominant to the tonic. Then the harmonic coloration moves from the tonic to the subdominant. There is no need to tell the learner in technical terms what is happening. This may or may not be done, according to his general stage of maturity and advancement. But there may well be excellent reasons for making him explicitly and clearly aware of the shifting values of the tonality and the harmony. Moreover these should primarily be presented not as intellectual problems, but as expressive agencies. The two that have been mentioned do a great deal to create the mood that Schumann intended. They are vital elements in the expressive and aesthetic content. As such the learner should be made conscious of them. He should listen to them, perhaps pull them out of context, imagine them. He should be helped to "see into" them. They are among the devices which make the composition what it is. To make the study of the work turn entirely upon its notes and its manipulative problems, is to fail to deal with either in musical or developmental terms—and indeed these two emphases really come to the same thing. *Träumerei* should be treated as an aesthetic projection, which, after all, is exactly what it is. And even a young or immature person, in studying it, should develop an insight into some of the constituent elements which make it so.

It would, however, be a great mistake to think that the study of *Träumerei* or any other piece or song must always involve a complete musical and aesthetic analysis. If one is working with a young or immature learner, a good way to accomplish nothing is to try to do too much. This may even be as bad as doing nothing at all, simply teaching the notes and the manipulations, and letting the musical content go neglected. If he gets *something* in the way of musical insight, we ought to be pretty well satisfied. If he sees, feels, learns, and comes to know some constitutive element or elements of the musical form, that is a great deal more than usually takes place. After all, there will be other pieces, other opportunities, other chances for revealing aesthetic analysis, and so we need not worry too much about the gaps in our pupil's musical insight. In the same way it would be a great mistake to approach such a study of *Träumerei* with our minds dominated by the presuppositions of systematic theory. We can find in *Träumerei* discords of various kinds, passing notes, modulations, and 'so forth. Must we refrain from calling the pupil's attention to them, and helping him to clarify them at least in auditory perception and imagery simply because such topics come rather late in the syllabi of courses in harmony? Clearly not. We are not teaching systematic harmony at all, but helping the pupil to clarify the beauties and values of a musical work. Which beauties, which values we pick out will

[199]

really not matter a great deal, so long as they are important and distinctive and determining in the work with which we are dealing, so long as they are revealing and appealing, so long as it is rewarding to clarify them. This, perhaps, will show what is meant by working for musical insight in a deliberately incomplete, unsystematic, and incidental fashion. The point that is essential is not systematic completeness at all, but vitality. It is certainly the great and disastrous lack in conventional schemes for the promotion of musical insight.

The ideas, principles, and practices which have been illustrated in connection with the study of *Träumerei* all apply, *mutatis mutandis,* to the study of any kind of music, all the way from a simple song to be learned by ear in the first-grade to a Brahms symphony in rehearsal in the senior high-school. In the first-grade song there is a falling minor third which is one of the distinctive aesthetic values of the melodic line. We may decide to feature it in the minds of the pupils. We do not tell them what it is. If we pick it out of context, we do so only for a moment. We are, at this stage, not trying to make them "minor-third-conscious" in general, but only to have them clarify an expressive musical relationship in terms of its immediate expressive value and beauty. The Brahms symphony, again, contains some striking and unusual chromatic effects. It is very unlikely that many of our orchestra members know enough to understand just how Brahms worked them out. To go into a highly technical systematic disquisition would certainly be a mistake, although these pupils can stand a good deal more in the way of abstract exposition than can first graders. But also it would be a mistake to pass these distinctive effects by without any attempt to clarify them, to have the pupils notice them, hear them, imagine them, and realize their expressive and aesthetic values.

You may be inclined to think it questionable to attack systematic treatment and complete analysis, and to indicate that in many situations it can be wrong. But there is a very definite positive reason for taking this position. The reason is that growth, as we have already seen, starts with the immediate, the concrete, the crude, the incomplete. Certainly a complete insight into every structural and expressive detail of Schumann's *Träumerei* or of the Brahms symphony is very desirable indeed. So is a logical and systematic grasp of all the tonal and rhythmic resources in the art of music. About these propositions there is no argument at all. They are self-evident and admittedly so. But the question is how to realize, how to achieve such things. There is only one way, and that is by a process of growth. If we could teach the whole range of systematic harmony, counterpoint, and form to

[200]

children in the grades, and if we could get these subjects really understood and grasped, it would be wonderful. But the children would be very different beings from what they actually are. As it is, they must grow towards systematic grasp by a multitude of experiences and learnings which are not systematic, although they have the germ of system in them. They must grow toward complete insight by a multitude of experiences which are very partial and limited but which still involve authentic insight and so always tend toward completeness. As a matter of fact, we are not doing a very successful job of teaching systematic harmony, counterpoint, and form even to conservatory students, who are relatively mature persons with a special interest. The reason is that they have not had nearly enough incidental but musically significant experiences and learnings to be able to grasp a systematic presentation of musical relationships in any but the most nominal fashion. They have been taught music. But usually they have not been taught it in a musical way. The emphasis has been manipulative, externalistic. It has not been upon aesthetic content and aesthetic values. In a word, it has not been developmental. And so, at a time of life when the fruits of musical growth should be manifesting themselves, there is very little but an arid desert. When theory teachers in the conservatory say that their students ought to be able to grasp a systematic exposition of musical content, that they ought to find such a study enriching and rewarding, they are perfectly right. But unfortunately the fact that something ought to be, does not make it so. What these teachers require could undoubtedly be done. It is possible enough. But it never will be done without a properly organized sequence of development in musical insight.

III

Musical composition can provide extraordinarily fruitful opportunities for the development of musical insight. In principle everything that has been said up to this point applies here, but the subject is so important, so interesting and so often and so grievously misunderstood that it deserves to be singled out for somewhat extensive treatment. It will be remembered that I definitely prefer to speak of musical composition rather than of "creative work" because the term involves no hedging or implied apologies, but says exactly what is meant, namely the projection of original music. This should undoubtedly be fostered all along the line—in the elementary-school, in general music courses, through informal curricular organizations, in applied music classes if possible, certainly in connection with theory, and indeed wherever opportunity offers.

The only intelligent foundation for practical procedures here is a clear understanding of the process of musical composition itself. This can be very simply stated. To compose music is to translate a way of feeling into an expressive pattern of tone and rhythm. It is to create a tonal poem. Here lies its very essence, all the way from its simplest to its most august manifestations. This is precisely what every composer does. One might say that composition is the completest of all musical acts, because it involves the use of all musical resources for an expressive purpose. In this lies its developmental value and its educational importance. The greatest composers have educated themselves musically in and through the act of composition. The youngest of children can be educated musically in and through the same act.

Now this idea is very rich in implications, and the implications are stringent. By way of bringing them out, let us consider the situation in which poetry is used as the starting point for child composition.[1]

1 The nature of the problem is evident. On the one hand there is the poem. This is a work of art very similar to music, except for its use of words and definite images. It uses certain resources to project emotional and aesthetic values. These values may be simple, and for children they must be; but they must be authentic, and they can be because authentic beauty can be simple. But a mere jingle will not do. The poem must appeal. The poem must charm. It must have beauty living and breathing in it. The children must feel this appeal, this charm, and must seek to release this music. The teacher's business is to encourage and help them to do it. So much is imperative. If it is not fulfilled, the whole value of the act is lost, and it had better not even be attempted.

To any teacher who thinks that this would be a very difficult thing to do I will make two points in reply. First, it is an exceedingly delightful and stimulating thing to do. Surely it is a far greater pleasure to help children to discover in its fullness and freshness, a beauty and a charm to which one responds oneself, than to labor through the steps of any formal lesson. Also one can be well assured that it is a far better thing to do. So much for my first point.

My second point is this. It is not nearly so difficult as it looks.

[1]This is not the only possible starting point, nor always the best one, but it is often used.

What it requires is something far other than pedagogical techniques. It requires that the teacher educate her own heart to be responsive to the power of poetic beauty. To try to make this more specific I have included in Appendix III several aesthetic critiques of poems, and also a reference to recorded readings of poetry. These, as I am well aware, are sophisticated beyond the level of children. But the same idea applies at all levels. Read the poem as a work of art. Have the children read the poem as a work of art. Feel its values, its emotional meaning yourself. Help them to feel it too. It must be dwelt upon, responded to, and loved. The music which comes from it must flower out of this response, this love, or the whole business is no good. All this, I repeat, is far easier than it seems. There is no difficulty in loving a poem. It is a very natural thing to do. And the music must blossom out of this love, and express its values. The act of composition is a magic which transforms what one feels in a poem into the medium of tone and rhythm.

2 Quite probably it will be necessary, at any rate at first, to help the children to pick out some one or other of the constitutive expressive elements of the poem as specific starting points. To see what those elements are you are again referred to the expository critiques in Appendix III. But some words of explicit advice may also be in order.

Beware of confining yourself to the metrical scansion of the poem. This is the rhythmic spine of the work, just as the beat is the rhythmic spine of a piece of music. But in and of itself it is not an independent expressive element. For instance, the first line of stanza four of Keats' *Ode to a Grecian Urn* scans as follows:

"Who are | these com|ing to | the sac|rifice?"

But it is actually felt somewhat as follows:

"Who are these || coming to the sacrifice?

Or again, examine the analysis of the famous *Song to Celia* presented in Appendix III, in which a musical pulse in 3/4 measures is set up for a line scanning into four prosodic feet.

Whatever element you catch and pull out, it must be *expressive*, not mathematical or mechanical. It may be the fluid sequence of the expressive rhythm; it may be the rise and fall of the voice in the speech tunes; it may be the speeding up and the slowing down; it may be the sheer sound of the words; it may be some suggestion still more evanescent, a hint of color, or light, or motion.[1] If you want to indicate the expressive rhythm by some sort of symbolism, this may have its uses.[2] The point, of course, is to give the children something to get hold of, something with which to make a start. But be sure that what they do get hold of is the right thing, and a true lead, and not the wrong thing and a false lead. Any genuine expressive element in the poem is the right thing, or one of them. Any merely mechanical or arithmetical component is the wrong thing, or one of them, and a false lead.

3 As to the tonal, and specifically the melodic resources of the children, the word of wisdom is this: *Do not worry!* Children have far more music in their systems than some teachers want to give them credit for. Some excellent people insist that "creative work" (sic!) should not be undertaken before the fourth-grade, because only by then will the pupils have a sufficient stock of phrase patterns. Indeed, I myself have, in times past, been guilty of advocating this very thing, an error which I now freely confess. The argument simply will not hold water. For one thing, the children have certainly experienced hundreds of times as much music outside the classroom as in it. For another thing, creative projection does not mean the fishing out of memorized stereotypes, like unfortunate trout from an artificial fish-pond. Where the creative mind gets its material is always a source of wonderment, not only to others, but often to that mind itself. Once the impulse is released, usable stuff is grabbed from anywhere and everywhere out of the psychic ether, moulded to a purpose, and

[1]Consider the wonderful plangent effect, so suggestive of tonal values, of the word "desolate" in the stanza just referred to from the *Ode to a Grecian Urn*, which reads as follows:

> Who are these coming to the sacrifice?
> To what green altar, O mysterious priest,
> Lead'st thou that heifer lowing to the skies,
> And all her silken flanks with garlands drest?
> What little town by river or sea-shore,
> Or mountain-built with peaceful citadel,
>   Is emptied of its folk this pious morn?
> And, little town, thy streets for evermore
> Will silent be; and not a soul, to tell
>   Why thou art desolate, can e'er return.

Poems of this caliber, to be sure, are not usually selected, but the instance holds.

[2]Such a device will be found in *A New Approach to Poetry*, by Chapin and Thomas, to which reference is made at the close of this chapter.

transformed. One sees this in writing and in painting, and it is undoubtedly so in music. One finds it not only in persons of genius, but in quite ordinary individuals as well. It is how the process has to work. So the idea that children must be furnished forth with certain ready-made stereotypes before they can compose is psychologically false.

More than this, it indicates an educational approach that is basically unsound. When certain music teachers say that it is "impractical" to introduce creative work before the fourth grade because a number of phrase patterns must be learned first, and that the thing cannot be done, the "thing" they have in mind is the fitting together of tonal jig-saw puzzles. But this is not musical composition at all, but mechanical manipulation, and it has no significant place in music education. A scheme of music education which centers on building up a set repertoire of tonal patterns is wrongly oriented from the ground up, and when so-called, or rather miscalled "creative work" is introduced into the scheme, the fault becomes glaring. The promotion of musical insight precisely does not mean the building up of a set tonal vocabulary. It means fostering a growing apprehension of the constitutive beauties of music wherever they appear. This is one of the things that class work ought to do for children, in contradistinction to the unguided extensive musical experiences that they have in daily life. Musical insight so fostered blossoms out very naturally into expression by way of composition. When musical composition is so conceived it becomes entirely "practical" not merely in the fourth grade, but right down into the nursery school. And as for tonal resources, it has been found that the expressive musicmaking of very small children contains in embryo a surprising number of the compositional techniques of mature composers—rhythmic variation, sequential progression, adaptations of rhythmic progressions to verbal forms and vice versa, recurrent refrains and primitive rondo forms, varying instrumentation, transfer of rhythms from one instrument to another, and so forth.[1] It is through such activities that genuine musical insight both expresses itself and is strongly fostered. But all such values are lost if musical composition is treated as the mere manipulation of stereotypes. Such work may not be "practical" before the fourth grade, and it is not worth doing anywhere.

[1]See Gladys E. Moorehead and Donald Pond, *Music of Young Children: II. General Observations*, p. 18. Pillsbury Foundation for the Advancement of Music Education, Santa Barbara, California, 1941.

4 An interesting and important question here has to do with the revision of the creative efforts of children. Should the first projection always be taken as final and satisfactory, no matter what it is? The answer is no. But it is always very important to understand the role of revision in the creative process. That process is by no means a mere arbitrary outpouring, but a giving of shape to emotional intimations. It is in itself a process of growth, and revision is always an affair of refining and making more explicit and effective those meanings and values at first imperfectly apprehended.

The whole case is contained in the illustration already given of the shaping up over a three-day period of the rhythmic refrain:

"You better watch out for your whole life!"

These little children were functioning exactly as the greatest creative artists function. They were evoking form out of the formless. That is how every art work, from the humblest to the most magnificent, is brought to birth. And when children compose music they are bringing a work of art to birth, or the whole affair is dust and ashes. So revision should always consist of helping the children to try to say better what they want to say. To guide this process is an exceedingly delicate matter, even with mature learners, for the tender plant can easily be killed. But it is important just the same. The child's growth in musical insight turns, at least in part, in a growing power of self-criticism, and the quest for expressive perfection is something to be treated always with profound respect. But revision should always be positive, not negative. The child's expressive idea is a living thing, and the endeavor should be to help it to grow into the most perfect shape possible.

5 It will be at once apparent that this whole indicated approach and treatment is as different as cheese from chalk from many conventional practices in so-called creative music. A crassly manufactured and sapless piece of verbiage, miscalled a poem, is set up. Then it is scanned. It is pretty sure to scan according to rule, this superficial feature being about its only resemblance to a real poem. Then the children are requested to ransack the filing-systems of their memories for a phrase which will fit the scansion of the first line. Then they "decide," not without some slight compulsion, to have a different kind of phrase-pattern for the second line, and this one is fumbled for and produced. So the process of carpentry goes on to its grim finale. The alleged poem, as the ghastly expression has it, is

[206]

"set to music." At least something that looks like a poem has been treated very firmly, indeed, until it has gotten well crammed into a Procrustean pattern which may or may not be music, but at least has notes. No doubt this is easy to do. But why do it? To call such assembly-line proceedings "creative music" or musical composition is nothing but a monstrous travesty.

6 In this discussion I have particularly emphasized musical composition which centers on the use of poetry. I wish to make it quite clear—and the point has already been mentioned—that this is by no manner of means the only approach. With very little children, for instance, it may be unsuitable, and instead of setting up such definite suggestions it may be much better to encourage a natural spontaneity. Also the composing of children and young people need not be limited to songs. But the universal values of this activity are well exemplified in the special illustrated procedure here chosen. Here we have an act which involves and reveals the whole essence of the art of music, and does so with extraordinary intimacy and persuasiveness. Its focus is sensitiveness to beauty and to emotional appeal and meaning. It reveals musical resources for what they are, namely resources of expressiveness. Whether verbal poetry or not, the act of musical composition is always an act of tonal poetizing. This is the heart of its developmental value, and the reason why it can do so much to promote authentic and vital musical insight.

Such endeavors and adventurings in musical composition should be begun at the earliest levels and continued all along the line. To be sure, the resources of the young composers will at first be limited. Also as they try their hands at more ambitious enterprises they will make the kind of mistakes which cause theorists to grit their teeth. It does not matter, so long as living growth is going on. The important thing is to encourage and help the pupils to try their musical wings. Those who object to such work because mistakes are sure to occur may be reminded that one can be so afraid of mistakes that one makes success impossible. Or they may be reminded of the parable of the wheat and the tares. No one wants mistakes, but every sensible person welcomes ambitious and even overconfident endeavor. That is the way people learn and grow, the way they develop into something. If work of this kind is continued the time will come when mistakes will fall away as the chrysalis falls away from the larva, and the outcome of musical growth stands revealed.

IV

The study of formal musical theory is a beautiful and revealing example of some of the most basic issues in the psychology of mental development. Its values, limitations, and problems only become understandable in terms of such pyschology. Mental growth, as we have seen, is a movement from the crude toward the precise, from the concrete toward the abstract, from the immediate toward the universal, from the vague toward the exact. Now musical theory is an abstract body of doctrine involving general or universal principles which convey definite and precise meanings. Thus, clearly, it belongs at the top level of the developmental sequence.

This idea has many important and interesting implications.

1 We must never think of the courses in theory as the place in the music curriculum where the teaching of musical insight ought to begin. Rather those courses are the place in the curriculum where a great mass of still somewhat inchoate and undeveloped musical insight is brought together, shaped up, and rationalized. It is precisely the neglect of this vital consideration that explains the weakness, even the futility of many courses in this field. To try to begin a developmental sequence with precision, definiteness, abstractness, and universal principles is quite hopeless. Such things are ultimate outcomes, not starting points. When we try to start with them what happens is that we never get started at all. The legal experts of the emperor Justinian did not invent out of their heads the whole *corpus* of Roman law. Indeed they could not possibly have done so. They pulled together and codified a vast body of more or less incoherent and imperfectly understood legal doctrine and practice. In the same way musical theory is a codification of musical experience. But such a codification is futile unless there is something to codify.

Thus it is that when theory teachers disparage and discourage attempts at composition because they are bungling and limited, or the musical analysis of pieces which students hear or learn to play because it is incomplete, incidental, and sometimes even incorrect, they are cutting the ground from under their own feet. Many of them fail to realize how much genuine musical maturity their work presupposes. They recognize its importance, which it has beyond all doubt. But they provide a pabulum suitable to persons musically almost grown-up, and then feel disconcerted when it is regurgitated by the musical babes in arms with whom they are really dealing. To

[208]

be an acrobat with one's fingers, or arms, or lips, or larynx does not make one a musically mature person. Such appearances are extremely deceptive. So theory teachers who know where their own interests and the true values of their subject lie will most certainly work in season and out of season for a genuinely developmental scheme of music education from the earliest years on. This, indeed, is their only ultimate hope.

2 To what extent and in what way theory courses should be, or indeed can be reorganized to meet psychological and developmental realities is very much of a question. In order to arrive at an intelligent answer, it is necessary to be quite clear about the nature of the problem.

The difficulty centers in the systematic, abstract, formal character of the study of theory as ordinarily conducted. There is no objection to systematic, abstract, formal study as such. Indeed, quite the contrary. For those who have already achieved a high level of development it is exceedingly beneficial. Some of the greatest composers, including Rimsky-Korsakoff, Tchaikovsky, Schubert, and Beethoven, undertook the most drastic, laborious, and abstract kind of work, going far beyond anything any school of music could conceivably require. They worked out hundreds of exercises in strict counterpoint, copied the music of other composers again and again, and so forth. For them such arduous discipline was repaying and fruitful. It extended their flexible command of musical resources, and contributed something they knew to be essential to their musical growth. I know of other musicians, of lesser caliber but of great maturity, who have benefited by similar work, voluntarily undertaken. But what for such persons is beneficial will almost certainly be stultifying and meaningless for those who are relatively immature. The reason is contained in our previous discussions of mental growth. Systematic study in music, as in all other fields, necessarily presupposes maturity, and cannot be repaying without it. For the immature person it is not an enlightening traffic with realities, but a mere manipulation of symbols, rules, and empty concepts.

This is why the mere denaturing or watering down of conventional theory, without any essential change of content or approach is not likely to meet the situation. There are a good many such plans more or less in operation. In some schools of music the study of theory means no more than diatonic harmony up to and including the dominant seventh. Also some textbook writers and teachers have tried

[209]

to convey the content of simple harmony in terms of some sort of game, which of course is nothing but sugar coating. Theory in the high school, again, often means merely a simplified and limited diatonic harmony systematically presented. But the trouble with all such plans is that they defeat the real purpose of systematization, which is precisely the achievement of a comprehensive, complete, organized grasp of musical resources and of the musical rhetoric in all its aspects. Unless this can be achieved, the whole affair becomes pointless. If we are going to be systematic at all, we had better make a thorough job of it.

Another attempt at reformation and adjustment turns upon changing the order of topics in systematic theory. To any student of educational psychology this looks like an old story, for the same thing has been done in a great many subjects, and without appreciable advantage. It is perfectly true that the conventional order of topics in theory is in no way sacrosanct. There is no reason why all the triads and their inversions must be studied before taking up the sevenths. There is no reason why the whole gamut of diatonic harmony must be covered before chromaticism is introduced. There is no reason why contrapuntal problems cannot be introduced much earlier than is usual, or why they must always be approached by way of strict counterpoint. Also, it is quite true that the order of topics as set up in conventional textbooks on theory does not correspond to the frequency of chords as they are used in music, though what relevance this has to learning is none too clear. Theory, like any other systematic subject, can be internally rearranged in numerous patterns and sequences, but how much good this is likely to do remains an open question. Certainly it cannot resolve the basic difficulty, which is that we have on our hands a subject well suited to the mature person, while we are actually dealing with the musically immature.

The constructive proposal would seem to be to organize a type of music study midway between the purely incidental and the purely systematic. Whether it should be designated as theory or not does not matter a great deal, except in so far as names have power. After all, we are dealing with students who, while their musical insights are undeveloped, have pretty well reached the age of young adulthood, who have usually had considerable musical experience of a kind, and whose musical interests and aspirations are strong and definite. This is a very different thing from dealing with children, although it is also a very different thing from dealing with musically mature persons. Such students could probably benefit very much from an explicit and organized consideration of the musical insights involved in the work they are doing—that is, in the music they are studying for performance, or in connection with appreciation and history. In fact such a study of theory, if such it is to be called, would verge toward what is ordinarily thought of as general music, though much more intensively conducted and much more explicitly focalized on musical insight than the usual general music course. To be sure, the systematic sequence of topics would have to be abandoned, since the work would turn on the direct study of musical instances, and would have to deal with whatever musical content happened to be involved. Also student composition would probably be encouraged in such work, because of the enlightenment that it can bring, and the fetish of formal correctness would have to go by the board. Such a study would not consist of denatured or rearranged systematic theory. Moreover it would not fill the place or realize the values of systematic theory, which to repeat are genuine and incontestable. But it might be well suited to the actual developmental level of a great many students. And if it did not give them all that could be desired, it would at least provide something better than the dust and dry bones of premature systematization for which their minds are palpably unready.

V

Workers in music education need to understand much more clearly than they usually do the importance and the true place of verbal and arithmetical symbols and of visualization in connection with the development of musical insight. Musical practice has developed a very remarkable symbolic mechanism, including various systems of syllabification, the designation of notes and chords by various types of names and numbers, and of course the notation itself. How remarkable, how valuable all this is one can see by contrasting music with the dance, where only rudimentary beginnings of anything of the kind exist. The influence of this apparatus upon the art of music is enormous, and although it involves the constant danger of manipulating tone by abstract analysis and visual plotting instead of by direct perception and imagery, it has immense and essential values.

But the psychological significance and the proper educational uses of this apparatus are persistently misunderstood. This is due to the prevailing externalism of music education at all levels. The chief point of teaching the symbols of the notation, the syllables, the numbers, and so forth is usually thought to be the development of a certain kind of skill, namely the ability to read with facility and accuracy. This, however, is a profound mistake. *The study of the symbolic apparatus should in the first instance be pointed to the development, not of musical skill, but of musical insight.* Reading itself, indeed, should be considered not as a sheer skill or knack, but as a manifestation of "musicianship."

Musical symbols are of three kinds, direct, intermediate, and indirect. The pattern of notes on the staff is a direct symbolic arrangement. It shows the rise and fall of the pitch, and so the arrangement looks more or less the way the music sounds. Clefs are intermediate symbols. They do not directly represent the sound of the music, but they designate the meanings of the lines and spaces. Their function is to bring about a visual orientation to the score, to show a person how to look at it. Time signatures and measure bars also belong in the intermediate category, since once more they do not directly represent the sound of the music, or transcribe it immediately into a visual medium, although they do show one how to look at the score. Key signatures, accidentals, and durational symbols (that is, note lengths and rests), in contrast to the foregoing, are indirect or conventional. Then of course there are the subsidiary symbols, such as slurs, staccati designations, tempo indications, and the like, which are usually, though not always, conventional rather than direct. This classification of musical symbols into three types based on their psychological functions is of great importance for an intelligent understanding and treatment of them.

By all means the outstandingly important consideration about this whole apparatus is that it is capable of giving us, within certain limits, a direct picturization of certain crucial elements in the tonal pattern. It enables a person, within limits, directly to see what he hears or images. This is the really great discovery. Indeed it is so great, so essentially "right," that we hardly think of it as a discovery at all, unless we begin to wonder how much could have been handled if it had never been made. This, beyond a doubt, is the point at which the symbolism makes its first natural contact with musical development. Little children, very early, should begin to see what they hear, to see what they image, to see what they sing. It is as simple as that! At first it is not necessary to use the standard notational symbols exclusively or even at all. What is wanted is simply the process of visualization, which is the very heart of the symbolism, and it should be developed with just as few confusing irrelevencies as possible. The use of posters on which children can pin little cut-out figures representing the notes, the drawing of curves made to parallel the melodic pattern, and suchlike simple devices are what one thinks desirable. They feature direct visual representation, and they eliminate everything else. When it comes to durational values, two possibilities exist. The different note lengths can be represented by different cut-out figures, which are *ad hoc* conventional symbols, or by the proportional spacing out of the figures or the curves, which is a direct symbolization. There is no reason why both cannot be used. The purpose in using such symbols is always to establish controls by way of musical insight, to enable children to realize, to hear, to image what they are doing by seeing it. Rhythmic accentuation, too, can be directly represented by pinning a larger or differently colored cut-out figure on the strong beat, by a thickening of the representational curve, by drawing short vertical lines through it, and so forth.

When the staff notation itself is introduced it is important to understand that new psychological processes come into operation. The visual representation of the pitch line becomes more precise, because of the use of a fixed system of co-ordinates. But new types of symbols are involved, and these present both difficulties and opportunities. The designation of the beat ceases to be direct, and becomes indirect. Probably one reason for the very common ailment of defective rhythmic development is due to the fact that teachers have not realized that there is a problem here. The child is challenged, not to see what he hears and feels, but to understand what he is supposed to hear and feel and deliver when it is wrapped up and conveyed in a quasi-mathematical and partly indirect symbolism. This is much more of a problem than is ordinarily recognized, and the usual outcome is that the child fails to understand, so that the time symbols are learned and manipulated for their own sake, without clarifying and supporting a direct rhythmic awareness. The answer, of course, is to postpone the use of the intermediate symbolism, to emphasize the rhythmic component by physical movement and by attention to it in singing and listening, and to support it by some kind of "homemade" symbolism as simple and direct as possible.

When it comes to the indirect symbolism, particularly key designations, everything becomes much more doubtful and difficult. Direct visualization can certainly mean something to children in terms of singing experience. It can shape up their musical insights by showing them more clearly what they are doing, and so enabling them to do it with more awareness and satisfaction. The same is probably, though not so certainly, true with the intermediate symbolism. But to go beyond this point without the experience of instrumental performance is a very dubious undertaking, and in all likelihood an impossible one. If we want to develop children's insights into key relationships and tonality relationships, it is almost surely necessary to have them play instruments. This, of course, is one of the arguments for simple instrumental experience in the grades. Such work may not be, in the literal sense, a direct preparation for instrumental study proper. In fact, children and older persons also should have experience with many media of musical performance with the least possible emphasis on technique, because of what it can do to musical insight. One way to make such work repaying is to connect it with the symbolism of the score, which should be thoughtfully examined and understood for the sake of high-lighting musical relationships.

The movable do system as developed by John Curwen involved among other things an attempt to deal with tonality realtionships in terms of direct symbolism. Curwen continually insisted that the syllables should always be used to bring out what he called "the mental effect," that is, the tonality trends and relationships of the music. Also he presented a scheme of hand-signs, associated with the syllables, intended directly to represent these trends—the upward tendency of the leading tone, the falling effect of the mediant, the trend of the dominant towards the tonic, the finality effect of the tonic, and so forth. He argues again and again that the hand-signs and the syllables should be used for this purpose. However, in our present-day practice in music education, this advice has been totally ignored, or almost so. The syllables are used as singable substitutes for note names, although they were intended to mean considerably more. Perhaps what Curwen advocated really cannot be done. Perhaps we cannot in any case or by any means develop an insight into tonality trends and key relationships with children in a setting of song. In any case it is undoubtedly true that the use of instrumental resources and experiences which were not available to Curwen can make all this far more feasible.

The clef symbols involve psychological and pedagogical issues of great interest. A clef, as we have seen, establishes a visual, and in fact a behavioral orientation. It keys a whole pattern of looking, thinking, understanding, and acting. It gives determinate shape and determinate meaning to an entire intricate and far-reaching configuration, just as a strong foundational line or mass can give shape to an entire picture. Quite probably the clef signs need to be supported by, and developed in, a context of instrumental experience, but their very interesting and striking psychological function needs to be understood. To even an elementary piano pupil the second line in the treble staff *looks* like G, the third space *looks* like C, and so on, and he behaves and acts in terms of these meanings. What neither he nor his teacher ordinarily realize is that all such interpretations, which seem so immediate and natural, are determined by an imposed visual attitude or slant, the *clou* of which is the clef sign. Since in the minds of most teachers the only point in the mastery of the notation is the ability to read, they never even think of using any clef orientations other than those required by the particular medium being studied,— piano, wood-wind, or what not. But if we say that the chief aim in the study of the symbolism should be musical development, or more specifically the development of musical insight, then it may be admirable practice to have the student familiarize himself with all the clefs. To do so would call, presumably though not essentially, for rudimentary experience in several media. It does not, of course, belong at the elementary level, but neither should it be considered as an exemplification of fabulous virtuosity. Judging from experience in other fields, it could be done far more easily than might be imagined, for visual orientations establish themselves very quickly, and have a most remarkable and pervasive effect upon action. Such a thing could be done incidentally and unsystematically at first, and perhaps brought to a head in the sort of intermediate theory course that I have tried to shadow forth. It would at once relieve transposition of most of its terrors, for these depend very largely on a rigid visual orientatior. And it would exemplify one use of the symbolism for its proper fundamental purpose, namely the development of flexible and effective musical insight.

There is one essential condition that under-runs everything that has just been proposed. The symbolism must always be taught in an authentic, rich, and varied musical setting. The direct, the intermediate, and the indirect symbols should always be used for the explication of musical values that are actually perceived, imaged, and felt. Abstract drills, here as everywhere else, are analytic procedures which have a certain usefulness to make things clear, but only an occasional and incidental one. They should never be regarded as staple procedures for the building of certain habits. It is not the symbolism which we should be trying to teach, but musical insight. The symbols can help greatly in the development of musical insight, for the reason that they can pull out and call attention to the constitutive elements of the tonal-rhythmic pattern. But they should always be taught and learned in the closest application to that pattern.

[215]

Children, and older students too, should be helped to see the music that they listen to, music that they sing and play, music that they image, in symbolic representations that are partly direct, partly intermediate, partly indirect. Such seeing should always be for the purpose of sharpening up auditory perception and imagery, and of more clearly realizing the beauties that the music contains, so that it can be better enjoyed and better delivered. It should be for the purpose of developing musical insight in the first place, rather than musical skill.

This analysis pretty well establishes our attitude towards the grand problem of reading which haunts all discussions of elementary music education. Its obvious suggestion is that this problem is quite wrongly conceived. What we ought to be thinking of and working for is not reading as such, but musical insight, for the promotion of which the symbolism is a very valuable instrumentality. In a direct sense it does not matter very much how many of the symbols children have learned by the time they get to the sixth-grade. What does matter is what happens to these children's musical insights. If it were possible to teach the whole gamut of the musical symbolism, including all the keys and all the clefs, and to teach it in such a way that all the musical meanings of the symbolism were effectively realized, this no doubt would be ideal. But it is not possible. It follows from this that we should prefer to do a few things well—that is, in terms of their real psychological function and purpose—than a great many things badly and externalistically. Simple informal visual representations of the pitch line and the phrase may be all that can be managed, but at least it is something, and until we are sure of having learned this much it is risky to rush on to other matters. Direct notational symbols should not be unattainable, and very often some of the clef orientations and the indirect symbolizations of tonality can be made meaningful in a musical sense. By all means we should try to go as far as we can; but to try to go too far is to risk frustration in everything. To set up in a course of study a plan for teaching a whole host of musical symbols without giving time and attention to developing their relevance to musical experience is sheer externalism. For, to repeat once again, the value of the symbols turns upon their instrumental use for the development of musical insight.

To some this may seem to shelve or dodge the whole problem of reading as a desirable skill. It is known that while language reading is, in one of its aspects, a sheer skill, it turns much more importantly upon comprehension. The vital question is not merely how fast a person reads, although this matters to some extent, but rather how well he reads, that is, how understandingly. Language reading is very far from being a mere knack. It is a complicated and profound psychological process, essentially a process of reasoning, or interpreting, or comprehending. The same is true, without a doubt, of music reading. What is proposed here is the development, in connection with the symbolism, of real and defined musical comprehension, real and defined musical insight. If this is done, the problem of facile reading is nine-tenths solved, and a great many other values are attained as well.

This whole discussion may be rounded off by referring to the extraordinary impediments to musical development encountered by blind students. The great and central difficulty is that the Braille notation does not yield any kind of direct musical symbolism. The musical patterns are not directly represented, but only indirectly conveyed. This makes it difficult to read, and difficult to remember. But above all, one of the most valuable supports of an evolving musical insight is missing. No one who has had contact with such students can doubt how much visualization can contribute to certain essential phases of musical growth, or that seeing what one hears is enormously helpful in coming to be able to hear it well.

QUESTIONS FOR DISCUSSION

1. What changes in organization, content, and presentation would be involved in the teaching of theory if it were regarded as musical rhetoric rather than musical grammar?

2. How is ear training related to growth in musical insight?

3. Just what do you understand by the term "musicianship"? At what stage in a person's musical education should it begin to be cultivated?

4. Should there be any essential difference in the process of musical composition as exemplified by beginners and by mature artists?

5. How do you account for the fact that children and older persons, when encouraged and helped to compose, will be able to use many musical patterns which have never been taught to them? What is its educational significance?

6. What other starting points for composition besides poetry can you suggest? Why is the use of poetry so specially revealing as to the nature of musical composition?

7. Why are the revision, or watering down, or sugar coating of systematic theory not likely to be constructive solutions to the problem of presenting this subject? How do they differ psychologically from the solution proposed in the chapter?

8. Devise a very simple visual symbolism that might assist the musical insight of young children dealing with a rhythm band piece, or a song to be learned by ear, or a little composition of their own.

9. Show that musical insight is the only sound basis of reading skill.

10. In the light of this chapter, discuss the inter-relationships of musical awareness, musical discrimination, and musical insight.

ADDITIONAL READINGS

WALTER ENGELMANN. "Beethoven and the Creative Law of Symphonic Art," *Musical Quarterly*, 1937, Vol. 23, pp. 56–63. (Seems remote from teaching children, but can give an authentic insight into the process of composition and the nature of musical insight.)

ADELE T. KATZ. "Heinrich Schenker's Method of Analysis," *Musical Quarterly*, 1935, Vol. 21, pp. 311–329. (Gives an account of the most thoroughgoing revision of musical theory. Not easy reading, but an excellent source for those who wish to understand the Schenker system.)

JAMES L. MURSELL. *The Psychology of Music.* W. W. Norton and Company, Inc., New York, 1937. Chapter 8, "The Psychology of Musical Composition." (Deals comprehensively with composition at a high level, but the ideas are applicable at all levels.)

JAMES L. MURSELL and MABELLE GLENN. *The Psychology of School Music Teaching.* Silver Burdett Company, Inc., New York, 2d Ed., 1933. Chapter 6, "Ear Training"; chapter 7, "Rhythmic Training." (These chapters assemble much psychological material bearing upon musical insight.)

CHAPTER TEN

Growth in Musical Skill

I

The fifth broad avenue of musical development is growth in musical skill. In all music education the problem of skill is crucial. So there is nothing in this whole field concerning which it is more important to establish an intelligent attitude and a proper way of thinking.

In the minds of some music teachers, skill is the supreme essential, the one indispensable outcome of worth-while music study. The ideal which dominates all their work is that of the technically well-equipped performer. They tend to go on the assumption that if only a person will achieve this much, all other things musical will be added unto him. Unfortunately this is very far from true. There are a great many skilled instrumentalists and vocalists whose musical awareness is narrow, whose musical initiatives are feeble, whose musical taste is deplorable, and whose musical insights are virtually nonexistent.

Then there are those who, while admitting that there are other possible values in music study besides the achievement of skill, feel that the demands of technique are so exacting that virtually nothing else can be attained or hoped for. This attitude manifests itself at all levels. It appears in the elementary-school supervisor who believes that the grade-school program should stress nothing but reading, in the high-school instrumental director who feels that he must concentrate on nothing but the fairly competent performance of a few numbers because even this is so hard to attain, in the studio teacher or the conservatory teacher who makes a halfhearted genuflection in the direction of work in theory and history, but in effect considers them interruptions to the real business of musical training.

Then, on the other hand, there are those who would set up programs of music education which place almost no emphasis at all upon skill. They insist that music has a rich cultural content, that it is inspiring and stimulating, that it is a force making for social values and the elevation of morale, that it is enjoyed by many and could be enjoyed by more. And they infer that the development of skill should have but little place in the content of a general program of music education. The reason they give is precisely the same as that offered by those who would concentrate on nothing else, namely that musical skill is very difficult and its acquisition very time-consuming.

Now there is a real element of truth in each one of these contentions. Musical skill is extremely important—so important that no one lacking it can be considered a well-rounded musical person. It is difficult to acquire, though as we shall see, not nearly so difficult as many people think, or as it is needlessly made by improper pedagogical treatment. Also there are a great many values in music and in music study which are not directly related to it. So the problem is to shape up an approach to the development of skill in music education which will do justice to all these three propositions instead of recognizing one of them and conveniently ignoring the others. How can we teach skill so that it will really be attained, and still keep a proper balance of values? That is the essential question.

The very heart of the answer lies in our working conception of the nature of musical skill, or musical technique. Externalistically considered, it is simply agility, or dexterity, and nothing more. Technique then means legèrdemain pure and simple. It has no more essential relation to musical responsiveness than have stenotype operating or juggling. Moreover when this conception is translated into pedagogical procedures, it makes difficulties instead of resolving them, for an externalistic approach to technique is inefficient from the standpoint of getting sheer technical results. But there is an entirely different, a sharply contrasting conception. According to this, *technique is the ability to project an intended musical effect in a given medium.* This is by all means the correct point of view. It is aesthetically sound, because no artistic technique is an end in itself, and cannot be understood or considered apart from the aesthetic content it is intended to realize. It is psychologically sound, because from a psychological point of view a skill of any kind is not merely a matter of quick and accurate movement, but rather the efficient motor realization of a meaningful purpose. It is pedagogically sound, because this way of approach minimizes difficulties and saves time and effort. And it characteristically expresses the developmental viewpoint, in terms of which musical skill must stem from and be controlled by musical responsiveness, and the development of skill must be at the same time the development, refinement, deepening, and sharpening up of musical responsiveness.

[220]

II

In dealing with skill there are two basic problems, the problem of control, and the problem of the action-pattern, that is, the pattern of movement needed to produce the desired result. The first of these, which we are now to consider, is by far the more usually overlooked. But it is of crucial importance.

In all musical technique the control should reside in the musical intention, the musical conception to be realized. In attacking a technical problem, either in individual or group work, the very first question is this: Is there a dominating musical conception? That conception cannot usually be clear at the start, but it should always be present and emerging into clarity. If this is not so, technical practice cannot be rightly oriented. Here is another application of the principle already stated: *Always go back to the music.*

I have watched a piano student labor, for what must have come altogether to many hours, on a couple of measure in Schumann's *Papillons.* It was one of those passages all too familiar to all of us who have studied music. When everything else had been pretty well mastered, it stubbornly refused to "come clean." The student pulled it out of context and worked on it in isolation. For a moment it would seem to have arrived, but the moment he put it back into setting, it was lost. He put the work away for a month, returned to it, and was defeated. He put it away for another month, and another. He worked at special technical exercises that seemed likely to help. He tried to strengthen certain muscles that seemed weak. He tried to analyze and reorganize the action-pattern. Then, following what was almost a casual suggestion, he realized that the passage consisted of the arpeggio of the E flat major triad with interpolated notes, that it was distributed in a distinctive fashion on the beat, and that it called for a crescendo and diminuendo in its expressive delivery. He embodied these considerations in his practicing, and the difficulty cleared up with amazing promptitude. Why had not this simple suggestion of going back to the music not been made long before? The whole secret lay in finding and establishing the right control.

The great trouble with an immense amount of technical work is that no effective controls are set up. The work consists essentially of blind fumbling, without any clear apprehension or intelligible goal. This cannot help but reduce efficiency enormously. Surely one cannot learn well if one only knows that one is wrong. Surely the important thing is to know what one is trying to do. Of course the goal cannot be perfectly clear at the beginning. But the process of learning must be a process of clarifying that goal, not merely of stumbling in a fog. To do this is like being put into an elaborate maze blindfold, without the slightest clue as to which paths to choose and which to avoid. Then one's only guide is the painful bang as one runs into a dead end. Perhaps if one keeps on long enough one may find the way. Also perhaps not! In any case it will take much time, toil, and grief to get there. If one could have possibly got a complete map, or at any rate a few constructive hints, one would surely get there much faster, and have a far happier time doing so. This is a good analogy to working at a technical problem in music. The musical effect one desires to produce corresponds to the clue. As one follows it up, it grows more and more significant. It co-ordinates all one's endeavors. It more and more clearly defines success, which is the supreme necessity. In other words, it is the control around which the action-pattern should be grouped.

This leads to a practical implication of the highest importance. *All good technical study is good music study.* If one is learning to sing or play a composition, or a passage in it, the prime necessity is to grasp, comprehend, and feel its expressive musical shape. Here we have nothing less than a constructive solution of the most baffling and refractory problem in music education, which is the problem of technique. It means two things. First, technical study so conducted achieves an immense saving of time, because the proper control is set up, which is an essential condition for efficiency, and the time so saved is available for other matters. Second, technical study itself ceases to be merely mechanical drill, and becomes a direct and powerful influence for the development of musical responsiveness. To learn to sing or play a composition in this way is to learn to grasp it musically.

In a developmental scheme of music education this attitude, this way of approach should be inaugurated from the very first, and reinforced in varied situations all along the line. When grade-school children sing a song by ear, one does not usually think of this as "technical work" at all. If this means that voice training drills, vocalises, and the like are probably undesirable and certainly should not be stressed, it is perfectly correct. But the children should be projecting an expressive intention in the vocal medium. They should feel the mood and its embodiment in the pattern. They should be responsive to the flow and undulation of the pitch line, the beginnings and ends of phrases, the integrating rhythm of the beat, the appropri-

[222]

ate and desirable tone quality. Of course an elaborate abstract analysis would be quite out of place, but these should be the controlling considerations. And this is the very essence of the business of learning to sing, the very heart of the vocal technique. Even to speak of a "technical approach" in dealing with young children in a grade group may seem offensive and wrong-headed. But this is due to a false notion of what technique really is, and of the conditions for its development. Technique is not externalistic and mechanistic skill, and the way to work for it is not through blind and mindless drill. It is the ability to project beauty, and the way to work for it is through an emerging conception of the beauty to be projected.

Exactly the same emphasis and approach should be continued and amplified in all work in musical performance—in classes in applied music, in individual lessons in applied music, in the rehearsal of vocal and instrumental ensembles. Not long ago I was listening to a senior high-school orchestra in rehearsal. They ran into a rhythmic nuance which they proceeded to botch. The director attacked the problem partly by exposition, partly by making some suggestions to various wind players about breath-control and embouchure, partly by sheer trial-and-error plugging. The situation was by no means ill handled. But the root of the difficulty was perfectly clear. These students did not know exactly what they were trying to say musically, and they were not in the way of finding it out. Most of them had enough skill to cope with the problem, but it was not a musically oriented skill. They could undoubtedly have solved it, and solved it quickly, if they had really envisaged it. If it had been tackled this way—that is to say, as a musical and expressive problem primarily—a technical result would have been forthcoming very soon, and something would have been done for their musical development. Of course if they had already come along through a really effective developmental program, they would have known in a flash just how this particular rhythmic nuance ought to sound, and they would have made it sound that way without more ado.

This basic principle, that any problem in performance or technique should be approached as a problem of projecting a musical meaning, is subject to violent misunderstanding and even to travesty. I once heard a fairly advanced piano student massacre a Beethoven sonata in public. His performance was sloppy, awkward, ineffective, inaccurate. Afterward he excused himself by saying that, as every other performer should, he was creating an effect, so that wrong notes and technical deficiencies did not matter. This, obviously, was quite

[223]

preposterous. The "effect" lies in the shape itself, and when the shape is hopelessly distorted, that effect is lost. A sonata by Beethoven, in particular, is a most exacting aesthetic problem, to be approached with reverence and humility, and a devoted determination to discover and realize, so far as one's limitations permit, the master's full intention. Yet this does not mean that its technical problems are merely drill problems, and that a good performance amounts to nothing more than not hitting any wrong notes.

One finds something pitiable and laughable in this student's point of view. Yet the same ideas appear altogether too often among people who should know better. Some choral directors, for instance, have suffered such a revulsion from an arid and mechanistic approach which they think of as a "technical approach," that they have swung to the opposite extreme. They point their activities toward what they call the "joy of singing," to "having a good time with music," to a crude and slapdash expressiveness that has no aesthetic meaning or validity. Now there is such a thing as the joy of singing; there is such a thing as having a good time with music. Both these things, moreover, are eminently desirable, and if they are lacking there is something very far wrong. But the joy of singing does not mean boisterous hollering, and having a good time with music does not mean romping with it as though it were a large and exuberant dog. Furthermore, a "technical" approach does not mean aridity or externalism. The fallacy of all such work as I have indicated is the same as was committed by the young pianist who murdered Beethoven. It is the idea that an interpretation or an expressive performance is something arbitrary, something imposed upon the music, instead of something intrinsic to it, embodied in it, derived from it —something to be realized and made explicit by patient and devoted yet most rewarding study of the refinements and values of its pattern. When a choir, when an orchestra, when an individual young or old studies music as it ought to be studied, then there is simply no gap between the technical problem and the process of musical and expressive realization. For the musical conception controls the technique, and technical study defines and refines the musical conception "How do I want this music to sound?" That is always the master question in approaching its technical problems.

III

The action-pattern—the movements and the successions and combinations of movements required to sing or to actuate a musical instrument—is what might be called the content of the technique as such. To some extent in all cases, but in differing degrees in different cases, it must be studied, practiced, and acquired directly. But its essential control is not within itself, but is located in the result intended, that is to say in the musical goal.

. A few simple illustrations from everyday life will make clear how profoundly an explicit goal affects a pattern of action, and how powerfully that goal shapes it up and influences it. If you are walking along the street and see a friend ahead of you whom you want to catch up with, you do not give careful thought to the movement of your hips, and knees, and ankles, and to the swing of your body, and then set yourself and increase your rate of motion. You merely speed up, and all these movements arrange themselves without your even thinking about them. If you are at the table and want the salt which is at some distance from you, the best thing is not to reflect that the arm should be lifted from the shoulder, that the hand should at first hang loosely from the wrist, and that a relaxed motion is always advisable. You merely reach for it, and the action-pattern comes along without any trouble. If you are talking to somebody and he says something that makes you angry and calls for a vigorous retort, you do not consciously set yourself, slightly hold your breath, carefully arrange certain facial muscles, and establish tension in the larynx. At least you do not do all these things deliberately, although they may all very well happen. So far as you are concerned, you have an annoying person in front of you, and your immediate response is a convincing flush, scowl, and snarl. Or again, if a typist has something very much on his mind while he is writing something else on the machine, the subject is very apt, as it were, to break through, so that he finds himself typing irrelevant words, phrases, and in extreme cases even whole sentences. Conversely, the mere thought of what he wants to put down does a great deal to control the motion of his hands and fingers on the keyboard.

The truth of the matter is that much of the most efficacious control of action is unconscious rather than direct. This does not imply any high-flown theory about the influence of the "subconscious mind." It involves only simple common sense. The body responds best when one thinks chiefly about the goal, about what one is trying to do,

[225]

rather than about how one is to do it. A tight-rope walker who began thinking about his movements and analyzing them would quite likely be in a dangerous predicament. But if he thinks simply about getting from here to there he gets across quite nicely, and his body behaves like a perfect gentleman.

It may seem that one crucial factor in the situation has been ignored so far. The action-pattern of a person who is hurrying to catch a friend, or reaching for the salt, or expressing himself angrily, or who is a good typist or a good tight-rope walker is already well established. It requires no attention in and of itself. All such a person need concern himself about is the goal before him, and the movements immediately run off efficiently. But what happens in the learning stages? Is it not necessary to attend to the action-pattern directly, to practice it independently for what may be a long time before it can be relegated to the subconscious? Must it not, in short, be made automatic before it will arrive when and as wanted without any thought being directed to it?

There is some truth in this, but it must be understood correctly. It is not the case that certain patterns of action are made habitual in isolation, and then and only then applied in functional situations where they come under the control of the intended objective. When a pattern of skill is being learned, a process of growth is going on. That process is not in reality one of habit building, but of progressive adaptation to a goal. To be sure there will be moments in the process when the attention of the learner is switched away from the goal and concentrated on the movements through which he is trying to attain it. These are the analytic phases of the growth-sequence. But to suppose that the whole sequence is made up of nothing but analysis is quite untrue. What actually happens is a rhythm of analysis and synthesis, in which the learner tries for the goal, finds that his aim is clumsy and uncertain, works for a while at the pattern of action which is the means through which he seeks his end, improves it somewhat, tries once again for the goal with a better aim, and so forth in a sequence of evolving efficiency. It is through this developmental drama that all skilled performance establishes itself. It follows, then, that to concentrate on nothing but the pattern of movement with the idea of making it fully automatic before using it in a functional situation is very bad practice. An over-all intelligible goal should most certainly dominate the whole process, and it becomes more and more effectively controlling as the skill develops. So the basic formula for the development of musical skill always is to set

[226]

up an authentic musical goal, to shape up action with reference to that goal, and to use whatever analysis, and whatever direct attention to the action-pattern itself may be necessary as this evolution takes place. How much analysis, how much direct attention to the action is necessary will vary in different situations, as we shall see.

1 Let us first consider the bearing of this discussion upon vocal pedagogy and the development of vocal technique. Here the expressive musical intention is of over-riding importance, and the direct analysis and shaping up of the action-pattern is comparatively subsidiary. For this there are two reasons.

A. *The voice is extremely responsive to the content, meaning, and purpose of what is being expressed, and to mood and feeling.* There is no need to go beyond everyday experience to prove this much. In ordinary conversation we do not have to think about making special vocal adjustments to convey surprise, inquiry, sadness, joy, love, anger, and so forth in the tones that we use. They come out unmistakably in tone quality, register, dynamics, steadiness or tremulousness of utterance, hesitations, changes of pace, the rise and fall of speech tunes, and so forth. The vocal mechanism adapts itself very swiftly, very flexibly to produce these effects, without our needing to give any thought at all to it.

Now the pattern of vocal action in speech is somewhat different from the pattern used in song, but not radically different, so far as we know. Indeed the main difference seems to turn on the nature of the control itself. In speaking, the control of the voice is chiefly brought about by the formation of words, although tonal and rhythmic components are involved also. In singing the control is chiefly in terms of pitch, although word formation is present too. The vocal action of a person who is speaking is dominated by the explicit meanings, the shapes, and the emotional values of the words he is using. The vocal action of a person who is singing is dominated by the expressive values and the relationships of the tonal patterns he is delivering. Thus expression is prepotent in both ways of using the voice.

B. *Almost nothing at all is definitely known about the nature of the action-pattern in the act of song.* It is, quite literally, a scientific and pedagogical *terra incognita*. No doubt plenty of voice teachers think that they know, claim that they know, and manage to persuade their loyal pupils that they really do know. But unfortunately teachers and experts of the highest eminence in this field are in flat disagreement on every major point having to do with vocal control and vocal action, which means that what we actually have before us is not scientifically well-founded knowledge, but only confident ignorance.

The extent and universality of these disagreements have been established in a very striking and unanswerable fashion in an extremely thorough investigation which covered the whole literature of vocal pedagogy published in English over a period of many years.[1] The author set up all the major concepts having to do with the control of the voice and its training. He then proceeded to collate the expressed judgments of the best authorities with regard to these concepts. The men and women whose opinions he examined included the most eminent teachers, singers, and experts in this field. Since he took their published statements, he had every right to assume that they represented the best and most responsible judgment of these persons. What he discovered was a flagrant mass of incredible contradictions. The human voice has only one register. It has two registers. It has three registers. The singer should pay direct attention to his breathing. The singer should pay no attention to his breathing. The singer should control his breathing by means of the diaphragm. The singer should not control his breathing by the diaphragm. The tongue should be kept low. The tongue should be kept free. The throat should be consciously controlled. The throat should not be consciously controlled. Head cavities are important as resonators. Head cavities are not important as resonators. Falsetto tones are legitimate. Falsetto tones are not legitimate. The singer should listen to his own tone. The singer should not listen to his own tone. So on at great length. These are only brief samples, and the reader who wants an adequate idea of the range of contradiction, which covers every important point in vocal pedagogy, should go to the study itself. Let it be remembered once more that these violently conflicting opinions are the considered judgments of the best workers in the field. The only possible inference is that none of them really know how the vocal mechanism acts, or what should be done to analyze it properly for the sake of training.

In view of all this certain very formidable questions force themselves upon us. How does anyone ever learn to sing? What is the best way of teaching him to do so, or perhaps better helping him to become able to do so? There seems to be only one possible answer. Emphasize, at all times and in all possible ways, the expressive musical

[1]Victor A. Fields, *Training the Singing Voice*. Kings Crown Press, New York, N. Y., 1947.

[228]

intent. Give the learner plenty of opportunity and plenty of encouragement. Do whatever seems best and whatever seems most helpful at the moment to get the vocal apparatus working properly and to overcome its impediments. Always remember, however, that any direct analysis, any direct attempt to control the action, for instance by freeing the jaw, or loosening the throat, or an upward or forward placement of the voice, or by management of the breathing is sure to be extremely superficial, extremely empirical, and that it is certainly not based on any established doctrine or certain knowledge. The devices used by singing teachers succeed if they succeed. That is about all one can say. Their success seems to depend very largely upon the personalities involved, and upon the happy chance of hitting upon something that somehow means something to the learner. The focus of endeavor should always be to develop the control of the voice in terms of expressive intention. This involves the kind of songs used, the way they are used, the response the pupil makes to their musical and aesthetic content and values. Beyond this all that can be said is that we are shaping up an unknown something, and working virtually in the dark. For how to control and train the voice by a direct analysis of the action of its mechanism is simply not known.

All this has a direct and very interesting bearing upon two very important issues. First of all, if we want to make a person into a fine singer we ought to do our very best to make him into a fine, responsive, sensitive musician. We have here a field of educational endeavor shamefully infested by quacks, and any voice teacher who neglects musicianship and substitutes some system of vocal gymnastics is open to the suspicion of belonging to this category. Vocalists have the reputation, only too often well-deserved, of being poor musicians. This is not a wholly accurate statement. Those who come through to some kind of success are apt to be, more precisely, limited musicians—limited in their musical responsiveness. Their vocal action is largely conditioned by an expressive tone-quality, an expressive melodic line, and by mood, which of course is established by the words as well as the music of their material. This is about as far as many of them go, and they may find it enough to please the public. But it is a very slender and precarious basis for the development of an artistic singer. Everyone who is seriously being taught to sing should be taught to sing *music*—music in all its completeness and subtlety. And if he is going to be able to sing music, he must know, not in concepts, or abstractions, or rules, but in terms of an intimate personal responsiveness, what music is.

Secondly, our analysis bears upon the singing of young children. Here the watchword should ever be musical expressiveness. The emphasis should not be upon conventional tone, or head voice, or a certain way of breathing, but upon saying something in the musical medium as appropriately and expressively as possible. Once more this involves the kind of song material used, the development of its mood-values and aesthetic content, the high-lighting of its appeal. A little analysis of the vocal action here and there may help. But in all probability its main effects are psychological—that is to say, it gives encouragement, stimulates confidence, focalizes effort. Certainly we cannot for one moment believe that it is possible to tell children the one right way to use their bodies in the act of song. But we can get children to sing, and to sing beautifully by continually emphasizing expressive insight and refinement, and by helping the voice along here and there as opportunity seems to offer, and as our own best wisdom and experience may suggest.

Observe in closing that this implies that there is not one kind of vocal pedagogy appropriate to the first-grade, and another appropriate to the junior high-school, and another appropriate to the senior high-school. All sound vocal pedagogy is the same in kind, though different in degree. Always it turns first and foremost upon the projection on the voice of a sensitively apprehended and felt musical conception. Thus the study of vocal technique becomes an avenue of musical growth.

2 When it comes to instrumental technique there is no doubt that direct attention to the action-pattern has a greater proportional importance, partly because it is more external and artificial, and partly because it is much more accessible to analysis. Nevertheless it is still true that the basic control and the conscious goal should be the musical intention.

In dealing with the action-patterns, which are the content of an instrumental technique, it is very important to approach them in the right way. If this is not done there is sure to be an enormous waste of time and energy, technical practice becomes mechanical rather than musical, and results come very slowly and doubtfully. The following are the crucial considerations here.

A. *A technical problem should always be approached as a problem to be analyzed and understood rather than as a challenge to mechanical repetitive drill.* Good technical action is *intelligent* action—action adapted to the efficient achievement of a goal. A skill, in fact, is intelligence expressing

[230]

itself in motor terms. So it should always be dealt with in terms of thought, experimentation, and insight.

Take, for instance, the playing of a scale passage on the piano. What is wanted is to be able to control the action in terms of a musical intention. The passage may be smooth and flowing; or it may be rough and broken; or it may be uniform; or it may involve much differentiation of stress; or it may be slow or fast, or soft or loud. What it should be depends upon the expressive demands of the music, and technical mastery means the ability to deliver it as desired. What is wanted, that is to say, is control for the sake of a contemplated musical result. According to the older piano pedagogy scales should be practiced with a high finger-action, and without any turning from the wrist as the thumb passes under or the hand passes over. This, however, is a very inefficient action-pattern, and it is based upon a most unintelligent analysis. Clearly the problem is to get the fingers laid out on the keys in advance as far as possible, and to keep them as close to the keys as possible. So we think of the scale, not as a series of separate notes to be played finger-wise one by one, but as a series of tetrachords ascending or descending. Any wrist movement is allowable which gets the hand quickly into position for the next tetrachord without lost motion. This is, at least in part, an analysis of the scale-wise movement as actually executed by virtuosi. And in learning to play scales, the student should not merely go over and over a routine, but should think about what he is doing, why he is doing it and how he is doing it. He should, that is to say, be continually and critically scrutinizing and analyzing the action-pattern.

But where does the musical intention come in? It is extremely important, and in very practical respects. Let us say that the problem is the two ascending parallel scales, to be played on a high dynamic level and with a strong emphasis on the culminating tone, which occur at the end of Chopin's *Ballade in G Minor*. The difficulty of these passages is partly motor. It is partly a matter of the right action-pattern. If one attacks them with the old-fashioned finger-wise, note-wise action they present a very serious problem indeed. If one attacks them by means of a free fluid action centering on the tetra-chords, one is well on the way toward ripping them off properly. These passages, like every other passage in music, contain a mental hazard too as the scales run through several octaves. They have to be executed under stress. There is a very strong impulsion towards the culminating note. This creates a very strong tendency to skip many intervening notes, make a leap, and grab the culminating tone with-

[231]

out more ado. Indeed, I have heard quite able pianists leave out as much as a whole octave in the passages in question. The enemy, then, is flurry. It is always the enemy. It always spreads a net for the feet of the performing musician, although it is unusually conspicuous here. How to overcome it? Merely analyzing the action-pattern will not do the trick, although if the action-pattern is wrong and clumsy there can probably be no salvation at all. One thinks of these scales, not as an embarrassingly large number of notes, but as built out of rhythmic or tonal sub-units, and one practices them in this way. This immediately has the effect of co-ordinating the action, just as a given expressive intention immediately co-ordinates the voice. As control increases, awareness of the sub-groups within the lengthy sweep of the passage may sink into the background. But its work has been done, and it can be revived wherever and whenever necessary. Thus musical practice can yield a result which is very hard to attain by mechanical practice. This is true in general. A fine and mature technician has a rationalized and efficient repertoire of action-patterns, but he also knows enough to co-ordinate these patterns under the control of a musical intention.

The objection to purely routine and mindless technical practice is that it is divorced both from intelligence and from musical values. Such practice multiplies difficulties because it puts a premium on stupid and bungling action, and because there is no over-all guiding control to shape the action up. Thus it is time-wasting from a purely technical point of view, and it is devoid of developmental musical values. So technical study should always involve movement analysis. Otto Ortmann, in his remarkable book, *The Physiological Mechanics of Pianoforte Technique*,[1] has broken down the pianistic action into eleven basic types of movement. This book is a rich mine of material for the piano teacher, and indeed for teachers of any medium of musical performance. It should, however, be said that the learner himself should be helped to do his own analyzing rather than simply being told the answers to his technical problems. Moreover, an action-pattern should be analyzed, not merely in its own interest, but with a definite musical result in mind, the primary reason being that this establishes the all-important control. For instance, the famous circular octave passage for the left hand in Chopin's Ab Major Polonaise involves an intricate problem of movement which should be attacked via intelligence. But it will shape up much faster if it is studied with conscious reference to the tonal, rhythmic, and dynamic values of the passage.

[1]E. P. Dutton & Co. Inc., New York, N. Y., 1929.

To sum the whole thing up, technical practice should always be interfused with thought. The student should not so much repeat as experiment. He should be constantly criticizing, rationalizing, reviewing, revising, and making more intelligent the actions he performs, not for themselves alone, but with a view to an expressive musical outcome.

B. *A vitally important, but much neglected, consideration in the establishment of effective action-patterns has to do with the framing or centering of the movement.* All specialized or detailed movements go on in a frame, or rather a series of frames which are themselves moving. One can see the same thing in a piece of machinery in which one moving part goes through its orbit in the setting of another and larger moving part, this one in the setting of a still larger part, and so on. It is this total interlocking co-ordination, rather than the small immediate motion, with which we have to be concerned. The pianist's fingers, the violinist's left hand and bowing arm do not function in isolation. The fingers function in the setting of the hand, the hand in the setting of the arm, the arm in the setting of the shoulders and ultimately of the entire body. In a proper centering of the specific movement lies a considerable part of the secret of its proper control.

What is required for a proper centering or framing of movement is not primarily a definite postural set. This is involved indeed, but only indirectly. The basic necessity always is an easy, unimpeded flow of movement. It must be remembered that the movements required to actuate a musical instrument are, anatomically and physiologically, extremely complicated. They bring into play a great many muscles, many of them remote in varying degrees from the muscles which have to do with the immediate moving parts themselves—the fingers, the hands, the "lip," and so forth. The action of this far-reaching muscular complex can very easily be self-impeding. It can be as though some of the larger moving parts of a machine were slightly out of line, so that the smaller moving parts directly in contact with the work performed inaccurately or were under stress. So when the violinist is learning to draw his bow, or the pianist is learning to play a trill, the whole body has to be co-ordinated, because the whole body is involved. A great many difficulties are created, or are solved very slowly or perhaps not at all, because of neglect here. This, to repeat, does not mean that a certain fixed pose must always be required, although an awkward, slumping pose may very well affect the action of the hands and the fingers themselves. Also when we get a pupil to reorganize his pose, this may pull things into line that previously were out of line, so that a better result is forthcoming almost at once. But the point to have in mind is not the pose itself, but its effect on action. It may be as though the wheels of a car could not be properly aligned because the frame itself was a little bit askew. Then we can work as long as we like at the wheels, and never get them quite right. But when the framework is adjusted, the wheels come into line easily enough. This is why a proper attentive posture can be of importance in a choral or instrumental ensemble group, in a grade-school singing group, or with an individual learner. The emphasis should not be on something that merely looks right and proper, but on a comfortable physical adjustment that enables the whole action-pattern to flow freely about a center.

Here, of course, is the heart of the problem of what is called relaxation, which is much talked about and little understood. If the body is in a state of complete relaxation, no movement at all can be made. Thus it is quite impossible to produce any kind of tone, even a soft one, let alone a loud one, without muscular effort and tension. No machine, similarly, could operate without a discharge of energy, which would be impossible without points of support unless the whole thing were to fall apart. In a machine there must be a system of thrusts and counterthrusts, and this cannot be avoided. The point, however, is to avoid internal friction as far as possible, and to prevent energy working against energy. That is exactly the problem of so-called relaxation in any skill in general, and in the musical techniques in particular. There never can be relaxation in the complete and global sense. There can, however, be a flow of energy either relatively impeded, or relatively unimpeded. So the thing to work for is not relaxed action, at least in any literal sense, but centered action, focused action, action intelligently concentrated upon a goal.

This is brought about partly by the kind of thoughtful, experimental, self-critical movement-analysis which has been indicated already. But here is only a part of the story. The goal itself has a very great effect. It is known for a fact that the efficiency of many skills depends upon the visual frame of reference. When a person can see what he is trying to do, he is able to line up his action better than when he cannot. The same is undoubtedly true of the musical skills, *mutatis mutandis*. When a person hears or images in auditory terms what he is trying to do, this strongly tends to pull the whole action together, and to make it go better. Many of the difficulties of so-called relaxation, which is really co-ordination, are due to the fact that the

[234]

performer has only a vague idea, or perhaps no idea at all, of what effect he is trying to produce. It is amazing, for instance, how often technical difficulties can be cleared up simply by giving the learner an effective sense of the rhythmic shape of the passage, or of the expressive moulding of the melodic line or the harmonic pattern. So once again the combination of a musical goal as the control with an intelligent analysis of the action-pattern appears as the essential formula for technical practice.

IV

All that has been said so far in this chapter can be brought to a head and expressed in terms of a co-ordinated and sequential program for the development of technique, as one of the main avenues of musical growth.

1 One should always think of the growth of technique, rather than of the building of technique. The command of technique is brought about by a process of organic development, not of mechanical construction.

It turns, first and foremost, upon the establishment of the proper controls. Musical performance is essentially an act in which the content, the expressive shapes, the aesthetic meanings and values of the music are translated into sound. Therefore it follows that the mind of the performer should be dominated, and his patterns of action controlled by an apprehension of this content and these values and meanings. No one can perform music as he should unless he is keenly aware of what it says and how it says it. No one can learn to perform music as he should learn it, unless every step of the way he is seeking to achieve musical insights and musical discriminations which are to be made audible and intelligible. This attitude of mind, this controlling direction of the attention, is the very heart of sound technical study.

It should be started right from the very first. Indeed, with little children, the technical side of music study should mean very little else. When they sing a song by ear, when they play a melody on toy instruments, when they realize the rhythm of a little piece in bodily movement, they should be consciously trying to express and project as beautifully and appropriately as possible what the music says. This is a very simple matter—so simple, indeed, that most people never think of it as having anything at all to do with technique. As a matter of fact it goes to the very tap-root of musical skill, and throws into high relief the central consideration so much overlooked in technical study. The point is not to try to make children into agile or facile performers, but to instill into them, by means of vital and revealing experience, a realization that in all musical utterance one should always be seeking to release the beauties and expressive meanings of the music.

This is not a hard thing to do with children. It is not something forbidding, or arid, or unenjoyable. On the contrary, such experiences can and should be full of rewarding delight. But the pleasure that they hold, which is that of discovering and experiencing a natural avenue of expressiveness, is not that of an unthinking musical romp. The experience of shaping up a simple rote song so that it is a pleasure to sing and a pleasure to hear has in it the living germ of an artistic challenge which can lead onward endlessly to ever higher ranges of achievement. To reveal with clarity and truthfulness the beauties of music is the true goal of every performing artist, never fully attained, always beckoning, always fascinating. Young children, at the very beginning of their musical education, should become conscious of its attractive and authentic power, for they too, in their measure, should be thought of as performing artists, and not as novices who must plod through a meaningless routine before the significance of what they are doing is revealed to them.

This same determining attitude which should be inaugurated from the very first should be continued, supported, and strengthened to the very end. A person who is studying music should always be studying how to make it beautiful, or rather how to reveal its beauties better. He can get a revealing glimmer of all that this means in his grade-school singing. The light should grow brighter and broader as he works with simple instruments, with standard instruments, with the piano, in the voice class, in the applied music class, in the choir, in the orchestra. This is always what music study ought to be when oriented toward performance. It is, to repeat, the very heart of technical study. And it is in this sense that the establishment of a technique should be understood as the outcome of a process of growth.

2 Direct analytic study of the action-pattern should begin very simply indeed, and should become more and more independent, penetrating, exacting, and extensive. In the early stages of a technical development, analytic work of this kind should take the form of nothing more than incidental and casual helps and hints, designed to assist the child to realize better his expressive intent, and to remove

immediate blockages and barriers. If a technical problem is to be studied at all in isolation from its musical context, this should be done only for a moment, and for the sake of improvement on the spot. Above all, a teacher should beware of becoming wedded to some system of movement-analysis, some fixed scheme of devices which can so easily begin to seem the only proper ones, the only correct and definite mode of treatment. A flagrant example of this is the indiscriminate insistence on "getting the voice up," or singing in the masque, which has been sanctified under the designation of the "head voice." Another flagrant example is the equally indiscriminate insistence on so-called diaphragmatic control, which has been pushed so far by some teachers that they actually tell children that the diaphragm is "the singer." It has already been pointed out that our concepts of vocal action are not based on fact, that they do not correspond to reality. The same is certainly true, though to a lesser degree, of many of our concepts of the instrumental action. But also it has been argued that specific suggestions, specific "prescriptions" of this kind may have psychological value. They may help a child to turn a corner. They may make a difficulty dissolve. This is just what is wanted. So it is very desirable for a teacher to have a large and varied repertoire of them, to be tried out as occasion seems to indicate. If they are inconsistent, if they do not hang together in the pattern of a theoretical system, this is even a good sign. They cannot be consistent anyhow, because they do not derive from an objective knowledge of the action-pattern. Thus consistency can only be forced upon them as a spurious and limiting influence. If one child sings better when you tell him to "get his voice up," and another child sings better when you tell him to center on his diaphragm, if one child plays better when you tell him to carry the instrumental phrases "on the breath," and another one plays better when you tell him to tap his foot, so be it! If such diagnoses are inconsistent, never mind! You are working empirically, and in the dark. But only this is possible. But through fumbling and guesswork you have touched the sensitive place in the action-pattern and brought about improvement. This is all that matters.

3 As musical and technical maturity advance, independent attention to the action-pattern comes to assume an increasing place As a matter of fact, a growing learner will demand it and benefit from it. This raises the very important issue of the proper use of formal technical materials, that is to say, exercises, scales, and studies. What

is implied here, by this whole discussion, may conveniently be summarized under a series of points.

A. *The staple material of technical study is always authentic music.* The main line of advance in the vocal technique is the musically intelligent study of songs. The main line of advance in the pianistic technique is the musically intelligent study of piano compositions. A violin pupil can get more real technical development out of practicing the second movement of the Mendelssohn Concerto than out of a whole host of formal studies and exercises, so long as he practices it as it should be practiced, with a constant concentration on its musical content and values. The reason is that such music has something to say, and that technical skill is the motor ability to say it. Its motor problems should be identified, docketed, pulled out of context, worked upon, put back into context once again in an interweaving, interlocking sequence of analysis and synthesis, all for the explicit and immediate purpose of achieving an expressive result. This is the substance of technical study. It may make very little use indeed of formal technical materials.

B. *Such materials, however, have a real place, although a subsidiary one.* They can, for instance, be used for warming up. This is a perfectly sensible and respectable purpose, but it obviously does not carry any very great developmental value, and no one should fool himself by supposing that it does. Also as musical and technical maturity increase, such materials take on an increasing interest in their own right. To study the action-pattern of the scale, the tremolo, of double-stopping, and so forth can have a definitely constructive meaning for the advanced student, and a great deal of meaning for the mature artist. This is why it often happens that such an artist will spend large amounts of time in practicing scales, exercises, and studies as an isolated task.

There are, however, certain cautions which it is essential to understand and observe.

(a) All such "formal" or isolated technical practice should be for the sake of clarifying and establishing the right pattern of action. In any skill it is always movement that must be shaped up and brought under control. From this standpoint nearly all published volumes of technical material are radically defective. They are actually compilations of musical figurations rather than classifications of movement problems. For instance, in nearly all books on piano technique, one

[238]

finds a section in which all the major and minor scales are laid out in various arrangements of parallel and contrary motion, according to the cycle of keys. From the standpoint of technique, however, the problem is not primarily to know all the scales, but to be able to deliver the proper scale-wise action in any situation. The cycle of keys, or the sequence from parallel octaves to parallel thirds to parallel tenths, which of course have an obvious abstract reasonableness, may not be desirable orders at all when it comes to clarifying the action. Teachers and learners should always remember that the authors of books on technique present their material in an order which may be quite irrelevant and even quite detrimental to genuine and intelligent action-analysis. What such books offer is source material, to be handled very judiciously, rather than study material arranged in the most helpful fashion.

(*b*) It is all-important that a learner use intelligence and judgment in his selection of formal technical material to be practiced, and in his ways of practicing it, rather than blindly carrying on this kind of study merely because he is told to do so, or because it is vaguely supposed to do him good. A good learner should always have before him a number of technical problems—of action problems—which exercise his mind, and at which he wants to get. It is not at all a bad idea to encourage students who have reached a certain stage of maturity to keep technique notebooks in which they set up, as page headings, the action problems which seem to them particularly challenging and important. Under each such heading they may write down an analysis of the exact nature and character of the required movement. They may be referred to published books on technique to search for helpful practice material. They may, at any time, choose for study any problem that they wish, keeping a log of the material they select, of the work they do, and of its efficacy or reverse, and bring their results to the teacher for review and suggestion according to their own initiative. This particular procedure may or may not recommend itself. But the point to bear in mind is that in all formal technical practice the great evil is unthinking routine, and the great virtue is a problemizing and analytic approach. Merely to talk about such things, however, is not enough. There must be some organized and intelligible plan for accomplishing them.

(*c*) Formal technical materials become stultifying and pernicious when they are imposed on immature learners simply because they are known to be of value to the mature artist. Many teachers know

[239]

that virtuosi usually practice scales, exercises, and studies a great deal, and so they infer that beginners ought to practice them as much as possible. Here is yet another piece of sheer externalism. Such teachers only see the outside of things. What they do not see is that the virtuoso, in all his technical practice, is dominated by his expressive intentions and recognized musical needs, and that this is what makes it fruitful. The real function of formal technical study is not to build a technique but to systematize it. In this respect it is an exact parallel to the study of musical theory, which systematizes the grasp of musical resources, but does not inaugurate it. And like any other type of systematic study, it belongs to the later and not to the earlier stages of development.

4 What does it mean to possess a fine technique? It does not mean merely great agility, or the power to produce astonishing fireworks. These may be manifestations of great skill, but they are not, in and of themselves, manifestations of musical skill. *To possess a fine technique means the possession of a great capacity for refined and expressive musical utterance.* As has been admirably said in another connection: "Now any technique acquired through the conscious expenditure of time and labour . . . becomes in large degree, as everyone knows, unconscious in its exercise. Step by step, through stubborn persistence in acutely conscious effort, it builds itself up below the field of consciousness, until at last consciousness, released through its own self-imposed subjection, is free to interpret or create at will."[1]

Such is the meaning of the whole process. It does not, however, indicate a long novitiate of mindless habit-building, but a continual adaptation of means to contemplated ends, in which the means become more effective, and the goals more clearly envisaged. It indicates a process in which a vital significance, apprehended at first in terms of the crude, the immediate, and the limited, realizes itself more and more completely—a process of growth in which musical responsiveness and musical skill advance hand in hand.

V

Before bringing this discussion to a close it seems desirable to show its bearing upon the teaching of music reading as an act of skill. This is a subject on which there is a great deal of decidedly tangled thinking, and since it is of much practical importance, an effort should

[1]John Livingston Lowes, *The Road to Xanadu*, p. 598. Houghton Mifflin Company, Boston, 1927.

be made to clarify it. Our knowledge of the process of music reading is incomparably less complete and exact than is our knowledge of the process of language reading. In the latter field there has been an immense amount of well-controlled and fundamentally significant research, in the former hardly any. Moreover the problem of music reading is intrinsically much more difficult from the standpoint of investigation than is the problem of language reading, for reasons that will appear below. Thus most of our analysis has to be based upon inference and analogy rather than upon objective data. Still it seems not impossible to arrive at reasonably reliable and assured conclusions, particularly if the whole matter is approached from the psychological standpoint developed in these pages.

Reading as a process of skill is known to involve a definitive action-pattern. This, to be specific, is a pattern of eye-movements. When a person is reading language material his eyes do not move continuously but discontinuously, that is to say, in a series of successive motions and pauses. The difference between a good and a poor reader declares itself in this action-pattern. The eyes of a good reader dealing with language material are thought always to move forward along the line, whereas the eyes of a poor reader often move backward or, as it were, hesitate. The eyes of a good reader make comparatively few pauses per line, while those of a poor reader may make a great many.[1] The eyes of a good reader will make very brief pauses, perhaps about one-twenty-fifth of a second, while those of a poor reader will make much longer ones. A forward movement, with few and brief pauses, has been established by very adequate research to be the desired action-pattern. The significance of these findings becomes apparent when it is understood that the reader actually reads during the pauses. When the eyes are in motion he sees nothing clearly. So it follows that the good reader actually sees less of what is on the page than the poor reader, which may seem paradoxical but is indubitably true. The point, of course, is that the good reader is able to pick out salient features, and to apprehend meanings by inference.

These findings no doubt apply to music reading, but only in a general way and with considerable differences. For instance, it is

[1]The eyes of an average reader dealing with clearly printed material of average difficulty will make approximately three pauses per line. The eyes of a poor reader may make scores of pauses. So will the eyes of an average reader dealing with very difficult material." On the contrary, an extremely efficient reader will make less than three pauses per line, and the pauses will be very brief.

[241]

extremely likely that there is more backward movement in good music reading than in good language reading. Moreover there is nothing in language symbolism that corresponds to the orienting symbols of clef, key signature, time signature, and accidentals. How they affect eye-movement is completely unknown, but that they must and should affect it is perfectly certain. Moreover the musical score has a dimension up and down which does not appear in language, so that in reading anything but homophonic music on a single staff there is a problem of vertical as well as horizontal movement, and quite probably this appears in single-staff reading as well. But virtually nothing is known of its characteristics, or of what the pattern should be to get an efficient result. The main reason why nothing is known about these important questions is that they are very difficult to investigate. The data on eye-movement in language reading have been obtained by photographing the eyes of readers with a motion-picture camera. But here the camera can be set up to focus on a horizontal line, and it will catch everything of significance. In music reading, however, this is not the case, and it is very expensive to construct a camera with a two-dimensional focal adjustment, and also very difficult to operate it. In one piece of research where this was actually done at great cost, the investigator had to spend months in learning to operate his instrument before he began to get any results at all.

The consequence is that it is possible only to make very general statements about the action-pattern of the reading skill in music. It is better to have few pauses rather than many pauses, short pauses rather than long pauses. That is really about all. What effects are produced by ascending scale passages, by descending scale passages, by ascending arpeggio passages, by descending arpeggio passages, by interpolated notes in a passage, by narrow skips, by wide skips, by accidentals, by key signatures, by time signatures, by the introduction of accompaniment figures, to mention a few obvious problems, is simply not known. This is why attempts to classify musical patterns in order of reading difficulty have no basis in ascertained fact. All we can say with any confidence is that the eyes of a good reader do not pause often or pause long, that they do not, as it were, fumble with the symbolism, but rather pick out its essential elements in a minimum number of brief, well-directed glances.[1]

[1]There have been a few pieces of published research dealing with some of these problems, and in the main they are well-conducted in a strictly technical sense. But they are extremely limited, and deal with highly artificial and restricted situations, so that they have very little general or practical significance.

Externally considered, language reading as a skill is evaluated in terms of speed. The more words per minute a person can read, the better, other things being equal. This is something that can be established quite readily. All one has to do is to have the subject read a passage or a series of passages for a given length of time, say one hundred and twenty seconds, and then count the number of words he has read. This will yield an index of his reading skill which is objective and meaningful within its limits. But here language reading and music reading part company. Language reading is silent reading. Music reading is not. So in music reading the desideratum is not maximum possible speed, but only optimum speed. If a person can only read very slowly this indicates poor skill. But it would not ordinarily be thought that the sign of a good music reader would be to run off an adagio passage at a presto tempo. So in the music reading tests on the market—and they are neither numerous nor good —the criterion set up is accuracy within the required speed. But this is by no means as simple as it looks. What is accuracy? What is an error? Supposing one person reads off a passage without any note errors but makes it sound like unintelligible gabble, while another person reads it with three mistakes on unessential notes but projects the musical shape, which is the better reader? Perhaps this is not an easy question to answer, but it is very certain that if we were dealing with the expressive oral reading of English we would not rate the result simply in terms of the number of separate words correctly pronounced. The truth is that note-wise accuracy is a very uncertain criterion of reading skill, for the reason that not all note-errors have anything like the same value. The inescapable conclusion seems to be that music reading as a skill is a far more intangible and ill-defined affair than many people imagine. We only know in a very general way what makes it work, and we have extremely uncertain criteria for evaluating it.

But there is another and most important aspect of the reading problem which has nothing directly to do with skill. In connection with language reading it is well understood that excellence expresses itself not only in speed, but also in comprehension, which is a very different matter. On the average the two go together, but the relationship is by no means perfect. In general a slow reader understands poorly, and a fast reader understands well. Conversely, a person who understands well will usually read fast, and one who understands poorly will usually read slowly. Moreover the difference comes out in different patterns of eye-movement. These relationships, however,

[243]

are far from invariable. Furthermore, two points have been established which really bring us to the root of the matter before us. First it is known that reading speed can be increased even as much as a hundred per cent without affecting reading comprehension at all. Second it is known that reading speed can be increased surprisingly easily so long as there is a reasonable level of comprehension, but that it is very difficult to improve reading comprehension.

In the light of all this, and particularly of the last two points, it now becomes possible to take a definitive position. *Skill in music reading must be developed on the basis of a development of musical insight.* As was argued in the preceding chapter, the study of the notation should be undertaken for the shaping up of musical responsiveness through the visualization of the expressive musical patterns. Such a study should not be pointed at developing nothing but a facility in dealing with a symbolism whose meanings are not properly comprehended. The efficient reading of language depends upon comprehension; so does the efficient reading of music. In both cases we are indeed dealing with a skill. But in neither case is it a pure or independent skill which, so to speak, stands on its own feet.

Even without sufficient investigation, which is certainly lacking, one can be pretty sure in general how the eyes of a person who is reading music ought to behave. The things that he ought to pick up as he looks at the score are not the separate notes, but the significant, integrated, expressive musical patterns. This is exactly what happens when a good reader deals with language. He does not center on the separate words, still less on the separate letters. He is able to pick out the crucial elements in the language-pattern, and is able to put them together and to understand what they mean. So, too, a good music reader ought to be able to pick out certain essentials at a glance —scale passages, arpeggio passages, interval skips, key alterations, rhythmic arrangements, and the like. But if he lacks musical insight he cannot pick these things out with his eyes, he cannot see them, because he does not even know that they are there.

This immediately explains a great deal and indicates a great deal. For instance, directors of musical organizations in high-school often say that groups of pupils able to read can do much better work than groups of pupils who cannot read. They usually think of this as due to a sheer difference in skill. As a matter of fact, however, there is a great deal more to it than this. The pupils who are able to read have almost certainly carried their musical insights much further than those who cannot read, because those insights have gone through a

[244]

considerable process of shaping up, even if it has been unintelligently conducted. What makes the difference is not merely the existence of a certain specific skill, but rather a differential level of general musical development.

Have we, then, on our hands an argument for a monopolistic "reading program" in the elementary-school? Not at all, at least in the ordinary sense. What all this actually comes to is an argument for a serious and authentic program of musical development in the elementary-school, which does not neglect musical insight, but which makes use of visualization and of the opportunities afforded by the symbolism as a means of engendering it. Let elementary-school children be taught to "understand" what phrases, and melodies, and chords, and keys, and rhythmic patterns really are. Let them "understand" these things in terms of perception, imagery, and expressive feeling. Let their "understanding" be reinforced by seeing these constitutive elements of the expressive pattern displayed before their eyes on the blackboard, on the page, in their own music manuscript. Then the reading problem will virtually solve itself. All this can be done without sacrificing other aspects and avenues of musical growth, of which the development of musical insight is only one. Many of the same experiences which promote musical insight can and should also promote awareness, initiative, and discrimination. What children in the elementary-school should always be doing is to experience and to study music as an expressive art, and to achieve a developing responsiveness to its verities. An integral, an essential part of this development, often indistinguishable from other parts, will be a growing capacity to identify, understand, and manipulate the elements of the tonal-rhythmic pattern in terms of their intrinsic logic and their expressive values. And this is our definition of musical insight.

Granted musical insight, reading skill is easy. Here the experience of workers in language reading is decisive. Speed can be brought along very fast if there is a foundation of comprehension. All that one does is to push for speed, to go forward at all hazards, to try to grasp meanings rapidly. Note spelling and note pointing must be thrown out of the window, because they are directly antagonistic to proper eye movement and also are irrelevant to musical insight. Children should be encouraged to read music that they like to read and want to read, because liking and wanting are important psychological components which are known to contribute to efficiency. They should be encouraged to try to read it expressively and in a

[245]

meaningful fashion, with correctness as a consequence and not a primary consideration. This is all possible granted a basis of comprehension, granted a basis of insight, but without such a basis it is not possible. When high-school music teachers speak up on behalf of a very formalized and monopolistic reading program in the grades, their emphasis is mistaken. They are the beneficiaries, not of a sheer development of isolated skill, but of a development of musical insight which could not be altogether avoided. Such a program actually fosters reading skill itself much more slowly and uncertainly and with far more casualties than ought to be or need be the case. Also it sacrifices the great values of a well-rounded, widely appealing musical development which is the best possible foundation for good work in the high-school.

Such sacrifices are entirely needless. There is no argument for abandoning reading altogether, or for pretending that it does not matter, or for slighting it to such an extent that it is reduced to an absurdity. There is every argument for putting it on a proper psychological basis. To be sure it does not matter very much if the specific reading skill itself is in a low stage of efficiency in the sixth-grade, so long as a genuine musical development has gone on, and so long as an authentic growth in musical insight has taken place. For we cannot, too strongly, insist that with this sort of background nine-tenths of the difficulty of the reading skill evaporates. Some pupils may hardly carry it forward at all, but they could if they wanted to. Others will get into situations where there is some real point in having it, and then they can learn to look quickly over the score, to understand what it tells them to do, and then to do it. The whole argument of this chapter has been that skill must be projected on an adequate basis of responsiveness, discrimination, and insight; and when we deal with the reading skill this is superlatively manifest and necessary.

QUESTIONS FOR DISCUSSION

1. What basic elements of technique are involved in teaching a song by ear to young children?

2. When a technical problem is being studied in isolation, what should be the basic control? Give examples from your own experience.

3. Why would it be better to describe technical development as a process of organization rather than of habit-building?

4. What is far more apt to ruin a child's voice than anything else is lack of musical intention. Discuss this statement in the light of what is presented in the chapter.

5. Since we have very little knowledge of what makes the voice work, should singing teachers pay any attention at all to the action-pattern?

6. Analyze and discuss the various factors involved in relaxation in playing an instrument.

7. In the light of what is presented in the chapter, criticize the widespread emphasis on "head voice" in dealing with children.

8. Analyze with specific illustrations the place of formal technical materials in the growth of musical skill.

9. Why is it impossible, on any basis of scientific knowledge, to arrange the topics bearing on the musical notation in an order from simple to complex?

10. Collating the material in this chapter with other references in the book, formulate the position taken with regard to music reading.

ADDITIONAL READINGS

OTTO ORTMANN. *The Physiological Mechanics of Pianoforte Technique.* E. P. Dutton & Co., Inc., New York, 1929. (The best action-analysis of a musical technique. This extensive and important work should be scanned for relevant material.)

JAMES L. MURSELL. *The Psychology of Music*, pp. 245–250. W. W. Norton and Company, Inc., New York, 1937. (Summarizes research material on musical skill.)

JAMES L. MURSELL and MABELLE GLENN. *The Psychology of School Music Teaching.* Silver Burdett Company, Inc., New York, 2d. Ed., 1933. Chapter 9, "Technique." (General summary and implications of research results.)

PART THREE

THE DEVELOPMENTAL PROGRAM

CHAPTER ELEVEN

The Point of View

I

Everything that has been said in this book up to this point indicates that a developmental program of music education must be planned and organized from the human point of view. It must be planned and organized with reference to and for the sake of the actual musical growth of actual human beings. This, and nothing else, is always the controlling consideration.

It is the easiest thing in the world to carry on educational planning in terms of stereotypes and conventions. A sequence of activities, endeavors, and learnings is worked out because they are generally accepted as desirable, because they are recommended by authorities, or for suchlike general reasons. Standards for the different grades, or for the elementary school, the junior high-school and the senior high-school are set up in the light of what is supposed to be the logic of the subject, and of what looks like a reasonable plan for its sequential mastery. The result as it appears on paper in the form of a course of study may look very orderly, and to the uninitiated and uncritical may seem very convincing. If the beautiful and elaborate scheme could really be transferred into the pupils' heads, it would be wonderful. But as a matter of fact it never is. What actually happens is that both pupils and teachers go through certain motions, and the contemplated results, if they are forthcoming at all, appear with only a very few individuals.

This may seem like a hard saying, but it is absolutely true, and can be proved up to the hilt with every subject in the curriculum, certainly including music. Look through any course of study in music that has been prepared in this way—and there are plenty of them—and ask yourself seriously and realistically to what extent the indicated outcomes are really appearing, and with what proportion of the pupils. If you are honest about it, you will have to give a discouraging answer, and if you applied the techniques of measurement to get at the facts,

[251]

you would almost certainly find that even a very cautious guess was extremely optimistic. I say this with great confidence, because this situation—the flat failure of such logical plans to do what they were supposed to do—has been revealed innumerable times. I know of one important school system where a most determined effort, worked out with the greatest of care, is made to teach children to read the notation in the elementary-school, almost everything else being sacrificed to this end. The authorities point with much pride to groups of "musically literate" students entering the high-school. But there are certain considerations which take a good deal of the gilt off the gingerbread. First, these alleged "musical literates" are at best a selected few, and one cannot say too much for a program of music education which brings salvation to ten per cent at the cost of condemning all the rest to outer darkness. Second, a great many of them are not nearly so "musically literate" as they are able to seem when they are brigaded with others in an *a cappella* choir, for any kind of really drastic individual testing would tell quite a different story. Third, many of the best of them acquired such "musical literacy" as they possess, not from the school program, but from private lessons in piano and violin. Now this is the most that can be expected under the most favorable circumstances of any scheme or course of study worked out primarily in terms of the logic of the subject. Most of the children simply do not learn to read, do not acquire any grasp of tonal and rhythmic relationships, any genuine confidence with the singing voice. The contemplated outcomes are forthcoming only in the most meager fashion, if at all. The program I have described represents the best that can be done with such a scheme, and a great deal more than ordinarily is done. I suggest that it is not good enough.

The trouble, of course, is that the planning is conducted from the wrong point of view. It starts with music as an abstract pattern, not as a human experience in the lives of the human beings with whom one is dealing. The inevitable outcome is a bed of Procrustes, which is a destructive and disastrous piece of furniture, however beautiful the cabinet work may be. Those who happen to fit do fairly well. But so far as the rest are concerned, who are sure to be the majority, one has to try either to stretch them out or lop them off, and neither procedure makes for musical health and growth, even though accompanied by all the lollipops and sugar coatings that the wit of man can devise. For there is only one proper starting point for educational planning, and that is not with music as an abstract system, but with the human beings with whom one is dealing.

[252]

Now this does not mean disorder, or casualness, or mere day-to-day extemporization. Planning from the human point of view is real planning. I have already mentioned this, and the idea will be developed much more fully in what is now to come. It is true that we have to plan deliberately for flexibility and scope. But this is perfectly practicable, although it means that we shall not be able to lay out a one-way track on paper and have everybody go along it. But a stockyard-like arrangement in which all the creatures follow one another down the selfsame chute is by no manner of means the only possible kind of orderly scheme. A developmental program has a genuine and compelling logic of its own, with which we now have to deal. That logic is the logic of musical growth. The way to put it into practical operation is to keep our minds fixed, first and foremost, upon the musical growth of the human beings with whom we are concerned.

II

In order to make this idea, and indeed this whole discussion of the developmental program of music education as concrete as possible, I here present at some length a very interesting case study of musical growth. It is an autobiographical account written by a student of mine, and I reproduce it here with a minimum of editing, because it seems to me to reveal very clearly some of the most fundamental issues involved.

My musical "education" began by my being farsighted enough to "select" two musical parents. My mother and father were both quite musical, though neither's musical education extended beyond being able to play hymns and simple secular songs at the piano and being able to sight read this type of music for singing. Nevertheless, I have since ascertained that both were naturally gifted above the average, so it follows that I, as one of their progeny, had little chance of being tone deaf or harmonically unresponsive.

As is the case with most if not all infants, my first awareness of music was the awareness of *tone*, the vocal tone of my mother's lullabies and cradle songs; her singing and humming as she went about her housework. Furthermore, I was fortunate in that this introductory tone was *good* tone, smooth, round, and unerringly on pitch. Thus from my earliest encounter with the medium of music I heard the accurate relationship of the tones of the scale, and I have subsequently realized that my tone-wise and scale-wise growth was based on a good foundation.

Although it is natural that my concern with music for many months was with tone and tone alone, according to my mother's report the phenomena of

[253]

melody and rhythm began to assert themselves ere too long. At about two years of age or shortly thereafter I began to sing back to her the tunes I heard her sing; the embryonic concept of rhythm was perforce shown therein.

Around the age of four or four-and-a-half years an awareness of harmony began to be manifested. I was given a harmonica and shown how it worked; and I began experimenting. Believe it or not, in a few days I was able to play "Home, Sweet Home"! I shall never forget how elated I was when I first showed my mother that feat. The fact that I was becoming aware of different harmonies is illustrated in this wise: the harmonica was in the key of C and contained no half steps outside the diatonic scale, so, in my experimenting with various tunes, I sometimes ran into spots where the tone could not be made, and I *knew* when the substitution or else the stopping point was reached. Of course the tone that I needed most frequently was the F♯ used in modulating to G, the dominant of the key of the harmonica. It is evident from this that I knew the difference between the C and the G tonalities.

The best elementary instruction in rhythm that I remember ever having gotten was in the game of bouncing a ball on the floor in time with my mother's playing or singing. This was an excellent way of getting the "feel" of the rhythm throughout my whole body. Though she was likely unaware that she was "instructing" me or helping me develop a feeling for rhythm, I have since thought what a pity it was I didn't continue ball bouncing rather than get involved in a *count*-wise approach to the notes of the score.

At the age of seven I started to school and simultaneously began private piano lessons. This was the beginning of my formal music education, and though *some* good undoubtedly came from it I feel that I possibly would have been better off had my contact with music remained "informal" and my learning incidental, at least until I might have come under the influence of a *good* teacher. Within the next five years I fell victim to three piano teachers, and, as well as I recall, their teaching techniques were practically identical, and practically stupid.

Before I continue in the discussion of these teachers, their methods and my receptivity, let me lessen the indictment against them somewhat by saying that I was the victim of what you call a tradition of "spurious masculinity." My home and school were located in a small town about the size to be called a hamlet, in a section of the country not too culturally advanced; and out of possibly two hundred elementary-school children I was the *only* boy taking piano lessons. Looking at the psychology of such a situation it is reasonable to conclude that I didn't *want* to succeed in learning the piano because then my "disgraceful" liaison with the "feminine" art of music would have become more widely known and discussed through my more frequent and successful public appearances. Such a situation is most regrettable and certainly rouses my indignation when I think of it now, but such was the situation, and there was apparently nothing I could have done to better it, except to ignore it, and I *didn't* succeed at that. Therefore I admit that Franz

Liszt himself *possibly* couldn't have made a pianist out of me, but I feel that Liszt would have made an attempt to eradicate some of the ignorance fostering such a condition. At least he would have appealed to my subsequently discovered *will* to be musical with some *good* teaching, and this, I think, would have seen me through that period of a distorted concept of values and saved me from the ranks of disappointed pianists.

I remember quite well my first piano teacher, nor can I forget the manner in which she tried to teach me. After introducing me to the lines and spaces, the F and G clefs, the fingering of the C scale and little or no more, she gave me some stupid music-less *piece* to learn for the Christmas recital program, and subsequent lessons up to that recital were spent in working on that piece. Of course I was concerned almost entirely with the mechanics of playing, getting the right finger on the right note at the right time. It was such labor for my unschooled fingers that there couldn't possibly have been displayed a sense of the complete whole, as though it were a piece of *music* and not just a string of notes. However, the notes were played at the recital, and then the same laborious, uninspired procedure began over, pointing toward the next recital.

For the next four years my lessons went on, though under two more teachers who showed no more insight into how to make the study of *music* an alive, growing thing than did the first. In fact, I believe that it is reasonable to say I wasn't taught *music*; rather, an attempt was made to teach me *piano*. Not one instance can I recall in which the teacher had me sing a chord, name a chord, or even sing the melody of the piece. Always the concern was with notes and fingering, and if an allusion was made to the rhythmic flow of the piece, it was always couched in such technicalities concerning the *count* that I must have missed the rhythmic contour altogether.

Learning anything about the score from the approach of *singing* was completely nil. There was no class of "public school music," and the singing we did was in assembly, or in preparation for some special program such as an operetta or a county choral contest. In such cases various ones were gathered together, taught the songs by rote, and when the program was over we were forgotten until the next program. There was absolutely no emphasis on good singing *tone*; the instructors likely knew very little about tone and its production, since they were primarily pianists.

Before I finished elementary-school, however, my naturally good "ear" began to show itself, and having developed a good singing voice, I began to sing "harmony" on the songs we happened to be working on for a program. I feel certain that the discovery that I had the knack of doing that, and the subsequent exercise of that knack on through school was the ear training, of an incidental nature, that has stood me in good stead since, and partially offset the utter lack of formal training along this line in my secondary-school work. I should never have learned anything about harmony had I continued my note-wise study of the piano, the technicalities of which precluded my really *hearing* what I was playing, to the exclusion of singing, which developed something far nearer "musicianship."

As I entered junior high-school my parents concluded that my attempts at becoming a pianist were less successful than that of becoming an athlete, so my lessons were suspended.

Throughout the remainder of my high-school days my *academic* musical education was at a standstill. Athletics remained my primary interest, and about the only musical activity I participated in was informal group singing or hymn singing in church. I always tried to sing "harmony" to the songs, though in some of the more difficult hymns and popular songs I found this not so easy.

This adolescent period was a most important developmental time in my life when my will to be musical should have been "in training," but unfortunately it was not. In fact, it was not awakened to the extent that prompted me to *do* something about it until about my senior year in high-school.

The day my father bought me a radio proved to be a turning point in my life. Prior to that time I had heard very little really fine music, and I suppose I simply hadn't realized what a powerful, moving force it could be. I began to realize it daily as I listened to the comparatively polished performances of the radio shows. The first stimulant of a specific nature I remember was an accordionist whose digital dexterity simply amazed me. That was a real "developmental experience" in my life. I wanted to get an accordion and start lessons; I talked about it to my parents, but they persuaded me to transfer my enthusiasm back to my old friend, the piano, and this I did with considerable success. I did not, and have not become a good pianist, but the job of digging out my old exercise books and pieces, and ordering more, and setting about relearning—or actually *learning*—something about music on my own was of invaluable aid to me later. I was not pushed toward a recital this time; I was not interested in playing silly little pieces for people; I simply wanted to *learn music* in the real sense of the term—and I did, far more than I had ever known before. In fact I found that upon entering college and beginning the study of "theory" and sight singing that I ranked very well with the students who had had considerably more pre-college training than I.

It is obvious from the foregoing résumé of my pre-college musical training that mine was a clear case of a thwarted and blunted natural musical inclination. The causes cannot be catalogued simply as bad teaching; rather the causes were manifold and complementary. Of prime importance, I should say, was environment. My home life was not sufficiently musical to substitute for the utter lack of musical culture in the school and community. Radio was in its infancy and was considered such an experimental luxury that its benefits were denied to me for many years. The era of "community concert series" was not yet, at least in my home area, so practically no fine music or musicians were heard. Furthermore, the ignorance of the people of the community about music and musicians fostered an attitude on their part

[256]

and their children's parts relating to the "manliness" of the art that was a definite blight on my natural inclination toward it. But all these negative factors were not enough; the teaching I was subjected to was also negative. Who would reasonably expect a musician to come out of this? Hardly anyone, I should think. The very fact that today I *am* one, in some degree at least, leads me to conclude that heredity, the innate will to be musical, is *primarily* responsible for my being so; still, that hereditary factor had to be reinforced by a favorable "change" in environment ere it began to assert itself earnestly. When at last I was given an insight into the realm of music as a real art, when I began to *hear* good music daily, the urge to be a creator of music became too powerful to ignore. An interesting commentary on the hereditary factor in music is seen in the fact that in my freshman year in college I took the Kwalwasser-Dykema and/or Seashore tests along with the other music students, and I came out with the highest score. This couldn't possibly have been a result of environment because my musical environment compared unfavorably with many or most of them.

I entered college with my mind firmly set upon becoming a "singing musician." I realized by the time I entered college that piano was not to be my performing medium, for I seemed to have too poor motor ability. Too, my voice had developed into a tenor of good quality, I had a fine ear and seemed to have the "feel" of singing, and certainly not of less consideration, I *enjoyed* singing profoundly.

Fortunately the institution I entered was a small private junior college in which the music department was small enough for consideration of each person as an individual, and each individual *did* get as much attention as he desired. Under these conditions I earnestly set about overcoming my deficiencies, for I realized that I had a long way to go before I could begin to think of myself as a musician.

I began the study of singing under a very competent and inspirational teacher. She began teaching me technique—voice "placement," diction, breathing and so forth, but at the same time she began to teach me a musicianly approach to singing through proper phrasing, attention to pitch and *listening* to how the voice part was fitted to the accompaniment. The application of technique was not limited to abstract vocalises and exercises. Rather, it was applied to songs of the better "popular" class and semi-classical types. Then little by little as my vocal ability and musical "appreciation" grew, she introduced me to the better things of vocal literature. This teacher certainly had an insight into the psychological aspect of growth, and could well be emulated by myself and other prospective vocal teachers.

As far as academic musical credits were concerned, the number earned in this institution was not ponderous, for the school was simply a liberal arts school, and practically all the music courses were designed to be elective. But the *intrinsic* musical credit I acquired was practically inestimable. I spent hours each day at the piano practicing piano and voice and exploring new material; I listened to all the phonograph records in the department library over and over; I avidly devoured all the books on singing and singers I could find; I attended all the concerts or events of musical interest that time and money would permit. In short I reacted to music as a vacuum does to air, except that I'm not yet filled.

Of great import in my musical training was the organization during my second year of a men's glee club of which I became president. Furthermore, from this group was selected a quartet, and I was chosen to sing first tenor in it. I had long since come to believe that some of the very best training a person may get, pointing toward a public singing career, is that of actually *singing in public*, and this quartet work proved to be a medium affording all of this opportunity one could desire. We were soon singing almost daily at some event—business clubs, funerals, radio, even our own full evening concerts. In fact, we proved so popular and such good advertising for the school that I was offered a scholarship for a third year of post-graduate work, which I accepted.

Since I was the only one of the four whose primary interest was in music, it fell to my lot to do any arranging or rearranging of our music we deemed necessary. In my second year I had begun the study of harmony and some elementary composition, and consequently was gaining some small idea about the structure of music. This type of work was an invaluable means of putting into practice my rapidly growing abilities.

After the third year at this junior college, when I had taken about all the music courses offered, and my fellow quartet members had graduated, I decided I wanted to continue my work at a conservatory, preferably in a large city where musical standards were higher and opportunities greater. I learned of a school in one of our largest cities that offered some partial scholarships; I applied for one of these, and on the strength of recommendations of my junior college teachers I received one.]

At this conservatory a whole new musical vista was opened for me. My vocal study was with an artist teacher who was an artist in the true sense of the word. She taught me new techniques; she opened fields of repertory with which I was unfamiliar and gave me advice on song interpretation which only a successful concert artist can give. I resumed private piano lessons, and this time progress was more commensurate with effort, though of course piano now was of secondary importance to me. I continued the study of harmony, form, and analysis, choral conducting, sight singing and dictation. However, in spite of the excellent academic training received there, I believe the thing of primary importance to me was the musical "atmosphere"—the omnipresent concerts, symphonies, operas, excellent radio musical productions and the like that afforded me opportunity to *hear* music. In relation to the average music student of junior college level I was considerably behind on familiarity with an abundance of material. A person may study music in an academic sense all his life without becoming a real musician if he doesn't have the chance to practice aurally what he knows or studies. Music, after all, is *sound*, a product of the "aural mind" of the composer transmitted to the "aural mind" of the listener. A person cannot become a musician by learning all the academic rules of the art in an abstract way. He must learn to hear those rules in actual musical application. In this wise my musical growth was enormous that year at the conservatory.

The next year I received an offer of a partial scholarship from a liberal arts college with which I was acquainted, in return for my work with its college quartet. For financial and other reasons I found it necessary to accept, though I realized that the musical "atmosphere" of the larger city would be sacrificed. However, there was the compensating factor of the public singing experience, the value of which I had already ascertained.

The quartet work proved to be on an even vaster scale at this institution, and my growth through the pursuit of it was certainly considerable. As is the case with all liberal arts colleges offering the Bachelor's degrees, "academic" requirements have to be met by musicians as well as biologists, so of course my music courses had to be interspersed with these "necessaries." However, when graduating, my total number of points credit in music was about 70 out of 120. Admittedly much of this work represented mere smatterings of various aspects of the art of music, but at least I had formed a "nodding acquaintance" with such more advanced things as counterpoint, form, analysis, conducting, and keyboard harmony. In my singing I had reasonably well progressed to the point where physical limitations imposed their rule.

Then came the war—and four years of musical inactivity. Since the war I have been primarily concerned with rebuilding my performing technique, since it seemed to have suffered more retrogression than the "theoretical" abilities.

In epitomizing the salient features of my musical growth I note that my first contact with music was favorable, and I reacted to it favorably, quickly assimilating tone, tonal relationship, and rhythm. However, upon commencing the study of an instrument, which was supposedly the way to go about learning music, those very faculties that I had developed and upon which my further growth should have been based were simply ignored. This was a most unfortunate breakdown in the sequence whereby I might have finished high-school well on the way to becoming a musician. As it happened I had to resume the sequence accidentally or "intuitively" of my own volition after altogether too many dormant years.

III

This is a human document of great interest, and it reveals many things of great significance. The writer's comments, his criticisms of the influences which were brought to bear upon him, and his self-judgments are very suggestive and enlightening. He tells a story of mingled failure and success. If you will put out of your mind the conventional stereotypes of music education, if you will simply ask yourself how you would go about organizing the best possible developmental influences for such a person at all points in his growth, and if you will remember that you have to deal not with one person but with many, you will be on the right track in planning a developmental program. We shall return to this concrete illustration many times, but before passing on there are three general comments to be made.

First, this man's musical growth has led him into a professional musical career. When he was a little child in the home, when he was in the elementary-school, even when he was in high-school there was no way at all of telling whether this would happen or not. Even when he was in junior college the issue was not decided. No one, then, could plan his early musical education with anything of the sort in mind. From the developmental viewpoint, however, this does not matter in the least. What the professional musician needs, and does not always have, is an adequate and rounded musical growth. This is also what everyone should get out of his musical education. That musical growth naturally issues in certain avenues of fulfillment, and whether one happens to make a living out of them or not is something that only the future can decide.

Second, the writer's belief that he has a more than average innate musical gift is interesting and probably correct. This, however, does not mean that he belongs in some special category of human beings. Everyone is musically responsive. The musical impulse, the will to be musical, is universal and normal. But in some people it seems stronger than in others. That, at least, is a reasonable position to take. But one needs to understand the real nature of the argument, and also its implications. The proof of this man's superior musical responsiveness lies in his persistence in the face of difficulties and his quick response to opportunities. Since other people did not respond or persist, one concludes that there must have been an unknown quantity, an "X," which made him behave differently. Now there is something to this argument, but it is certainly not watertight. Above all, we do not know in the least what this unknown causal factor, this "X," really is. To call it hereditary is simply to say that we know nothing at all about it, that it has eluded our observation. Conceivably, though again not certainly, the real cause of this man's persistent musical behavior might have been various subtle and hidden personal influences and attractions, for instance his reactions to his parents or to his teachers or to some of his friends. A psycho-

[260]

analyst would assuredly not rule out such possibilities. So we must beware of saying that this man grew musically when he had the chance and overcame adverse circumstances simply because he was talented, for the word "talent" is the equivalent in psychology of the term "unknown quantity" in mathematics.

I present this analysis, not for its own sake, but because of its implications. One of the most dangerous fallacies that any teacher or educational planner can commit is to say that pupils who do not respond well to certain educational influences are lacking in talent. Boiled down to its logical essentials this amounts to saying that they do not respond, and we do not know why. Yet it can be, and, in fact, is used as an excuse for any and every kind of bad teaching. Quite possibly the trouble may be with the influences, and not with the pupil. To his early piano teachers this individual probably presented the picture of an untalented person. Yet when constructive opportunities came along he blossomed out. Is it not reasonable to believe that there may be plenty of people whose potentialities are as good as his, and for whom music might mean as much as it does to him, who fall by the wayside never to rise again because of persistently and banefully stupid influences, or because they never have the luck to come under good ones? Our business is certainly not to set up an arbitrary scheme, and then to say that those with whom it misses fire must have come from parents with the wrong chromosomes. Our business clearly is to organize the best influences at all points all along the line, so that so far as possible no one shall be lost to music, or lose the good gifts music can bring, because of our stupidity.

The third, and for our purposes the most important thing to notice about this account is its revelation of the real conditions of musical growth. Whenever the poetic and aesthetic values of music were stressed and revealed, musical growth went forward. Whenever those values were obscured and negated, it came to a halt. Listening to his mother sing, singing back to her, bouncing a ball to her singing and playing, becoming a member of a performing organization, coming under the influence of musically inspiring teachers, enjoying the musical atmosphere of a great city, discovering music by means of his radio—these were developmental influences in this man's career as a person. The stereotyped piano lessons, on the other hand, were not. It is perfectly clear which kind of influences ought to be built into the texture of a developmental program. Notice that some of the most effective influences were also the most informal and apparently casual, and that some of the most ineffective were of the type ordinarily considered desirable. One cannot escape the suspicion that if this man's parents had encouraged him to take up the accordion when he wanted to, instead of influencing him to go back to the piano, it might have done a great deal more for him in the long run. Does this seem like a shocking suggestion? It should not. There is no doubt that as a musical medium the piano is far more important than the accordion. But it is not the abstract or general desirability of an experience that matters, but its actual psychological effect upon a growing person in his actual situation and stage of development. If the accordion, at that moment, could have revealed more about music than the piano, it was at that moment the better choice in spite of all general and abstract arguments and conventional prepossessions. So a developmental program of music education will be hospitable to any and every kind of activity or endeavor so long as it is musically revealing and impelling—so long as it is a true developmental influence—and compared to this, its conventional respectability or abstract importance will not matter one whit.

In this connection notice too how all the main lines of musical growth work together and reinforce each other. The vocal quartet in the junior college created a whole host of "initiative situations"— situations in which this man had to make musical choices on his own responsibility. These immediately acted as challenges for the development both of musical skill and of musical insight. The radio which came as a gift during his senior year in high-school, and also the musical opportunities of a great city later on, opened up expanding vistas of musical awareness, and this in turn was a powerful dynamic making for general musical growth. It is interesting to observe that the writer has nothing at all to say about growth in musical discrimination. The reason probably is that he simply took it for granted, for it is very certain that it actually took place. Still more significantly, when skill and nothing but skill was stressed, there was virtually no growth at all, even in skill itself. This leads to a further point of major importance in the planning of a developmental program. We should try to organize activities, experiences, and learnings each of which carries forward and activates musical growth along all its main avenues. No doubt in this situation or in that, one or another of these lines of growth should be chiefly and explicitly in focus. But if any one of them is completely ignored, there is something wrong, and growth even in the specifically desired direction is sure to suffer. This, as we shall see, provides an operating criterion for the planning and organization of the developmental program. Awareness, initia-

[262]

tive, discrimination, insight, and skill are not independent objectives to be promoted in isolation from one another. They are organically related aspects of integral musical growth, not one of which can be slighted without weakening the rest, not one of which can be fostered as it should be fostered without helping all the others along.

FOR FURTHER STUDY

The human document here presented should be used as an opportunity to review, reconsider, and bring to a new synthesis all the ideas that have been presented so far in this book. Moreover it can also be used as a preview for the planning of a program of music education by asking oneself how such a case could best be dealt with, how the problems indicated by the writer could best be met, and what would be the most constructive influences the school could bring to bear.

CHAPTER TWELVE

The Developmental Program:
Its Content

I

It is illuminating to think of a developmental program of music education as consisting of a general sequence, with the various specialties such as the orchestra, the band, the *a cappella* choir, the high-level offerings in applied music, the courses in theory, and so on, stemming from it as branches stem from the trunk of a tree. Although this conception is thoroughly sound and very helpful in organization and planning, it is somewhat novel and requires a redefinition of some familiar terms and notions. In particular it involves a great expansion of the notion of general music. This term, as ordinarily used, refers to a course usually offered in the junior or senior high-school, running sometimes for one semester, sometimes for two, and sometimes for as many as four. As understood here, however, it means a sequence of work and offerings, dominated by a definite point of view, beginning in the nursery-school or kindergarten, and continuing through the elementary-school and into the secondary-school and even the college. In this chapter we shall deal first with the controlling ideas and the content of general music as so conceived, and then with the typical specialties as outgrowths of it.

II

General music, understood in this way, is the core of the developmental program. It should have the following broad characteristics.

1 General music is "general" first in the sense of being a planned sequence of activities, endeavors, and learnings designed to promote comprehensive and rounded musical growth. Here is one respect in which it differs from the specialties. To be sure, musical

growth is a primary concern in the orchestra, the choir, the band, the courses in theory, and so forth. But in such situations there is bound to be a special emphasis, and properly so. An orchestral rehearsal, for instance, can and should do something to foster musical awareness, but here there is a special purpose which ought not to be unduly sacrificed. The same is true of courses in theory or in the history of music. Such offerings are indeed related to musical growth in all its aspects, but they are necessarily concerned with growth in some special direction. General music, on the other hand, deals with music as such and with musical growth as such. In it the time devoted to the development of awareness, or initiative, or discrimination need not be stinted for the sake of developing insight or skill. On the other hand, the persons carrying on the sequence in general music will not feel bound to ignore either insight or skill for the sake of avoiding what is called a "technical approach."

It is very important to see that general music, properly understood, involves a positive and not a negative idea. As actually taught in the form of a specific secondary-school course it is often treated as a sort of catchall, a place in the program where people do a little of this and that, and nothing very well, an opportunity for the "non-specialist." This at once deprives it of driving power, and indeed, of educational respectability. One unfortunate result is that trained music teachers who are assigned to handle it feel themselves somewhat at a loss, because the only idea they have is that they must avoid any kind of specialized or technical difficulty. Clearly, however, this is an impossible foundation for any kind of constructive work. The proper policy is entirely different. The true purpose of general music is to promote and foster in the most comprehensive way possible the over-all musical growth of the particular group of people with whom one has to do, without the limitations which become necessary in the specialties. And to repeat, work so conceived and so organized belongs not only in the secondary school, but throughout the entire music program from the very beginning to the very end.

2 Again, general music as so conceived is "general" in the sense of having the widest possible appeal and value. It very often happens that in many senior high-schools not more than about ten per cent of the pupils are effectively reached by the music program. The clear reason is that the offerings actually consist of an array of specialties on the highest attainable level. Opportunities are limited, and so inevitably appeal is limited also. Now even those who may bog

down on the proposition that music can have meaning and value for one hundred per cent of the human race will hardly argue that its significance is confined to only one person in ten. It is just conceivable that only one person in ten is suitable material for membership in an orchestra or an *a cappella* choir, though even this would certainly look like a very pessimistic estimate, and one may well believe that if proper stimulation and opportunity were provided, the ratio would be very different. But the point is not to gather recruits for orchestras and choirs, or to treat such activities as the ultimate ends of a musical education. The point is to do everything possible to stimulate and evoke the musical responsiveness which exists in most, if not in all, normal human beings. One may confidently maintain that in every school population there is an enormous potential interest in music, which all too often remains untapped. The idea of general music is to set up a sequence of activities, endeavors, and learnings designed to reveal the power and significance of the art to just as many people as possible. In some high schools the music teachers who have done this have been amazed at the avalanche pried loose. I know of some cases where teachers have struck this particular rock, and have been almost drowned in the resulting flood. And to repeat once more, work organized on this principle belongs not only in the high school, but all along the line.

3 The pattern of general music as here characterized stands on its own foundations, maintains its own values, and makes its own contribution. It is not an inferior substitute for specialized studies and activities, nor is it in a direct sense a preparation for them. It ought to be possible for a person going through a school system to get a well-rounded musical development of real significance and value without becoming a member of any official performing organizations, without taking private or class lessons in applied music, and without going into any courses in theory or music history. Such a person, to be sure, would lack something, but so do we all. He would lack certain expert and specialized refinements. But the specialized musician often lacks a rounded musical development, which is also quite a defect! Moreover it is very likely that as such a person came along in a vital developmental sequence, he would want to branch out into this or that specialty. But the point is that general music should be thought of as an educational pattern intrinsically independent of and prior to the specialties, and with intrinsic and independent values of its own. Specifically this means that general music

[266]

in the elementary school should not be for the sake of training recruits for a secondary-school music program consisting chiefly of performing specialties, but for the sake of over-all musical growth. Also it means that in the secondary school it should not be regarded as a poor relation of the performing organizations, and that membership in such an organization should not be regarded as a satisfactory substitute for general music, since it too has something vital to contribute. General music is the trunk. The specialties are the branches. That is the true relationship.

Such, then, are the broad characteristics of general music as here conceived. Before passing on to specific matters, a few further comments remain to be made.

First, the idea is psychologically sound. This you may see if you will refer to the case study of musical growth presented in the last chapter. In the writer's early life all the favorable influences—singing at home, ball-bouncing, the harmonica, the radio—belonged to the pattern of general music. They were all influences making for a broad musical development without any confining specialization. When an attempt was made to channel his musical growth in terms of a specialty, by means of piano lessons begun about the age of seven, everything went wrong. Perhaps more intelligent piano instruction would have yielded happier outcomes, but even so there would have been limitations. Even at his conservatory, the "atmosphere" of which he speaks so highly belonged in the category of general music. Now it is quite understandable that a person could get a very good, repaying, and significant musical education out of nothing but such general influences, assuming of course that they were intensified, organized, and planned. The writer of the case study, however, became a specialist and made a professional career. If he had been under the influences of a really vital sequence of general music until he was well into his teens, what would have happened to his specialty? In all probability it would have benefited. He would have been a quicker, more effective, more intelligent learner. He would have had a firmer foundation, a wider outlook, a greater vitality in his later work in music. To think that general music activities are trivialities, and that specialization alone is serious business is a capital fallacy. Broad and free musical growth is the most important single thing for anybody in this field, whether he is going to be a specialist or not.

Second, the idea of general music, as here characterized, is good educational strategy. Music education in this country has gone a very long way, and has scored a most remarkable success. But it has done so by riding the specialties, and it has just about come to the end of that road. But there is another path to be followed. There are other fields to be reaped, and they are ripe unto harvest. School administrators and curriculum workers are well aware of this, even if music educators are not. There is little argument against the proposition that music has potentially enormous value and potentially vast appeal. But this value and this appeal must be released, and such release is impossible by means of a program oriented chiefly toward the specialties. A good program of music education can and should mean something far more than and something far different from producing and maintaining fine performing organizations at the upper levels. So far as it goes, this is admirable, but it can only go just so far and no farther. What the most forward-looking general educators want and are willing to support is a program of music in the schools which will reveal the far-ranging significance of the art in human living. This means a program oriented, not toward the specialties, but toward broad and many-sided musical growth. If music educators find this idea hard to comprehend and to realize, it can only indicate that they are to some extent the prisoners of their own success.

This leads directly to the third pertinent comment. A great many trained musicians undoubtedly suffer from a blind spot in their thinking. To them music means a specialty, and musical effectiveness means specialized expertness. This is all that they can see. What they fail to see is the great art of music itself, the art of tonal poetry, as a vital element in human culture and individual experience. They accept it as axiomatic that children should be started on a specialty as soon as possible, and that standards are determined by expert achievement in a specialty. To such people, general music is a *terra incognita*, to be regarded with suspicion. When they try to deal with it, they are very apt to fail. This is why enthusiastic amateurs, who have less skill but a more direct and realistic attitude, often make better teachers of general music than trained professionals. Surely, however, this cannot be other than a great reproach. To bring the art of music, with all its poetic values, vitally home to those who, whether they know it or not, are hungry for it, should be a most inspiring challenge to any musician. This argument for general music broadly conceived as the core of the developmental program, is precisely a plea for the abolition of the blind spot, and for a recognition of the authenticity and value of a broad and rounded musical growth.

[268]

As to the actual content of this developmental core, it cannot be completely determined in advance. What should be done at any given time in any first grade, or third grade, or ninth grade will depend largely upon the human factors of the situation—the backgrounds, interests, and personalities of the pupils, the personality and equipment of the teacher—and also upon the opportunities that present themselves. Thus it is not possible to lay out a stereotyped course of study, and there should be much freedom and much flexibility. Nevertheless our understanding of musical growth provides us with a basis of order and criteria for choice. The content of the sequence in general music must consist of activities, endeavors, and learnings designed to foster musical awareness, musical initiative, musical discrimination, musical insight, and musical skill. They should be thought of and planned as developmental experiences. In planning and choosing them for pupils at various levels of maturity, the controlling considerations should be the characteristics and rhythms of the process of growth.

It is convenient and in many respects illuminating to think of the activities, endeavors, and learnings which make up the program under the three headings of performance, listening, and composing. But this classification can be seriously misleading. It is, by no manner of means, hard and fast, and the three divisions are in no sense watertight compartments. In actual practice the three types of activity should constantly merge and interfuse flexibly and naturally, so that in a given unit, or lesson, or period all three may be involved. The very last thing we want is to set up three self-contained sequences, for the paramount consideration is not whether a child is performing, or listening, or composing, but whether the development of his musical responsiveness is being effectively fostered. Still, if this proviso is kept in mind—and it is of the very highest importance—the threefold classification does have its uses in the orderly organization of our thinking and planning. But to repeat once more, the developmental program is a program of musical growth, and not a program of performing, listening, and composing. These latter are means and instrumentalities only, and not ends in themselves.

III

We now turn to consider some sample illustrations of activities in the category of performance as they may appear in the developmental program.

[269]

1 Moorhead and Pond have given an admirable summary of what musical performance should mean for very young children.

Music for young children is primarily the discovery of sound. Their deepest interest is in tone color. Their first need is for a wide variety of sound-making material. The instruments with which they are provided must be those that they can use most efficiently for their own purposes, should present no technical problems that are beyond their intellectual and physical powers of solution; as many as possible should be portable; the children should be allowed to use the instruments when, where, and how they wish so long as no harm is done to them, and all should possess intrinsically valuable timbres. Nothing is less correct than the idea that second-rate toy instruments are sufficient to fill the child's needs, and instruments are not enough. No restrictions other than those absolutely necessary should be placed in the child's way to hinder him from using any of the potentially soniferous materials of his everyday environment. He needs opportunity to experience and use the sounds of wood, metal, pottery, glass, stretched skins, strings, blown tubes and reeds and other materials which are present or can be given to him. . . . He must be allowed to use his voice naturally. Not only the conventional singing voice and notes within the commonly (and errone-ously) accepted compass of his voice, but all cries and vocalizations of any kind whatsoever and notes of whatever pitch he can sing them are parts of his musical vocabulary.[1]

Here we have, in embryo form, the whole meaning of musical per-formance in a developmental program of music education. Notice how musical development along all its five avenues is directly fos-tered. Musical awareness is cultivated by means of a wide range of very immediate, concrete, attractive, and purposive experiences. Mu-sical initiative is strongly encouraged, for the children are not told to do this or that, but are put into situations which offer many easy and attractive choices which promise successful and significant out-comes. Musical discrimination is evidently involved, for the children begin to discover through direct, immediate, concrete experience what a good instrumental tone and a natural singing tone mean. Musical insight, too, is fostered, since the children have to do with tonal media of various potentialities, and begin to find out the ex-pressive potentialities of the voice through the imitation of cries and vocalizations and the singing of melodic fragments. Musical skill also is not neglected, for as we have seen, the matrix of all technique

---

[1]Gladys E. Moorhead and Donald Pond, *Music of Young Children. II. General Obser-vations*, p. 17. Pillsbury Foundation for the Advancement of Music Education, Santa Barbara, California 1942.

is the control of action in terms of musical responsiveness. When one watches a group of little children playing and experimenting with tone and rhythm in such ways as these, the spectacle may strike one as exceedingly simple. Yet one should not miss its significance. They are dealing with music, on their childish level, exactly as the best and most sensitive of virtuosi deal with it—as an expressive medium to be explored, used, and enjoyed with freedom and confidence. Those who admire the flower should not despise the bud!

2 The organized rhythm band and the organized toy orchestra belong to a higher stage of maturity, because more is demanded in the way of specific controls and of considerations beyond the level of sheer immediacy. There is instrumentation to be decided upon. There are parts to be laid out. There is perhaps the teacher's performance of a simple piece on the piano to be apprehended and followed. It may even be that some kind of simple visualization of the music in an easy "homemade" notation is introduced to help things along. But all the same values should be present. The same five avenues of musical growth should be fostered, although they are now taking more definite form. Initiative is the great desideratum here. All possible choices should be left to the children. What instrumentation sounds best? What contribution can be made by nonmelodic instruments? What variations can be introduced when a phrase appears several times? How fast or how slowly should the music be played? How can its expressive and mood values be brought out? The teacher should refrain from deciding such matters, and use her skill for the sake of helping the children to reach decisions satisfactory to them. Clearly such "initiative situations" and challenges involve awareness, discrimination, insight, and the basic matrix of skill.

There are several general comments to be made about activities of this kind.

A. *While classified here under performance, it is clear that listening and composing may also be involved in varying degrees and in various ways.* Sometimes a toy orchestra may undertake to play a set piece, but even so the children should listen to it, think about it, experiment with it, and make decisions about the best instrumentation. Sometimes the decision may be to have the toy orchestra or the rhythm band accompany a song, and then there is a wider area of choice. Sometimes it may be best to have the children actually make up the music *de novo*. These, of course, are only suggestions and indications. What

[271]

they are intended to make clear is that rhythm band work and toy orchestra work should not be stereotyped under any one rubric.

B. *The setting of a musical project with the rhythm band or the toy orchestra may have a great deal to do with its developmental value.* If a set piece is imposed as a sort of music lesson, awareness and initiative are reduced to the vanishing point, and other values will be impoverished too. Suppose, however, that the children have been learning about the Pilgrim Fathers, and that they undertake, with the teacher's help, to find and organize for performance a little piece expressing, let us say, their joy at the first harvest, or even to make one up. Then it is clear that we have a project of an entirely different order, and of much greater potential fruitfulness. In such an undertaking all five lines of musical growth are far more effectively promoted.

C. *It is an error to think that in rhythm band work and toy instrument work the teacher should make the decisions, or that she should allow the textbook to make them, because by so doing a better performance will result, and because the group will get somewhere much faster.* The aim is not to produce a good performance for its own sake, but to foster musical growth and musical responsiveness, and this is best brought about by the children's own experimenting, choosing, and purposing. Here, as always, it is a capital mistake to sacrifice developmental fruitfulness for the sake of an immediate and quick result.

D. *It is an error to think of rhythm band work or toy instrument work as in any sense a direct preparation for instrumental study "proper."* On the contrary, such work has authentic values of its own, and if it is preparatory in any sense, it is only so because of its power to foster general musical growth. What children ought to get out of experimenting with and playing simple instruments is a revelation of the potentialities of tone and rhythm which purely vocal experience cannot afford. Just how much such simple instrumental experience can mean and how much value it can have is clearly shown in the case study cited in the last chapter, the writer of which recounts that first the harmonica and then the accordion opened up for him whole new vistas of musical possibilities.

3 Coming now to singing, no one can doubt its importance and value. Yet there is good reason to believe that we have been altogether too uncritical in accepting it as the paramount activity of the general music program from the kindergarten on. In general, singing has been far too narrowly conceived, and far too monopolistically handled. A vital program of music education is a great

deal more than a program of song singing without any further qualifications, even though the songs selected may be good ones. The setting in which the songs are presented, and the emphasis in presenting them are considerations of determining importance.

For instance, a certain third-grade had been studying the lives of famous personalities in the history of the United States. In connection with this work they found out a great deal about Stephen Foster and his life and music. This presented an opportunity for learning and singing by ear a great many of his songs. The children made drawings to illustrate the songs, and listened with keen delight to recordings of his music whenever the chance to do so presented itself.

Once again, a sixth-grade was preparing a Greek play as part of their work in Social Studies. They wanted the other sixth grades to help out with the musical end of the program. It developed that the music teacher was able to make good suggestions as to suitable material, for she was aware that the sixth grades were studying Greek life at the time, and had made special preparation. So a choice of Greek folk songs was on hand. Opportunities naturally presented themselves for bringing to the children information about Greek education and Greek music, about the early Greek flute and lyre, and for listening to a fine recording of *The Hymn to Apollo*.

It is quite true that the singing of songs need not and should not always or perhaps even usually be "integrated" with other subjects in the curriculum. But the singing of songs should always be "integrated" with genuine and vital interests and meaningful concerns. It should be a cultural and developmental experience, not simply a self-contained music lesson. The reason for this is clear. Musical responsiveness, as we have seen, is responsiveness to the poetic values and meanings of music, to music as an essentially expressive art. With children the expressive content of the song must be made very concrete, very immediate, or it will not be grasped. With older persons this is not so necessary, particularly if they have had a sound musical development. For them a musical composition tends to create its own interest and convey its meanings directly. But if we do not develop these considerations very explicitly with children, the learning and singing of a song is almost sure to become little more than a formal and technical problem, and most of its developmental values are dissipated. At all levels, however, everything depends upon what David Barnett calls the "imaginative approach" to the singing of songs.[1]

[1]David Barnett, *They Shall Have Music*, Chapter 2. George E. Stewart, Publisher, Inc., New York, 1944.

[273]

The following are the chief developmental values which should accrue from experiences in singing in the sequence of general music.

A. *Such work can do much to develop musical awareness through the singing of many songs of many types, with their expressive values and poetic meanings always emphasized and made apparent.* The development of musical awareness, as we have seen, turns upon exploration, and the illustrations already given serve to suggest what can be done to stimulate children to seek, find, and enjoy a wide range of musical experiences in connection with the singing they do at school.

B. *There are many ways in which singing can be organized to promote musical initiative.* The request from the sixth-grade to other sixth-grades for help in the preparation of their Greek play is a case in point. It is worth noticing that in this instance the teacher was wise enough not to supply the answers out of hand, but that she simply made resources available. That, of course, is always the proper policy. One creates "initiative situations," where perhaps a program is to be presented, or material found and examined for some purpose, or by opening up problems of interpretation for discussion and decision, or by encouraging individuals to bring to school songs that they know and like. Then one makes it one's business to see that the initiatives are feasible, that they lead to success rather than frustration.

C. *The developmental experience of learning and singing a song should, among other things, foster musical discrimination.* Here the quality of the song will be a paramount consideration. As we have seen, a piece of music is "good" whether or not it rises to the height of greatness, in so far as it embodies and projects authentic emotional intimations. Also a performance is "good" in so far as it sincerely and genuinely conveys the emotional values of the music. Good taste is developed by dealing with musical content and musical performance in terms of these criteria, and to do so is not only possible but also necessary from the very beginning. At first this is a very simple matter. It means letting children discover by direct experience what it means to sing artistically significant songs in an expressive and appealing fashion. Little by little the constitutive expressive elements in the music come increasingly under conscious attention and control, and the sequence of experience through the grades and into the secondary-school should be pointed toward an apprehension of what artistic singing, artistic songs, and artistic music mean.

[274]

D. *Some of the most important developmental values to be derived from singing have to do with musical insight.* There is no medium which can so well convey the expressive flow of melody and phrase. Also the experience of properly directed singing can lead to a grasp of the expressive value and meaning of good tone quality. It must be remembered, however, that good vocal tone quality is expressive tone quality. This is what should always be emphasized, rather than conventional tone, and particularly the kind of unnatural, hushed, breathy conventional tone so often idolized as "head voice" or "child voice." This kind of conventional emphasis points straight toward false standards of discrimination and erroneous musical insights. Once again, singing can and should help in the development of harmonic insights. The principal means of bringing this about is to use some kind of accompaniment, usually on the piano, and to call attention to it. The belief that children should always sing unaccompanied is a most peculiar fallacy, for it means that they are having a musically incomplete experience in song. Of course the accompaniment should not be used simply to cover up the singers' defects. It should and can be used as an important opportunity to develop certain significant musical insights, notably those having to do with the harmonic content of music. The use of the rhythm band, the toy orchestra, or some simple instrumental ensemble for accompaniment purposes can also point in the same direction, and such procedures can also have value in developing a grasp of the rhythmic structure as an expressive element in the song.

There are, however, certain types of musical insight for the development of which purely vocal experience is not well adapted. The melodic flow, tone quality, harmonic and rhythmic content, and expressive tonality trends are well within the range of possibility. But it must be remembered that the voice always tends to deal with music in terms of total expressive patterns rather than note-wise. This is its peculiar value, its "genius" so to speak. There is a great deal in the musical score which does not naturally or directly become meaningful in a setting of vocal experience. To try to teach note reading through the agency of singing is certainly to create difficulties, and probably insuperable difficulties, no matter what ingenious devices are used. We should by all means confine ourselves to the natural potentialities of the medium, and not try to force it to the service of essentially alien ends. To graph the up and down of the pitch, the beginnings and endings of phrases, and some of the durational values, at first in simple "homemade" symbolism, and later on in the notational symbols can be very helpful. But it is dubious if one should try

[275]

to go much further in connection with singing alone. And even so the purpose is not to establish a reading facility, but to point up musical insight by having the young singers see what they are trying to do and what they are experiencing.

E. *Ample experience with the expressive singing of artistically significant and appealing songs is one of the best possible starting points for the development of musical skill.* Yet one must be clear about what such an experience can and cannot do. What can and should be done is to establish an attitude toward musical utterance that is capable of being carried over into other media of performance. What cannot be done and should not be contemplated is to build vocal expertness as an end in itself. The controlling objective of this work is not voice training or vocal technique, but ample and convincing experience with expressive song. As we have seen, one of the great weaknesses of a great deal of technical study is lack of genuine musical control, which makes it mechanical, musically unintelligible, and in effect inefficient. Plenty of experience with the right kind of singing can do a great deal to rectify this defect, and to render later endeavors in the learning of specialized techniques more fruitful.

4 Has instrumental work "proper," that is, work with the standard instruments including the piano, any place in the sequence of general music? It certainly can have such a place, and it should be included wherever possible, for it has very great potential developmental values. The intention, however, should be not to develop specialized instrumental techniques, but to use the instruments for the sake of broad and many-sided musical growth.

For instance, little children can very well be allowed and helped to examine the piano, to look at its insides and to see how they work, to see what the sustaining pedal does, to experiment with the keyboard. Opportunities to examine an organ console, to explore some of the mysteries of the instrument, to watch it being played, and perhaps to try it out for themselves can be very rewarding and exercise a lasting and long-remembered constructive influence. Later on, when they are learning about the band and orchestral instruments, it is a very good idea to have some of the actual instruments available, to allow the children to handle them and operate them, and to give them just enough help and instruction so that they can produce some very simple music, even if this is no more than a few notes. It is perfectly possible in a very short time to enable children to make instruments "sound," to find out what it means to manipulate them, and in some cases to play simple and familiar tunes on them. The same is true of the piano. Experiences of this sort are likely to be very captivating and can be exceedingly fruitful. They open up a vital awareness of instrumental potentialities which may never be developed even by a great deal of listening. They can be the starting point for many valuable initiatives, for they very often suggest self-chosen avenues of study. They can very quickly establish discriminations in connection with listening which are difficult to inaugurate in other ways. They can do much to advance various phases of musical insight, for even a very little direct instrumental experience can reveal many things about the content and organization of music which do not readily come out in a purely vocal setting. And to have made even a few tones, or played a few simple tunes on a string instrument, or a wind instrument, or a clavier instrument is to have gained a new grasp of the meaning and significance of musical skill.

In terminating this discussion of what may be classified as the performance aspects of the general program, it should be understood that what is here presented is in no sense a complete scheme, and that it is not so intended. The purpose has simply been to suggest the kind of things that may and should be done, and to use sample illustrations of work that has been found successful and suitable in certain situations but might not be appropriate in others. The thing to remember is that musical performance in the sequence of general music should always turn upon the experience of expressive musical utterance rather than upon the development of specialized technique. The whole setting of this phase of the work should be oriented toward this end. With this in mind, it is clear that the more diversified the media and opportunities for making music can be, the better. The developmental value of many and varied samples of significant musical activity is quite obvious. Experiences of this kind are sadly lacking in the background of a great many trained musicians. There can hardly be two opinions as to their values and potentialities.

IV

The encouragement of composition should most certainly be an element in a sequential program of general music at all levels. This can be accomplished, and in fact is being accomplished in so many different ways that to reduce it to a standard procedure is an impossibility. Perhaps the best mode of dealing with the subject will be to describe briefly various ways in which the thing is done successfully, and then to indicate the values to be expected and the errors to be avoided.

With very little children musical composition means the simplest, most direct, most spontaneous kind of musical projection, using the voice or the simplest kind of mechanical means. The dramatization of music, that is, the acting out in movement and pantomime what it "says," also belongs in this general category. All that is needed is suggestion, encouragement, opportunity, and recognition. With older children poetry may be effectively used as a starting point for composition, in the manner that has already been described in these pages. A poem, too, can be the starting point for an instrumental composition as well as a song. In David Barnett's work he used music that was heard and enjoyed as the incentive for creative effort. Thus he would present mazurkas of different types, whimsical, melancholy, pompous, or graceful, and bring about a situation in which some child would decide that he wanted to compose "one like that." Also he has made much of utilizing the poetic experiences of everyday life—the rain, the wind, the sunshine, and so forth—as points of origin for composition.[1] Again, the members of a certain third grade, having found much satisfaction in writing their own words to a "Song Without Words," went on to make up their own tune to another piece of self-made poetry. In doing so they found out much about the flow and movement of music, about the up and down that makes a pretty and expressive tune, and about the possibilities of the piano part, which may be the same as the singing part, or play a second tune which sounds well with the voice part. Again in a certain high school an enterprising teacher organized a course with the title "Music for Fun," which was on an elective basis. She began with singing, listening, and so forth, but as soon as a momentum had been established she started to urge and stimulate creative endeavor, and soon obtained a very good response. Some of the pupils could manage nothing more than a four- or eight-measure phrase, but with the help of the teacher these were always expanded and developed. As a usual thing it was necessary for her to give assistance in harmonization, the development of accompaniments, and so forth, but the outcomes of the year's activity were very creditable indeed. In fact, the class was able to give a composers' concert, which attracted much attention and interest in the school and among the parents. These,

[1]David Barnett, *Living with Music*. George E. Stewart, Publisher, Inc., New York, 1944.

of course, are only samples and suggestive instances, presented to indicate some of the many ways in which musical composition can be promoted as part of the general program.

As to the values of such undertakings, everything once more turns on what David Barnett calls the imaginative approach. The act of musical composition is the translation of feeling into tonal and rhythmic form. The actual circumstances under which a composition is born, the literal circumstances of the "inspiration," may differ enormously. This has certainly been the case with the great composers, and there is no doubt that it is just as true with children in school. Here is the reason why no one set procedure can be recommended, and why many diversified modes of approach may all be good. The point always is to stimulate the imagination and to motivate the attempt. And when children, or adolescents, or adults actually make the attempt under proper stimulation, and with some help and guidance available, they find that musical composition is incomparably more feasible than it is ordinarily supposed to be. To compose authentic music, which genuinely captures and conveys feeling, does not demand special talent of a very high order. It is a perfectly normal expression of musical responsiveness, and a powerful influence for developing that responsiveness. Moreover it is likely to be a very engrossing and captivating form of activity. Music teachers who have promoted it commonly find that the music period ceases to be nearly long enough for all that the pupils want to do. This powerful evocation of purpose is one of the surest of signs that we are dealing with a true and effective developmental experience, and fulfills an essential condition for the fostering of musical growth. Moreover to compose on one's own account brings one into contact with the realities of the art of music in a peculiarly intimate and vital manner. If a person is to grasp what music really is, and how it expresses and conveys poetic values, there is nothing like making some of it for himself. So musical composition is a potent influence in the development of musical insight. That initiative is involved in many ways is also very evident. And since stimulation, suggestion, and inspiration may come from other music, and from the endeavors of other people around one, musical awareness is involved as well. So much for the psychological and educational values of activities of this type.

Turning now to dangers and misconceptions to be avoided, there are three of them which call for comment.

First, the purpose of musical composition is not to teach the notation. When one puts the proposition bluntly in this form, it certainly seems obvious, and the opposite point of view looks nothing less than preposterous. But in some school systems, so-called "creative music" is in fact carried on as a separate activity for the stated reason that it is a good way to teach children to read music. Surely, however, this is putting the cart before the horse with a vengeance. It is perfectly true that if activities in the way of musical composition are promoted at all levels in the program, children are extremely likely to learn a great deal about the score by the time they get to high school—about key signatures, clefs, time signatures, measure bars, accidentals, rests, and so forth——which they rarely grasp in a setting of purely vocal experience, and which even instrumental experience easily leaves pretty vague. But these are incidental although genuine benefits, not main controlling purposes. Moreover when one has a musical idea and wants to put it on paper, one learns the symbols, not mechanically or parrot-fashion, but in terms of actual and genuine musical insight. But once again, musical composition is not an exercise in writing down music and using the notation. Indeed if it is treated as anything of the kind, its values are immediately and fatally extinguished, for it becomes formalized and routinized, and loses the imaginative quality and content in which lies its vitality.

In the second place, musical composition as here advocated and described, is not directly related either to the concomitant or the later study of theory. Its relationship to theory is rather like the relationship of toy instrument work to instrumental study "proper." That is to say, it is an agency for general musical development. Now there is no doubt whatever that any theory teacher would have cause to bless his stars if he could face a class of beginning students whose musical insights were already mature and only needed organizing. That is exactly what the systematic and extensive promotion of musical composition tends to offer. If every student who entered a conservatory had, for some years past, been composing music of his own under guidance, and if this were considered just as normal and natural a part of his musical education as singing or piano playing, the work of the institution would be transformed. And for those who will not enter a musical career, who are not going to be pianists, who are not going to be vocalists, but who can get immense values from being brought vitally into contact with the art of music, what more fruitful experience can there be than the experience of musical composition?

In the third place, in the promotion of musical composition by pupils we must not be dominated by the fetish of formal correctness.

[280]

Such activities are golden opportunities for pupils to find out by their own experimentation what sounds well and what does not sound well, what is expressive and what is not. Our business is to assist such experimentation, to see that it gets somewhere even though it does not reach perfection, not to kill initiative and confidence by excessive direction and pedantic restrictions. One of the main reasons why much of the teaching of theory is so ineffective is that students come to it with no background of musical experimentation, which means no adequate development of musical insight. Thus it is mistaken policy to stereotype musical composition in the elementary school by requiring the use of certain phrase patterns, or to stereotype it later on by requiring the use of diatonic harmonic resources only, or by treating consecutive fifths with a blue pencil. Let the pupils make their own mistakes. Let them find out that they are mistaken. Help them to see where the errors lie and what to do about them. Let them discover and try out whatever tonal resources they will. Help them to find and use new tonal resources. Remember that musical composition, which is always the projection of feeling into a pattern of tone and rhythm, is an agency for bringing about learning and growth, not an act to be attempted only after learning and growth have been completed.

V

Experiences in listening should appear in the developmental program at all possible points. Sometimes they should be expressly and directly organized as such. But many of them should be informal, casual, and incidental. Every opportunity to bring in such experiences should be taken. Children should listen to the singing and playing and compositions of other children. They should be given many chances to listen to the music making of the teacher. When one or two songs or pieces are being chosen to illustrate a social science unit or a dramatic project, as much music as possible should be heard, and the matter should not end merely with the teacher's picking out of appropriate material and having it learned for performance. There should be all possible encouragement given to out-of-school listening, on the radio, by means of the phonograph, at the movies, and in "live" performances. There should be free aesthetic discussion of music that has been heard and enjoyed. Children who have been fortunate enough to have had some special listening experience, as for instance attendance at a concert, should be asked to tell about it.

At the upper levels, books, magazine articles, and newspaper reviews may be used to stimulate and direct listening activities, to indicate possibilities, and to reveal standards of discrimination. It is not too much to say that a developmental program of music education should be saturated with listening.

The reason is that an expanding musical awareness is perhaps the most essential of all aspects of musical growth. Not only is it important in and of itself; it provides a basis for developing initiative and discrimination, and orientation for both insight and skill. One of the crying defects of much of our conventional music education, both in classrooms and studios is an extremely limited and narrow contact with the art of music itself. How can we expect boys and girls in their teens who have hardly ever, or perhaps never, heard a fine performance of fine music, and who have no notion of its values, to be good learners in matters of skill and insight, or to develop effective standards of taste and discrimination? What single influence can more powerfully promote the musical growth of a child than to bring him a varied wealth of musical experiences by way of listening? And if we wish really to make music live in the lives of those multitudes who will never go far in the direction of expertness, is it not far wiser to open up to them the treasuries of the art than to insist narrowly upon techniques which they hardly acquire and will never use?

Any restriction, deliberate or accidental, upon the range of listening experiences in a program of music education can only be considered baneful, narrowing, and antagonistic to musical growth. There are some school systems and many studios where practically no encouragement whatever is given to listening, and this is very bad indeed. There are other schools where listening is, as it were, canalized by being restricted to lists of material drawn up in advance and considered suitable for this grade or that, and on the secondary level by being organized into, and pretty well confined to courses in appreciation. This at least does involve a measure of explicit recognition, but listening experiences should overflow any such boundaries. In the ideal situation there will be a wealth of resources, both personal and mechanical, those resources will be readily available, and they will be drawn upon with the utmost freedom and flexibility. A good teacher of poetry will have a wealth of poetry at his command, and will use it on all sorts of occasions and for all sorts of purposes. Exactly the same thing is true of a good teacher of music.

There should be the freest possible interplay between listening and performance and between listening and composing. Listening to

[282]

music should stimulate the desire to perform, should suggest choices of music to be performed, and should help to establish standards of discrimination in judging one's performance; and it should be pointed up to fulfill these purposes. When one learns to perform a piece or to sing a song, it may be eminently desirable to hear it performed by others, or to listen to similar or related music. And the same relationship should obtain in connection with composition. To listen to much music, to listen in many ways and in many circumstances, to think about it, to discuss it, to carry it in one's heart and one's head is a developmental influence of the highest potency. The less standardized, the less formalized such experiences can be, the better. Here is something indispensable in any program of music education devoted to the promotion of musical growth.

VI

A turning point in this exposition has now been reached, so a moment's stocktaking is in order. The core of a developmental program of music education should be a sequence of vital musical experiences, activities, endeavors, and learnings, including performance in many media; musical composition, ample and diversified listening, reading books and articles about music, discussing music, musical doings outside school. This sequence should begin in the nursery school or the kindergarten, and continue on through the grades into the secondary school. Its prevailing purpose should be to promote all-round musical growth, to bring music home to large numbers of pupils, to make them musically responsive, sensitive and discriminating persons. The sequence can very well be called general music, for this describes it accurately. What should be done in the secondary-school course, ordinarily designated by that name, does not differ from what should be done in the kindergarten or the first grade, either in purpose or essential content. The only difference lies in the differing maturity of the human beings with whom we have to deal. Out of this sequence of general music the specialties stem, and this is the topic now to be considered.

The controlling general principle here is that of developmental continuity. To begin the study of applied music, to enter a class in theory, to become a member of a high-school orchestra should not mean a fundamental shift of emphasis, interest, and methods of working. It should be a continuation, in a specialized setting, of the process of musical growth already inaugurated. This principle of continuity has three important and, indeed, determining implications. The specialties should carry forward the same concern for broad musical development that characterizes the general sequence. General music should support the specialties. The specialties should reflect back upon and help to vitalize the sequence of general music.

1 The same concern for broad musical development that characterizes the sequence of general music should appear in all specialized musical studies and activities.

A. *It should appear in the work in applied music.* What this means in practice is shown very well in an account presented to me by a teacher of singing at a very famous school of music. He writes as follows:

Of course in private voice teaching one does not have to deal with the child who is in school because there is a social must. My students are at —— because they desire to be singers or teachers of singing. Here they have a purpose but at the same time there is still the necessity of keeping the interest high and strengthening that purpose by presenting as interesting and varied a program of teaching as possible. This does not only refer to the materials and procedure followed in the studio. Much encouragement should be given to attendance at concerts and opera. I have also found it profitable to suggest readings in non-controversial books on singing, such as Plunket Greene's *Interpretation of Song.* Another suggestion I would like to make as a device invaluable in maintaining interest and presenting the very necessary incentive to learn to the student is the practice of having a solo class at intervals of every three or four weeks. All private students are encouraged to attend this class in order to present an audience situation for individual performing students. Where does a singer receive more impetus in his voice work than when he is pointing to a performance? At the same time this class presents a varied and interesting experience for the learners.

This gentleman, of course, is dealing with mature students who are paying high fees for their work, and so he is quite right in saying that there is a special and powerful motivation. It is all the more noteworthy, therefore, that he finds it desirable to do a great deal more than emphasize vocal skill, and vocal skill alone. Many of his suggested practices could certainly be taken over to good advantage by teachers of applied music in ordinary school situations, not only in the field of voice, but also in that of piano, and of the various band and orchestral instruments. And there are a great many other things of that same sort that can also be done advantageously.

[284]

In particular, class instruction in applied music lends itself very well indeed to a broad musical approach. It is a great mistake to think that an applied music class is simply a device for uniform teaching, or for the giving of what really amounts to a series of very short individual lessons with all the pupils gathered together at one place and at one time. The class is a social situation with many potential social values, advantage of which should certainly be taken. It should, in essence, be treated as a sort of seminar for the study of the medium concerned, in which materials and musical values are discussed, technical problems are displayed and analyzed, the students listen to one another's work and are encouraged to offer suggestions and help. Thus it is not necessary that everyone should be doing the same assignment at the same time, and indeed, there are very few real values in having several pieces of music, or parts of them, considered and criticized at the same session. Nor is it necessary for all the members of the class to be even approximately on the same level of advancement, or for the teacher to do all the teaching. Indeed, so far as this latter point is concerned, the very reverse is desirable. Just recently I came in contact with a piano class five of whose members were advanced students while one was almost a beginner. Yet all of them were getting a great deal out of it, because the group was pervaded by a very helpful spirit, and because there was a very free interchange of ideas about technical and musical problems. Another great advantage of class instruction is that it provides a constant audience situation, and this is not only a standing incentive, but also makes playing or singing in the presence of other people a perfectly natural thing to do. In scheduling the meetings of such a class there should be considerable flexibility. On one day all the time may be taken up by the presentation of a lengthy work in an almost finished condition by a single individual, and by discussion and criticism of what he has done. Next time there may be four, five, or more short presentations. Next time there may be no presentation at all by any of the pupils, but rather an organized general discussion of problems relating to discrimination, or insight, or technical skill, or methods of practicing, or perhaps an experience of listening to and analyzing recorded music. The idea that "music lessons" always mean individual coaching is a very curious and entirely unreasonable mental stereotype, for class situations are exceedingly rich in potential developmental values.

It may be asked whether applied music taught with this broad emphasis does not sacrifice the development of skill for the sake of other values which, however admirable in general, are nevertheless

[285]

beside the point. To this the answer is: Certainly not! Wide and consistent experience decisively shows that well-directed class instruction in applied music, which consciously fosters awareness, initiative, discrimination and insight will get as good results in the matter of skill as the very best of private instruction, and much better results than average private instruction. The reason is that all the lines of musical development reinforce and support each other. When the attempt is made to cultivate skill in a narrow setting, and without any reference to anything else, things tend to go slowly and badly. For the basic control in musical skill is musical responsiveness, and the presence or absence of such control is a crucial factor in determining progress.

B. *Coming to orchestral, band, and choral rehearsals, many of the same considerations apply here also.* Time is by no means wasted when these occasions are treated not simply as drill sessions, but as occasions for music study, of course with special purposes and definite outcomes in mind. It very often happens that members of high-school choral groups do not know even as much as the titles of the compositions on which they are working, let alone having any understanding of their musical values or their expressive form. Very often, too, band and orchestra members know absolutely nothing but their own individual parts, which clearly implies that they must play in the most routine and mechanical fashion, and without any appreciable musical controls whatsoever. Also one very often finds a choral or instrumental ensemble being drilled on a difficult passage by sheer and unintelligent repetition, without any attempt to give the performers an aural conception of how the passage ought to sound. All this makes for slow learning, dubious results, and uncertain performance. From the standpoint of the practical director of a chorus, or a band, or an orchestra, musical responsiveness is a great deal more than a pretty and nebulous idea. It is one of the very greatest helps that he can possibly have in his own operations, and he should welcome its development in the sequence of general music and carry it forward to greater precision and definiteness in his work. Time and energy devoted to fostering it, for instance by having his organization hear one or perhaps more than one recording of a composition that they are taking up, by discussing problems of technique and interpretation, by building up and listening analytically to unusual harmonic effects, by encouraging them to do some out-of-school listening and reading, is likely to be repaid manifold in rapid progress and assured and certain grasp of the music.

[286]

C. *An organization of small instrumental ensembles can provide an interesting and valuable liaison between the general sequence and the specialties.* Activities of this kind can properly belong to either category. They can range all the way from very elementary to very advanced levels. They can include unusual instrumental combinations. They offer excellent opportunities for the exploration of musical literature and for the discussion of problems relating to taste and discrimination, because they are not under the same pressure of performance responsibilities as the orchestra. Also they offer many opportunities for musical initiative in the choice of materials, and volunteer presentations, and so forth, and because a good deal of the handling of such an organization can often be entrusted to students. They can supplement orchestral experience in valuable ways by offering chances for the players of inner parts. And they are effective seminars for the cultivation of musical skill.

D. *The course in theory in the secondary-school should be more than and different from a systematization of musical insight.* The reason for this is not that systematic study is worthless. As has already been pointed out, the very contrary is true. But students in high-school, even with a good developmental sequence behind them, are probably not mature enough to find such work repaying. Just as a class in applied music should be a music-study seminar with particular emphasis on skill in a specialized medium, so the course in theory should be a music-study seminar with particular emphasis on musical insight. This means that it should be organized, not about a systematic logical presentation of the subject, but rather about music that the students bring in —music that they have heard, music that they are learning to play, music that they have composed. Since the argument for an offering of this kind has already been put forward and developed at some length it will not be repeated here. All that need be said in addition here is that such a course would obviously tend to foster musical awareness, musical initiative, and musical discrimination, and to provide the basic control of musical skill, while its focal emphasis would be upon musical insight.

2 A vital program of general music is the most effective support that the specialties can receive. What it means is that large numbers of pupils come out of the elementary-school with a strong interest in music, a strong desire to continue with it, definite ideas about what they would like to do, and enough musical maturity to be

good learners when they enter some special phase of music study or activity. This is about as favorable a state of things as could be asked, and over the years it cannot help but affect the situation in many practical ways. The curriculum as it actually operates is not drawn up by a group of educators seated in the upper room of an ivory tower. It is the resultant of many forces. One of those forces is certainly created by the stable interests and desires of the student body. These interests and desires reflect themselves in the attitude of the community, and affect the decisions of the board of education and the administrative staff. Thus a strong program of general music builds support for music in general and for the musical specialties in particular in a most constructive fashion.

Moreover it is entirely in accord with sane and forward-looking educational thinking. There is at the present day a strong and eminently reasonable interest in what is called general education, a belief that the curriculum of the public schools should consist largely of broad cultural studies and activities. One immediate implication is that monopolistic specialties of every kind are likely to come under very critical scrutiny. There are unmistakable signs that a critical scrutiny of this kind is beginning to be directed toward the specialties of the music program. Administrative officers and general educators who in the past have been much impressed by the publicity value and pulling power of bands and orchestras are clearly beginning to ask themselves how much allotment of time and money and how much credit recognition should go to activities which, after all, are relevant to the needs of only a comparatively small proportion of the students. But if these activities can be shown, not by verbal arguments but in actual practice, to be natural outgrowths of a broad developmental sequence, then they are at once put on a different and far sounder footing.

There are certain ideas about the relationship between general music and the specialties that need to be clarified.

A. *Is it the function of general music to discover talent on the basis of which students should be guided into the special musical activities and studies?* The answer here is by no means perfectly simple. If it is thought that there is just so much innate musical talent in the entering first-grade population, and that the business of general music is simply to bring it to light, then the idea is probably wrong. There is strong reason to believe that a vital sequence of general music actually fosters talent. It opens up the world of music to the pupil. It stimulates musical

[288]

awareness and musical initiative. It encourages him to make constructive musical choices and discoveries. It brings him varied experiences of success with music. That is to say, its whole tendency is to create and strengthen the will to be musical. It may very well be that if we are dealing with a supremely gifted individual, nothing can stop him. But there are a great many people who are capable of a very effective musical response—as capable, let us say, as the writer of the case study presented in the last chapter—who might very well be discouraged forever by consistently adverse circumstances. After all, the writer in question did have the very great advantages of a musical home, and believed, probably quite rightly, that he owed a great deal to it. To say that for the vast majority of children, who do not quite come up to the level of natural-born and unstoppable Handels or Mozarts, circumstances have nothing to do with what we call talent—whatever it may be—is certainly a very extreme position.

Whatever the abstract psychology of the situation, its practical bearings are perfectly clear. A vital developmental sequence of general music in the elementary-school provides a setting in which musical interest is likely to be created, and in which it can manifest itself. And it is well known that continuing and growing interest is one of the best and surest indications of aptitude.[1] Such an interest will not show how much of a given aptitude a person possesses in comparison with other people. But it will tend to reveal the profile of his own aptitudes, and it is something that every properly instructed guidance counsellor will certainly heed. Thus, there is no better way for a child to reveal his musical bent than to give him a real chance to discover music and to discover himself musically. This is exactly what is contemplated in a developmental program of general music in the elementary-school, and it is exactly what is apt not to happen in the case of ordinary music lessons, or in a mechanistic elementary-school program.

B. *Should general music properly be considered a recruiting ground for the secondary-school musical organizations?* Here the answer is easier and more decisive. Not in the direct sense! High-pressure efforts at recruitment in the elementary-school are apt to do more harm than good. One gets a certain number of candidates, but one loses a great many others. And such children are likely to be lost, not only to the band or the orchestra, but to any further music whatsoever.

[1]For a fully documented discussion of this point see James L. Mursell, *Psychological Testing*, pp. 253–260. Longmans, Green & Co., Inc., New York, 1947.

To be specific, this issue frequently centers in instrumental classes in the elementary-school. Enthusiastic instrumental directors often inaugurate such classes with the thought that they are a valuable proving ground for recruits for the performing organizations later on. But if they look at the human aspect of the situation in a realistic way, they have to admit that a great many children who are enrolled in such classes by one means or another do not in fact go on as contemplated. Many a child who is induced, perhaps by rather high-pressure tactics, to take class lessons in cornet or saxophone in the elementary-school makes very little out of them, and quits music for good immediately thereafter. This is a state of things which we cannot, in good conscience or indeed in ordinary prudence, afford to ignore, for in the course of time it is pretty sure to bring its own revenge. Moreover it is not necessary. For children in the elementary-school to have instrumental experience—to learn about the instruments, to see them, to hear them, to discuss them, to experiment under guidance with playing them—is very valuable indeed. This, however, should not take the form of conventional class lessons, narrowly concentrated on specialized instrumental skill. It should be one of the influences making for general musical growth. If so, it has much of interest and value for everyone whether he is a prospective specialist or not, and also it is the right starting point for the specialist. In connection with such experiences a considerable number of children will almost certainly develop a strong interest in instrumental specialization. *These are the ones who should get it.* And it *should* be made possible for them to get it, both for their own sake, and for the sake of the special activities of the program later on. At the same time, their instrumental training then and later should be more than instrumental training. It should be a rich and developmental musical experience, and it should not take them completely away from general musical influences. This is the best way to make them into effective instrumentalists, which is a worthy aim although a limited one. And it also accomplishes something far more important. For after all, the purpose of music education is not simply to produce good band and orchestra players in high-school, but to bring music into people's lives as a lasting value.

C. *Is it the function of general music to prepare for the specialties? Certainly not in the specific sense.* It may be taken as a universal educational principle that a broad and vital general development is the best possible approach to specialization. This holds true in all walks of life, including music. A vitally interested and broadly equipped person can go amazingly fast in a specialty, and also go amazingly far. It is this broad general vital development with which the general sequence is concerned, and which constitutes its contribution to the specialties.

What has already been said about instrumental classes in the elementary school applies here. But there is another relevant and specific issue that must be noticed. It is that of sight reading. The general sequence which has been envisaged in this chapter, and which is implied in this whole book, is precisely not organized for the sake of producing an ability to read. Yet there is no ability which is more consistently demanded of the elementary-school teachers by the secondary-school specialists. How, then, can we resolve this contradiction?

A developmental sequence of general music in the elementary school does not specifically contemplate reading skill. But it most emphatically does contemplate musical comprehension, which is the only valid basis of an effective reading skill, and granted this, the reading skill itself is easily acquired. It proposes to foster musical insight, beginning from the very start, and continuing all along the line. It contemplates a developing capacity to identify, understand, and deal with the elements of the tonal-rhythmic pattern in terms of their intrinsic logic and their expressive values. It proposes to transform this capacity from vagueness to definiteness, from crudeness to precision, by means of a continuous sequence of activities, endeavors, and learnings pointed toward this end. As a means of freeing musical comprehension from the immediate and the concrete, that is from direct experience "by ear," it proposes to use visualization, beginning with very simple homemade or child-made symbolic devices, and later using some at least of the symbols of the regular notation. Such visualization is introduced in connection with all sorts of experiences, all sorts of activities, for what is wanted is not drill on the notation, but musical comprehension. A certain outcome of such rich and varied experiences, pointed up and supported in this way, is that children will get a far better idea of how music is put together, of what makes it expressive, and what the symbols really mean, than most of them will ever get from direct drill on the elements of the score. Thus elementary-school general music does not and should not offer reading skill to the secondary-school specialists. It offers something far better, namely musical comprehension which can be developed into effective skill in musical reading very readily indeed when the need arises.

3 The specialties should help to vitalize general music, and I put this, not in the form of a question, but as a statement, for it seems self-evident though it is often enough ignored. To have fine orchestras, fine bands, fine choirs, and perhaps successful composition classes in the secondary school, and not to use them for constructive educational purposes and for the vitalization of interest in the entire student body seems the height of perversity. Yet it certainly happens! Why not have an orchestra club, or a band club, or a choral club, one of whose functions would be to spread the news of what is being done by personal word of mouth? Why not have groups of elementary-school children attend rehearsals from time to time, and have matters explained to them by the director, or by members of the organizations? Why not have members of the organizations come into the elementary-school classrooms from time to time, and tell about their work or about forthcoming performances, and discuss the music, and demonstrate their instruments? Would not these be valuable developmental experiences for givers and receivers alike? Why should not the members of a theory class in the senior high school be asked to compose an occasional song or piece to meet the needs of some elementary-school situation, and then come and teach it to the children? The senior high-school organizations are not, or should not be regarded as remote, semi-professional music-making machines, completely out of contact with anything in the life of a first-grade child. They are the final flowerings of a process of musical growth in which everyone is engaged. And it is far from unreasonable to imagine that a bud may get considerable help and stimulation from contact with a flower!

I am well aware that many instrumental and choral directors in the secondary schools may regard this plea for general musical growth, and this critique of specific preparation and specific recruitment with grave misgivings. They know of many situations where the whole success of the high-school organizations seems to depend upon instrumental classes and high-pressure recruitment in the elementary school. But what is almost certainly lacking in such situations is a really vital sequence of general music, issuing in dynamic musical growth, and the effective arousal of musical interest and will. When this is lacking, the whole relationship breaks down. But if there is in the schools a program intelligently and energetically directed to making people musical, then the specialties will derive more benefit than from all the special training and high-pressure recruiting that the wit of man can devise or elementary-school principals will tolerate.

Moreover it enables the specialist to avoid the reproach of sacrificing the interests of the many for the sake of a selected few. Here, beyond a doubt, is the wave of the future in music education. It is the thing for which everybody ought to work, specialists included!

QUESTIONS FOR DISCUSSION

1. Show that the idea of general music here presented is simply an expansion or extension throughout a wide age-range of what ought to be done in a good general music course in high school.

2. The musical education of most music students consists of an array of specialized studies. What benefits might such a student get from considerable work in general music?

3. If the limited appeal of many high-school music programs is due not to the limited appeal of music itself, but to the way it is organized, what are some of the limiting factors?

4. To what extent must and should the specialties of the music program sacrifice broad musical growth for special ends?

5. Should singing be the core activity of the elementary program? If so, in what sense should it not be "monopolistic"?

6. What are the arguments for and against unaccompanied singing by children?

7. Is there any reason why a person should not "take" composition lessons much as he "takes" piano lessons as part of his normal musical education?

8. Does the argument of this chapter leave any place for the conventional course in appreciation?

9. Document from your own experience the values claimed for class instruction in applied music. How may such values be established? How are they often dissipated?

10. Suggest ways of using high-school musical organizations to promote musical interest throughout the school system. To what extent would this solve the problem of recruitment and preparation for those organizations?

CHAPTER THIRTEEN

The Developmental Program: Organization and Administration

I

The administration of a developmental program of music education requires an organically integrated staff. An organically integrated staff is a group of workers diverse in outlook, talent, personality, training, and background, but unified in terms of a common conception which is shared by all, and which really and effectively determines their activities.

Organic staff action is not achieved by setting up various kinds of work and activity in music—bands, orchestras, small ensembles, instrumental classes, choruses, choirs, voice classes, courses in general music or appreciation or theory or history, sequences in the elementary school, the junior high school, and the senior high school—and allocating to each a reasonable share in the budget, the time schedule, and the physical facilities. What usually happens then is that all these lines of work go on independently, or with a very superficial and external relatedness. Nor is it achieved merely by amiable and co-operative relationships within the staff. The vocal director may feel quite free to approach the orchestra director for a joint concert without getting his head bitten off. The elementary supervisors may rejoice in kind words of commendation from the band director instead of smarting under his unpleasant wise-cracks. The whole music organization may be a "happy shop" under the benign aegis of its top administrative officer. This is all to the good, but it is not organic integration, because it amounts to an amiable collaboration of sovereign entities rather than a real fusing and meeting of minds. There is merely diversity without clash. There is not diversity in unity.

When there is genuine organic unity, however, all types and levels of work become different ways of doing the same thing, and are recognized as such. They mutually reinforce one another, and contrib-

[294]

ute, each in its own fashion, to the furtherance of a central common task. Does the band director have any considerable sense of shared responsibility for the work in general music, even though he may not participate in it directly? Does the orchestra director take any constructive interest in what goes on in the elementary schools, beyond trying to push instrumental classes and grumbling a little because the children do not learn to read better? Do people in the vocal field concern their minds, to any extent, with what is done in the instrumental field? Do the elementary supervisors and the grade teachers know what musical influences operate in the secondary schools, or consider such things in any manner within their sphere of responsibility? Are the various specialists affected in any way by what those outside their specialty are doing or thinking? Is there any mutual interplay of mind on mind, and plan on plan? Is there any tangible idea, specific enough to afford real and practical guidance, of what the whole business is about in the corporate mind of the staff? Is there, in any genuine sense, a corporate staff mind at all? These are the kind of questions that tell the story. They are very searching. They unmistakably reveal the degree of vital co-ordination, of organic planning and thinking, exemplified in the program.

There is only one idea sufficiently inclusive and far-reaching, and at the same time sufficiently specific in its bearing upon all aspects of music education to provide the basis for organic planning, and for the organic integration of the working staff. This is the idea of musical growth. Without it the music program is simply a collection of various types of work and activity, held together by purely external relationships. But the moment each person on the staff comes to realize that, in his own line of activity, he is doing what everybody else is doing—namely, fostering a five-fold pattern of musical development—all this begins to change.

Consider, for instance, some of the effects that this can have on the doings of the band director, who is often the most toughly independent nut of all. He wants to foster musical growth. He does it, of course, primarily through his own organization, which is perfectly proper. This at once affects everything he does with his band—his management of rehearsals, his choice of music, the way he deals with it, his approach to problems of technique, the use he makes of public occasions, his disciplinary procedures, his whole influence upon the pupils. But also his interests are carried beyond the limits of the band itself. He thinks it part of his job to do something about the musical development of the children in the elementary schools. Ob-

[295]

viously, he cannot take personal charge himself. But he can do a good deal of missionary work, in staff meetings and elsewhere, and also he can make arrangements for some of his band members to do a bit. He can bring to the grade-school children an awareness and an appreciable degree of discrimination about his organization and its activities, about the instruments it uses and their problems, about the music it plays. This can be done by direct demonstrations and contacts that have some fire and life in them. Once again, he will work for a vital and co-ordinated program of musical influences in the secondary schools, to which his organization can contribute, and which can contribute to it. He will think it all to the good when members of his organization want to take work in general music, or theory, or history, and he will feel a concern in helping to see to it that there is the right kind of work for them to take. He ceases to be simply a band director, and becomes an educator working with music. He wants the members of his organization to become musical persons, not simply performers on certain instruments. And as one result among many, his band does not suffer!

This is an instance of how vital, organic co-ordination can work out. It is by no means intended as a specific recommendation suitable for all situations, but merely as an example of the kind of thing that needs to be accomplished. Every course, every activity, every musical organization should be conducted as an instrumentality for musical growth, both among its own members, and in the whole student body. Endless ways of bringing this about can be devised, and one successful venture is almost certain to suggest a flock of others. Specialists remain specialists, as of course they should. But they conduct their specialty in the light of the whole and of its determining idea.

Let it not be thought that such talk about the organic integration of the working staff is nothing more than cloudy educational philosophizing. The issue is an exceedingly practical one, and the outcomes are constructive to the highest degree. To come in contact with a music program which, in all its diversity, has the unity of a set of variations on a single theme, and with a group of workers who, in all their different activities, are consciously doing just one thing, can be a real eye-opener. Students, general teachers, administrative officers, and ultimately the constituency become aware of what is going on, and cannot fail to be impressed. And to work on such a staff is itself a precious and revealing experience of very great developmental value.

The management of such a vitally co-ordinated program is no mean administrative and educational task. The man at the top cannot do it by sitting in his office, issuing directives, and manipulating the budget. He can do it only by exercising the supreme function of the administrator, which is to organize the progressive self-education of the working staff. It is a toilsome job, and sometimes a heart-breaking one, for some of the brethren seem to take a very long time to see the light—and they may be useful and worthy brethren too. But it is the only way. Organic integration does not arrive all in a moment. It cannot be imposed. It can only be achieved as the workers themselves grow to a clearer and more convinced vision of a common central task, which is to foster, each in his own fashion, the process of musical growth.

The staff which is achieving a genuine organic integration in and through its work will be concerned with problems in four major areas. These have to do with internal aspects of the program, external aspects of the program, evaluation, and general planning. Let us consider them in order.

II

It has been pointed out many times in these pages that a developmental program of music education cannot be stereotyped, although most emphatically it must be orderly. This expresses itself in its internal organization. The controlling idea is always that of the promotion of musical growth. In order that this may be done, there must be an organized sequence, an organization of physical resources, and a utilization and development of human resources.

1 It is impossible to lay out the sequence of a developmental program of music education on a hard-and-fast gradewise basis. To do this is always tempting, because it looks plausible and seems efficient. Moreover there is no doubt that in the practical sense it is the easy thing to do. Teachers are asked to draw up a course of study in music. With a few groans they get to work. First of all they argue for a while about some general objectives, since something of the sort is fashionable and likely to make a good impression on the curriculum staff and the superintendent. With that out of the way, they get down to real business. The first consideration that forces itself upon them is that they are dealing with a school system organized into annual levels called grades. From then on this dominates their thinking. Just what can and should be fitted into each one of

these grade levels? That becomes the determining question. Their natural tendency is to look for topics and sub-topics which can be arranged in some kind of sequential order, and to assign them to the various grade levels on some, not too unreasonable, basis. Materials are suggested for the sake of handling these topics, and grade standards are defined, either explicitly or by implication, in terms of "covering" or "mastering" them. Since the notation lends itself better to such treatment than anything else in music, the emphasis is very likely to center here. However "appreciation," or to be more specific, listening, is similarly organized, compositions being listed on the basis of their supposed suitability for this grade or that. The outcome is a thoroughly characteristic administrative and supervisory instrument. The course of study is a specific, stereotyped working plan, which purports to tell a teacher exactly what ought to be done each year, and sometimes even undertakes to say what ought to be done each week. The function of supervision then becomes to see to it that everyone is living up to the schedule.

That this mode of approach is fundamentally wrong has already been pointed out many times in these pages. It gives the teacher no elbow-room. It leads directly to mechanistic procedures. In appearance it is orderly, but that orderliness is at best superficial and usually spurious, for it exists on paper rather than in practice. The basic objection to it is that the musical growth of human beings, not their grade placement, must determine any vital and effective scheme of music education. Given two third grades in successive years, or in two different schools, or indeed in the same school at the same time, the proper thing to do may well be quite different in the two cases. Or again, two different teachers might very well do quite different things if they were handling the same third grade situation, and both might be excellent. As a matter of fact, courses of study of the familiar kind just described never operate as contemplated. They are merely nightmares on paper, in spite of all the police efforts of supervisors. But if, in some fantastically improbable situation, it were possible to make everything go exactly according to the blueprint, right down to the last detail, one might be sure that everything would be wrong!

What, then, is the alternative? It is organization on an entirely different basis. The three structural ideas in the internal organization of the developmental program are developmental lines, developmental levels, and developmental influences. The first thing to do is to determine the lines of musical growth that it is intended to promote, and to make them as specific as possible in the way that was indicated

[298]

in the chapters on awareness and initiative and suggested by implication in the treatment of discrimination, insight, and skill. What specific types of awareness, initiative, and discrimination, what specific factors of insight and skill are to be fostered? This is the first question to be answered. We wish, let us say, to cultivate a discriminating responsiveness to tone quality and rhythmic precision as expressive elements in music, an insight into the expressive values of chord color and melodic configuration, an attitude of controlling musical action with reference to expressive intention and musical shape, this being the matrix of skill, an awareness of many types of music, initiative in listening to radio programs and in selecting new directions for music study. These are a few sample instances of the sort of developments we want to have take place. They are, so to speak, the vertical columns of our organized structure. They run right through it from top to bottom.

Next comes the question of how to promote them at different levels. Many, if not all of them, will be present in the kindergarten and the early grades as well as in the senior high-school, but procedures for dealing with them will be very different in the two cases. Here we draw upon our understanding of the characteristics and rhythms of growth. At the early developmental levels, responses of the kind indicated will naturally be crude, unformed, indeterminate, immediate, and for this we will make provision. With little children a toy orchestra will be better than a violin ensemble for conveying rhythmic precision and feeling for tone quality and harmonic color, the singing of folk songs will be better than piano study for conveying a feeling for melodic configuration. We will recognize and accept all this, not because we value limitations, but because we are aware that growth must be a continuous unfolding, that it must be purposive, and that it must be meaningful, and because experiences that are prematurely precise, or definite, or abstract are inevitably meaningless.

This leads to the third question. What developmental experiences shall we bring to bear in order to foster musical growth along the indicated lines? As we have seen, a developmental experience is arresting, impelling, revealing, fulfilling, and conscious. Within the scope of this prescription lies an enormous territory, all of it fruitful. As the staff works on its program, a great range of activities, endeavors, and learnings with these characteristics will be accumulated, some of them actually tried out, others suggested or contemplated. Their value and the conditions of their effectiveness will be analyzed and recorded, and their appropriateness for this or that developmental

[299]

acquire a high degree of skill, although this too has happened, and it is far from an impossibility, but they have commonly found music an extremely rewarding pursuit. The obstacles are indifference, lack of confidence, and the competition of other interests and claims upon time and energy. This is demonstrably true even of adults in their sixties, and it is most certainly the case with adolescents in high school. There is nothing impossible in such people doing excellently with music. Second, the older beginner is able to orient himself and to learn better than the child beginner. The common idea that the capacity to learn is greatest when one is very young, and that it declines with the years is definitely known to be false. Thus while the older beginner undoubtedly loses something, and perhaps irreparably, he is able to make up a great deal of leeway. The case study presented in Chapter Eleven is a good instance of this. The writer unquestionably lost a certain freedom with music, a wide awareness, a naturalness of approach, a range of choice, because of his restricted and unfortunate experiences as a child. But once his enthusiasm was aroused and well directed, he was able to travel both fast and far. Third, the kind of influences from which the older beginner will benefit most are precisely the general developmental influences with which this book has dealt so extensively. This again is very well exemplified in the case study just mentioned. So it is altogether reasonable to believe that a vital and well-organized course in general music in the first year of secondary-school can meet this human problem, while at the same time contributing to the musical development of those who have had the advantage of similar influences throughout their whole school career.

2 The assembling of a rich and diversified collection of teaching materials of all kinds is a most important factor in the practical management of a developmental program of music education. One of the surest signs of alertness and a progressive professional attitude on the part of the individual teacher is the systematic and imaginative assembling of such materials for use in his own work, and the same is true of the staff as a whole. Materials of this kind should include music books and song books both published for school use and commercial use, sheet music, scores, phonograph records, pictures, maps, charts, film strips, motion picture films, books, magazine articles, newspaper clippings, accounts of interesting and significant projects and activities in music education carried on in the home system or observed or reported from elsewhere, samples of student work such as

compositions, recordings, and so forth. They should be made readily accessible, usually in a centrally located library or depository where they can be conveniently shelved and filed, and made available by a proper catalog with ample cross-references. So far as possible a plan should be developed by which they can be loaned out promptly for teaching use or for examination and study by members of the staff. There should be periodical bulletin announcements giving information as to what is on hand.

The development of such a resource collection should not be the sole responsibility of the office of the director of music, or indeed of any one person assigned to the task, although the work must head up somewhere. Essentially it ought to be considered a concern of the entire staff. From time to time there should be staff discussions of the material, in which various items are actually handled and examined and evaluated, and experiences in using them are presented. Discussions of this kind are likely to raise far-reaching and illuminating issues, and they are all the more valuable because they turn on some concrete and specific point. Moreover, they have the effect of arousing staff interest in the whole matter, and of getting individual staff members to thinking about it, and arousing in them a sense of responsibility for it. An outcome of such a policy is to produce a rich flow of contributions, suggestions, and evaluations through which there is built up a collection of curriculum materials of very great and steadily increasing value. For the collection should not be an inert physical mass, but a living and constructive influence upon the work.

3 Another major consideration is the utilization and development of human resources. In a developmental scheme the background, the personality, the bent, the enthusiasms of the individual teacher are dynamic influences of indispensable importance, and everything possible should be done to give them constructive opportunity. Good teaching is the vital interplay of mind on mind, and of spirit on spirit, and it cannot be done by human automata. The teacher's personal idiosyncrasy is precious, and he should be helped and guided towards making his own unique contribution, in his own way, within the total setting. A developmental scheme of music education is sufficiently broad and flexible, and has a sufficient intrinsic reasonableness to give scope to a great variety of talent.

An organically integrated staff is itself a group of learners—of learners who are discovering through their classroom activities, their personal study and reflection, and their contacts and discussions with their colleagues what musical growth and its effective promotion really means in actual practice. No human being knows the whole story. There are always partial and mistaken views to be corrected, new things to be found out, new insights to be achieved, wider horizons to be envisaged. Thus organic integration is not something that can ever be finally attained. It is something that is always evolving and developing, and the moment that development, evolution, and advance ceases, it begins to evaporate. And in and through this evolution, the individual staff members achieve their growth. This is the absolute condition of vitality, for no one can possibly teach well unless he himself is learning and growing. Such a person may, and indeed certainly will, have faults and weaknesses. As he looks back upon his own endeavors of five years ago he may be astonished and appalled at their defects and limitations. This in itself, however, is a most healthy sign, for it means that he is moving, which is the great desideratum, for neither an immobile object nor an immobile personality can convey motion to others. Thus the most hopeful of all signs in a member of a teaching staff is a growing comprehension, sensitiveness, imagination, and ability to contribute to the total scheme. And the most fatal of all symptoms is the stubbornly closed mind, for which all problems are settled, and to which all answers are satisfactorily and finally known. The stimulation of this all-important personal, professional, and musical growth on the part of each is the concern of all. It is a crucial factor of staff relationships and staff action, and a crucial concern of the leadership. The supreme function of administrative leadership is not the orderly conduct of routine business, but the steady promotion of staff enterprise and staff thinking. Thus the dynamically integrated staff is in essence a self-educating group of workers.

In this connection there are two matters of considerable importance to which some attention should be given.

A. *Teachers outside the field of music—grade teachers in the elementary-school, teachers of other subjects in the secondary-school—are a rich, potential, human resource for the music program.* In a routine and mechanistic scheme of music education, narrowly centered on skills, and concerned chiefly with specializations, they have little or no part to play. But in a developmental scheme of music education, with its core sequence of general music, there are many contributions they can make.

Workers in music education worry and debate a great deal about the relationship of the general teacher, particularly in the grades, to

[304]

their program. Unfortunately a great deal of what they have to say is nonsense. They aim at reading in the elementary-school, at performance in the secondary-school, and virtually nothing else. Then they wonder how the general teacher can help. The answer is easy. He cannot! In all probability he is not even sympathetic. But even if he likes the idea, there is little he can do about it, because he cannot read much, and cannot sing much, and cannot play much. But does this mean that he is necessarily a total musical loss? Far from it! There is a whole range of possible activities, particularly at the elementary-school level, which are not only well within the capability of many general teachers, but also very fruitful developmental influences. To ask that our teachers colleges equip all their prospective teachers with enough musical skills to function virtually as old-line music supervisors, albeit on a low level of efficiency, is to seek the fantastically impossible. To say that these prospective teachers can be shown a hundred interesting, repaying, and fruitful things to do with music, and that the school staff can show them a hundred more after they are on the job, is well within the limits of the feasible. So too at the high-school level, a mathematics teacher who is a live musical amateur is a precious asset upon whom the music director should cast covetous eyes. He may never be able to rehearse the orchestra. But he may be able to do with great effect, something of which many a good orchestra man hardly dreams—promote a broad and vital musical growth in the school, which can be a benefit to the pupils and a major source of strength to the entire program.

B. *Constructive relationships with the private music teachers of the community are decidedly worth developing.* A dynamic program of music education in the schools tends to build for them a very practical support, and recognition of the work they do is entirely reasonable. Yet the music staff has a responsibility which forbids it to accept any and every kind of music teaching without due discrimination. The policy of establishing a list of accredited private teachers is sometimes followed, but it has obvious difficulties and dangers. Another plan is to accept private music study for school credit on condition that the pupil passes a satisfactory examination conducted by the music staff, and that he receives a certain minimum amount of instruction, usually fifteen hours per semester. Neither of these plans, however, goes to the root of the matter, which is that private music teachers often have an entirely different point of view from that which animates the music staff of the school. What ought to be done is to establish personal and professional relationships, so that private teachers whose work is to be recognized shall understand and sympathize with the developmental conception exemplified in the school program. When music education is consciously organized on a constructive basis, criteria are established to which those associated with it must be expected to conform. If private teachers are unwilling to do this, then the instruction they offer ought not to be recognized. Those who desire such recognition should be willing to attend say two or three conference meetings with the music staff each year, so that ideas can be exchanged, and a comprehension of what is being done in the schools shall be gained by those outside.

III

There are a number of problems relating to the external aspects of the program which are necessarily matters of concern to the organically integrated staff.

1 First there is the question of public performance, on which there should be a definite and constructive staff point of view. Public performance has obvious and great publicity values, but its educational values are clearly the chief concern, and if these are consistently and courageously emphasized, the rest will certainly be added in the long run.

Opportunities to perform music in public, on occasions ranging from the simplest to the most elaborate and formal, should always be thought of and planned with reference to their developmental effect upon the performers themselves and the entire student body. They should be thought of as opportunities for fostering musical awareness, musical initiative, musical discrimination, musical insight, and musical skill. For instance, it is well for the performers, wherever possible and as far as possible, to have a hand in the selection of the program. When certain items have been chosen, the preparation of them should mean a great deal more than simply drilling on the right notes and blindly following the interpretation imposed by the director. The cultural setting of the selections, their aesthetic content and values, and their expressive form should all be made matters for attention. Also it may be desirable and feasible to discuss various alternative interpretations. Sometimes a committee of students may be asked to prepare program notes, or to make a brief oral exposition to the audience. And when the event is over, there should certainly be a guided discussion of what has been done, turning upon whether the intended values have been really and effectively projected, what has gone well, what has gone badly, and why. The thing by all means to avoid is the sort of public performance which is the culmination of interminable routine drilling on a very small repertoire of compositions whose musical content and cultural significance are neither emphasized, understood, nor appreciated. The more of the right kind of public performance that can be organized in connection with the music program the better, for it is a developmental influence of great power and value. After all, to share with others the music that one loves and understands is a natural and vitalizing experience, and this by all means should be the spirit pervading all such occasions. If they are organized and managed with this in mind, they are real challenges, real stimuli to musical growth. But if they are allowed to degenerate into forced displays by more or less—and usually less—well-trained robots, then there is no doubt that their influence on many of the persons concerned is highly detrimental.

2 Closely related to the question just considered is the much more vexed issue of contests. What should be the attitude, what should be the policy of an organically integrated staff committed to the developmental point of view in regard to this matter?

There is no doubt that the expansion of music education in America owes a great deal to the contest system. The competitive motive has great pulling power, and many directors of music have played it up for all it is worth for perfectly obvious reasons. The music staff will recognize this, and will feel a good deal of hesitation about disparaging or attempting to eliminate so potent and dynamic an influence, for they will know that in educational work anything that has vitality is precious and also none too common. On the other hand, they will be aware that there is a strong reaction against the contest system, probably more marked among general educators than among music educators; that it has led to serious abuses; that some people have undertaken to ride to glory on it; that it has been not untainted with commercialism; that it often results in much bitterness and very destructive and undesirable attitudes.

The path of wisdom would seem to be to work for the reform of the contest system rather than its abandonment. There is nothing intrinsically wrong with the motive of competition as such. Ever since the days of the Greeks it has figured as a cultural force, and often a constructive and beneficent one. Furthermore it is in no way blameworthy for a teacher or a director to seek to gain a reputation

[307]

by doing good work. The developmental viewpoint requires us to recognize the realities of human nature, not to ignore them. Competition only becomes destructive when it is exacerbated, when its negative aspects are forced into prominence. This, to be sure, happens often enough but it is not unavoidable. So far as music contests are concerned, there is certainly a great deal that can be done. A wider range of performing organizations can be recognized. The repertoire of contest numbers can be liberalized. Standards of adjudication can be broadened and a much greater emphasis can be placed on aesthetic and cultural values. Far more can be done to prepare the ground in advance, so that everything does not turn on the snapshot judgment of a small number of individuals voting *in camera* on criteria imperfectly understood, or not understood at all, by the performers. The plan of straight-line ranking, often on small and debatable points of difference, can be radically modified. Comments and criticisms can be made prevailingly helpful and constructive, and pains can be taken to enable the performers to recognize the force and implications of what is said about their work, so that a genuine process of well-founded self-evaluation is set up. In general, the cut-throat features of the contest can be reduced and subordinated, and the occasion can be transformed into one where performers come together to display their work, to compare themselves with others, and to submit themselves to objective and revealing judgments. This, of course, is the essence of what is often called the "festival idea" in contradistinction to the "contest idea." About the potential helpfulness of such occasions there cannot be much doubt.

This, broadly speaking, is what a staff committed to the developmental point of view is likely to favor. It will see great potential values in bringing performers and performing groups together from over wide areas. It will believe that occasions of this kind can be managed in such a way as to promote genuine and broad musical growth. And the fact that such a staff is organically integrated means that the band director, the orchestra director, and the choir director, who in the past have been the chief sponsors of the contest system and to some extent a law unto themselves, are learning to point their admirable and successful energies toward long-range constructive ends and the good of the whole.

3 One other matter which deserves at least passing mention is the promotion of amateur musical organizations and activities in the community. This is a legitimate and valuable function of the

music staff of the school system. It need not, however, be a kind of fifth wheel, for the point is that such activities need not, and indeed should not, be entirely separate from the school music program itself. It is, for instance, often possible to draw adult amateurs in the community into active collaboration with some of the musical organizations in the schools. This has been done with the happiest results in connection with small instrumental ensembles. Interested amateurs in the community can be a great source of strength to the program, and musical collaboration between them and the students can have very valuable effects on both sides.

IV

The organized system of evaluation has a profound and far-reaching effect in any working educational scheme. It affects the procedures of the teachers, the attitudes of the pupils, and all the outcomes of the work. The reason is that it determines the prevailing emphasis, whether the persons concerned are or are not fully aware of its influence upon them. No staff, which approaches its task in a realistic fashion, can fail to give it the most careful and thoughtful consideration.

1 The marking system is our conventional and universally accepted instrument of evaluation. This creates a very real dilemma for the music staff. Many of the effects of the marking system are unfortunate, and this is particularly evident in such a subject as music. On the other hand, marking is unavoidable, at any rate above the level of the sixth grade, because it is our universal method of educational bookkeeping, and is used everywhere for the recording and transfer of credits on which status in school depends. The music staff, therefore, is compelled to use a system which is in many ways alien to their purposes, and which can very easily have a disruptive effect upon their work. What, if anything, can be done about it?

The first thing is to understand clearly just what the marking system is and how it operates. This is something about which a great many teachers are far from clear, yet it is simple enough. The whole idea of marking turns on comparative straight-line ranking on a single uniform criterion. A certain standard of achievement is set up. Testing situations are devised in order to show how well the indicated standard is being met. Everyone is ranked on the results in ascending and descending order of excellence. Then everyone's standing in the rank order is converted into a certain symbol called his mark. The tests may be formal or informal, written or oral, of the "objective" or the "essay" type. The symbols may consist of numbers running from 100 to 0 with a passing point at 60 or 70 or elsewhere, or of three, five, or six letters unmodified or modified by plus and minus signs, or of some other arrangement. These details are the accidents of the system, not its essence. Its essence is a process of ranking on some uniform criterion of achievement, and the expression of this ranking by means of symbols whose meaning is known. This is the thing always to keep in mind. The basic logic of the marking system would be displayed as clearly as it ever could be if we reverted to the old-fashioned spell-down. We would have a uniform criterion to begin with. We could line up the pupils around the room, ranked in the order of their success. We could assign marks by calling the top five per cent A, the next twenty per cent B, the next fifty per cent C, the next twenty per cent D, and the bottom five per cent E or F, or by proceeding on some other plan which would give our symbols a clear meaning. If this sort of thing were actually done, it would give teachers a much clearer notion of what the system involves than they often seem to have.

Now the objection to marking is not that it shows up degrees of excellence. Differences in human ability and achievement are facts, and very important facts too. It is perfectly right, and indeed very desirable that they should be known, and any system of evaluation which ignored them would be preposterous. The objection to marking is its narrowness and mechanical uniformity. One cannot rank people, or for the matter of that inanimate objects, in ascending and descending order except on a uniform criterion. One can take into consideration only a single kind of excellence, and one has to ignore all other kinds as irrelevant. This is why the marking system tends to place such a heavy premium upon routine results and memory work, an emphasis which affects both teachers and learners. A child may show great initiative, great originality. He may make excellent progress. He may bring to class some creative achievement of real merit. But in strictness the marking system is incapable of expressing the values of what he has done, because there is no basis for making a straight-line comparison between his achievement and that of the rest of the class. Bringing this to bear upon the situations that arise in music, there is no way of making a straight-line comparison between the tympanist and the concert master in an orchestra, or between one child who sings very well, and another child who has not found his singing voice but does beautifully with simple instruments. In all such cases the marking system fails, not because there may not be real and important differences in excellence, but because it cannot express them since they are not uniform or in a single dimension.

It is quite true that, as a matter of fact, teachers do not stick to the rigor of this logic. They take into consideration attitude, interest, effort, progress, previous preparation, and indeed all sorts and kinds of factors, and they allow them to affect the marks they finally assign. It is perfectly right that such things should be recognized, for they are of very great importance. But the point is that the marking system cannot take cognizance of them properly. When they are allowed to affect a mark, the system is misused, because its whole operation is based on the assumption of a single uniform standard of excellence. And the danger of the system is that it constantly tends to force upon teachers and pupils alike a narrow and mechanical uniformity, and a covert assumption that anything outside the straight-line predetermined sequence is unimportant.

Now the first step in avoiding this danger is to recognize it for exactly what it is, and this is a long step too, for the situation is far from hopeless. With regard to marking, the music staff can adopt an intelligent and constructive policy. They should work for a reform of the marking system of the school in which there is a reduction of the number of subdivisions. A system of letters with plus and minus signs is better than a numerical system running from 100 to 0; a system of five unmodified letters is better still; a three-letter system is the best of all. The reason is that the fewer the pigeon-holes into which people have to be classified, the greater the flexibility. Then they should work for the abandonment of all marking in the elementary-school. This is a practical possibility, because the problems of transfer and accumulation of credits do not arise, and it is being successfully put into effect in a number of places. Then, very frankly and consciously, they should mark in an impressionistic rather than in a strictly logical fashion. This may seem rather like recommending sabotage, and in a certain sense it is. But the unavoidable truth is that developmental teaching becomes impossible unless the stifling uniformity, which is the chief curse of the marking system, is avoided somehow.

2 Beyond all this it is a very good idea for the music staff to establish its own orderly and organized system of evaluation independent of the marking system. The time and effort involved may impose limitations here, but the idea is well worth consideration. In ideal, at any rate, every individual pupil should be a matter of concern and interest to the music staff, in all aspects of his musical activities and his musical growth. Moreover this ideal should not be allowed to remain nebulous and hanging in the air. It should not just be something to be talked about, but embodied in a concrete, practical plan of action.

The general outline of such a plan is reasonably clear. For every pupil there should be set up a developmental folder, in which there accumulates a record of his musical reactions, activities, and doings. It should contain informal jotted comments by the various teachers who have had dealings with him, regarding his responses to different situations and stimuli, his probable abilities and limitations, more formal notations of achievement, records of his musical doings both in and out of the regular curriculum, samples of his work wherever they are available, and over-all interpretations and appraisals made at periodical intervals by members of the staff who know him particularly well. What should really be brought together is a log of his musical growth. Moreover there is every reason why the pupil's own opinions, self-judgments, appraisals, and expressions of interest and desire should also be included.

Such a scheme can have very great values. It is a businesslike plan for the cultivation of human material. It provides for evaluation on a broad and realistic basis, which turns upon the recognition of many-sided musical development. If material accumulating in folders of this kind is from time to time studied and discussed by the staff, many splendid opportunities for constructive work will present themselves which otherwise might very well be missed. Also it acts as a continual check-up and review of the real effectiveness of the whole program. No one thing is more important for a working staff than to study and understand the human material with which it is dealing.

Moreover, the scheme can have a pervasive and beneficial effect upon the pupils. Teachers often tell pupils not to work for marks, but there is a certain insincerity in such advice so long as the marking system is the only organized instrumentality for evaluation. But if it is known that all kinds of musical response, and all evidences of musical development are matters of concern and interest, then there

[312]

is a realistic and constructive substitute. When pupils know that this is so, and when they are given opportunities to collaborate actively in the appraisals that are being made, it is an influence making for the guided self-evaluation which is certainly the true objective.

V

In the actual planning of the year's work, or the semester's work, or of the single unit, or lesson, or project, the people actually on the job should always have a hand. This applies all the way from the general musical activities in the first-grade to the doings of the senior high-school orchestra. The reason is that good collaborators tend to make good learners. This, of course, means that the whole organized scheme must be flexible, so that any teacher working with any group of learners may have elbow-room and at the same time effective direction. This is precisely the intention in defining guide-lines in terms of musical growth, and in providing a wealth of suggestions and of resource material out of which developmental experiences of many kinds can be organized. To take time out to talk over with pupils what the group can do and how it can do it may seem a startling idea to many teachers. However much experience has indicated that this can be time very well spent indeed, so long as judgment and discretion are exercised, and well-considered plans emerge. A teacher who learns to operate in this way will have the highly satisfactory experience of having his pupils genuinely with him in what is undertaken. This in itself will have a more beneficial and vital effect, and do more for authentic musical and personal development than the most meticulously elaborated standard plan imposed from above. For although musical growth is recognizable, and although its manifestations can, to a large extent, be specifically defined, there are a very great many different ways in which it can take place, and it depends, beyond everything else, upon the personal enthusiasm and drive of the individuals concerned.

QUESTIONS FOR DISCUSSION

1. Make suggestions as to what some grade teachers known to you could do with music, even though they are not skilled in it.

2. Is it true that the music program often represents a viewpoint out of harmony with that of the school as a whole and of the general teachers? How serious is this? What should be done about it?

3. Show what good constructive effects upon the staff as a whole might come from (a) building up a body of resource materials (b) operating a definite plan of evaluation.

4. Public performance may be a helpful or a harmful influence. Confirm this from experiences of your own. How may it be made helpful?

5. If conferences with local private teachers were inaugurated, what might be some of the problems to come up?

6. Can you give any specific accounts of unfortunate effects produced by music contests? How might they be avoided?

7. Discuss the idea of junior high-school general music as a re-synthesis.

8. Are unfortunate attitudes apt to be created among pupils by setting up music as a required subject? How may they be avoided?

9. Consider in detail why it is better to begin planning in terms of development than grade-wise. Is the idea practicable?

10. With some specific group of pupils in mind, suggest ways in which you might plan musical activities not merely for them but with them.

ADDITIONAL READINGS[1]

R. WILL BURNETT. "The Science Teacher and His Objectives." *Teachers College Record*, 1944, Vol. 45, pp. 241–251. (A very instructive account of developmental planning in another field, but entirely applicable to music.)

H. H. GILES. *Pupil-Teacher Planning.* Harper & Brothers, New York, 1941. (This book is full of concrete instances of co-operative planning.)

RUTH STRANG. *Every Teacher's Records.* Teachers College, Columbia University, Bureau of Publications, New York, 1936, pp. 13–43. (A very direct practical account of the use of developmental folders.)

JAMES L. MURSELL. *Education for American Democracy.* W. W. Norton and Company, Inc., New York, 1944. (Many of the chapters in this book deal with program development, evaluation, and administration, bringing together much material.)

[1]These readings have to do with general problems of program-building and administration, and have reference to the entire third part of this book.

APPENDIX

I
Recommended Readings

The following is a list of readings especially recommended for those who wish to broaden and deepen their understanding of the developmental approach to the teaching of music. It is very different from the list of professional readings ordinarily found in educational books. Indeed it contains no treatise or textbook on methodology at all, and it is not even confined to music. Frankly, too, it is a very heterogeneous list, with items ranging from the simple and popular to the technical and difficult. But every item it contains will repay study, and above all meditation and reflection, for all of them are relevant to the great subject I have tried to present in these pages, and can help to provide a basis for intelligent comprehension and enlightened action.

BARNETT, DAVID, *Living with Music*. George E. Stewart, Publisher, Inc., New York, 1944.

BARNETT, DAVID, *They Shall Have Music*. George E. Stewart, Publisher, Inc., New York, 1944.

CHAPIN, ELSA, and RUSSELL. THOMAS, *A New Approach to Poetry*. University of Chicago Press, Chicago, 1929.

CHRISTIANI, ADOLPH, *Principles of Expression in Pianoforte Playing*. Harper & Brothers, New York, 1885.

COWELL, HENRY, "The Process of Musical Creation." *American Journal of Psychology*, 1926, Vol. 37, pp. 233–236.

DISERENS, CHARLES, *The Influence of Music on Behavior*. Princeton University Press, Princeton, N. J., 1926.

DREW, ELIZABETH, *Discovering Poetry*. W. W. Norton and Company, Inc., New York, 1933.

ENGELSMANN, WALTER, "Beethoven and the Creative Law in Symphonic Art." *Musical Quarterly*, 1937, Vol. 23, pp. 56–63.

FERGUSON, DONALD N., *On the Elements of Musical Expression*. University of Minnesota, Minneapolis, Minn., 1944.

GESELL, ARNOLD, and AMATRUDA, CATHERINE S., *Developmental Diagnosis*. Paul G. Hoeber, Inc., New York, 1941.

HELSETH, INGA OLLA, *Living in the Classroom*. Edwards Brothers, Inc., Ann Arbor, Mich., 1939.

KATZ, ADELE T., "Heinrich Schenker's Method of Analysis." *Musical Quarterly*, 1935, Vol. 21, pp. 311–329.

LEE, VERNON, *Music and Its Lovers*. G. Allen & Unwin, Ltd., London, 1931.

LUSSY, MATHIS, *Musical Expression*. H. W. Gray Company.

McGRAW, MYRTLE, *Growth: A Study of Jimmy and Johnny*. D. Appleton-Century Company, Inc., New York, 1935.

MATTHAY, TOBIAS, *Musical Interpretation.* Boston Music Company, Boston, Mass., 3d. Ed., 1914.

MOOREHEAD, GLADYS E., and POND, DONALD, *Music of Young Children: I. Chant.* Pillsbury Foundation for the Advancement of Music Education, Santa Barbara, Calif., 1941.

MOOREHEAD, GLADYS E., and POND, DONALD, *Music of Young Children: II. General Observations.* Pillsbury Foundation for the Advancement of Music Education, Santa Barbara, Calif., 1942.

MURRY, JOHN MIDDLETON, *Studies in Keats, New and Old.* Oxford University Press, New York and London, 1939.

MURSELL, JAMES L., *The Psychology of Music.* W. W. Norton & Company, Inc., New York, 1937.

OGDEN, R. M., *Hearing.* Harcourt, Brace and Company, New York, 1924.

REES, HELEN M., *A Psychology of Artistic Creation.* Teachers College, Columbia University, Bureau of Publications, New York, 1942.

SHEEHY, EMMA D., *There's Music in Children.* Henry Holt and Company, New York, 1946.

UNGER, MAX, "From Beethoven's Workshop." *Musical Quarterly,* 1938, Vol. 24, pp. 323–340.

II
Recorded Readings of Poetry

The following aesthetic analyses of poetry are presented to illustrate numerous points which occur in the book. The close relationship between music and poetry, due to the fact that both are expressive arts, is one of the main contentions here put forward. The reader will be able to observe, by examining the instances here presented, and comparing the material with the discussions in the text, how strikingly similar are many of the expressive devices used both in music and in poetry. Moreover it is hoped that he will use the material in this appendix only as a starting point for explorations of the art of poetry which can cast much revealing light upon the sister art of music.

CORWIN, NORMAN, *Masterpieces of Literature.* (Set E-S, Columbia Records, 6 10-inch records)

EVANS, MAURICE, *Shakespeare, William: Hamlet,* four examples. (Columbia Records 11135 D). *Macbeth,* excerpts. (Victor Records M 878)

FROST, ROBERT, *Poems* (by the author). Epic Picture Consultants; also Encyclopaedia Britannica Films, Inc.

GIELGUD, JOHN, *The Voice of Poetry,* Volume 2. (Columbia Records M 419–5)

GULLAN, MARJORIE, various poems. (Halligan Studios, 475 Fifth Avenue, New York, N. Y.; 4 10-inch records)

It will be found interesting and illuminating to compare these presentations of poetry from the standpoint of projection and interpretation. The readings by Corwin, though clearly enunciated, are distinctly lacking in poetic feeling and aesthetic insight. In some cases the recordings are at present off the market, but they are available in many loan collections.

III

Aesthetic Analysis of Poetry

These examples of aesthetic analysis are cited from Lennox Gray, *Syllabus for English 130*, Third Preliminary Ed., University of Chicago, 1933:

DIRGE IN WOODS: GEORGE MEREDITH

A wind sways the pines,
  And below
Not a breath of wild air;
Still as the mosses that glow
On the flooring and over the lines
Of the roots here and there.
The pine-tree drops its dead;
They are quiet, as under the sea.
Overhead, overhead
Rushes life in a race,
As the clouds the clouds chase;
  And we go,
And we drop like the fruits of the tree,
  Even we,
  Even so.

When we read this short poem of George Meredith's we are aware of several currents which merge in the complete flow of the experience the poet is seeking to communicate. The images and the rhythms are two distinct elements. The one strikes the eye and the other strikes the ear. Yet in effect they are one and the same thing. Through their combination we see the picture, and at the same time are made to feel that there is something behind the picture, and that this is the essential idea of the poem. Certain harmonies of sound, moreover, add to the harmony of image and rhythm.

The first step toward a critical appreciation of any harmony is to distinguish the relationship of the notes forming it. We do this for several reasons. When we first hear a song or a poem we take pleasure in discovery. When we hear it again the first glow of discovery may be gone, but there is another pleasure which comes from familiarity and anticipation. With critical insight into the several currents in a poem, as in music, we constantly find new surprises and deeper familiarity. Without it, we find our resources for enjoyment soon exhausted, and a once vivid experience may become stale because we have no way of refreshing it. So we seek to distinguish the various currents of sensation, sound, feeling, and idea—not to "tear apart" but to build up, as the creative imagination of the poet has built up the poem.

How does "Dirge in Woods" proceed to build up our feelings of sober exaltation? The swaying of the uneven lines at the start, with the to-and-fro movement of the *abcb* rhyme, makes us feel the swaying of the pines. The tendency to stress pairs of words in "wind sways" and "wild air" gives a suitable force to the idea. This is accompanied with an expressive fluency of *r*'s, *w*'s and *l*'s, pitted against resistant *p*'s and *b*'s. Thus the impression from the first few lines owes something to rhyme, to rhythm, to image, and to consonance. In the three lines which follow the first three, the clipped statement of the start has given way to an uninterrupted run, with no end-stopped lines and with hardly a pause:

> Still as the mosses that glow
> On the flooring and over the lines
> Of the roots here and there.

Here the imagination can follow the flowing line of the ground free of underbrush; or it can go beyond that to a feeling of unimpeded openness and freedom of spirit. And then, "The pine-tree drops its dead"—short and final with its *p*'s and *t*'s and *d*'s, and yet with weighty stress on four out of six syllables. The freedom has become the infinite freedom of death; and a quiet, balanced, reflective line follows:

> They are quiet, as under the sea.

Then with repetition of "Overhead, overhead," and with a couplet rhyme ("race . . . chase"), and with insistent *h*'s, *s*'s, *sh*'s and *ch*'s, the poem rushes with the wind again. And again, as at the start, it falls away with the short line and with the hush where the pine needles and the pine-cones fall:

> And we go
> And we drop like the fruits of the tree,
> Even we,
> Even so.

If "Dirge in Woods" had no more than this to reveal, it would be a poem of no great distinction and would not be worth more critical attention. Yet it is a primary requirement in art that the idea and feeling and form shall be only different aspects of the same thing. In "Dirge in Woods" this identity is found, and shows greater depths wherever we look. We can make our approach variously through idea or feeling or form. Since ideas and feelings are widely variable and often intangible, however, and since criticism aims to be as definite and explicit as possible, the surest critical approach is through form. It is form, after all, which makes poetry immediately distinct from prose, and it is form which gives poetry much of its peculiar power.

In prosody (the technique of verse-form), "Dirge in Woods" is notable, we say, for its use of anapaestic dimeter with variant lines of anapaestic monometer. To the reader who knows the meaning of the terms this description marks out certain features which would probably pass unnoticed, or as uncertain impressions, if it were not for the recognition given by a name. To those who know only the bare definitions of the terms, of course this description is not much more meaningful than to those who do not know the terms at all. The *meaning* of the terms anapaestic and dimeter must include not only the recognition that here is the rhythm of a three-syllable foot with stress on the third syllable, as in "And below," and that dimeter is a line of two feet; it must include first a recognition of the probable effect of these together, and then in connection with the idea of the poem. *Anapaestic dimeter* should clearly indicate several things in connection with such a title as "Dirge in Woods."

In the first place, the anapaestic is a "rising rhythm," frequently found in galloping poems like Browning's "How They Brought the Good News from Ghent to Aix." It is not a usual or conventional measure for dirges. In the second place, dimeter is a very short line, not frequent in English poetry; and monometer is even rarer. Here again it is unconventional. On the face of it, then, our dirge must be either a light dirge, or it must be heavily weighted by extra stresses and retarding sounds, and compressed in phrase, to avoid a lilting effect. Almost surely, it will combine sobriety with uplift in feeling. To the alert reader the title itself, "Dirge in Woods," will suggest several of these things, as a title should: through shortness of phrase ("Dirge in Woods," not "A Dirge in the Woods"); through stress on two syllables out of three; through the predominance of consonant sounds.

The mood has been described as "sober exaltation." It is clear that much of the exaltation or lift of feeling is due to the unusual

[322]

rhythm. The rhythm interprets or confirms ideas in the poem which are strongly implicit but which cannot always be fixed in any one word or phrase of the poem. We are made to feel the exaltation which man usually derives when he reduces life and death to the dimensions of the Biblical mustard seed or to Omar Khayyám's bird that has but a little time to flutter. For the moment we can stand away from life, like lesser gods, and see all things in proportion. We are masters of it, in our imagination; even of the sober thought of its ending. The mastery is not so much in the words as in the rising undercurrent. It makes little difference whether we reflect that the dropping "fruit" of the pine may be a symbol of life as well as of death; or that peace may be good after the rushing wind; or that life is tree-like. Within limits, the poem allows various interpretations. What it does not warrant is any pious or sentimental interpretation. It preaches no moral. Its short statements avoid the sentimental fluency of ana-paestic lines like "When you come to the end of a perfect day." It gives a man's feeling about something of universal significance. Mer-edith has unmistakably felt the substance and rhythm of this pine wood with the wind overhead and the quietness below; his sure knowledge of this recommends his knowledge of the other things which seem to him comparable with it.

SEA FEVER: JOHN MASEFIELD[1]

The "Feel" of the Sea in Masefield's "Sea-Fever"

John Masefield's "Sea-Fever" is neither wholly song nor dramatic lyric, but is a combination of both.

Like a great body of English songs it goes to the ballad for its basic rhythm,—appropriately so, recalling sea adventure and sailors' chanties. At first glance the three long-line (14–16 syllables) quatrains, rhyming *AAbb*, do not appear to be ballad stanzas. But when the first two lines are broken at the caesuras, the pattern becomes clear.

> I must go down to the seas again,//
> to the lonely sea and the sky,
> And all I ask is a tall ship//
> and a star to steer her by;

Thus an alternating four-stress and three-stress pattern emerges, and an *abcb* rhyme. Yet like descriptive and reflective lyrics it varies its rhythm (within singable limits) according to feeling. As in most of

[1]From *Poems*. Copyright 1913, Harper & Brothers; 1914, The Century Company and by the McClure Publications; 1912, 1913, 1914, by The Macmillan Company; 1915, 1923, 1924, 1926, 1930, 1931, 1932 and 1935 by John Masefield.

Masefield's poems the expressive rhythm is the most remarkable feature; and here as elsewhere (often in poems of the land like "The West Wind") it is most remarkable for the rhythm of the sea.

Taken as a whole, it has a long ground-swell, gained in part by the regular use of a single-syllable rhyme in the first two lines of each stanza and by the two-syllable rhyme with falling stress in the last two: "Sky . . by . . shaking . . breaking . . tide . . denied . . flying . . crying . . life . . knife . . rover . . over." The vowels here are regularly long and sustained. This long sweep is both aided and interrupted by the cross-current of refrain "I must go down to the seas again" in each first line, and the variable "All I ask," now in the second line, and now and again in the third.

Even more notable than this, however, is the roll and heeling of the individual lines. After Masefield gains his imagined "tåll shíp" in the second line (the only spondee up to that point), the lines are sustained running crests of spondees and troughs and pyrrhics with the appropriate extra fullness and then the retard on the seventh wave, in "shaking" and "breaking."

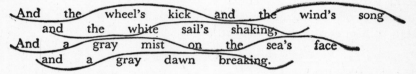

And the wheel's kick and the wind's song
and the white sail's shaking,
And a gray mist on the sea's face
and a gray dawn breaking.

At the start of each stanza, moreover, the return to iambics and anapaests assists the words to remind us that the sea is remote; and so the nostalgia deepens.

This nostalgia is the dominant emotion. It is universally understood by English-speaking people, even when their contact with the sea lies several generations back. And even for those whose personal experience might induce a feeling other than nostalgia, there is a fresh sea-wind, here as in "The West Wind," which has power to clear the head. Against a tonal background of misty short *i*'s and flat grayish *a*'s, the wind sings in moaning *o*'s and shriller *i*'s and *e*'s:

> And all I ask is a windy day with the white clouds
> flying,
> And the flung spray and the blown spume, and the
> sea-gulls crying.

These sounds are restlessly varied in sequence until the end, where a final even assonance and consonance (the repeated *l*'s and *m*'s, and the lingering *r*) are resolved in harmony with the feeling:

And all I ask is a merry yarn from a laughing
　　fellow-rover,
And quiet sleep and a sweet dream when the
　　long trick's over.

This comes in interesting contrast to the onomatopoetic effect of the
smacking k-sounds and the buffeting explosives in combination with
liquids and sibilants—sky, wheel's kick, sail's shaking, breaking, clear
call, sea gulls crying, clouds; tall ship, flung spray, blown spume.
The particular poignancy of "and the sea-gulls crying" is due in no
small part to this musical preparation, coming sharply after the heav-
ier sound of "flung spray" and "the blown spume."

From all this it is apparent that "Sea-Fever" can hardly be called
a reflective lyric "recollecting emotion in tranquillity" (Wordsworth's
definition of poetry), though the action takes place only in thought.
Its theme is adventure, not thought. Its images are communicated,
not interpreted. The fleeting thought about immortality at the last
is simply one of those immediate associations which the sea holds
eternally for men.

Historical Note. Masefield owes something to the long tradition of
English sea poetry. In his use of the ballad it is inevitable that he
should write with memory of such pieces as "Sir Patrick Spens,"
"The Mermaid," Cowper's "The Castaway," Coleridge's "Rime of
the Ancient Mariner," Peacock's "Three Men of Gotham," Southey's
"Inchcape Rock," Longfellow's "Wreck of the Hesperus," Kingsley's
"The Three Fishers" and "The Sands of Dee," Kipling's "McAn-
drew's Hymn," as well as numberless sailor's chanties of "men who
go down to the sea in ships," whose idiom he echoes. Particularly
notable is his recollection of the *kennings* of the Anglo-Saxon *Beowulf*
and "The Seafarer" in "the gull's way" and "the whale's way."
Yet Masefield's rhythm is his own, sometimes reminiscent of Coleridge's skillful effects in the "Rime of the Ancient Mariner," but more
authentic than Coleridge at his most nautical:

　　The fair breeze blew, the white foam flew,
　　　　The furrow followed free;
　　　　　　"Rime of the Ancient Mariner," ll. 103–104

It seems fair to say that Masefield makes history in sea poetry as well
as derives from it.

Biographical Note. Biography amply supports here what is evident
in the poem. Masefield (1878–　　) went to sea when he was fourteen. We know how, when he was in America (1895–1897), his read-

[325]

ing of Chaucer and old literature turned him toward poetry; and this helps to account, in spirit at least, for the *kennings*, "the gull's way" and "the whale's way," and also for the ready use of forceful vernacular in "I must go down," "wheel's kick," and "the long trick's over." One would expect to find Whitman, Kipling, and Conrad listed among the moderns who have influenced him, and one does.[1]

SONG TO CELIA: BEN JONSON

Drink to me only with thine eyes,
  And I will pledge with mine;
Or leave a kiss but in the cup,
  And I'll not ask for wine.
The thirst that from the soul doth rise
  Doth ask a drink divine;
But might I of Jove's nectar sup,
  I would not change for thine.

I sent thee late a rosy wreath,
  Not so much honoring thee
As giving it a hope that there
  It could not withered be,
But thou thereon didst only breathe,
  And sent'st it back to me;
Since when it grows, and smells, I swear,
  Not of itself but thee.

If we know D'Artagnan in *The Three Musketeers*, or Romeo in *Romeo and Juliet*, or François Villon, or Cyrano de Bergerac, we need no elaborate explanation of the general feeling. Graceful manners and courtly speech are not foremost among modern ideals, but we like to imagine that we command them, or that we could. We like to imagine ourselves socially adroit, never at a loss for the effective gesture or word. We like this cavalier feeling of gracefulness, of quick wit and light foot, for it represents a mastery of a phase of life which may be less profound than that in "Dirge in Woods" but no less real. If the poem has a little of that mockery which goes with high gallantry, it has the added grace and zest of humor as well. If we can say, then, that the poem is graceful in feeling, idea, and form, we justify it enough; here is the complete experience of grace and gallantry in three dimensions.

[1]John Matthews Manly and Edith Rickert, *Contemporary British Literature*, Revised Edition, pp. 218–221. Harcourt, Brace and Company, New York, 1928.

The ingenious idea, or "conceit" (with sustained conception in the figure of speech: "Drink . . . pledge . . . cup . . . wine . . . thirst . . . drink . . . nectar sup"), is fanciful play, apparently easy, and yet keenly alert. The allusions and images are familiar, yet each is turned neatly out of the normal course which it would take in our minds. Our Elizabethan courtier shows his abundant skill, finally, by expressing his idea not merely once, but twice, and in quite different images.

A study of the form could anticipate many of these impressions. The form is at once familiar and unfamiliar. The first four lines are basically the alternating iambic four-stress ($\cup'|\cup'|\cup'|\cup'$) and three-stress ($\cup'|\cup'|\cup'$) of the popular ballad stanza, with the ballad rhyme *abcb*. This is the most familiar song measure in English poetry, found alike in drinking songs and hymns. But Ben Jonson changes the character of the stanza by doubling the length and repeating the same rhymes, *abcbabcb*, creating a familiar-unfamiliar effect with echo and surprise. To make it still more complex, the composer of the musical accompaniment has set it to waltz time (sic), giving a three-beat movement in contrast with the two-beat iambic. When we forget the tune, again, and observe the verbal melody which makes this a "song" even when we do not sing it, we see that Jonson has his own interwoven patterns of contrasting rhythm and tone. Against the strong tendency to read the line in strict iambic pattern, with stress (') on syllables usually not stressed in every-day phrasing

$$\text{Drink } \overset{\cup}{\text{to}} \mid \text{me } \overset{\frown}{\text{on}}|\overset{\cup}{\text{ly}} \overset{\frown}{\text{with}} \mid \text{thine } \overset{\cup}{\text{eyes}}$$

—there is the other tendency to read it expressively, as we should speak:

$$\overset{\frown}{\text{Drink}} \overset{\cup}{\text{to}} \overset{\cup}{\text{me}} \mid \overset{\frown}{\text{on}}\overset{\cup}{\text{ly}} \mid \overset{\cup}{\text{with}} \overset{\cup}{\text{thine}} \overset{\frown}{\text{eyes}}$$

—or perhaps, keeping nearer to the basic four-foot, four-stress pattern—

$$\overset{\frown}{\text{Drink}} \overset{\cup}{\text{to}} \mid \overset{\cup}{\text{me}} \overset{\frown}{\text{on}}|\overset{\cup}{\text{ly}} \overset{\cup}{\text{with}} \mid \overset{\frown}{\text{thine}} \overset{\cup}{\text{eyes}}$$

We are aware of different currents, as we are aware of the contrasting yet harmonizing movement of the air and the accompaniment in music. The sound-effects of vowels and consonants carry this further, even while they are faithful to the quality of the feeling, which is light. The resonance of long vowels and certain consonants (particularly *m* and *n*) in "only . . . thine . . . divine . . . might . . . Jove's . . . thine," is effectively lightened by the short vowels and the sharp, clicking, clinking, or alliterative consonant sounds in "Drink . . . pledge . . . but . . . a kiss but in the cup . . . look . . . thirst . . . Doth ask a drink divine. . . . But might I of Jove's nectar sup. . . ." The variation in the pitch of the vowels, as in notes in music, is particularly noticeable in the combination of the deep o's and high e's in the second stanza (the more melodious though less striking of the stanzas), with its "rosy wreath . . . so . . . thee . . . hope . . . be . . . only breathe . . . me . . . grows . . . thee." This contrast in pitch of o's and e's is evident in the first lines of many famous songs: "Weep you no more, sad fountains," "Sigh no more, ladies," "Sweetest love, I do not go," "Her eyes the glow-worm lend thee," "Gather ye rosebuds while ye may," "Go, lovely rose," "Flow gently, sweet Afton," "Green grow the rushes, Oh," "Oh to be in England," "I must go down to the seas again." In these and in the "Song to Celia" there are, of course, many intermediate and linking harmonies that are as much a part of the effect as the rhythm and images are. All combine in the feeling of gracefulness and refreshing lightness, for which this song exists.

Nothing has been said about love, in talking about idea and feeling in the "Song to Celia." This is because love has little to do with it, except in providing a suitable occasion for gracefulness. If there is love here, it is under excellent rhetorical control. Is it "sincere"? We can judge of this, if we care to only when we know something about Jonson and about the ways of his time, and when we define what we mean by "sincere." "Conceits" were conventional, and it was conventional also to address such complimentary poems to ladies at court. That Jonson was sincere as a *poet* there can be no doubt, whatever his actual feelings toward Celia. Sincerity is not a matter of depth of passion. If sincerity in the poem should mean that it must be unmistakably addressed to a particular person, then there is no evidence of sincerity, for it might be addressed to any woman. If it means, however, that the poet sets out to express his ideal for this type of graceful love-message, and that he spares no art in composing his compliment—so that the conventionally named Celia enjoys its adroitness and so that even today we recognize its near perfection— then it is as sincere as it needs to be.

Aesthetic Analysis of Music

The material presented in this appendix is cited, with the author's permission, from *On the Elements of Expression in Music*, by Donald N. Ferguson. It consists of an extensive and brilliant aesthetic exposition of a brief passage from Wagner. Its special interest here is that it provides illustrations for many of the expositions in the text. More generally, it indicates an aesthetic approach to the whole art of music. The reader will find in it concrete examples of many of the constitutive expressive factors of music which are discussed in the text. He will notice how the musical structure—the expressive form—is treated in terms of rhetoric rather than of grammar. And although such an elaborate analysis as the one offered here is far beyond the scope of children and beginners, the approach to music through its expressive and aesthetic values which it exemplifies is just what is desirable at all developmental levels. Mr. Ferguson's analysis follows:

Our first example is from Wagner:

We shall, of course, look for the elemental suggestions before considering the values given by the accessory factors of expression. And because the motor outlet of emotion is more objective than the nervous stress, and the element of ideal motion is therefore more clearly visible than that of tone stress, we shall reverse the order in which our elements were discovered, and shall discuss first the element of ideal motion.

The sense of motion is here conveyed, less by marked rhythmic pulses than by the continuous flow of the melodic line. Every detail of that line is thus significant. The long initial A flat, unimpeded, but also unimpelled by any external rhythmic factor, undergoes a sort of tremor (the "turn" in 32d notes) which itself seems to be the impulse causing the melody to rise to the high F—the moment of greatest rhetorical (not rhythmic) stress in the theme. Motion more fluid and effortless than this could not be imagined. The melodic point poises itself here, at the peak of its curve, for a time (a dotted quarter) as long as was its easy flow before the tremor began; and this stationary maintenance of the achieved height is characteristic of the whole curve of motion. (Imagine the F as an eighth-note, and the whole character is changed.) The quality of motion that is now established is maintained to the end. The descent to C, the ensuing rise to E flat, and the final swift descent (it seems swift because of the length of the drop to F) complete an undulating curve in which the ease and fluidity we noted are only once in the slightest degree abated (with the E flat, whose quality we shall examine more minutely).

This will suffice to fix in our minds the motion character of the melodic line itself. But if there is no rhythmic propulsion, whence comes the effortless power with which the melody moves? Are there tonal influences within the melody itself which can account for this power, and which must thus be seen as motor facts, although their primary interest may be within the field of tone stress? We noted above, that the high F formed a point of highest rhetorical stress in the curve. It forms also the point of highest altitude in pitch; and although nothing in the pitch relations of the melodic note A flat to this high F can be found to explain the rise to F, the rest of the curve, having regard to the length of F, will be seen as a consequence of the upward portion of the curve. The fact of direction in motion is so essential a part of the whole phenomenon of motion that the sense of relative height and depth in pitch, although it is itself a species of tone stress, has important motor suggestiveness.

But there is a more subtly suggestive tone-relation than that of height and depth: the relation of activity and rest. These words, activity and rest, although we have thought of them chiefly as describing a relation of tension in tones, also palpably imply motion. We may seek here, then, what we have so far sought in vain—the explanation of the rising energy of the rhythmically unpropelled A flat. It will be seen that, since the music is in the key of E flat, every note of consequence in the theme is active except the E flat; and this note is itself *made* active by the surrounding harmony, for E flat does not and can not belong to that harmony. A flat, the note with which we are immediately concerned, is felt as active at the very outset. Strictly, it should resolve to the nearest rest tone. Actually, it may be said to do so; but the fact of resolution is hardly perceptible because of the brevity of the G to which A flat moves. Neither this G nor the B flat following conveys any sense of rest, for the apparent motion of the 32d-note figure is too swift to suggest even the slightest sense of rest. If A flat is "seen" to touch G at all, it is only as if it rebounded, like a soap-bubble, and suffered a change of direction, but no loss of momentum, in doing so. There is nothing in the purely musical activity of A flat to cause it to rise to F; but the rise itself is visible evidence of intrinsic energy great enough to effect that motion.

By the principle governing the progression of active tones, the descent from F, again, should be to the rest-tone E flat; and again it really is so, but circuitously, in a gracious dip and rise whose shallower curve is not only exquisite as line, in relation to the soaring curve preceding, but is a vivid representation of the quantum of energy that remains, after the F, in the moving melodic point. And the final descent from E flat to F seems to be compelled, not merely by the implications of direction in all the preceding line, but also, and chiefly, by the peculiar, artificial activity of the E flat itself.

So far, we have attempted to deal with the element of ideal motion. But the facts of activity and rest which determine that motion are also perceptible as relations of tone-stress, indicative of nervous tension of a certain degree and character. The words we have used to describe that part of the apparent motion which is due to activity and rest in tone relation will also have suggested the nature of the stress conditions simultaneously represented. So fluid a motion, in a curve so gracious, could never result from nervous tension of any violent nature. But there is in this music a still further suggestion of tone stress: one that pervades the whole musical substance, and so contributes not only its intrinsic hint of nervous condition, but adds also to the vividness of the motor impulse. This, of course, is the one almost unchanging harmony which surrounds the whole theme: the chord of the dominant ninth. Having no half-step discords, this harmony is soft, not harsh; having five notes of different letter name, it is rich; having as its root a primary tone (the dominant), it gives a certain sense of quietude because of its close relation to the tonic. These qualities of softness (the dynamics are also soft, but we are speaking of a harmonic quality), of richness, and of quietude persist unchanged until the fourth beat of the measure. (The general slight *crescendo* prescribed by the composer heightens but does not change the tension-character depicted.) At this fourth beat, a new factor is added to the harmony in the shape of a passing-note, E flat, in an inner voice. This note, however, produces no half-step discord, for D does not persist, but itself moves to this E flat. This new note, the first definite rhythmic impulse that has occurred outside the melody, subtly intensifies the harmonic stress. It also anticipates, and so prepares our ear for, the E flat that is to come in the theme. For the increase of harmonic energy or tension is assimilated by the melodic note, E flat, which also occurs at the rhythmic crisis of the theme, the first beat of the second measure. And it is this increased tension which compels the long descent of the melodic tone, E flat. We felt no loss of power as the earlier F dropped to C, even though the inner voice took E flat an instant before the eighth-note C occurred in the melody; for that passing-note did not of itself change the character of the harmony, and the C might have been followed by a still higher leap if the general harmonic intensity had remained unaltered. But when E flat appears also in the melody, taken by skip from C, on the strong beat of the measure, and as the natural note of resolution of the preceding active tone, F, we feel a tiny stab of harmonic pain that, slight as it is, is enough to account for the sudden drop of the melodic line to the low F.

The reader is doubtless appalled at the use of so many words to describe nine notes and a single chord of harmony. We can only ask him—so far as is necessary by playing, but ultimately by *thinking* this music (for it is not easy to utter) to translate our clumsy descriptions into musical concepts. The expressive qualities we are observing are in the musical idea, not in our words, and neither ideal motion nor tone-stress nor any of the accessory values still to be studied can be rightly sensed until the whole substance of the music is felt as a living musical thought. Our microscopic examination has necessarily magnified all the details by several hundred diameters. No ordinary act of hearing could assimilate all this complexity of suggestion at its magnified value and at the normal rate. Yet those contributory values are *there*, and even in their natural proportions they affect our normal perception of the whole value to which they contribute. . . .

We have now sufficiently considered the elemental suggestions of motor impulse and nervous stress, as they appear in their musical form. We have been careful to offer as little comment of an expressively interpretative nature as possible, in order that we may later observe the interpretative process as a separate fact. It may be well, before going on, to sort out and arrange the many varied impressions we have received, classifying them into the two general groups which are indicated by the nature of the elements themselves. These impressions, if our hypothesis is sound, are the raw material of emotional

[332]

representation to which the secondary factors, still unobserved, may add much of vividness. Still avoiding the use of interpretatively suggestive words, we may summarize thus the values established so far:

1. A representation of motion, effortless and poised, which through a single slight impediment loses, at the end, something of the eager freedom with which it began.
2. Representations of stress of three sorts:
   a. Indications of relative height and depth, suggesting a certain general tension between high and low tones, but also, through the conveyed impression of traversed space, suggesting a path of motion;
   b. Indications of "activity" which, while they contribute still further to the motor idea, are also suggestive of intrinsic tensions of feeling;
   c. Harmonic discord, chiefly suggestive of nervous condition, but in itself perceptible as rich, sweet, and soft. This discord, however, also supplies motor energy.

We have argued that the function of the accessory factors of expression is to intensify the primary intimations of expressive sense offered by the elements. Before we can observe these secondary factors, then, we must draw from our observation of the elemental suggestions some tentative emotional inferences; for otherwise we can hardly judge the purpose and meaning of the lesser factors.

Assuming that the music is intended to represent or suggest emotion, we shall at least agree that with so much of ease in motion and so much of richness and sweetness in the facts of tone-stress, the emotion depicted is pleasurable, not painful. Leaving the reader, for the moment, to circumscribe for himself the particular region of pleasure indicated, we may even now observe the secondary factors as contributing definition to our idea of that region. The tremulous vibration of the tympani (hardly a fact of motion, yet appearing as a gentle, pervasive tremor) is taken over at the second bar by the violas; the clarinet, which has the important inner part with the first dissonant E flat, passes, in this progression, from the *chalumeau* to the middle register; the horns, bassoon, and bass clarinet which sustain the harmony are smooth and mellow in tone; and the theme itself, against this background of tone is sounded in the clear, vibrant beauty of the violins. These values of tone, prescribed by the composer and realized through the fine discrimination of trained performers, were chosen and distributed for the purpose of vivifying not only the sensuous interest but also the expressive meaning of this phrase. As we hear them, these tone-surfaces, like the well-modulated inflections of the

[333]

speaking voice, may seem to contain the thought itself; but it will presently be more clearly apparent that they were chosen for more than a purely aesthetic purpose.

The reader will perhaps accept as sufficiently accurate our description of these elemental and accessory suggestions, which we have put (as far as we were able) into factual terms indicative of motion, stress, and timbre. These suggestions, by our hypothesis, are interpretable as representative of emotional character. The reader himself will have had little difficulty in perceiving emotional suggestion in some, at least, of the indicated facts. But it is not through such individual hints, however vivid, that an actuality of expression is conveyed. Rather, it must be through the simultaneous impression made by all the suggestive factors. Moreover, a certain imaginative or inferential effort is necessary on our part: an effort that will relate the whole hint of feeling character to some type of human experience out of which such feeling may have been generated; for we cannot know emotion wholly apart from experience. Let us, then conceive, in terms of physical or imaginative experience the hints of motion, tone-stress and color we have so slowly accumulated.

The motion of our theme, untrammeled, poised and effortless, may be visualized as a curve, traced by some ideal object in ideal space; or it may be felt as the imagined flight of one's own body. What state of mind could arouse in us such an impulse of motion? For the music does more than delineate this exquisite pattern: It commands us imaginatively to enact this impossible flight. Considered dynamically and with full liberty of imaginative response, such motion as this can hardly suggest less than a condition of ecstasy—of being, indeed, "outside oneself." But there is described also a condition of nervous tension, presumably akin to the motor impulse just observed. Sensation that is warm and rich is the synaesthetic correlative of wider perception of the same character. What state of mind or feeling is as warm and rich as this; is expectant, as the gentle persistence of discord in this theme is expectant; and is tinged with pain, as this music is tinged, by the darker throb of the two E flats? For so strong are the initial impressions of warmth and ecstasy, and so gently is the sense of pain blended with them, that there is here no hint of bitterness or foreboding, but only the agony of overmuch delight.

To a considerable extent, what we have just set forth is doubtless an individual interpretation of the suggestions of motion and tension given by this music. We have almost compelled the reader to follow us in this interpretation; but we hasten to offer him the utmost liberty of criticism. We have only the right to ask that the elemental suggestions be received at their full value as implying motion and tension of clearly defined character. Even if the reader be inclined to view all musical substance as aesthetic creation purely, he is still obliged to observe these facts of motion and tension as existent, and as essential to structural coherence. We ask him, merely, to see these same facts as representing, also, possible conditions of feeling and motor impulse; and if the musical facts themselves have been so observed, we have little fear that his own account, verbal or imaginative, of their expressive meaning will differ materially from our own.

But even if assent be offered to our argument thus far, it is still necessary to add a further sharpness of definition to our awakening concepts of meaning before a fact of true expression can be said to have been achieved. We have still to establish a relation between the subjective facts represented—almost directly—by this music, and the objective conditions of experience which presumably might give rise to such feeling as is here portrayed. This relation, however, is not directly suggested by the music itself, nor does it exist among those more immediate implications of feeling which we have just discussed, and which we believe to be actually resident in the musical substance. This final definition of expressive character must be made by inference from the already established idea—by an inferential effort, that is, analogous to that which we had to make if we were to realize the significance of the meeting between Richard and Lucy. That, of course, was an inference of feeling from fact; this must be an inference of fact from feeling; but it will be seen that the inversion of the direction of our effort imposes no insuperable difficulty. . . .

Our present example, however, created by a mature artist of almost incomparable powers, and definitely intended as the expression of an idea already existent in verbal form, probably presents nothing that is superfluous, either aesthetically or expressively. If, then, we rapidly fuse into a single impression the observed suggestions of ecstasy, anticipation, warmth, poignance, and the like, together with whatever of clearer definition we have derived from the accessory factors of expression, our result will be at one with our first intuitive estimate of the character of this music, only our judgment will be more detailed in its certainty. The qualities here represented can relate only to the passion of love.

But is this all? Have we here merely love music in general, suited to every manifestation of the passion, or will our analysis have added to our awareness of the music's character a definition also of the pos-

[335]

sible circumstances under which such love as this can occur? Love is tender; but have we here the languishing tenderness of Tristan and Isolde in the garden? Love is expectant; but have we in the hesitant, wondering expectancy of this music any expression of the terrible, yearning eagerness of Isolde as she quenches the torch? Love is ecstatic; but is this the piteous, self-forgetting ecstasy of Isolde as she sings her life out in the *Liebestod*?[1]

We know at once, from the music itself, that the passion here expressed burns in the heart of quite another character than Isolde. Yet we can hardly *know*, in our own experience, the love of which this music tells. It is too pure in essence, too lacking in physicality, and above all too *young* to be quite credible as the experience of one living on the ordinary plane of human passion. Still, to think of this love as young, in the sense of immature and callow, is also impossible. It is not a mere childish dream of love; it bears the unmistakable stamp of emotional reality. Real as it seems, however, we can only infer that this is the love that is felt by someone not quite human.

Fortunately, we can test this inference. We are supposed to have heard the earlier dramas of the "Ring" cycle. The history of Brünnhilde's defiance of Wotan is fresh in our minds. We have seen her bound in that enchanted sleep from which she may be awakened only by him who dares to pass through the ring of fire. We have seen that awakening. Brünnhilde is to us now no longer the war-maiden. She is a woman—the woman from whom Wotan's kiss took godhood away, and in whom Siegfried's kiss has awakened not only humanity but love. How feeble are all our words about tenderness, expectancy and ecstasy—how feeble are any imaginable words—beside this instantaneous embodiment of the passion of a woman for whom both love and the world have been new-created!

Not all this vividness of expressive meaning can be said to have been conveyed by the music itself. If the reader had by any chance been unacquainted with our illustrative theme, but familiar with the story itself, he would doubtless have experienced a great illumination of his slowly acquired sense of musical meaning at that instant when

[1]The same figure, an upward leap from a turn, does indeed serve as the expression of the more ecstatic climax of Tristan and Isolde's duet, in the second act, and is also a feature, profoundly pathetic by reminiscent association, of the *Liebestod* music. The implications here are many, and will be discussed in a moment. It will suffice here for us to observe that the continuation of the phrase is other than that which appears in our example, and that its rhythmic character is far different from that which we have been observing.

the association became established between the music and the known experience. Yet if our deductions up to that point were justifiable, it is true that the music alone in its wonderful revelation of feeling character, implied the general nature of a very unusual type of experience. But if the fact of expression, through the elemental means we have described, be admitted, many incidental problems will at once appear.

If our hypothesis is sound, expression is conveyed by the representation of knowable conditions of nervous excitement or motor impulse. The musical representative of the given condition is a recognizable pattern or relation of tones; and this pattern, in its expressive aspect, becomes a symbol of the thing represented. It should also follow, then, that a given pattern or type of suggestion, appearing in quite another context, should still retain a clear indication of its original expressive value. No rhythmic pattern, of course, will attain to verbal concreteness of rhythmic definition. . . . Yet if the original pattern persists—that is to say, the original motor suggestiveness, not the structural shape, of the pattern; for this latter may be so altered by augmentation or diminution or other structural processes as to have quite a new motor value, although its design is still recognizable—if the original pattern persists, something of its original value of motor suggestion should persist also. Indeed, it would appear incumbent upon us to show that it does persist; for otherwise our element of ideal motion would lose its status as an element of expression.

This can be briefly done. In the theme just considered, the motion character is largely, though not wholly, established by the melodic progression from the opening long note, through the turn, to the high F at the peak of the curve. Precisely the same melodic pattern, at practically identical speed, but with every supporting factor altered, including the very different conclusion, occurs in the following familiar theme:

Remembering always that we are observing only the fact of motion suggestion, note the stability of the tonic rest-tone as initial note, in comparison with the active A flat of the earlier theme. Compare also the rhythmic decisiveness of this accompaniment—the tramping bass, the punctuating chords, the march-like progress of the whole—with the absence of all rhythmic propulsion in the other. The effortless freedom of motion is gone, for the melody itself is affected by the motion of the accompaniment; and with it is lost that sense of ecstasy which we derived from the inimitable fluidity of movement in the melody. The quiet, persistent warmth of the nervous tone (suggested chiefly by the ninth-chord) in the earlier theme is changed to fluctuating tension alternating between rest and activity. The high B, corresponding to the earlier F, is also, as it happens, harmonized by a dominant ninth-chord; but this chord is now in its first inversion, and so is far more unstable than was the root position of the other. In contrast to the preceding rest-chord, this is highly active; it produces, accordingly, in the high B a sense of kinetic yearning very different from the passive ecstasy of the F of the other theme. The succeeding melodic curve, also, shows not so much undulation as that in the Brünnhilde motive, but only uninterrupted descent: motion without lilt, that is, and nervous tension of a far more sober, depressed type. The theme from "Rienzi" is the product of a far less mature imagination than that which conceived the wonderful characterization of Brünnhilde; but even here the motor aspect and the nervous tension of aspiration—of the mood of prayer—are convincingly depicted, and the kinship of aspiration to ecstasy is vividly illustrated in the single type of motor-pattern.

We have seen the native buoyancy of the original motor suggestion darkened and depressed by other factors. In the following theme, from Bach, we may see how buoyancy, with hardly an attendant hint of other feeling, may become the predominant character in the same pattern:

The initial note (G sharp, still a rest-tone, but now dominant, not tonic, and so less stable) is short and unaccented. The figure of the turn, in consequence, is not a mere tremor of anticipation, preparatory to the leap to E sharp, but is a delightful antic in itself. The leap, thereafter, is so natural an outcome that, with a somewhat similar preparation (the first three notes of the second bar), it becomes the principal feature of the dainty motion of the whole theme. But even if it be no more than the obsession of the dance, the feeling here expressed is also akin to ecstasy.

In this, from Weber:

the same (dominant) rest tone at the beginning is strongly accented, so that the turn would appear less vital to the whole motion impulse if it were not repeated at once, on a higher level, and as if in joyous anticipation of the attainment of the high E. In this music, the quality of excitement is more pronounced, for it depicts Agathe's joy in recognizing the approach of her belated lover; but at this lower level we can still employ the very inexact word, ecstasy, to describe a feeling which is far more clearly defined by the music itself. (It will be remembered that at its climax this melody also leaps a sixth to an active note, exactly as does the Wagnerian theme.)

Finally, as we have already noted, the same figure appears in the duet in the second act of *Tristan and Isolde*. There, as an expression of the ecstasy of the two lovers at the culminant moment of their passion, its suitability is obvious. Yet the feeling here expressed is very different from that which is made to appear characteristic of Brünnhilde, so that many differences occur, both in the background of the theme and in the pattern itself. The pattern is not, in the Tristan music, a separately announced, carefully prepared theme. Rather, it appears as if spontaneously, representing the last incandescence of a passion whose gradual exaltation from a quiet longing for death has been fully set before us. The motion of the music, accordingly, has, in all the notes of the figure save the turn, a swiftness that would ill accord with the quiet ecstasy of Brünnhilde. The absence of the undulation (noted also in the Rienzi theme) is significant also, for that undulation could not occur without destroying the essential swiftness of the apparent motion. The harmony, moreover, is highly active, is constantly shifting its tonal base as the figure is repeated, and is thus far more varied in color. The figure itself, too, is somewhat obscured in prominence because it seldom occurs in the vocal utterance, but is mostly kept in the orchestra where it is over-ridden by the long, passionate phrases of the singers. And when this same

[339]

figure reappears in the *Liebestod*, it is not intended to be understood as an immediate musical expression of Isolde's dying ecstasy. It has, indeed, an even higher pathos, for it brings into the scene of death that memory of joy which the great poet spoke of as the bitterest of griefs.

These illustrations will suffice to show that kindred emotional states are often expressed in kindred musical terms by different composers, and that while a given figure may have an elemental or intrinsic value of suggestion, the possibility of appropriate musical variation is as great as the variety of mood that demands expression. Indeed, if we compare the highly various utterances of feeling we have just examined, and consider that we have found it possible, if not obligatory to characterize them all by the one term, ecstatic, we shall perhaps perceive as clearly as in any other way the high exactness of musical expression. We are not attempting to erect a verbally definite meaning upon the foundations of suggestion inherent in the expressive elements. Yet it is obvious that there is, in the meaning value of the figure we have examined so minutely, a clear analogy with the etymological values of word-roots. Indeed, the variations in expressive character produced by the varieties of treatment we have observed are hardly less great than are the variations of meaning in the root itself of such words as *log*ic, pro*logue*, ana*log*y, *log*arithm, produced by combination of the root (Gr. *logos*, a word) with other roots or suffixes.[1]

[1]Ferguson, Donald N., *On the Elements of Expression in Music*, pp. 53–61. University of Minnesota, 1944.

INDEX